TALES OF MYSTERY & THE SUPERNATURAL

General Editor: David Stuart Davies

JACK THE RIPPER
The Whitechapel Murderer

Jack the Ripper
The Whitechapel Murderer

Terry Lynch

WORDSWORTH EDITIONS

For my husband
ANTHONY JOHN RANSON
with love from your wife, the publisher.
Eternally grateful for your unconditional love,
not just for me but for our children,
Simon, Andrew and Nichola Trayler

Readers who are interested in other titles from
Wordsworth Editions are invited to visit our website at
www.wordsworth-editions.com

For our latest list and a full mail-order service contact
Bibliophile Books, Unit 5 Datapoint,
South Crescent, London E16 4TL
Tel: +44 020 74 74 24 74
Fax: +44 020 74 74 85 89
orders@bibliophilebooks.com
www.bibliophilebooks.com

This edition published 2008 by
Wordsworth Editions Limited
8B East Street, Ware, Hertfordshire SG12 9HJ

ISBN 978 1 84022 077 3

© Wordsworth Editions Limited 2008

Wordsworth® is a registered trademark of
Wordsworth Editions Limited,
the company founded by Michael Trayler in 1987

Typeset in Great Britain by Roperford Editorial
Printed by Clays Ltd, St Ives plc

CONTENTS

PREFACE

The following statement was issued as a reflection on the riots which had taken place in Trafalgar Square, after a mass protest by the unemployed, on 13 November 1887. This demonstration was referred to in later years as 'Bloody Sunday'.

Less than a year ago the West End press was literally clamouring for the blood of the people. Hounding Sir Charles Warren to thrash and muzzle the scum who dared to complain that they were starving . . . behaving in short, as the propertied class always does behave, when the workers throw it into a frenzy of terror by venturing to show their teeth.

Whilst we conventional Social Democrats were wasting our time on education, agitation and organisation, some independent genius has taken the matter in hand.

George Bernard Shaw

That genius came to be known as 'Jack the Ripper'.

INTRODUCTION

This manuscript unquestionably represents the strongest and most comprehensive book ever written on the subject of Jack the Ripper. It explores whole new concepts which have previously gone unrecognised, and analyses existing information from a variety of new angles.

As a quick illustration of the strength of the book could I request that initially you just read the evaluation of a previously unpublished Jack the Ripper letter on pages 244 to 256?

Also I would ask that you read the final two pages of the book concerning the report written by Sergeant White which is held in the Public Records Office, and consider the contents of his report and its inferences.

This is another point where nobody has taken the trouble to read between the lines as to the implications on the Ripper investigation of the contents of the report.

I have endeavoured to present the facts in a chronological fashion, and guide the reader, whilst allowing them to digest the information and formulate their own opinions.

I have attempted to represent the known particulars of the case fairly, and have introduced compelling arguments as to why the present accepted thinking is mistaken.

An example of this is the supposed double murder of Elizabeth Stride and Catharine Eddowes on the same night. With regard to this one event, I have challenged accepted opinion by using the medical evidence of 1888 to categorically prove that the knife used in each murder was different, and seeing that both murders were allegedly committed within one hour of one another, then why would the Ripper use a different knife to kill the first victim (Elizabeth Stride), and yet use the same knife that was used for all of the other murders to kill the second victim (Catharine Eddowes) one hour later? If your usual weapon is already about your person, then why use another one to commit a murder, unless the Ripper did not commit the first murder.

Again, to do with the Eddowes murder. The only piece of evidence ever left by the Whitechapel murderer was a portion of the dead woman's apron, which he threw away in Goulston Street. Why cut off a piece of apron, and abandon it at least one hour later, in a place only ten minutes walk from the murder site. Nobody has suggested this before, but I believe that the Ripper cut himself while he was mutilating the body (most probably his right hand), and wrapped the piece of apron around the wound, only throwing it away when the bleeding had stopped. (It was definitely a portion of the apron, because it cross-matched a repair on the section left with the body).

I have named a new suspect, and in doing so explained why there weren't any murders during the month of October 1888.

Previously, all of the letters except for the accepted few have always been regarded as fraudulent for various reasons. I have included more of the letters within the book than most previous publications, and have analysed each letter individually.

In doing this, I have unearthed among other things, a piece of prose which makes very interesting reading, but until now has never previously been untangled and interpreted. This verse was received by the police exactly one year to the day after the last Ripper murder, which was that of Mary Kelly. How, if it wasn't from the Ripper, did the writer know that there had been no more Ripper murders after the 9th of November 1888?

As you will see from the book, a number of murders occurred during the 12 months following the murder of Mary Kelly. None has survived the test of time to be still attributed to the Ripper, but in 1889 they were all still regarded as victims of the Whitechapel Murderer, and only the culprit would have known to send a letter outlining his reasons and motivation exactly one year after the murder of Mary Kelly, knowing for certain that she was the killer's last victim.

In the book I have included a table of the movements of each victim, allowing the reader to easily follow the night of each murder.

I have, I believe, established beyond reasonable doubt that the murders were committed by a left-handed person, and through careful analysis of two photographs, have ascertained that Montague John Druitt (a prominent suspect) was also left-handed. Part of my reasoning for this is that his tie is tied by a left-handed person, i.e. left over right, and a further photograph, depicting him reading a book, shows him to be leaning on his right elbow, allowing him, if required, to turn the pages of the book with his left hand. In this same photo, he is also sat with his left leg crossed over his right. It is much more comfortable the other way round if you favour your right side; one reason is that right-sided men have a tendency to dress on the left.

Nobody else has ever noticed these things, and within the book there are lots more examples.

I know that I am biased, but I believe that I have written the best ever book on the subject, and I hope that after reading it, you do too.

Please take time to read the book. In places I have highlighted certain sections which are specifically important, and which have been misinterpreted up until now. Even if these sections are the only ones you read initially, I am sure that they alone will prompt you to read the whole book.

The 'Whodunit' section is unique, and you will see the reason for this towards the end of that chapter.

The 'Medical Evidence' chapter and its analysis of the information are more comprehensive than any as yet written.

Any spelling and punctuation errors are deliberate, and are duplications of similar mistakes in the original papers. They are not the consequence of any lack of education.

To conclude may I state that I believe that I know more about this subject than anyone alive, and assure you that all the reported facts are accurate and correct. Until I researched the subject I could not believe the amount of information that has been ignored.

Thank you, and I sincerely hope that you enjoy the book.

TERRY LYNCH

ACKNOWLEDGMENTS

In the first instance I most sincerely thank all the previous authors who have blazed the trail in a subject which I found it easy to devour and which with every publication intrigued me that little bit more.

They are: Robin Odell; Colin Wilson; Tom Cullen; Daniel Farson; Richard Whittington Egan; the late Professor Francis Camps; Philip Loftus; Philip Sugden; Nick Warren; Jon Ogan; Stewart P. Evans; Keith Skinner; Martin Fido; Donald Rumbelow; and Paul Begg.

I cannot differentiate between the importance I attach to each particular book, and my own book contains a lot of individual research, but also I acknowledge with grateful thanks the research that I did not need to complete owing to it having previously been done for me.

I must also give my gratitude to all of the following concerns for answering my queries and supplying me with the information which I requested of them. Also, for their insight into passing me on to persons and places where I could glean my requirements, when they could not supply the information personally.

They are: the Public Records Office; the Tower of London; the Corporation of London Records Office; once again the Ripperana magazine and Nick Warren; Scotland Yard; City Police; Home Office files and pictures; *The Times* and *The Telegraph* newspapers from which enclosed articles were extracted; and finally the Daniel Hay Library, Whitehaven.

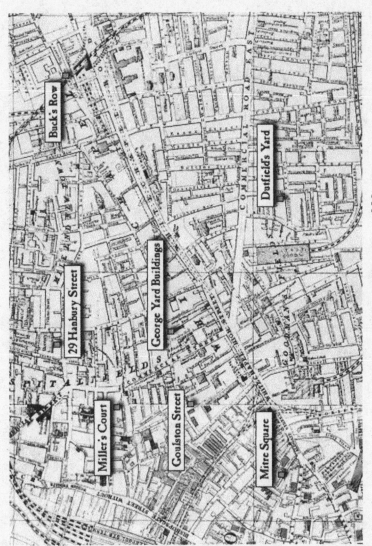

Buck's Row

Dutfield's Yard

29 Hanbury Street

George Yard Buildings

Miller's Court

Goulston Street

Mitre Square

MAP OF WHITECHAPEL IN 1888

*This book is dedicated to the love of my life,
the best armchair detective that
I have ever met.*

PART ONE

The Murders

CHAPTER ONE

Two unlikely victims

'Fairy Fay'

Terence Robertson, the author of *Madman who murdered Nine Women*, reported in *Reynold's News* of 29 October 1950, that 'Fairy Fay' was the first victim of Jack the Ripper and that she died on Boxing Night of 1887, in the back streets behind Commercial Street, having taken a short cut home from a public House in Mitre Square.

Inspector Reid is credited with leading the enquiry into the murder, which was apparently shelved after a few weeks due to the lack of information.

Indeed, there is a distinct lack of corroborating evidence to endorse the killing, and yet the description of the slaying by Terence Robertson appears to possess enough specific information in it to have the ring of truth.

An American journalist (reputed to be Tom Cullen) unearthed a reference to the incident whilst doing research, but he is no longer in possession of the case notes that were taken or the sources consulted, so the incident at present remains unsubstantiated.

No report of the incident has yet been discovered, either written by Inspector Reid or any of his contemporaries, and this coupled with the fact that there is no mention of the murder in the Home Office Files or those of Scotland Yard, gives rise to an element of doubt as to whether the incident ever took place.

However, certain questions arise which require addressing before the incident can be dismissed or any realistic conclusions can be formed, and it could be intimated that the reason for the apparent lack of information is that the murder of Fairy Fay never took place.

Questions which arise from the information that is available include the following.

What was the name of the public house in Mitre Square, from which we are informed that the victim was taking a short cut home?

Was the body mutilated in a fashion similar to the Ripper victims? When and how was the murder carried out?

A doctor's report needs to be unearthed, in order that the stereotyping and the extent of the injuries can be ascertained. This will allow the modus operandi of the murder to be compared with that of later Ripper victims.

The fact that the available information lends itself to the victim taking a short cut from Mitre Square, and that the short cut involved her going home via the vicinity of Commercial Street, tells us that at some time in the past her address must have been known. In establishing this, the murder site may also be identified.

We must also explore the possibility that homosexuals were known as 'fairies' in late Victorian England; and if so, are we looking in the wrong direction, and was Fairy Fay a man?

The name 'Fay' is a diminutive of 'Faith'. Was anyone with the Christian or surname 'Faith' murdered during the time when the Whitechapel murders were taking place, or was anyone of that name murdered in the year preceding the start of the Ripper murders?

Have any references been uncovered in the newspaper obituaries or death registers for the previous and ensuing months, and for similar periods in the years before and after?

Why was she supposedly murdered in the back streets behind Commercial Street? Surely the streets of London were sufficiently infamous and dangerous to encourage a woman alone to stick to the main thoroughfares; that is, unless she was a prostitute and had entered the back street of her death in order to entertain a client.

The answers to these questions would greatly assist in defining whether Jack the Ripper did indeed commence his killing spree on Boxing Day of 1887, or has this murder just been added so that his record was more impressive?

Let us now look at the police officer who is credited with leading the investigation.

Inspector John James Reid was born in 1846 and joined the Metropolitan Police Force in 1872. He succeeded Inspector Abberline as the head of H Division C.I.D. in 1888.

He was a conscientious police officer, being described by the *Weekly Despatch* as 'one of the most remarkable men of the century', making balloon ascents and parachute jumps. He received a medal for attaining a record altitude in the year of 1883. If, as is postulated, he was the officer in charge of the case, then it is possible that the murder was committed under the jurisdiction of J Division (Bethnal Green) as he was the Divisional Inspector in charge of this division at the time quoted for the murder.

My own opinion is that if Inspector Reid was in charge of the investigation then he strikes me as the sort of individual who would have been intelligent, conscientious and methodical and would undoubtedly have kept records and logs of any involvement he had with the case.

I further believe that the case would still have remained fresh in his mind, and therefore, if the injuries sustained by the victim were of a similar nature to those inflicted by the Ripper, or the method of killing was in any way comparable to that of the Ripper, then immediately on the commencement of the Whitechapel murders, Inspector Reid would have made the association, informed his superiors and requested that the case be reopened.

My conclusion therefore is that the murder of 'Fairy Fay', if it ever happened, was never seriously treated as a Ripper murder, and does not exist in the 'Ripper files', despite the fact that these files hold references to the Pinchin Street murder, the Rose Mylett murder and slaying of Frances Coles, even though it was never seriously entertained that they were Ripper victims.

Emma Elizabeth Smith

Emma Elizabeth Smith was born in 1883 and at the time of her demise was a widow of 45 years of age. She lodged in Fournier Street in Spitalfields, where she earned her living as a prostitute, and had gained a reputation as a bit of a brawler.

2 April 1888 was a Bank Holiday Monday and Emma had spent her evening soliciting around the Whitechapel High Street and Commercial Street areas. Early on the morning of 3 April, Smith was walking along Osborn Street when she was accosted by three youths. She herself put the age of the youngest at no more than 18 years.

Osborn Street was the bottom part of Brick Lane and ran from Wentworth Street to the Whitechapel High Street. It was notorious in Victorian days, and a number of gangs frequented the area. The youths had followed her from Whitechapel Church and confronted her at what is the commonly accepted site, on the corner of Brick Lane and Wentworth Street, opposite Taylor Brothers Mustard and Cocoa Mill.

The three youths raped her and forced a blunt instrument into her vagina, so brutally that it tore the flesh between her vagina and her anus. She staggered to her lodgings where the Deputy persuaded her to go to the London Hospital for treatment. On examination the doctors defined the extent of her injuries and Emma lapsed into a coma. On 5 April 1888 Emma Elizabeth Smith died from peritonitis.

Her inclusion as a Ripper victim is probably attributed to Walter Dew, who was a Detective Constable in the Whitechapel C.I.D. at the time of the murder, and who subsequently wrote in his memoirs that he believed that both Emma Smith and Martha Tabram were victims of Jack the Ripper.

It was suggested in an article in the *Sun* newspaper in 1972 that a criminal going by the name of 'Fingers Freddy', who performed conjuring tricks whilst associates picked the pockets of the audience, was involved, together with Emma Smith, in a blackmail attempt on an illegal abortionist, who in retaliation arranged for the murder of the guilty parties.

Superintendent Arthur Butler, who supplied the information for the article to the *Sun*, further stated that Fingers Freddy disappeared shortly after the murder of Emma Smith

There is no corroborative evidence to support this story and the information must therefore be taken with a pinch of salt. However, in order totally to eliminate Smith as a Ripper victim we must summarise our findings and look at the following information and questions.

Was there an inquest into her death, and are the hospital records still available?

How long did it take Emma to go comatose after her admission to hospital, and what did she say during her dying days?

All the Scotland Yard files on Emma Elizabeth Smith went missing from the Public Records Office in December of 1983. If any reader is responsible or knows the whereabouts of these files, would he please return them to me at the address provided on the last page of this book. If he declines to do this then I would greatly appreciate it if he would photostat the records and send me a copy for research purposes.

Nobody who describes the Ripper in later murders makes any mention of a youth, and yet it was only seven months later in November that the final murder of Mary Jane Kelly heralded the end of the Ripper killings.

Emma described her attackers. This was not an attack by a single killer like Jack the Ripper, but by a gang of young thugs. Only if one of the youths graduated to become Jack the Ripper could this be attributed to our Whitechapel murderer.

The instrument used was of a blunt nature, and no mutilations were evident.

My own opinion is that to kill Emma was not part of the plans of the gang of youths. It was a Tuesday morning the day after a Bank Holiday. The youths were probably broke and decided to rape and mug Emma purely for the kick of it, and so I do not believe that Emma Elizabeth Smith was a victim of the Whitechapel murderer.

CHAPTER TWO

Martha Tabram

Martha Tabram was also known as Martha Turner, having adopted the name of William Turner, with whom she had lived on and off for approximately nine years.

She was the estranged wife of Henry Samuel Tabram, who worked as a foreman furniture packer and lived in East Greenwich.

Samuel Tabram was a man of short stature who dressed well and sported a moustache and imperial. He had separated from Martha around 1875, supposedly because of her excessive drinking, but he did continue to pay her maintenance of 12 shillings a week, reducing it to half a crown on discovering that her way of life was that of a prostitute.

Martha had at one time issued a warrant against him which had resulted in his imprisonment for non-payment of maintenance. Suffice to say that in 1879, on discovering that she was living with William Turner, he discontinued supporting her in any way.

William Turner, a slovenly-dressed young man, had been employed originally in the trade of carpenter, but at the time of the murder had worked for a number of years as a hawker. He also found Martha's drinking to be a problem and hence their relationship was decidedly stormy.

The pair of them had lodged for a time at Number 4 Star Place, Commercial Street. This was verified by one Mary Bousfield who had been their landlady. They had absconded owing two weeks' rent, and at the time of her demise Mary had ceased cohabitation with Turner and was lodging alone at Number 19 George Street, Spitalfields.

On Saturday 4 August, William Turner met Martha in Leadenhall Street and gave her one and sixpence; this was to be the last time that he would see her alive.

On Bank Holiday Monday 6 August, Martha went out in the evening with a friend called Mary Ann Connolly (otherwise known

as Pearly Poll). Connolly was an unmarried prostitute
known Martha for a number of months under the name of
Turner. She was a big woman with a face that was flushed by d
and at the time of the murders was fifty years old.

She said, when testifying at the inquest, that they had gone into the
Two Brewers public house for a drink at around 10 p.m., where they
had met two soldiers and had drunk with them in several pubs until
approximately 11.45 p.m. At this time they had separated; Connolly
had gone with the corporal up Angel Alley to have sex, whilst Martha
had gone with the guardsman to George Yard (today it is called
Gunthorpe Street) for a similar purpose.

The public house, the Two Brewers, was identified by Daniel
Farson as being in Duke Street, Limehouse, but modern opinion
lends itself to its location having been in Brick Lane.

This is no disrespect to Daniel Farson, who is viewed with reverence as the Ripper researcher who discovered the very important
document the 'Macnaghten Memorandum' and also revealed the
identity of the initials M. J. D. as being those of a leading Ripper
suspect named Montague John Druitt.

Connolly stated that she and the corporal separated from Martha
and the guardsman at the corner of George Yard at about 12.15 a.m.
on Monday 7 August. After being questioned, Connolly disappeared.
She was traced by Sergeant Caunter (nicknamed Tommy Round-
head) to her cousin's, a Mrs Shean who lived at Number 4 Fullers
Court, Drury Lane.

Connolly subsequently attended an identity parade of the Scots
Guards at the Tower of London but failed to recognise anyone. She
then remembered that the soldiers had white cap bands and so was
taken to another identity parade at the Wellington Barracks in
Birdcage Walk. At this identity parade of Coldstream Guards, she
identified guardsmen George and Skipper. Both proved to have
firm alibis and this avenue of enquiry came to an end.

At approximately 2 a.m. Police Constable Barrett whilst patrolling
his beat saw a young Grenadier guard in Wentworth Street.
He described him as aged 22 to 26, about 5 feet 9 inches tall, with
a fair complexion, dark hair, and a small brown moustache turned
up at the ends. It is interesting to note that PC Barrett did not state
that he was a corporal, and also that he failed to record the soldier's
name.

On questioning the soldier he ascertained that he was waiting for
a chum who had gone with a girl. Based upon the testimony of

imate of the time, he must have been there for
ninutes, but this does however appear to be too
e for it not to have been the soldiers who had
and Connolly in their pub crawl.

oss as to how two ladies could spend a number
any of two gentlemen without having discov-
names. How had they communicated with
more importantly, how had the guardsmen
addressed one another? It must further be mentioned that PC
Barrett had found it necessary to question one of the guardsmen as
to why he was loitering in the area, and yet he also had neglected to
note the guardsman's name.

At 3.30 a.m., Alfred George Crow, a cab driver (of cab number
6600) who lived at George Yard Buildings, noticed what he thought
was a tramp sleeping on the first-floor landing, but paid it no heed.
This was probably the body of Martha Tabram.

At 4.45 a.m., another tenant of George Yard Buildings, John
Saunders Reeves, a waterside labourer with a dark beard who wore
earrings, left his residence at Number 37, and came downstairs
where he encountered Martha's body lying in a pool of blood. He
immediately went to find a policeman and returned to the scene of
the murder accompanied by PC Barrett.

Timothy Robert Killeen, a doctor with a surgery at 68 Brick Lane,
was called to examine the body at 5.30 a.m..

He estimated that death had occurred about two hours previously,
which would put the time of the murder at around 3.30 a.m..

There were thirty-nine stab wounds to the body, including five
in the liver, five in the left lung, one in the heart, two in the right
lung, two in the spleen and six in the stomach; the breasts, belly
and sexual organs being the main targets. He further stated that
thirty-eight of the wounds had been inflicted by a right-handed
person, and that only one wound could not have been caused by an
ordinary pen-knife. The exception was a wound to the sternum
which he ascertained had been made by a dagger or sword bayonet.

It has been suggested that Doctor Killeen may not have been
aware that the old triangular bayonet had been withdrawn from
infantry issue the previous year and that the new bayonet was quite
capable of inflicting wounds similar to those evident on the body of
Martha Tabram.

The author Jon Ogan points out that it was not believed for very
long that a bayonet was a possible assault weapon.

In the Aberconway version of the Memorandum, Melville Macnaghten stated that he did not regard Tabram as a Ripper victim.

Conversely, Doctor Robert Anderson (Later Sir Robert Anderson), who was the Assistant Commissioner of the Metropolitan Police C.I.D. did however regard Martha Tabram as the first victim of Jack the Ripper, a view with which I concur, and a view incidentally which is not shared by the majority of knowledgeable Ripperologists.

I consider that anyone who could stab his victim a total of thirty-nine times in a murder which was performed outside, must have done so whilst in a killing frenzy, or at the very least a fit of intense anger, and this could have served as the trigger to the killer. This in turn initiated the need to seek out further victims, in order to satiate a lust that was cyclical.

This murder would serve to satisfy his lust but only temporarily, and it would also have cultivated a need which made it necessary for him to kill again in order to alleviate the torment from which he now suffered.

If one takes a look at the succession of atrocities inflicted on a succession of victims by Jack the Ripper, then this would be a logical first incursion by him into the theatre of murder.

If Martha Tabram is accepted as the first Ripper fatality we can draw certain conjectures from the information available, the first being that one of the two guardsmen could therefore have been the Ripper.

PC Barrett did not specify if the guardsman whom he saw and questioned was a corporal.

A possible scenario would be that after separating from Connolly after sex, the corporal made his way to Wentworth Street (a distance of only 400 yards), where he met his colleague with Martha Tabram. He, the corporal, then went back into George Yard with Tabram for sex and then murdered her after an argument, probably about payment. During this period PC Barrett arrived on the scene and confronted the guardsman, who was standing in the street awaiting the return of his colleague.

This however would not ordinarily account for the length of the time lapse, so we must question the estimate of the time of death.

In 1888 they did not have the depth of knowledge and the technology to assist them with their estimation and so they relied on loss of body temperature and physical signs, so it would not be unusual for the time of death to be wrongly estimated. I have been informed on this matter that an error of up to two hours could be accounted for in this way. This would have rendered it more likely for one of the two soldiers to have been her assailant.

Doctor Killeen estimated that the body had been dead for about two hours, thus putting the death at around 3.30 a.m. This was an hour and a half after PC Barrett encountered the guardsman and over four hours since the two couples had separated.

If Doctor Killeen's estimate of the time of death was accurate, then another explanation is allowed, this being that Martha picked up another customer after separating from the guardsman, and this man proved to be her murderer. This was not unlikely as it was a holiday weekend and more people than usual would have been on the streets.

A number of questions arise which would assist in our enquiry, and would have been of undoubted assistance at the time of the murder.

PC Barrett also attended the identification parade, and neither of the two soldiers identified by Connolly was also recognised by the police officer.

Can any evidence be supplied as to the whereabouts of the two suspected guardsmen for the nights of the subsequent Ripper murders?

What was the extent of the investigation into the alibis of the two guardsmen? Soldiers literally close ranks when one of them is accused of anything, and are notorious for sticking together.

On surveying the extent of the wounds, it must be noted that a high percentage penetrated critical areas. Did the killer possess an element of anatomical knowledge enjoyed by soldiers in the field, or was the requisite anatomical knowledge exhibited in the murder greater than this, or could this high percentage be accounted for by chance?

How much anatomical knowledge did soldiers possess in 1888? Obviously they would be instructed in bayonet killing areas.

Did Connolly lie through vanity when she said that she went with the corporal and Tabram with the guardsman? Whilst Tabram was no beauty, it is perhaps pertinent that she was ten years younger and by description more attractive than Connolly. This would also lend credence to the guardsman having been seen by PC Barrett. The corporal would pull rank when taking his pick of the girls.

Furthermore, when questioned under caution as reported by Inspector Reid, Connolly identified two private soldiers, one of whom did have good conduct stripes on his arm, but this man was proved to have been with his wife at the time of the murder.

I do not believe that the soldiers were included with those paraded. If they had been confronted with both Connolly and PC Barrett they would have revealed their identities voluntarily so as to avoid a guilty confrontation.

In his assessment of the weapon used, Doctor Killeen specified that one of the wounds had been inflicted by a dagger or sword bayonet. Was it possible that all of the wounds were capable of being inflicted with the same weapon?

Had the murder already been committed when PC Barrett encountered the guardsman, and was the guardsman acting as a lookout?

If both of the guardsmen murdered Martha Tabram together then this would explain Doctor Killeen's assessment that two weapons were possibly used in the fatal assault.

When PC Barrett stated that he saw a guardsman in Wentworth Street and did not specify the rank of the soldier, this must be looked at from the perspective that even in those days a policeman was trained to notice detail, and would most likely have specified the rank of the soldier as corporal had it applied. It is the first thing that a layman notices on a uniform.

Martha Tabram was murdered by a sadistic homicidal maniac of a similar nature to Jack the Ripper. He stabbed her a total of thirty-nine times, a high percentage in critical areas of the body. If she wasn't the starting-point for the Ripper murders then why didn't this killer carry on to kill again?

His attack was frenzied and prolonged, with the breasts and sexual organs as the primary areas of attack, and I suggest that after inflicting ten to fifteen stab wounds the assailant would have attained a level of sexual passion. He then carried on to penetrate the body a further twenty-five times, and may have reached a sexual climax before ceasing the onslaught.

Has the possibility of William Turner as a Ripper suspect, or at the very least, the murderer of Martha Tabram ever been investigated or entertained?

Let us take a look at the last hours of Martha Tabram's life.

Witness	Where seen	With whom	Time
Mary Connolly	Two Brewers	Two guardsmen	10 p.m.
Mary Connolly	Two Brewers	Two guardsmen	11.45 p.m.
Mary Connolly	Corner of George Yard	Martha went with the guardsman	12.15 a.m.
PC Barrett	Wentworth Street	Saw a young guardsman alone	c. 2.00 a.m.
PC Barrett	Wentworth Street	He questions the guardsman	2.00– 2.05 a.m.
Alfred George Crow	George Yard Buildings	Notices what he thinks is a tramp asleep on the first floor	3.30 a.m.
John Saunders Reeves	George Yard Buildings	Came downstairs and discovered body	4.45 a.m.
Dr Killeen	Scene of crime	Called out by police	5.30 a.m.

To summarise and evaluate the known information, I believe that the murderer of Martha Tabram was a client whom she picked up after having separated from the guardsmen and whilst still in the proximity of Wentworth Street. I suggest that Martha took that client to one of her usual places nearby, which was George Yard, where after an argument or on impulse he killed her and mutilated the body. Gaining a perverse satisfaction from his actions he returned home where he was filled with horror at the thought of what he had done.

This remorse, dread and self-denial was gradually replaced with elation as over the following days he realized that he had escaped detection for the crime, and the thrill of the risk and suspense of the murder gradually overcame his trepidation until the dominant thought in his mind was to duplicate the kick he had gotten and so he had to kill again. But this time it would be deliberate. He would go out prepared to kill. So was born the legend of Jack the Ripper.

I propose the inclusion of Martha Tabram as a Ripper victim primarily because her killer was not of a normal disposition and the attack on Martha may have been the trigger which started this deranged murderer on his quest to kill. Undoubtedly frenzied in his attack on Tabram, he had the capability of stabbing his victim a total of thirty-nine times, the final thirty of which would unquestionably have been inflicted on an already dead body.

This was the work of a maniac, who if he was not closely linked to the murdered woman (a spouse or lover could have killed her in a fit of temper, and might never have killed again) was a danger to society. This could have resulted in the appearance of a second

Ripper on the streets of Whitechapel, as I am of the opinion that this man, if he was not Jack the Ripper, would almost certainly have killed again.

As this was not the case, then I suggest that Martha Tabram may have been the first victim of our killer, Jack the Ripper.

CHAPTER THREE

Mary Ann Nichols

Mary Nichols was born in 1845, the daughter of Edward Walker, a locksmith, who later earned a living as a blacksmith. Edward originally lived in Dean Street Fetter Lane, but at the time of Mary's death was residing at 16 Maidswood Road in Camberwell. As a matter of interest he was grey-haired and sported a beard.

The last time that Edward had seen his daughter was in June of 1886. Mary had lived with him between March and April of 1883 but her drinking had caused problems and she had left.

In 1864 she married a printer of Bouverie Street by the name of William Nichols, and later she moved with him to Peabody Buildings in Lambeth. At the time of the murder he was employed as a machine printer by Messrs Purkiss Bacon and Co. of Whitefriars Street, E.C. and was living at 37 Coburg Row, Old Kent Road

The marriage produced five children born between 1866 and 1879, but in 1880 the marriage broke down irretrievably and the couple separated.

The eldest boy took his mother's side and he and the youngest boy moved in with Mary's father, and were still living there in 1888. Both insisted that the cause of the breakdown had been William leaving Mary for another woman. Nichols himself maintained the break-up was due to Mary's excessive drinking, and in reality one probably instigated the other. Suffice to say that the eldest boy did not speak to his father until after his mother's death.

There must have been an element of truth in the drinking rumour as her father had also highlighted this as being a problem, during Mary's stay with him. Suffice to say that by 1877 Mary had begun to drink heavily and after the break-up of her marriage her lifestyle was in steady decline.

Initially Nichols paid Mary an allowance of five shillings a week, but ceased these payments in 1882 on learning that she was earning a living by prostituting herself.

Mary issued a summons against her estranged husband for maintenance, but lost the case when William proved that she was living off her immoral earnings.

The details of her movements after the break-up of her marriage are exceedingly comprehensive and well documented. They include that from 24 May 1883 until 2 June 1887 she lived with Thomas Stuart Drew who was a blacksmith and had a shop at 15 York Street Walworth. She also worked for a Samuel and Sarah Cowdry from 16 April 1888 until 12 July 1888, from where she absconded, stealing clothing worth £3 10s. Whilst in this position, she wrote a letter to her father saying that they were very nice people and expressing her satisfaction with the position. In the letter she requested that her father please reply telling her how they all fared. This he did, but ceased any further communication. It is also known that she spent a number of spells in the Lambeth Workhouse.

Let us now move forward. The last two places in which Mary lodged were Number 18 Thrawl Street where she shared a room with three other women. The room contained two beds and Mary shared a bed with Ellen Holland. The cost to each woman for a night was fourpence.

From 24 August up until the night of her murder Mary stayed in a dosshouse which allowed men and women to sleep together.

This was known as the White House and was situated at Number 56 Flower and Dean Street in Spitalfields. Flower and Dean Street is I believe the most important street in the hunt for the Whitechapel murderer. It ran from east to west between Commercial Street and Brick Lane and was described by some as the foulest and most dangerous street in the whole of London. Today the geography of the area has changed, leaving only a short part of the western side remaining.

On Thursday 30 August, Mary spent the evening in various public houses in and around Whitechapel Road. At 12.30 a.m. on Friday 31 August she was supposedly seen leaving the Frying Pan on the corner of Thrawl Street and Brick Lane. It was a frequent haunt of Mary's and is now an Indian restaurant.

At 1.20 a.m. she went to a dosshouse at Number 18 Thrawl Street; she was slightly drunk and did not have the required fourpence needed for a bed, and was turned away. She laughed as she left and said 'I'll soon get my doss money'. She further remarked on the new bonnet which she was wearing.

Some time after 2.00 a.m. she was met by Ellen Holland at the corner of Whitechapel High Street and Brick Lane. At this time she was drunk and staggering about. She informed Ellen that she had earned her doss money more than once that night, but had spent it in the Frying Pan on drink, and she refused to return to Thrawl Street with Ellen saying that she was off to earn it again and adding that she wanted to go to a place where she could share a bed with a man. Ellen Holland put the time of this conversation at 2.30 a.m.

At 3.40 to 3.45 a.m. Charles Cross, who lived in Doveton Street in Bethnal Green and was employed by Pickfords of Broad Street as a carman, saw what he thought was a tarpaulin lying on the ground opposite Essex Wharf, Buck's Row. He went across to examine it and discovered it was a woman. He was joined by Robert Paul, a carter who was on his way to work.

The body was lying with the skirts pulled up and on feeling the hands and face Paul said that he thought she was breathing but it was very little if she was.

The two men then went in search of a policeman and found PC Mizen in Hanbury Street, informing him that they had found a woman lying dead in the gutter in Buck's Row.

Buck's Row is situated to the east side of Whitechapel and runs from Brady Street to Baker's Row. It consisted of a wide section which narrowed at the site of a Board School, which was still there up until the 1980s when it burnt down. The narrower section consisted of newly built terraced houses on one side, and warehouses, or wharves as they were known, on the other.

A stable yard stood between the Board School and the terraced houses, and Mary Ann Nichols's body was discovered in front of the stable yard gate. After the murder the name of the street was changed to Durward Street, and most of the buildings have now been demolished.

In the meantime and totally independently PC John Neil whilst walking his beat eastwards along the Row towards Brady Street had also discovered the body at a time he later put at approximately 3.45 a.m. By using his lamp to signal, he summoned Police Constable Thain to his assistance when Thain was passing the bottom of the street, and the two were joined by PC Mizen who had been directed there by Cross and Paul.

As was the custom, the first attending officer remained with the body, while PC Thain was despatched to get Doctor Llewellyn and PC Mizen went to fetch an ambulance. An ambulance was not anything like what we would associate today but merely a glorified cart on which to transport the body.

Doctor Llewellyn testified at the inquest to say that he was called from his surgery at Number 152 Whitechapel Road at 4.00 a.m. and on attending the body he pronounced her to be dead. He noticed, as he put it, that there was only a wine glass and a half of blood in the gutter, but was in no doubt that the murder had been committed at that spot.

PC Thain reported that on his return to the scene, he discovered that PC Neil had been joined by two slaughtermen named Tomkins and Mumford, and yet when giving evidence both Tomkins and Mumford stated that PC Thain had informed them about the murder, and Tomkins further stated that another slaughterman called Charles Brittain had accompanied them to view the body.

Doctor Llewellyn instructed that the body be taken to the mortuary at Old Montague Street Workhouse Infirmary. It must be noted that while Doctor Llewellyn was examining the body in Buck's Row, an unknown man passed the scene of the crime and despite police appeals to the public this gentleman did not come forward.

Patrick Mulshaw, who worked as a night porter for the Whitechapel Board of Works, and who was called as a witness to the inquest, said giving evidence that he was on duty watching the sewage works at Winthrop Street (Winthrop Street ran parallel and converged into Buck's Row) that between 3.00 a.m. and 4.00 a.m. he saw and heard no one, except one man who passed by and said *'Watchman! Old man, I believe somebody has been murdered down the street.'*

On being further questioned Mulshaw admitted to dozing during the night, but assured the court that he had been awake during the time in question. It is therefore likely that this was the man who had passed the scene of the crime while Doctor Llewellyn was examining the body.

Whilst Llewellyn conducted his initial examination of the body, Sergeant Kerby arrived at the scene and with the assistance of PC Neil and an unnamed officer from H Division removed the body to the mortuary on the ambulance.

PC Thain assisted in lifting the body onto the ambulance and whilst so doing noticed that the back of the dress was covered in blood, some of which got onto his hands.

PC Thain remained at the site awaiting the arrival of Inspector Spratling, who had been sent for. Spratling stated that he arrived at the scene at 4.30 a.m., as the blood was being washed away by James Green. He then went to the mortuary, where he was taking down a description of the body while it was being stripped to be washed. When the skirt was lifted he discovered the extent of the mutilations. He recalled Doctor Llewellyn.

Inspector Abberline did provide a number of written reports which were most comprehensive in content and are held in the Scotland Yard Files. A typical example of these is the account describing the events which occurred immediately after the murder of Mary Nichols. It reads:

About 3.40 a.m. 31st ult, as Charles Cross, carman, of 22 Doveton Street, Cambridge Road, Bethnal Green, was passing through Bucks Row, Whitechapel (on his way to work) he noticed a woman lying on her back on the footway (against some gates leading into a stable yard). He stopped to look at the woman when another carman (also on his way to work) named Robert Paul of 30 Fosters Street, Bethnal Green, came up and Cross called his attention to the woman, but being dark they did not notice any blood, and passed on with the intention of informing the first constable they met. On arriving at the corner of Hanbury Street and Old Montague Street, they met PC 55H Mizen, and acquainted him of what they had seen, and on the constable proceeding towards the spot he found that PC 97J Neil (who was on the beat) had found the woman and was calling for assistance.

PC Neil had turned on his light and discovered that the woman's throat was severely cut. PC 96J Thain was also called and sent at once for Dr Llewellyn of 152 Whitechapel Road who quickly arrived on the scene, pronounced life extinct and ordered the removal of the body to the mortuary. In the meantime PC Mizen had been sent for the ambulance and assistance from Bethnal Green station and on Inspector Spratling and other officers arriving, the body was removed to the mortuary. On arriving there the Inspector made a further examination and found that the abdomen had also been severely cut in several places, exposing the intestines. The Inspector acquainted Dr Llewellyn, who afterwards made a more minute examination and found that the wounds in the abdomen were in themselves sufficient to cause instant death. *He further expressed an opinion that they were inflicted before the throat was cut.*

The body was not immediately identified. On the clothing being carefully examined by Inspector Helston, he found some of the underclothing bore the mark of Lambeth Workhouse which led to the body being identified as that of a former inmate named Mary Ann Nichols, and by that means we were able to trace the relatives, and complete the identity. It was found she was the wife of William Nichols of 37 Coburg Street, Old Kent Road, a printer in the employ of Messrs Perkins, Bacon and Co., Whitefriars Street, City, from whom she had been separated about nine years through her drunken immoral habits, and that for several years past she had from time to time been an inmate of various workhouses. In May of this year she left Lambeth Workhouse and entered the service of Mrs Cowdry, Ingleside, Rose Hill Road, Wandsworth. She remained there until the 12th July when she absconded stealing various articles of wearing apparel. A day or two after, she became a lodger at 18 Thrawl Street, Spitalfields, a common lodging house, and at another common lodging house at 56 Flower and Dean Street up to the night of the murder.

About 1.40 a.m. that morning, she was seen in the kitchen at 18 Thrawl Street when she informed the Deputy of the lodging house that she had no money to pay her lodgings. She requested that her bed might be kept for her and left stating that she would soon get the money. At this time she was drunk. She was next seen at 2.30 a.m. at the corner of Osborn Street and Whitechapel Road by Ellen Holland, a lodger in the same house, who seeing she was very drunk requested her to return with her to the lodging house. She however refused, remarking that she would soon be back and walked away down the Whitechapel Road in the direction of the place where the body was found. There can be no doubt with regard to the time because the Whitechapel Church clock chimed 2.30 and Holland called the attention of the deceased to the time.

We have been unable to find any person who saw her alive after Holland left her. The distance from Osborn Street to Bucks Row would be about half a mile. Inquiries were made in every conceivable quarter with a view to trace the murderer but not the slightest clue can at present be obtained.

By the time the doctor arrived back at the mortuary the body had been stripped and washed by two mortuary attendants, James Hatfield and Robert Mann. This was the cause of great indignation to Dr Llewellyn, who expressed his anger at the police. The police in turn insisted that the mortuary had been instructed to leave the body as it was until the doctor arrived.

Now let us review Mary's movements for the evening of the 30th and 31st of August.

Witness	Location	With whom	Time
General knowledge	Leaving the Frying Pan	Alone	12.30 a.m.
The Deputy	Dosshouse at 18 Thrawl Street	Said she was off out to get her doss money, commented on her new hat	1.20 a.m.
Ellen Holland	Corner of Osborn Street	Alone	2.30 a.m.
Charles Cross & Robert Paul	Bucks Row	Alone and dead	3.40 a.m.

At the inquest *The Times* reported Dr Llewellyn's medical testimony thus:

Five of the teeth were missing and there was a slight laceration of the tongue. *There was a bruise running along lower part of the jaw on the right side of the face that might have been caused by a blow from a fist or pressure from a thumb. There was a circular bruise on the left side of the face which also might have been caused by the pressure of the fingers.* On the left side of the neck about one inch below the jaw, there was an incision about four inches in length, and ran from a point immediately below the ear. On the same side but an inch below, and commencing about one inch in front of it, was a circular incision which terminated at a point about three inches below the right jaw. That incision completely severed all of the tissues down to the vertebrae. The large vessels on both side of the neck had been severed. The incision was about eight inches in length. The cuts must have been caused by a long-bladed knife moderately sharp and used with great violence. No blood was found on the breast, either on the body or the clothes. There were no injuries about the body until just about the lower part of the abdomen. Two or three inches from the left side was a wound running in a jagged manner. The wound was a very deep one and the tissues were cut through. There were several incisions running across the abdomen. There were also three or four cuts similar running downwards on the right side, all of which had been caused by a knife which had been used violently and downwards.

The injuries were from left to right and might have been done by a left-handed person. All the injuries had been caused by the same instrument. (See also *The Modus Operandi of Jack the Ripper*.)

The Central News Agency reported that

'. . . scarcely has the horror and sensation caused by the discovery of the murdered woman in Whitechapel some short time ago had time to abate, than another discovery is made, which, for the brutality exercised on the victim, is even more shocking, and will no doubt create as great a sensation in the vicinity as its predecessor.

The affair, up to the present, is enveloped in complete mystery, and the police have as yet no evidence to trace the perpetrators of the horrible deed. The facts are that as Constable Neil was walking down Buck's Row, Thomas Street, Whitechapel, about a quarter to four o'clock this morning, he discovered a woman, between thirty-five and forty years of age, lying at the side of the street with her throat cut right open from ear to ear, the instrument with which the deed was done tracing the throat from left to right. The wound was about two inches wide, and blood was flowing profusely; in fact, she was discovered to be lying in a pool of blood. She was immediately conveyed to the Whitechapel Mortuary, where it was found that, besides the wound in the throat, the lower part of her person was completely ripped open.

The wound extends nearly to her breast, and must have been effected with a large knife. As the corpse of the woman lies in the mortuary it presents a ghastly sight. The victim measures 5 ft. 2 in. in height. The hands are bruised, and bear evidence of having engaged in a severe struggle. There is the impression of a ring having been worn on one of the deceased's fingers, but there is nothing to show that it had been wrenched from her in a struggle. Some of the front teeth have also been knocked out, and the face is bruised on both cheeks and very much discoloured. Deceased wore a rough brown Ulster, with large buttons in front. Her clothes are torn, and cut up in several places, leaving evidence of the ferocity with which the murder was committed. The only way by which the police can prosecute an enquiry at present is by finding someone who can identify the deceased, and then, if possible, trace those in whose company she was when last seen. In Buck's Row naturally the excitement prevails, and several persons in the neighbourhood state that an affray occurred shortly after midnight, but no screams were heard, nor anything beyond what might have been considered evidence of an ordinary brawl. The woman has not yet been identified. She was wearing workhouse clothes, and it is supposed she came from Lambeth. A night watchman was in the street where the crime was committed. He heard no screams and saw no signs of the scuffle. The body was quite warm when brought to the mortuary at half past four this morning.

Police Constable Cartwright was ordered by Inspector Spratling to conduct a thorough search of the murder site and the surrounding neighbourhood, which he did without success.

Presiding over the inquest on Mary Ann Nichols was Wynne Edwin Baxter, who was forty-four years of age at the time of the murder.

Baxter was generally regarded as a talkative, well-dressed man. He used the telegraphic address 'Inquest, London' and conducted the proceedings in the Whitechapel Working Lads Institute. He criticised the police for their failure to detect the abdominal injuries while the body was still at the murder site and further for allowing the body to be washed without their supervision. This criticism was contested by Inspector Helsen and Detective Sergeant Enright who insisted that they had left strict instructions that the body was not to be touched. These instructions were disregarded and the body was washed and laid out by Hatfield and Mann at their own volition.

It was probably a lapse of memory on the part of James Hatfield which instigated the washing of the body. He had a notably poor memory, proven by the fact that a juror pointed out that Hatfield had denied that the body wore 'stays' when in point of fact he had personally shown them to the jury members when they had visited the mortuary.

Sarah Colwell of Brady Street claimed that she had been awakened during the small hours of the morning by the noise of a woman who was running and screaming. She stated that it appeared that the woman was being struck as she ran, but there was no noise of following footsteps. This would give credence to the tradition that the Ripper wore rubber strips on his shoes. The police started to do a similar thing so that they could not be heard when approaching a scene and so alert any suspects.

A railway signalman named Thomas Ede gave evidence at the inquest saying that he had seen a man in a two-peaked cap with the blade of a knife protruding from his pocket, outside the Foresters Arms in Cambridge Heath Road. At a subsequent visit to the inquest on 22 September he related that he had identified the man as being Henry James, a man who frequented the area of Whitechapel and who was considered to be a harmless lunatic.

Mrs Emma Green, who lived with her daughter and two sons in New Cottage, Buck's Row, the residence which adjoined Brown's stable yard gate, said when giving evidence, that she and her daughter slept in a room which nearly overlooked the murder site, and that she herself was a light sleeper, but had heard nothing unusual on the night of the murder until such time as the police arrived at the newly discovered body. It was her son who had washed the blood away from the gutter.

Mary Ann Monk attended the inquest and testified that the body in the morgue was that of Mary Ann Nichols. She was called after a Lambeth Workhouse laundry mark was discovered on Mary's petticoat. Monk had stayed at Lambeth Workhouse at the same time as the murdered woman.

Walter Purkiss, the Manager of Essex Wharf which stood directly opposite the murder site, stated in his evidence that he went to bed around 11.00 p.m. and awoke at various times during the night but heard nothing. His wife who was pacing the bedroom at the time of the murder also testified that she heard nothing. This would tend to cast doubt on the evidence given by Sarah Colwell.

Inspector Spratling stated in his evidence that he and Sergeant Godley, an officer who was prominent in all of the Ripper murder investigations, had searched the murder area, especially the East London and District Railway embankment and lines and also the Great Eastern Railway Yard. In both cases they had discovered nothing of any interest concerning the case.

Ellen Holland, who was a friend of Nichols and who had lived with her at times in a room at Number 18 Thrawl Street, was told by Mary Ann Monk that the body in the mortuary may be that of Nichols (Whom she knew as Polly). Ellen Holland went to the mortuary and positively identified the remains as those of Mary Ann Nichols. She was also the last person other than the murderer to see Nichols alive.

She went on to explain that she had been to see the fire on the docks (she referred to a fire which started at Messrs Gibbs & Co.

Engineering Works and spread to Gowland's Coal Wharf where it consumed 800 tons of coal). She returned some time after 2.00 p.m. and encountered Nichols at the corner of Osborn Street and Brick Lane. She had asked Nichols to return to Thrawl Street with her but Mary had refused, and they had parted at a time put by Holland at 2.30 p.m.

Later on in the investigation of the Ripper murders, Doctor Thomas Bond, the police surgeon for A Division of the Metropolitan Police, was asked by Doctor Robert Anderson, the Assistant Commissioner, to produce a report on the killings. *In this account he stated that in his personal opinion Mary Nichols had been attacked from her right-hand side.*

Ellen Holland described Mary as a very clean woman and this opinion was supported by Doctor Llewellyn who during the autopsy commented on the surprising cleanliness of her thighs.

Mary Ann Nichols was buried at Ilford Cemetery on 6 September 1888.

My own opinion as to how the murder was committed and after consultation and discussion with certain parties is:

The woman was described as being extremely drunk and as such would not have been a difficult target.

I believe that the Ripper probably punched his victim hard enough for her to fall. He then got on top of her and put his hands on her throat, left above the right (*remember the position of the bruises, this would account for the description*), and pressing down on her neck, squeezed the life out of her. After she had ceased struggling he pushed the neck up by using the heel of his right hand on her chin, and then proceeded to cut her throat using his left hand and directing any flow of blood away from him. He then commenced the mutilation of the body.

I feel that I should point out that Mary was described as having greying hair and with high cheek bones and grey eyes. Her two front teeth were missing but she was still described as looking ten years younger than her actual age.

Certain facts and questions become evident after reviewing the available evidence.

The report by Doctor Llewellyn specified that there were five teeth missing and slight laceration of the tongue. Was he implying that three teeth had been removed or was it more likely just a passing observation?

The bruise running along the lower part of the jaw on the right hand side, if caused by a blow from her assailant, would indicate that her attacker was left-handed. A right-handed man would tend to hit the left side of the victim's face. If the bruise was caused by fingers or thumb pressure then it would also indicate that the killer was left-handed. When applying pressure to the neck of a victim lying on the ground face up, then a left-handed person would initially place his left hand over his right. During strangulation killers frequently adjust their hold, but to begin with he would start with his left hand over his right. To include all possibilities, then, the bruise could have been caused by a small stone on the ground and the Ripper pressing her face into this stone.

Whilst I do not believe that he is the only suspect for the killer, it must be noted that a leading suspect at the time of the murders named John Pizer, alias 'Leather Apron', was staying at Crossman's lodging house in Holloway on the night of the murder. Crossman's lodging house is close to the scene of the crime.

Pizer was cleared of suspicion in the murders, but we will review this situation later in the book.

Doctor Robert Anderson took up his post at Scotland Yard on the day of the murder, and specified in his memoirs that this was 'the second of the crimes'. This suggests that he also regarded Martha Tabram as the first victim of Jack the Ripper.

CHAPTER FOUR

Annie Chapman

Annie Chapman was born in Paddington in 1841 as Eliza Anne Smith. Her father George was a Lifeguardsman who married her mother Ruth Chapman in 1842.

Annie married John Chapman, a domestic head coachman and a relative of her mother's. The marriage took place on 1 May 1869 at All Saints Church in Knightsbridge. The couple had three children, two daughters and a crippled son. One of the daughters died in 1882.

In 1881 the couple were living in Windsor and John was working for a company at St Leonard's Mill Farm Cottage. In 1882 the couple separated shortly before the death of their eldest daughter Emily, Annie having abandoned the family and returned to London.

The police stated that the marriage had broken down due to Annie's drunkardness and immoral ways, but it is worth mentioning that documents show that John Chapman died of cirrhosis of the liver and dropsy, on Christmas Day of 1886, which must cast doubt on his temperance and question the police evaluation. Friends and acquaintances described Annie as only an occasional drunk.

Chapman paid Annie 10/- a week, albeit not absolutely regularly, but nevertheless discharged his responsibilities.

Timothy Donovan, a witness at the inquest, alleged that a Mrs Pearcer of Hackney, who claimed to be a friend of Annie's, had told him that John Chapman had been sacked from his position as a valet to a Bond Street gentleman because of Annie's dishonesty.

Annie continued to make a precarious living by selling crochet work, matches, flowers, supplemented by obtaining money from male friends and occasional prostitution.

In 1886 she was described as living with a man called Jack Sivvey at Number 30 Dorset Street, Spitalfields.

After May of 1888 Annie lived primarily at Crossingham's lodging house, 35 Dorset Street. This building stood opposite Miller's Court, the site of the murder of Mary Kelly, the Ripper's last victim, and was managed by Timothy Donovan who had the job of Deputy.

Annie was of a stout build, having dark brown hair and standing about five feet tall. She had a rounded face, a broad nose and blue eyes.

Some time during the first week of September Annie had a fight with Eliza Cooper. The cause of the fight is debatable but it has been suggested that Annie had informed a chap known as 'Harry the Hawker' that Eliza had stolen a florin from him and replace it with a halfpenny. Eliza's story differs from this; she maintained that the fight had started because Annie had thrown the halfpenny at her as payment for a bar of soap which she had borrowed for a man named Ted Stanley to use.

Ted Stanley was a bricklayer who periodically paid for Annie Chapman's bed at Crossingham's. The rumour was that Stanley was an army veteran who received a pension from the Essex Regiment; however this was denied by Stanley when he was questioned about it.

The fight had taken place in the Britannia, a public house on the corner of Commercial Street and Dorset Street. The licensee was Walter Ringer, but this was in name only and in actuality the pub was run by his wife. It was demolished in 1928 to cater for extension work to the Spitalfields market.

The scrap had then continued in the kitchen at Crossingham's. The result was that Annie received a beating, and finished the fight with a black eye and bruising to her chest. Amelia Palmer said at the inquest that it was Annie's intention to attend the infirmary in order to receive treatment for her injuries.

She did not, by all accounts, gain admittance to either the Whitechapel Infirmary or the Spitalfields Workhouse Infirmary, but she may have received treatment as an outpatient.

Doctor Bagster Phillips reported that at the time of her death she was suffering from chronic disease of the lungs and brain membranes, was undernourished and would before long have died of these causes.

On 7 September she was admitted to the kitchen of Crossingham's by the deputy Timothy Donovan at 11.30 p.m. She was still there at 2.10 a.m. when she was seen by a painter called William Stevens who lodged at Crossingham's. He stated that 'she had taken drink' and that while he was present she removed a box of pills from her pocket, the box broke and she picked up a piece of envelope from the floor and put the pills inside it.

Frederick Stevens, also a lodger at Crossingham's, told the *Star* newspaper that he had drunk a pint of beer with Annie at half past midnight and that she left the lodging house at 1.00 a.m.

At 1.35 a.m. on the morning of 8 December, Donovan the Deputy reported that Annie was back at Crossingham's lodging house and that he had seen her in the kitchen eating a baked potato. He asked Annie for her doss money and she told him that she was weak and ill and had been to the infirmary. She asked that Donovan let her stay on trust, which he refused, and she left Crossingham's saying that they were to keep her a bed and she would be back soon.

John Evans, an elderly man nicknamed 'Brummie', who worked as nightwatchman, verified the time as being 1.35 a.m. and further added that she had told him she had just been out for a pint of beer adding that she had been to her sister's in Vauxhall. She said she didn't have the money to pay for a bed and Evans watched her walk down Little Paternoster Row in the direction of Broomfield Street.

At or around 5.30 a.m. Annie was seen on the pavement outside 29 Hanbury Street by a Mrs Darrell (she testified at the inquest under the name of Elizabeth Long). She was talking to a man a little taller than herself and foreign looking. Darrell heard the man say 'Will you?' to which Annie replied 'Yes' and Mrs Darrell then passed on.

John Davis, an elderly carman, who was employed in Leadenhall Market and who occupied the third floor front room of Number 29 Hanbury Street together with his wife and family, said he got up out of bed just after 5.45 a.m. on hearing the Spitalfields Church clock strike, and he then went into the back yard (probably to urinate). He discovered the body lying on her back parallel to the fence with her head adjacent to the back door steps. Her dress was pulled up over her knees and her intestines were laid across her left shoulder. He shouted for James Green and James Kent, who both worked for a packing case company called John and Thomas Bayley, who traded from Number 23a Hanbury Street, and sent them off to find a policeman.

Inspector Joseph Chandler, who was the Duty Inspector at Commercial Street Police Station, spotted the two men running up Hanbury Street, at a time he put at 6.02 am.

They told him the particulars and he went to the murder scene and also sent a runner for Doctor Phillips. On arriving at the site and seeing the situation, he sent back to the station for an ambulance and assumed the responsibility for informing Scotland Yard. It is further understood that he covered the body with a piece of canvas or sacking.

Inspector Chandler took charge of the site at approximately 6.05 a.m. He conducted a local search of the murder site and in so doing he found a section of a torn envelope and two tablets wrapped tightly in a piece of paper. He also informed the court that there was a standpipe in the yard, and that beside it was a folded leather apron (see the section of the book devoted to John Pizer for a further explanation as to the significance of this).

Doctor Phillips said in evidence that he was summoned to examine the body at 6.20 a.m.. His first observation was that at the feet of the body there was a piece of muslin cloth and a comb in a paper case which he assumed had come out of the torn pocket in Annie's dress.

Annie, on being approached by the Ripper, will have negotiated a price for her services, and will have undoubtedly requested settlement before intercourse was allowed to take place. I believe it is logical to assume that, as no money was found on the body, then the Ripper must have retrieved his money before leaving the scene of the crime. This statement applies in all cases. They didn't charge much for their favours, but only farthings were found at the scene of any of the crimes, and even these ladies charged more than that.

On attending the inquest on 14 September 1888 in the Whitechapel Working Lads Institute, he submitted this evidence under examination:

The left arm was placed across the left breast. The legs were drawn up with the feet resting on the ground and the knees pushed outwards. The face was swollen and turned to the right, so exposing Annie's left profile. The tongue protruded between the front teeth but not beyond the lips, and was much swollen. The teeth were perfect as far as the first molar, both top and bottom, and very fine teeth they were. The body was violently and terribly mutilated.

The stiffness of the limbs was not marked but was evidently commencing. I noticed that the throat was deeply dissevered; and that the incisions through the skin were jagged, and reached right round the neck.

On the wooden paling between the yard in question and the next, smears of blood corresponding to where the head of the deceased had lain were to be found. These were about 14 inches from the ground and situated immediately above the place were the blood lay that had flowed from the neck.

I should say that the instrument used at the throat and abdomen was the same. It must have been a very sharp knife with a thin narrow blade, and must have been at least six to eight inches in length, probably longer. I should say that the injuries could not have been inflicted by a bayonet or sword bayonet. They could have been done by such an instrument as a medical man may use for post mortem purposes, but ordinary surgical cases might not contain such an instrument. Those used by slaughtermen, well ground down might have caused them. He thought that the knives used in the leather trade would not be long enough in the blade. There were indications of anatomical knowledge, which were only less indicated in consequence of haste. The whole body was not present, the absent portions being from the abdomen. The mode in which these portions were extracted showed some anatomical knowledge. He should say that the deceased had been dead for at least two hours, and probably more when he first saw her but it was right to mention that it was a fairly cool morning and that the body would have been more apt to cool rapidly from it having lost a great deal of blood.

There was no evidence of a struggle having taken place. He was positive that the deceased had entered the yard alive. A handkerchief was around the throat of the deceased when he saw it early in the morning; he should say it was not tied on after the throat was cut.

On Saturday p.m. Doctor Phillips performed a post mortem examination of Annie Chapman's body at The Whitechapel Workhouse Infirmary Mortuary, which was in a poor condition, an observation which was not lost on the doctor.

The autopsy findings were reported as follows:

He noticed the same protrusion of the tongue. There was a bruise over the right temple. On the upper eyelid there was a bruise, and there were two distinct bruises, each the size of a man's thumb, on the forepart of the top of the chest. The stiffness of the limbs was now well marked. There was a bruise over the middle part of the bone of the right hand. There was an old scar on the left of the frontal bone. The stiffness was more noticeable on the left side, especially in the fingers which were partly closed. There was an abrasion over the ring finger, with the distinct marking of a ring or rings. The throat had been severed as before described. The incisions into the skin indicated that they had been made from the left side of the neck (again pointing to the use of the knife in the left hand). There were two distinct clean cuts on the left side of the spine. They were parallel to each other and separated by about a half an inch. The muscular structures appeared as though an attempt had been made to separate the bones of the neck. There were various other mutilations of the body, but he was of the opinion that they had occurred subsequent to the death of the woman, and to the large escape of blood from the division of the neck.

At this point in the proceedings Doctor Phillips said that as from these injuries he was satisfied as to the cause of death, he thought that he had better not go into further details of the mutilations, which could only be painful to the feelings of the jury and the public. The Coroner decided to allow that course of action to be adopted.

Doctor Phillips continued saying that the cause of death was apparent from the injuries which he had described. From these appearances he was of the opinion that the breathing had been interfered with previous to death, and that death arose from syncope or failure of the heart's action in consequence of loss of blood caused by severance of the throat.

He was then subjected to further questioning by the Coroner, and continued:

The deceased was far advanced in disease of the lungs and membranes of the brain, but they had nothing to do with the cause of death. The stomach contained a little food but there was not any sign of fluid.

There was no appearance of the deceased having taken alcohol, but there were signs of great deprivation and he should say she had been badly fed. He was convinced that she had not taken any strong alcohol for some hours before she had died.

The injuries were certainly not self-inflicted. The bruises on the face were evidently recent, especially about the chin and sides of the jaw, but the bruises in the front of the chest and on the temple were of longer standing – probably of days. He was of the opinion that the person who had cut the deceased's throat took hold of her by the chin and then commenced the incision from left to right. He thought that it was highly probable that a person could call out, but with regard to an idea that she might have been gagged, he could only point to the swollen face and protruding tongue, both of which were signs of suffocation.

It was whilst the body was being removed to the mortuary that the effects of Annie were discovered in a neat pile. They consisted of a piece of coarse muslin, two combs and two farthings.

The existence of the coins is questionable, as they survive in the press reports, but no mention of them was made at the inquest.

Annie Chapman had been wearing two or three rings and, as testified, these were missing from the body and abrasions of absence were evident. Despite the appeals in the press and widely publicised police enquiries, these rings were never found or handed in to the authorities.

For this reason I would be tempted to say that the Ripper himself removed the rings, but if so why didn't he remove the finger. My own suspicions lean towards those who attended her body in the mortuary.

The body was laid out and washed by a nurse called Mary Elizabeth Simonds assisted by Frances Wright and on the orders of the Clerk to the Parish Guardians.

On 10 September a summary was included in *The Times* which reviewed the situation thus:

So far as we know, nothing in fact or fiction equals these outrages in their horrible nature and in the effect which they have produced upon the popular imagination. The circumstances that the murders seem to be the work of one individual, that his blows fall exclusively upon the wretched wanderers of the night, and that each successive crime has gained something in atrocity upon, and has followed closer on the heels of its predecessor. These things mark out the Whitechapel murders, even before their true history is unravelled, as unique in the annals of crime. All ordinary experiences of motive leave us at a loss to comprehend the fury which has prompted the cruel slaughter of at least three, and possibly four women.

By this article we can see that *The Times* certainly regarded Martha Tabram as a victim and felt warranted to include Emma Smith as a possible casualty of the Whitechapel murderer.

Eliza Cooper and Elizabeth Allen were reported in *The Echo* of 20 September as having given a clue to the police as to the possible identity of a suspect. It is thought that this information was a repeat of that reportedly given by 'Pearly Poll/Mary Ann Connolly' which supposedly implicated one John Pizer, otherwise known as 'Leather Apron'.

Joseph and Thomas Bayley ran a packing case manufacturing business from Number 23a Hanbury Street; in reality this was the yard of the Black Swan public house.

On 11 September a piece of paper saturated in blood was found in the yard. This piece of paper was used to lend credence to the Laura Sickings story reported in the papers of the next day, in which she said that she had found a bloodstain left by the Ripper on the fence of Number 25 Hanbury Street. This was interpreted in conjunction with the bloodstained paper as indicating the escape route of the murderer to be across the fences of the intervening houses, enabling him to leave the scene through the passage of Number 25 Hanbury Street.

The police investigated this possibility and asserted that the piece of paper had not been there on the day of the murder, and Inspector Abberline supported this by confirming that the stain seen by Laura Sickings was indeed urine.

Doctor Phillips was requested to re-attend the inquest on 19 September at the behest of the Coroner Wynne Baxter.

On resumption Baxter stated that the doctor must give a more comprehensive explanation as to the after-death mutilations, and carried on to say that certain medical opinion was in disagreement as to whether the mutilations were indeed posthumous (although it was admitted that some of them must have been).

During his evidence the court was cleared of women and children owing to the hideous content of the evidence, which included the following information.

The abdomen was completely laid open and the intestines separated from their attachments. They had been lifted out of the body and placed on the shoulder.

The uterus, its appendages and a portion of the vagina and bladder had been entirely removed and none of these parts of the body were found. Doctor Phillips said that in order to accomplish this, the Ripper's incisions had consisted of precise cuts, avoiding the rectum, and dividing the vagina at a position which avoided injuring the cervix.

When questioned about the length of time which the perpetrator would have needed to carry out the atrocities, Doctor Phillips intimated that it would have taken him at least a quarter of an hour to inflict such injuries, and that if performed in a theatre environment it would have taken the best part of an hour.

Doctor Phillips was of the opinion that the mutilations were performed by an expert, or at least someone with comprehensive anatomical knowledge. He said that the primary basis for this assumption is the precise way in which the extraction of the pelvic organs was undertaken. This also determined the construction of the instrument used for the job, as having a blade at least five to six inches in length and probably greater, and very sharp.

Albert Cadoche, a carpenter born in 1865, was living at Number 27 Hanbury Street at the time of the murder. He testified that he went into the yard of his house at 5.30 a.m. on the morning of the killing, and that he heard from the yard next door at Number 29, a voice say 'No!' A few minutes later he heard what he thought was something falling against the fence. He stated that he heard no more and went to work. But how long was that after he heard the noise? He further stated that as he passed Spitalfields clock on his way to work the time said 5.32 a.m., and added that he saw no one in the street as he left the house.

In his summation on 26 September the Coroner Baxter said that Cadoche had been mistakenly reported as hearing the cry at 5.15 a.m. The question must be asked, did Cadoche at some time put the time that he heard the voice at 5.15 a.m., as this would fit in a lot better with his arrival at the Spitalfields clock at a time he put at 5.32 a.m.

Mrs Amelia Richardson and Mrs Annie Hardyman occupied the ground and first floors of Number 29 Hanbury Street together with their two sons, but neither reported hearing anything prior to the discovery of the body.

Henry John Holland was on his way to work at Chiswell Street when he was told about the murder by John Davis. He attended the murder scene and then went in search of a policeman. This was done at his own volition or possibly under the instruction of Inspector Chandler. He located a constable on point duty at Spitalfields Market, but the policeman refused to accompany him. Holland reported the conduct of the policeman at Commercial Street Police Station on the afternoon of 8 September.

Amelia Palmer, who lived at Number 30 Dorset Street, cleaned houses and took in washing in order to make a living. She said that she had known Annie Chapman for a number of years and had seen her several times during the week preceding the murder. Annie had complained of feeling unwell and had stated that she was not eating regularly. Palmer had given her twopence and elicited a promise that she would not spend it on drink. She further added that on meeting Annie later in the week, Annie had said that she was feeling unwell again but must pull herself together and get some money, otherwise she would have nowhere to sleep.

Annie's own brother stated at the inquest that he had seen Annie shortly before the murder and had given her two shillings. If this was true, then the fact that Annie had two shillings at the time of her murder was never reported, and if she was in possession of two shillings then what was she doing wandering the streets when she could have quite easily paid for a bed?

Another resident of Number 29 Hanbury Street was a Mr Thompson who was employed as a carman at Goodson's in Brick Lane. He stated that he had got up and gone to work at 3.30 a.m. on the morning of the murder, and seen nothing. He did not enter the yard, but this was two hours before the murder.

Emily Walter, a prostitute, told the *Star* newspaper that she had been propositioned by a man to go with him into Number 29 Hanbury Street and as such provided a description of the man wanted for questioning.

John Richardson lived at Number 2 John Street in Spitalfields. He was the son of Amelia Richardson and was called as a witness at the inquest. He stated that he worked as a porter at Spitalfields Market and was on his way to work on the morning of 8 September.

At about 4.45 a.m. he had called in to Number 29 Hanbury Street to check the cellar door padlock. He explained that there had been a break-in a number of months earlier, and a saw and a hammer had been taken. He stated that the street door and the one accessing the passage to the yard were never locked and that this was also the case on that morning. On being questioned, he verified that on occasion it had been used by prostitutes and that he at one time had found a man and woman on the stairs.

He said that on the morning of the murder he saw no one and had sat down on the step in order to trim a piece of leather from the sole of his boot. He added that he had left the yard after about three minutes.

The knife was inspected and it was found that it would have been impossible to commit the murder with it. Richardson further confirmed that the leather apron discovered near the standpipe was in fact his.

Annie Chapman was interred in a secret ceremony at Manor Park on 14 September 1888. The funeral was attended by members of her family and was arranged by undertaker Harry Hawes of Number 19 Hunt Street, Spitalfields. Smiths Undertakers of Hanbury Street supplied the hearse for the occasion.

When analysed and if accepted, this evidence once again helps to confirm that Doctor Phillips must have been mistaken about the time of death. In mitigation it must be appreciated that the methods used to determine the time of death were very basic when compared to modern techniques, and were primarily dependent upon an estimate of the rate at which the body was cooling and the effects of rigor mortis.

Doctor Phillips when giving evidence repeatedly expounded that the murderer had an element of anatomical skill, and depending on the part of the body being described uses such phrases as 'expert' and 'great anatomical knowledge'. He further says that the body had been dead for two hours, and yet Mrs Darrell and John Richardson both professed that this could not be. I therefore suggest that the coolness of the morning influenced Doctor Phillips's reckoning

Additional facts and questions emerging from the available information are:

The time given by Mrs Darrell is referred to as around 5.30 a.m., and we must appreciate that all of the action took place within hearing distance of Spitalfields Church clock. However if Mrs Darrell had heard the clock chime the half hour surely she would have been more adamant in her assessment of the time. Furthermore if she is to be believed, then she passed close enough to Annie Chapman and the unknown man to catch part of their conversation, and as the victim was well known to her, it is highly unlikely that this is a case of mistaken identity. This information, when coupled with the discovery of the body at approximately 5.50 a.m. (Mr Davis got up after hearing Spitalfields Church clock chime 5.45 a.m.), indicates to me that the man they described was extremely likely to have been Jack the Ripper.

Let us now evaluate the testimony of Albert Cadoche. The only time factors to be positively identified are Mr Davis getting up at 5.45 a.m. and Mr Cadoche passing Spitalfields clock at 5.32am. If we now subtract the time taken to walk from Number 27 Hanbury street to the Spitalfields Church and then accept that a few minutes elapsed between his hearing the woman's voice say 'No!' and the noise of something falling against the fence, then this suggests that the onslaught commenced at approximately 5.20 a.m. and that Mrs

Darrell did see Annie Chapman outside 29 Hanbury Street, but at a time closer to 5.15 a.m. and not 5.30 a.m. as she approximated the time to be.

The following sequence is offered as a suggestion . . .

Time a.m.	Activity
4.45–4.50	Richardson is in the yard of 29 Hanbury Street and sees nothing.
5.15	Mrs Darrell sees Annie Chapman talking to Jack the Ripper.
5.17–5.18	Annie and the Ripper go into the yard.
5.20	Cadoche hears someone in the yard say 'No!'
5.22	The Ripper commences assault and strangles Annie.
5.24	Cadoche hears the body fall against the fence.
5.25	The Ripper commences the mutilation of the body.
5.27	Cadoche sets off for work and sees nobody in the street.
5.32	Cadoche passes Spitalfields Church.
5.35–5.40	The Ripper completes the mutilations and leaves the murder scene.
5.48	John Davis comes down into the yard, finds the body, and raises the alarm.

We must now look at the way in which Annie was murdered and the effect of the bloodletting on the perpetrator's person and clothes.

Could the Ripper have inflicted the first wound in the chest, and after the initial surge of blood then proceeded to cut the throat? This would allow the clothing to act as a barrier and prevent a lot of the blood from marking the murderer. He could then have set about his business knowing full well that the blood would cause minimal staining to his hands and clothes.

It is already accepted that the Ripper strangled his victims prior to the mutilations, so therefore the heart would already have stopped pumping the blood around the body, and on penetration of the body with the knife there would have been no fountain effect, which would have been the case had it been a still beating heart.

As stated above (page 35), parts of the body were missing and Dr Phillips, when giving evidence at the inquest, itemises the absent pieces. The Ripper must therefore have had a bag or some form of receptacle in order to carry away the trophy pieces.

Doctor Phillips expounded the fact that the killer had a degree of anatomical knowledge. Could the Ripper have been present at the inquest, and hearing the evidence have deliberately mutilated his subsequent victims in a more haphazard fashion so as to reduce the suspicion of him possessing anatomical knowledge? It is definitely true that later victims did not illustrate distinct anatomical know-how to the extent shown in the murder of Annie Chapman.

The bruise on the chin could probably have been caused by an initial attacking blow, either with a fist or a blunt instrument. This would have allowed the killer to maintain the element of surprise and quickly gain a stranglehold on the throat and so explain the apparent lack of noise.

The long-term bruising can be ignored and is probably the result of her fight with Eliza Cooper, but the position of the fresh bruising is significant and could help us to a decision as to which hand the Ripper favoured.

The bruise on the right side of the chin and the right hand of Annie could indicate a left-handed assailant. Modern books on the murders have expressed a preference for a right-handed Jack but initially the evaluation was that the Ripper was left-handed.

Let's take the two bruises identified. A person, in this instance Annie Chapman, would normally attempt a defence against a left-handed blow by the use of a right hand parry, and conversely a left-handed attacker would inevitably make his first assault with his left hand.

Dr Phillips stated that the stiffness was more pronounced on the left, especially in the fingers. I have since been informed by a leading expert in forensic medicine that no importance should be attached to this.

The body had been turned on to the stomach at some time during the attack, in order that the two cuts down the left side of the spine could be performed. This is possibly the time when the rear portion of the neck was assaulted.

In his summing up, Coroner Wynne Baxter suggested that the motive for the murder may have been the extraction of the uterus and the subsequent sale of the uterus to an anonymous American doctor. The reason for this statement was that at the time rumours circulated that such a person had been offering substantial sums of money for specimens.

The Coroner was praised in the press of the day for giving promin-ence to this observation and so highlighting the authorities to the possibility that the practice of 'Burking' had restarted.

'Burking' was a practice whereby persons were suffocated and when dead, their bodies sold to anatomical schools for research purposes.

It was named after William Burke who was executed for this type of murder in 1829.

The final information which I will include on Annie Chapman is the report by Inspector Chandler who wrote:

I at once proceeded to No. 29 Hanbury Street and in the back yard found a woman lying on her back, dead, left arm resting on left breast, *legs drawn up*, abducted, small intestines and flap of the abdomen lying on right side above right shoulder, attached by a cord with the rest of the intestines inside the body; two flaps of skin from the lower part of the abdomen lying in a large quantity of blood above the left shoulder; throat cut deeply from left and back in a jagged manner right around the throat.

I at once sent for Dr Phillips, divisional surgeon, and to the station for the ambulance and assistance. The doctor pronounced life extinct and stated the woman had been dead at least two hours. The body was then removed on the police ambulance to the Whitechapel Mortuary.

On examining the yard, I found on the back wall of the house (at the head of the body) and about 18 inches from the ground, about six patches of blood varying in size from a sixpenny piece to a point, and on the wooden paling on the left of the body near the head, patches and smears of blood about 14 inches from the ground.

The woman has been identified by Timothy Donovan, deputy of Crossinghams lodging house at 35 Dorset Street, Spitalfields, who states he has known her about 16 months as a prostitute, and for the past four months she had lodged at above house. At 1.45 a.m. 8th instant, she was in the kitchen, the worse for liquor and eating potatoes. He (Donovan) sent to her for the money for her bed, which she said she had not got and asked him to trust her, which he declined to do. She then left stating that she would not be long gone. He saw no man in her company.

Description: Annie Siffey, aged 45; length 5 ft; complexion fair; hair wavy, dark brown; eyes blue; two teeth deficient in lower jaw, large thick nose.

Dress: black figured jacket, brown bodice, black skirt, lace boots, all old and dirty.

A description of the woman has been circulated by wire, to all stations and a special enquiry called for at lodging houses etc., to ascertain if any men of a suspicious character or having blood on their clothing entered after 2 a.m. 8th inst.

In conclusion may I say that in my opinion Annie Chapman was undoubtedly a victim of Jack the Ripper, and I would like to add that I believe that at a time of around 5.15 a.m., Mrs Elizabeth Darrell/Long saw the Ripper talking to Annie Chapman in the street outside the murder site and probably at a time within fifteen minutes of her death.

CHAPTER FIVE

Elizabeth Stride

Elizabeth Stride was born in 1843, the daughter of Gustaf Ericsson and his wife Beata, of Torslanda near Gothenburg, in Sweden. As was the custom, she was known thereafter as Elizabeth Gustafsdottir.

In 1860 she moved to the Carl Johan Parish in Gothenburg where she had obtained work as a servant to Lars Frederick Olofsson. By 1862 she had moved to Cathedral Parish and was still giving her occupation as domestic servant.

In 1865 she had made the transition to prostitute and in that same year she gave birth to a child who was stillborn.

Elizabeth moved to London some time in 1866 or 1867 and is initially thought to have worked as a servant for a family living in the area of Hyde Park. This is based on the story which she gave to friends and acquaintances.

In 1869 she married John Thomas Stride at St Giles in the Field church.

Stride was born in 1821, the son of a shipwright, and he himself worked as a carpenter at the time of the marriage and resided at Munster Street in Hampstead.

From 1870 to 1877 he was the proprietor of a coffee house, first at Upper North Street, Poplar, for the first two years, next at 178 Poplar High Street, where he stayed from 1872 until 1874, and thereafter at Crisp Street, also in Poplar.

By 1882 the marriage had broken up, and little is known of Mr Stride until 1884 when he died of heart failure in Bromley Sick Asylum. His address at the time of his death was given as 'Poplar Workhouse'.

Elizabeth laid claim to the fact that she and her husband were employed on the steamer *Princess Alice* which sank off Woolwich in 1878, and whilst this would fit in with known data of their movements there is no proof to support this claim.

She further said that her husband along with two of their children had perished in the tragedy but this does not tie in with the previous paragraph and nothing has been unearthed to support this narrative.

Wynne Baxter, the Coroner at her inquest, stated that there was no trace of any connection in the available documents concerning the *Princess Alice* tragedy.

It is not known exactly when the marriage broke down, but it is known from the evidence given by a Mrs Elizabeth Tanner, the Deputy of a common lodging house at Number 32 Flower and Dean Street, that Stride had lodged there on and off for approximately six years.

In 1881 Stride had been treated for bronchitis at the Whitechapel Workhouse Infirmary, indicating that she was already in the area and that the marriage had probably broken down by this time.

In 1885 Stride was living with Michael Kidney, a 33-years-old labourer, at 33 Dorset Street. Kidney stated that Stride lived with him for most of the time, though she frequently absented herself when she was drinking. He further admitted that their relationship was at times of a stormy nature.

In his inquest statement he stated that:

Stride was subject to going away whenever she thought she would. During the three years I have known her, she has been away from me about five months. I've cautioned her same as I would a wife. It was drink that made her go, but she always came back again. I don't believe she left me on Tuesday to take up with another man, and I think she liked me better than any other man.

On 6 April 1887 Elizabeth took an action for assault against Kidney. The case was dropped because she failed to appear at court to give evidence. However, we do have corroborated information that Kidney was imprisoned for being 'drunk and disorderly' in July of 1888.

Elizabeth was also frequently arrested for drunkenness and during the last year of her life was convicted no fewer than eight times at the Thames Magistrates Court. One of these convictions was for being drunk and disorderly at the Queen's Head, which was a public house on the corner of Commercial Street and Fashion Street.

The most informative book ever written on this subject is called *The Jack the Ripper A–Z*, written conjunctively by Paul Begg, Martin Fido and Keith Skinner. In the book it is noted that in 1886 Stride made two claims for financial assistance to the Swedish Church of

Radcliffe Highway, and gave her address at this time as Devonshire Street, Commercial Road.

At the inquest it was commonly concurred by all who knew her, that Elizabeth spoke fluent English, without the trace of any foreign accent. It was also mooted that she had at least two children by John Thomas Stride. At the time of writing there is no documentary evidence to support or deny this.

We do know however that at the time of her death Stride was staying at the lodging house at Number 32 Flower and Dean Street. She had not stayed there for the previous three months, but this fits in with the fact that Michael Kidney stated that he had not seen her for five days.

On 29 September, Mrs Tanner, the Deputy of the lodging house, paid Liz sixpence for cleaning some rooms at the house. At 6.30 p.m. Liz went to the Queen's Head public house, returning at around 7.00 p.m., when she borrowed a clothes brush from Charles Preston, a barber who was a fellow inmate.

Preston stated in evidence that he had seen her in the kitchen of the lodging house between 6.00 p.m. and 7.00 p.m., at a time which was confirmed at the inquest by Catherine Lane, who said that she was in good spirits and gave her a piece of velvet to keep until she returned.

She left the lodging house not much later. At 11.00 p.m. she was seen leaving the Bricklayer's Arms, a public house in Settles Street, by two men. The first of these was Mr J. Best, a labourer who lived at Number 82 Lower Chapman Street; the second was John Gardner, who lived at Number 11 Chapman Street, who further volunteered that she had at that time a flower pinned to her dress. She was in the company of a man they described as of a clerkly appearance, and they continued that Stride and the man set off in the direction of Commercial Road.

The next sighting of Liz was at 11.45 p.m. when she was again identified as being in Berner Street by a Mr William Marshall, a bootmaker, who resided at Number 64 Berner Street. He was of the opinion that the gentleman she was with was English.

Mr Marshall stated in evidence that he was stood outside his house for about ten minutes at around 11.45 p.m. and that he saw a man and a woman opposite. He described the man as being about 5 feet 6 inches tall, of stout build and as Best and Gardner said, of clerkly appearance. He said the man was dressed in a small black coat, dark trousers and was sporting a peaked cap.

He said the man spoke, saying 'You would say anything but your prayers', and Marshall said that the voice was of a mild disposition and had an English accent; he added that the two then moved in the direction of Dutfield's Yard.

Dutfield's Yard was situated between Number 40 Berner Street, which was the headquarters of the International Working Men's Educational Club, and Number 42. It was accessed by an alleyway approximately 20 feet long and 12 feet wide.

In the vicinity of Dutfield's Yard lived Matthew Packer, who plied his trade as a greengrocer at Number 44 Berner Street, where he lived with his wife and two lodgers, Harry Douglas and Sarah Harris. All of these were questioned on the day of the murder as part of the house-to-house enquiries, and all declared that they had neither seen nor heard anything suspicious.

In conflict with this, in an article in the *Evening News* of 4 October it was reported that two private detectives named Grand and Batchelor had interviewed Mr Packer, who had told them that a woman with a white flower pinned to her jacket accompanied by a stout man of clerkly appearance about 5 feet 7 inches tall, who was wearing dark clothes and a 'Wide-awake' hat, and possessing a sharply commanding manner, had purchased a half a pound of black grapes and had stood across the road in the rain for about half an hour, eating them. He said they were talking and that they then crossed the street glancing at the Working Men's Educational Club, where community singing could be heard.

In a later visit to the murder site, Grand and Batchelor recovered a grape stalk from the drain where police had washed down the yard.

We know nothing of the credibility of Grand and Batchelor, nor whether the stalk was genuinely recovered from the yard. They may have been using the murder to drum up business or discredit the police, and I would therefore view this incident with a degree of caution.

Packer was an unreliable witness who variously stated that the time of the sale was 11.00 p.m. and 11.45 p.m., and if placed against the earlier evidence the 11.45 p.m. may even be an early estimation.

According to PC William Smith, who was walking his beat on the night of the murder, at about 12.30 a.m. he saw Elizabeth Stride in Berner Street with a man. He placed the sighting as opposite Dutfield's Yard. The man was described as around 5 feet 7 inches tall, clean-shaven and about twenty-eight years old. He said that the man looked respectable, was wearing dark clothes and a felt deerstalker hat. He also confirmed that Liz was wearing a flower in her jacket.

If PC Smith is correct in his estimation of the time, then he did not mention seeing Mr Packer closing up his shop, and equally, Matthew Packer failed to mention that he had seen a constable, but seeing that Stride and the man were still standing opposite Dutfield's Yard, I would argue that Matthew Packer's shop was still open (he stated that he saw the couple cross over the road to the working men's club). Either this is the scenario, or else it must have been after 12.30 a.m. Another somewhat bizarre solution would be that Stride and the unknown man had re-crossed the road to Dutfield's yard, and when PC Smith passed, Packer's greengrocer's was already closed.

At Number 36 Berner Street lived Mrs Fanny Mortimer, who said that she was standing at her door for about ten minutes on the night of the murder, listening to the singing from the working men's club, at a time she put variously at 12.30 a.m. to 1.00 a.m., and stated that she only saw one person in Berner Street. This turned out to be an innocent pedestrian named Leon Goldstein. She also said that she heard the 'measured heavy tread of a policeman passing the house'. If this was the case then the only policeman who came up Berner Street was PC Smith, who was in Berner Street at 12.30 a.m. as previously testified. In order for Mrs Mortimer's evidence to coincide with that of the other witnesses, the correct time for her ten-minute sojourn outside must have been between 1.45 a.m. and 1.55 a.m.

At 12.45 a.m. in Fairclough Street, James Brown, who testified at the inquest, said that he was on his way home to Number 35 Fairclough Street when he saw a woman he was almost certain was Liz Stride talking to a man about 5 feet 7 inches tall, of stout build and wearing a long coat. He said that Stride had her back to the wall, and the man was leaning with his arm against the wall as if to stop her leaving and heard her say 'No, not tonight, maybe some other night'. He stated that he did not see the face of the man and failed to notice whether she had a flower in her jacket (this could have been obscured by the body of the man lounging against the wall). He said he then carried on home, and about 15 minutes later while he was eating his supper he heard the cries of 'Murder!' as the body was being discovered. These circumstances could support the opinion that the time that had lapsed was slightly in excess of 15 minutes, if we are to allow for him walking home and getting settled, and then sitting down and being presented with his supper. It would probably have taken him nearer twenty to twenty-five minutes before he was sat down enjoying the meal.

If we project backwards from the time at which the alarm was raised, this would put the time at which Brown saw Liz Stride at around 12.40 a.m., and this would fit in with the fact that Israel Schwartz also claimed to have seen Liz, at 12.45 a.m., being thrown to the pavement outside Dutfield's yard.

A probable explanation could be that Stride was indeed in Fairclough Street, having crossed Berner Street in order to ward off the advances of the unknown man. He followed, and they carried on walking into Fairclough Street; it was less than fifty yards. This is where Brown witnessed the man propositioning Liz, and her rejection of his proposal with the words. 'No! not tonight, maybe some other night.' Could this have been in answer to the question 'Are you coming back home?' which may have been posed by Michael Kidney? Stride then left the man and made her way back to Dutfield's Yard to pick up another man who came out of the pub. I suggest that the unknown man did not accept the rejection and followed Liz back along the road, accosting her and throwing her to the ground just as Israel Schwartz came on to the scene.

All the times now fit into place, and it must not be forgotten that a man named Morris Eagle passed through the yard at 12.35 a.m. and Liz Stride definitely was not in the yard at that time.

Joseph Lave, a Russian-born immigrant who lived at the International Workingmen's Club, testified that he left the Workingmen's Club to get some fresh air at a time estimated to be 12.40 a.m., and returned to the club five minutes later. He stated that the passage was so dark that he had to grope along the wall back to the entrance to the club. Lave was probably back in the club before Schwartz arrived in the street.

Israel Schwartz, a Jewish immigrant from Hungary who lived at Number 22 Ellen Street, in giving evidence at the inquest stated:

> that at 12.45 a.m. on turning into Berner Street from Commercial Road, and having reached the gateway where the murder was committed, he saw a man stop and speak to a woman who was standing in the gateway. The man tried to pull the woman into the street then turned her round and threw her down on the footway. The woman screamed three times but not very loudly. On crossing to the opposite side of the road in order to avoid the conflict, he saw a second man who was stood

lighting his pipe. The man who threw the woman to the ground called out, apparently to the man across the road, 'Lipski' (this was the name of a murderer and was used as an anti-Jewish insult). Schwartz then walked away, but finding that he was being followed by the second man, he started to run and didn't stop until he reached the railway arch. But the man did not follow him this far. Schwartz could not determine as to whether the two men were together.

As a point of order: there is no evidence of Schwartz having given evidence at the inquest, but in a draft reply to a Home Office question, Robert Anderson refers to the evidence given by Schwartz at the inquest. This is held in the 'Scotland Yard files'.

Schwartz attended the mortuary where he positively identified the body as that of the woman he had seen. He described the two men thus . . .

First man – aged about thirty, height 5 feet 5 inches, complexion fair, hair dark; dress – dark jacket and trousers, black cap with peak, broad shouldered, and sporting a moustache.

Second man – aged about thirty five years, height 5 feet 11 inches, fresh complexion, hair light brown; dress – dark overcoat, old black hard felt hat with wide brim.

The police report implies that Schwartz's statement was undoubtedly believed. It is then probable that all of the witnesses were describing the same man, and that James Brown was slightly mistaken in describing the dress; anyway, how long is a long coat, and would a frock coat be so described?

If Stride was trying to rid herself of the man, then when she walked off in Fairclough Street the man could have gone up Backchurch Lane and along Commercial Road and been on his way down Berner Street when Israel Schwartz fell in behind him. This would be borne out by the interview which he gave to the *Star* newspaper, which reported the interview thus:

Information which may be important was given to the Leman Street Police Office yesterday, by a Hungarian, concerning this murder. This foreigner was well dressed and had the appearance of being in the theatrical line. He could not speak a word of English, but came to the police station accompanied by a friend, who acted as an interpreter . . .

As he turned the corner from Commercial Road, he noticed some distance in front of him, a man walking as if partially intoxicated. He walked on behind him and presently he noticed a woman standing in the entrance to the alleyway where the body was found. The half-tipsy man halted and spoke to her. The Hungarian saw him put a hand on her shoulder and push her back into the passage, but feeling rather timid about getting mixed up in quarrels, he crossed to the other side of the street. Before he had gone many yards however, he heard the sound of a quarrel and turned back to find out what was the matter. But just as he stepped from the kerb, a second man came out of the doorway of the pub a few doors away, and shouted out some sort of warning to the man who was with the woman and rushed forward as if to attack the intruder. The Hungarian states positively that he saw a knife in the second man's hand, but he waited to see no more and fled.

This was slightly different from the other version, but we must remember that this was through an interpreter, and could have changed slightly in translation.

Let us now review the information we have been given.

Witness	Where seen	With whom	Time
Mrs Tanner	32 Flower & Dean St lodging house	Mrs Tanner	6.00 p.m.
Mrs Tanner	Liz went to Queen's Head	Mrs Tanner	6.30 p.m.
Mr Barber	32 Flower & Dean Street	Mr Barber	6.00–7.00 p.m.
Chas Preston	32 Flower & Dean Street	Chas. Preston	7.00 p.m.
J. Best & John Gardner	Leaving Bricklayer's Arms in Settles Street going towards Commercial Road	With unknown clerkly man	11.00 p.m.
William Marshall	Berner Street	Clerkly English man	11.45 p.m.
Matthew Packer	44 Berner Street	Man of clerkly appearance	11.00 or 11.45 11.45 p.m.
PC Smith	Opposite Dutfield's Yard	28 years old clean-shaven, presentable	12.30 a.m.
Morris Eagle	Passed through Dutfield's Yard	Seen nobody	12.35 a.m.
James Brown	Fairclough Street	Similar description	12.40 a.m.
Joseph Lave	Dutfield's Yard and Berner Street	Seen nobody	12.40–44 a.m.
Israel Schwartz	Dutfield's Yard	Similar description, possibly with a second man	12.45 a.m.
Mrs Mortimer	36 Berner Street	Saw Leon Goldstein pass	12.45–12.55

The police files hold a report by Sergeant Stephen White primarily containing the statement of Matthew Packer. It testifies:

I beg to report that acting under the instructions of Insp. Abberline, I, in company with PC Holding, C.I.Dept., made inquiries
at every house in Berner Street, Commercial Road, on 30th ult,
with a view to obtain information respecting the murder. Any
information that I could obtain, I noted in a book supplied to me
for that purpose. About 9 a.m. I called at 44 Berner Street, and
saw Matthew Packer, fruiterer in a small way of business. I asked
him what time he closed his shop on the previous night. He
replied, 'Half past twelve in consequence of the rain. It was
no good for me to keep open.' I asked him if he saw anything
of a man or woman going into Dutfield's Yard, or saw anyone
standing about the street about the time he was closing his shop.
He replied, 'No, I saw no one standing about, neither did I see
anyone go up the yard. I never saw anything suspicious or heard
the slightest noise, and knew nothing about the murder until I
heard of it this morning.'

I also saw Mrs Packer, Sarah Harrison (most probably Sarah
Harris) and Harry Douglas, residing in the same house, but
none of them could give the slightest information respecting the
matter.

On the 4th inst, I was directed by Inspector Moore to make
further inquiry and if necessary see Packer and take him to the
mortuary, I then went to 44 Berner Street and saw Mrs Packer,
who informed me that two detectives had called and taken her
husband to the mortuary. I then went towards the mortuary
where I met Packer with a man. I asked him where he had been.
He said 'This detective asked me to go and see if I could identify
the woman.' I said, 'Have you done so?' He said, 'Yes, I believe
she bought some grapes at my shop about 12 o'clock on Saturday.' Shortly afterwards they were joined by another man. I
asked the man what they were doing with Packer and they both
said that they were detectives. I asked for their authority. One of
them produced a card from a pocket book, but would not allow
me to touch it. They then said they were private detectives.
They then induced Packer to go away with them. About 4 p.m. I
saw Packer at his shop. While talking to him the two men drove
up in a hansom cab, and after going into the shop they induced
Packer to enter the cab, stating that they would take him to
Scotland Yard to see Sir Charles Warren.

From inquiry I have made there is no doubt that these are the two men referred to in the attached newspaper cutting who examined the drain in Dutfield's Yard on 2nd inst. One of the men had a letter in his hand addressed to 'Le Grand & Co., Strand'.

Matthew Packer's statement is printed later in the chapter.

About 1.00 a.m., Louis Diemschutz drove his horse and cart into Dutfield's Yard having been out all day selling cheap jewellery at Westow Hill Market. The time was taken from the tobacconist's shop in Commercial Road. It was normally his practice to unload the cart, leaving the goods in the care of his wife, prior to stabling the horse in Gunthorpe Street at George Yard.

On entering the yard, the pony turned to the left and hesitated, refusing to move forward. Using his whip Diemschutz felt something behind the gates; he got down from the cart, lit a match and found what he first thought was a drunken woman lying on the ground. He at first feared that it might be his wife and so immediately went into the club to check. He informed those inside the club and went back outside into the yard accompanied by a group of several persons. There, they discovered Elizabeth Stride lying on the floor with her throat cut.

Diemschutz and another member of the club went off in the direction of Fairclough Street to find a policeman, and Morris Eagle went off in the opposite direction shouting 'Police!' Eagle met two policemen, PC Collins and PC Lamb, with whom he returned to the murder scene. He stated that on getting back to Dutfield's Yard a number of people were already there.

PC Lamb, on reaching the scene, sent a constable, referred to only as 426H, to fetch Doctor Blackwell, and despatched one of the men at the scene to the police station to fetch help. He then closed the gates and commenced a search of the yard and the interior of the club. He remained on the scene until daybreak.

Doctor William Blackwell was called to the scene and arrived at 1.16 a.m.. He determined that Stride had been dead no longer than twenty minutes.

He believed she had been killed whilst standing, her head being pulled backwards using the handkerchief scarf about her neck, and her throat cut. He also intimated that the blood on her hand was caused by the struggle with her attacker.

Dr Phillips, the police surgeon for H Division, was summoned at 1.20 a.m., arriving at the scene of the crime at approximately

2.00 a.m. via the police station in Leman Street. In his report he stated:

The body was lying on the near side, with the face turned towards the wall, the head up the yard and the feet towards the street. The left arm was extended and there was a packet of cachous in her left hand.

The right arm was over the belly, the back of the hand and the wrist had on it clotted blood. The legs were drawn up with the feet close to the wall. The body and the face were warm, the hand cold. The legs were quite warm. Deceased had a silk handkerchief round her neck, and it appeared to be slightly torn. I have since ascertained it was cut. This corresponded with the right angle of the jaw. The throat was deeply gashed and there was an abrasion of the skin about 1½ inches in diameter, apparently stained with blood, under the right brow. At 3.00 p.m. on Monday afternoon at St George's Mortuary, Dr Blackwell and I made a post mortem examination . . .

Rigor mortis was still thoroughly marked. There was mud on the left side of the face and it was matted in the head. The body was fairly nourished. Over both shoulders, especially the right, and under the collar bone and in front of the chest there was a bluish discoloration, which I have watched and have seen on two occasions since. There was a clean-cut incision on the neck. It was six inches in length and commenced 2½ inches in a straight line below the angle of the jaw, half an inch over an undivided muscle, and then becoming deeper, dividing the sheath. The cut was very clean and deviated a little downwards. The artery and the other vessels contained within the sheath were all cut through. The cut through the tissues on the right side was more superficial, and tailed off to about two inches below the right angle of the jaw. The deep vessels on that side were uninjured. From this it was evident that the haemorrhage was caused through the partial severance of the left carotid artery. Decomposition had commenced in the skin. Dark brown spots were on the anterior surface of the left chin. There was a deformity in the bones of the right leg, which was not straight but bowed forwards. There was no recent external injury save to the neck. The body being washed more thoroughly, I could see some healing sores. The lobe of the left ear was torn as if from the removal or wearing through of an earring, but it was thoroughly healed. On removing the scalp there was no sign of bruising or extravasation of blood. The heart was small, the left ventricle firmly contracted, and the right slightly so. There was no clot in the pulmonary artery, but the right ventricle was full of dark clot. The left was firmly contracted so as to be absolutely empty. The stomach was large and the mucous membrane only congested. It contained partly-digested food, apparently consisting of cheese, potato and farinaceous powder. All the teeth on the left lower jaw were absent. Examining her jacket, I found that while there was a small amount on the right side, the left was well plastered with mud . . .

[in answer to the coroner's questions]

The cause of death is undoubtedly from the loss of blood from the left carotid artery and the division of the windpipe. The blood had run down the waterway to within a few inches of the side entrance of the club. Roughly estimating it, I should say there was an unusual flow of blood considering the stature and the nourishment of the body.

Doctor Phillips was recalled to the resumed inquest on 5 October and answered further questions thus:

He had made a re-examination with regard to the missing palate, and from very careful examination of the roof of the mouth he found that there was no injury to the hard or the soft palate. He had also carefully examined the handkerchiefs, and had come to the conclusion that the stains on the larger handkerchief were those of fruit. He was convinced that the deceased had not swallowed the skin or inside of a grape within many hours of her death. The apparent abrasion which was found on washing the flesh was not an abrasion at all, as the skin was entire underneath. He found that the deceased was seized by the shoulders, pressed to the ground, and that the perpetrator of the deed was on the left side when he inflicted the wound. He was of the opinion that the cut was made from left to right of the deceased, and from that therefore arose the unlikelihood of such a long knife having inflicted the wound described in the neck. The knife was not sharp-pointed, but round and an inch across. There was nothing in the cut to show an incision of the point of any weapon.

He could not form any account of how the deceased's right hand became covered in blood. It was a mystery. He was taking it as a fact that the hand always remained in the position he had found it in, resting across the body. Deceased must have been alive within an hour of his seeing her. The injuries would only take a few seconds to inflict; it may have been done in two seconds. He could not say with certainty whether the sweets being found in her hand indicated that the deed had been done suddenly. *There was a great dissimilarity between this case and Chapman's.* In the latter the neck was severed all round down to the vertebral column, the vertebral bone being enlarged with two sharp cuts, and there being an evident attempt to separate the bones.

The murderer would not necessarily be bloodstained, for the commencement of the wound and injury to the vessels would be away from him, and the stream of blood, for stream it would be, would be directed away from him and towards the waterway already mentioned. He had reason to believe that the deceased was lying on the ground when the wound was inflicted.

Doctor Phillips attended the post mortem of Catharine Eddowes, which was carried out by Dr Frederick Gordon Brown, *and ascertained that the murder was not by the same hand that killed Stride.*

The Lancet of 15 September provided an insight into the profile of the murderer in the eyes of medical opinion. It stated:

The theory that the succession of murders which have lately been committed in Whitechapel are the work of a lunatic appears to us, to be by no means well established. We can understand the necessity for any murderer endeavouring to obliterate by the death of his victim his future identification as a burglar. Moreover, as far as we are aware, homicidal mania is generally characterised by the one single and fatal act, although we grant this may have been led up to by a deep-rooted series of delusions. It is most unusual for a lunatic to plan any complicated crime of this kind. Neither, as a rule, does a lunatic take precautions to escape from the consequences of his act. The truth is that under the circumstances nobody can do more than hazard a guess as to the probable condition of the mind of the perpetrator of these terrible tragedies. Until more evidence is forthcoming, it appears to us to be useless to speculate upon what can only at present be regarded as problematical.

At Number 50 Eagle Street, Red Lion Square, lived Mrs Mary Malcolm, who originally claimed that the body was that of her sister, and identified her from the mark of an adder bite on her leg. The wrongful identification collapsed when her sister, Mrs Elizabeth Stokes, appeared at a later hearing and denied everything.

Police Constable Walter Stride, the nephew of her late husband, testified at the inquest that the dead woman was indeed his late uncle's wife.

The private detectives Grand and Batchelor attended the City Mortuary accompanied by Matthew Packer. In order to test whether he was telling the truth, they showed him the body of Catharine Eddowes instead of Stride (Eddowes having been murdered the same night). Packer, on being shown the body, stated that he had never seen her before. The press of the day took this as undeniable proof of his authenticity, and said that Packer had seen and spoken to the murderer of Stride. They further printed that 'No detective or policeman has ever asked me a single question nor come near my shop to find out if I knew anything about the grapes the murdered woman was eating before her throat was cut.'

On 4 October, Packer went to the mortuary of St George's in the East, and identified Stride as being the woman who he had seen, and who had been with the man who had bought grapes at his shop on the night of the murder. On his return to his home he met Sergeant White. White interviewed him, and at 4.00 p.m. of the same day, he took a hansom cab, along with the detectives Grand and Batchelor, to see Sir Charles Warren, the Metropolitan Police Commissioner at Scotland Yard.

Sir Charles Warren took Packer's statement, and in his own hand wrote:

Matthew Packer keeps a small shop in Berner Street, has a few grapes in the window, black and white. On Saturday night about 11.00 p.m., a young man from 25 to 30, about 5 feet 7 inches tall, with a long black coat, buttoned up . . . soft felt hat, kind of Hunter hat . . . rather broad shoulders, rather quick in speaking, rough voice. I sold him ¼ lb. of black grapes, threepence. A woman came up with him from Back Church End (the lower end of the street). She was dressed in black frock and jacket, fur round the bottom of jacket, a black crêpe bonnet; she was playing with a flower like a geranium, white outside and red inside.

I identify the woman at the St George's Mortuary as the one I saw last night . . . they passed by as if they were going up Commercial Road, but instead of going up, they crossed to the other side of the road, to the Board School, and were there for about half an hour till I should say 11.30 p.m. talking to one another. I then shut up my shutters. After they passed over opposite to my shop, they went near to the club for a few minutes, apparently listening to the music. I saw no more of them after I shut up my shutters.

I put the man down as a young clerk. He had a frock coat on, no gloves. He was about 1½ inch or two or three inch . . . a little higher than she was.

The statement is initialled CW and dated 4.10.88.

This conflicts with the statement which he gave to Sergeant White, and proves that his evidence (only with regard to the times) was unreliable.

There are too many references to the grapes from other parties for that part of his story to be disbelieved. He was not called as a witness to the inquest.

Matthew Packer was, I detect, a sensation seeker, as he made further approaches to the press, claiming on one instance that he had seen the man getting on a tram in Commercial Road, and at a later date that the Ripper was the cousin of a man he knew, and that he, the Ripper, was in America.

Grand and Batchelor were employed by the Whitechapel Vigilance Committee, and also the *Evening News* after the double murder. They discovered that a Mrs Eva Harstein who lived at Number 14 Berner Street had seen a blood-soaked grape stalk and some white flower petals in the passage into Dutfield's Yard. They then recovered the grape stalk from the yard and made the link with Packer, who at that time had not thought to mention it at his initial police interview.

Walter Dew, a highly respected policeman (he caught Crippen), recalled that as a Detective Constable he remembered that detectives searching the yard found several grape skins which had been spat out.

There were a variety of other people who offered information in order to assist the police in the investigation. Among them was Charles Letchford who lived at Number 39 Berner Street. He told the *Manchester Guardian* that on the night of the murder, he had walked up the street at about 12.30 a.m., when, as he put it, everything seemed to be normal.

Another who volunteered was William West. He worked as a foreman printer for 'Arbeter Fraint's office', situated at the back

of the workingmen's club. He gave evidence at the inquest, the gist
of which was that at about 12.30 a.m., he had left the side entrance
of the club and gone into the printing office (passing through
Dutfield's Yard), in order to return some literature. He returned
to the club after which, he, his brother, and a man called Louis
Stanley, left the club by the Berner Street entrance and walked
towards Fairclough Street. Though short-sighted, he testified that
he had looked towards where the body was found, and had seen
nothing untoward.

A horse-keeper by the name of Edward Spooner, who resided at
Number 25 Fairclough Street, gave evidence at the inquest.

He stated that he was standing outside the Beehive public house
between 12.30 a.m. and 1.00 a.m. when Louis Diemschutz and another man came running towards him shouting 'Murder! Police!'
He then went to Berner Street where he saw Elizabeth Stride with
blood flowing from her throat. He stated that she had at that time a
flower in her jacket and some cachous in her hand. When questioned
he said that he did not see the grape stalk.

Thomas Bates, in giving his evidence to the inquest, testified that
Stride had left the lodging house at about 7.30 p.m., and that he
knew her by the nickname 'Long Liz'. He said that she made her
living 'charring'.

Catherine Lane, a charwoman, was resident at 32 Flower and
Dean Street, and had known Stride for a number of years. She said
Liz had had a quarrel with Michael Kidney when she came to stay at
the lodging house, and added that she had seen Stride on the night of
29 September between 7.00 p.m. and 6.00 p.m.

On 1 October, in the Infirmary at St George's in the East, a
prostitute stated that she was absolutely sure of the identity of the
murderer. She went on to describe how a foreigner was blackmailing
unfortunate women, and threatening to rip them up. She described
her suspect as around forty years of age, of fair complexion, and with
a stout build. It is commonly thought that this is just another version
of the 'Leather Apron' story which is covered later in the book.

The wife of Louis Diemschutz was reported in *The Times* of
2 October 1888 as saying 'Just about 1.00 a.m. on Sunday, I was in
the kitchen on the ground floor of the club and close to the side
entrance. I am positive that I did not hear screams or sounds of any
kind.' This was also corroborated by a servant.

Thomas Coram lived in Plumber's Row, and was called as a witness
to the inquest. He found a bloodstained dagger with a 9- to 10-inch

blade, and with its handle wrapped in a bloodstained handkerchief tied with string, on the doorstep of Mrs Christmas's Laundry in Whitechapel Road. He alerted PC Joseph Drage to his find and they went to the Leman Street Police Station.

The press of the day sensationalised the find, but Dr Bagster Phillips maintained the improbability of it being the knife that killed Elizabeth Stride. It did however have the rounded end which Dr Phillips had stated was one of the requirements of the knife that killed Stride, but it did not meet the specifications of the knife which the Ripper used on the other four prostitutes, and it couldn't have been used to kill Stride because it was found at 12.30 a.m., and Stride was alive until well after that. She was identified by Israel Schwartz as late as 12.45.am, and was probably alive for at least ten minutes after that.

The inquest was presided over by Wynne Edwin Baxter, and was held in the Vestry Hall in Cable Street on 1, 2, 3, 5 and 23 October.

On evaluation of the available material, it appears as though a number of the witnesses all saw the same man, and all recognised Stride but not her escort. This could eliminate some of the suspects as they were resident in the area and would have been known by some if not all of the witnesses.

I doubt very much that the Ripper would pick up a prostitute inside a public house. He doesn't want to be recognised, and doesn't want to be caught, so he would approach an unaccompanied woman on an empty street.

The knife wounds do not conform to those of the other Ripper victims, and the injuries are described as being caused by a short-bladed, broad and possibly somewhat blunt knife, whereas the other victims are all recorded as being killed with a long-bladed pointed sort of instrument.

There were no abdominal mutilations. They say he was disturbed, but even if he did not have the time to mutilate as extensively as with the other victims, he would still have made a token one-stroke cut of the stomach.

Dr Phillips stated that the murder of Eddowes was not by the same hand that killed Elizabeth Stride. If this is to be believed, and there is no reason why it should not be believed, then Stride was not a victim of Jack the Ripper, because Catherine Eddowes definitely was.

In answer to a question from the coroner as to whether there was any similarity between this and the Chapman case, Doctor Phillips replied 'There is a great dissimilarity. In Chapman's case the neck was severed all round down to the vertebral column, the vertical bone being marked, and there had been an evident attempt to separate the bones.

My primary reason for the statement that 'as far as I am concerned I do not believe Elizabeth Stride was a Ripper victim', is based on a number of observations, by far the most compelling of which, is that within the hour Jack the Ripper murdered and mutilated Catherine Eddowes. He did so with the same knife that he used on his other victims. My contention is that the doctors in the late Victorian era were not as accomplished as they are today, but they were competent physicians and when examining an injury could quite accurately assess the way in which the damage was inflicted and the construction of the instrument used to inflict it.

If we look at all the inquest and post mortem evidence, we find that the only departure from the description of the weapon comes in the murder of Elizabeth Stride. All the others describe a similar instrument.

As they do in the courtroom, I now put to you the following conjecture. Jack the Ripper definitely murdered and mutilated Catherine Eddowes. The modus operandi confirms this. He did so with his normal/usual knife, approximately three quarters of an hour after the murder of Elizabeth Stride was discovered. So, if he murdered Stride (and because of the later murder of Catharine Eddowes we are certain that he was carrying his usual knife at the time of Stride's murder), why therefore use a different knife to kill Liz Stride, and then 45 minutes later use your usual knife to slit the throat and mutilate Catherine Eddowes? It doesn't make sense.

Jack the Ripper did not kill Elizabeth Stride.

I believe that the police accepted Stride as a Ripper victim because they did not want to alarm the public even more than they were already, by admitting that there were two killers on the loose in the same patch and in such a short time space.

The killer of Elizabeth Stride was the man seen by Israel Schwartz, and I concur with A. P. Wolf, the author of *Jack the Myth*, who nominated Michael Kidney as the likely murderer of Liz Stride.

On 1 October Kidney turned up at Leman Street Police Station, accusing the police of incompetence and saying that if he had been the constable responsible for the beat on which on which Stride was murdered, he would have committed suicide. When questioned about this at the inquest, he claimed he had heard something that led him to believe that he could have trapped the murderer and caught him in the act, if he had command of a force of detectives and had the authority to position them where he thought fit. He later retracted this claim saying that he had no information.

This murder was prompted by Kidney's efforts throughout the evening to convince Stride to return to live with him and go back home. Her statement, as heard by James Brown, 'No! not tonight, maybe some other night,' is the typical response to a come-home plea. Again at Dutfield's Yard, where Israel Schwartz saw the man throw Stride to the ground and stated that *she screamed three times though not very loudly*, this again seems to be the response of a woman, confronted by someone she wanted rid of, but did not feel sufficiently threatened at that time to yell at the top of her voice.

In *The Jack the Ripper A to Z* the authors express doubt as to the credibility of the Elizabeth Stride murder being attributed to Jack the Ripper, but emphasise the fact that all the people involved with the case accepted Stride as a Ripper victim. They do however draw attention to the connections which cast doubt on this conclusion.

They are highly respected Ripper researchers and whilst I accept their arguments as to the thoughts and the assumptions of the senior police on the Ripper case, I place more importance on the opinion of Doctor Phillips, who did not regard Stride as a Ripper victim and highlighted what I regard as the main point, which is that the knives used in the two killings of that night were totally different weapons. There is a further reason why it would be in the best interests of the police to blame the Ripper for the murder of Stride. The police were receiving a lot of criticism for not having apprehended the Ripper, but the situation could have been much worse if they had admitted that there were two killers in the area of Whitechapel at the same time, so they may have chosen to blame the killing on the Ripper to maintain what credibility they still retained.

I will conclude the evaluation of the death of Elizabeth Stride with Donald Swanson's report to the Home Office, dated 19 October, which states:

I beg to report that the following are the particulars respecting the murder of Elizabeth Stride on the morning of 30 September 1888.

1 a.m. 30th Sept. A body of a woman was found with the throat cut, but not otherwise mutilated, by Louis Diemschutz (secretary to the Socialist Club) inside the gates of Dutfield's Yard in Berner Street, Commercial Road East, who gave information to the police. PC 252 Lamb proceeded with him to the spot and sent for Drs Blackwell and Phillips.

1.10 a.m. Body examined by the doctors mentioned who pronounced life extinct. The position of the body was as follows:
lying on the left side, left arm extended from elbow, cachous
lying in hand, right arm over stomach, back of hand and inner
surface of wrist dotted with blood, legs drawn up, knees fixed,
feet close to wall, body still warm, silk handkerchief around
throat, slightly torn corresponding to the angle of right jaw,
throat deeply gashed and below the right angle apparent abrasion
of skin about an inch and a quarter in diameter. Search was made
of the yard but no instrument found.

The report then goes on to identify the remedial steps taken by the
police in respect of the gruesome murder, and specifies that these
actions are a continuation of those which have been agreed as appropriate actions to be taken with regard to the murders. He concludes:

The body was identified as that of Elizabeth Stride, a prostitute,
and it may be shortly stated that the enquiry into her history did
not disclose the slightest pretext for a motive on behalf of her
friends or associates or anybody who had known her. The action
of police besides being continued in the directions mentioned
in the report respecting the murder of Annie Chapman was as
follows.

A. Immediately after the police were on the spot the whole of
the members who were in the Socialist Club were searched, their
clothes examined and their statements taken.

B. Extended enquiries were made in Berner Street to ascertain
if any person was seen with the woman.

C. Leaflets were printed and distributed in H Division asking
the occupiers of homes to give information to police of any
suspicious persons lodging in their houses.

D. The numerous statements made to police were enquired
into and the persons (of whom there were many) were required
to account for their presence at the time of the murders and
every care taken as far as possible to verify the statements.

Concurrently with enquiry under heading 'A', the yard where
the body was found was searched but no instrument was found.

Under heading 'C', 80,000 pamphlets were issued to local
residents, and a house-to-house enquiry made, not only involving the result of enquiries from the occupiers, but also including a
search by police. This search was completed with a few excep-
tions, and instigated in a way so as not to convey suspicion. It

covered the area bounded by the City Police boundary on the one hand, Lamb Street, Commercial Road, Great Eastern Railway, and Buxton Street, then by Albert Street, Dunk Street, Chicksand Street, and Great Garden Street to Whitechapel Road, and then to the City boundary. Under this heading also, common lodging houses were visited and over 2000 lodgers were examined.

Enquiry was also made by Thames Police as to sailors on board ships in docks or river, and extended enquiry as to Asiatics present in London. About 80 persons have been detained at the different police stations in the Metropolis and their statements taken and verified by police, and enquiry has been made into the movements of a number of persons estimated at upwards of 300 respecting whom communications were received by police, and such enquiries are being continued.

Seventy-six butchers and slaughterers have been visited, and the characters of the men employed enquired into, this embraces all servants who have been employed for the past six months.

Enquiries have also been made as to the alleged presence in London of Greek gypsies, but it was found that they had not been in London during the times of the various murders.

Three of the persons calling themselves cowboys who belonged to the American Exhibition were traced and satisfactorily accounted for themselves.

Up to date, although the number of letters daily is considerably lessened, the other enquiries, respecting alleged suspicious persons, continues as numerous.

They were certainly leaving no stone unturned in their quest to apprehend the murderer, but it all proved to no avail. I must therefore conclude that Elizabeth Stride was not a Ripper victim.

One point of interest is that the attendance at Elizabeth Stride's funeral was minimal. She was buried in the East London Cemetery, in a pauper's grave, and yet when Catherine Eddowes's funeral took place the public lined the streets. Did the public also believe that Catherine Eddowes was a victim of Jack the Ripper and that Elizabeth Stride was not?

CHAPTER SIX

Catharine Eddowes

Catharine Eddowes was born in Wolverhampton in 1842. She was the daughter of a tinplate worker named George Eddowes and his wife Catherine (née Evans). The whole family moved to Bermondsey when Catharine was only a toddler. Her mother died when Eddowes was thirteen years old and this led to Catharine along with most of her family being placed in the Bermondsey Workhouse. She was educated at St John's Charity School in Tooley Street.

Research by others has determined that she was removed from the workhouse and placed in the custody of her aunt who lived in Wolverhampton, where she recommenced her education at the Dowgate Charity School.

In her late teenage years or early twenties, Catharine left her home with a man called Thomas Conway. Conway had been formerly enlisted in the 18th Royal Irish Foot regiment, from whom he was in the receipt of a pension. Catharine assumed the role of his common law wife from this time. They lived together in Wolverhampton where Catharine had three children by him, and also at some time she had his initials tattooed onto her arm. She also claimed during this period that Conway and she were legally married, though no records have yet been traced to substantiate this claim. It is thought that Conway wrote what were known as 'chap books' (light books or pamphlets on a variety of subjects), and that the couple then sold them to make a living.

In 1880 the so-called marriage broke down and they separated. The eldest child Annie, who had been born in 1865, went with her mother, and the two boys stayed with their father. Various reasons have been given for the breakdown. Her daughter said that it was due to Catharine's drinking coupled with the fact that she frequently went missing; however, Catharine's sister put the blame of the breakdown at Conway's door, stressing his drinking and violent conduct towards her sister, as the reason. It is sufficient to say that at the time of the murder the two had not seen one another for a number of years.

In 1881 Catharine commenced cohabitation with a market porter called John Kelly and went to live with him in his lodgings in Flower and Dean Street.

Kelly was of the Catholic religion and described by those who knew him as quiet and inoffensive with fine features and sharp and intelligent eyes. It appears that he had a beneficial effect on Catharine as when she attended the Whitechapel Infirmary with a burned foot she volunteered her religion as Catholic. Kelly was not a man in good health and by 1888 he had a chronic cough and suffered from a kidney complaint, which could in itself indicate that he drank excessively.

On 9 September 1888, Catharine went to a place near Maidstone in Kent, hop-picking with Kelly. They remained in Kent for over two weeks and during this period earned very little money. The trip having been declared a failure, they returned to London accompanied by Emily Birrell and her husband.

Her daughter Annie had by this time met and married a man named Louis Phillips who was employed as a 'lamp-black packer'. Catharine frequently sought out her daughter with the purpose of borrowing money from her. This necessitated, according to Annie, that they frequently moved house in order to avoid the scrounging of her mother.

At the time of Catharine's murder they were living at Southwark Park Road, and had not seen Catharine for a period of 25 months, at which time Annie had been pregnant and was being attended by her mother, for which service she was being paid.

It was on 28 September that Eddowes and Kelly reached London, having walked back from the hop fields of Kent. They had only a tanner (sixpence) between them, of which Kelly kept fourpence in order to pay for a bed at Cooney's lodging house in Flower and Dean Street. He gave the remaining twopence to Eddowes, who went off to secure a bed at the Shoe Lane Workhouse where she was well known to the regulars.

Catharine informed the Superintendent that she had returned in order to name Jack the Ripper and to claim the reward as she thought she knew who he was. The Superintendent cautioned her to look out for herself in case the murderer got her, and she replied that there was '*No fear of that*'. She stayed the night of the 28th at the workhouse. On the morning of the 29th September Eddowes was turned out of the Shoe

Lane Workhouse supposedly because there had been a bit of trouble. She went to Cooney's lodging house in search of Kelly.

They agreed that Catharine should take a pair of Kelly's boots and pawn them in order to get some money, and Eddowes then went off to Church Street, where she pawned the boots for 2/6d in the name of Jane Kelly. They then went out to buy some food, plus tea and sugar, and around 10.00 a.m. they were in the kitchen of Cooney's where they had some breakfast.

A half crown was a reasonable amount of money in those days but nevertheless by mid-afternoon they were broke again. They separated in Houndsditch and Catharine went in search of her daughter in Bermondsey in order to borrow money from her. It is known from the inquest testimony of Annie Phillips, her daughter, that she did not find her, and consequently did not borrow any money from her. This is as maybe but at 8.30 p.m. Catharine was arrested by Police Constable Louis Robinson for being 'drunk and disorderly and causing a disturbance' outside 29 Aldgate Street, where she had attracted a crowd with her antics and was among other things imitating a fire engine. She then lay down on the pavement to go to sleep.

I would like you to be aware that a friend of Eddowes witnessed her arrest and, as you will see, told John Kelly that she had been taken into custody.

With the assistance of Police Constable George Simmons, PC Robinson removed Eddowes to Bishopsgate Police Station. When questioned Eddowes gave her name as 'Nothing' and she was duly locked in the cells by Station Sergeant James Byfield at approximately 8.45 p.m.

PC Robinson checked the cell five minutes later to find Eddowes sound asleep and the cell smelling strongly of drink.

At 9.45 p.m. Police Constable George Hutt started his shift at the station and inspected the cells at regular intervals throughout the evening. He stated that she was singing at around 12.15 a.m. and by 12.30 a.m. was calling out demanding to be let out. PC Hutt informed her that she would be released when, in his opinion, she could take care of herself.

At 1.00 a.m. he judged her to be fit to release and Eddowes asked him the time. Hutt replied that it was too late for her to get any more drink, and she said 'I shall get a damn fine hiding when I get home.' This indicates that even though Kelly was described as being of an inoffensive disposition, he did on occasion beat Eddowes.

She gave her name as Mary Ann Kelly, and her address as Number 6 Fashion Street. PC Hutt said 'This way Missus' and asked her to close the door after her, and he said she departed with the words 'Good night old cock' as she left the station. At 1.30 a.m. she was in the vicinity of Duke Street, and at approximately the same time three men left the Imperial Club at Numbers 16 and 17 Duke Street. They were Joseph Lawende, Joseph Hyam Levy, and Harry Harris.

At 1.35 a.m. the three men saw Eddowes standing in the entrance to Church Passage, which leads to Mitre Square.

Mitre Square was a small enclosure in Portsoken Ward on the eastern edge of the city. It was contained on each side by Mitre Street, King Street, Aldgate and Duke Street; Church Passage was on the Duke Street side. A warehouse owned by a company called Kearley and Tonge was situated to the northwest side of the square and next to it stood the house of Police Constable Richard Pearce. Between King Street and Mitre Square lay St James's Place, which was known in those days as 'The Orange Market'. The Square was accessed by a gas-lit opening from Mitre Street, by Church Passage from Duke Street (a narrow covered entrance) and from another covered passage from the St James side.

To the right of the Mitre Street entrance stood three cottages; the body was found on the pavement in front of the cottages.

Joseph Hyam Levy was a 47-year-old butcher who lived at Number 1 Hutchinson Street, Aldgate. He was a witness at the inquest and stated that he had left the Imperial Club at 1.34 a.m. in the company of Mr Lawende and Mr Harris. At the entrance to Church Passage he had seen a woman talking to a man, and had remarked to the others 'I don't like going home by myself when I see these sorts of characters about. I'm off!'

In the *Evening News* of 9 October, it was reported 'Mister Joseph Levy is absolutely obstinate and refuses to give the slightest information. He leaves one to infer that he knows something, but that he is afraid to be called at the inquest.'

On attending the inquest Levy testified that he saw a woman outside Church Passage with a man about three inches taller than her, though he did not take any notice of them. He added that persons standing at that time of the morning in a dark passage were not up to much good!

It must be noted that Levy sponsored Martin Kosminski's application for naturalisation. Kosminski was a very prominent Ripper suspect. Did this enhance his hesitations and his reluctance to co-operate at the inquest? We must question the fact that he recognised

the man and chose through fear or friendship to withhold the information. At the present time however, no research has been unearthed
that sheds light on this situation either way.

Mr Harry Harris was a Jew who earned his living as a furniture
dealer, from premises in Castle Street, Whitechapel. He also said
that he left the Imperial Club at approximately 1.34 a.m. and at
Church Passage saw a man and a woman talking. He added that
he paid scant attention and intimated that he would not be able
to identify either of the two persons. When speaking to the *Evening News* of 9 October, he stated that neither of the others saw
anything more than himself; they could only have seen the back
view of the man.

Joseph Lawende was born in Warsaw in 1847 and came to England in 1871. He married Anne, and they had nine children and lived
at 45 Norfolk Road, Dalston. He worked as a commercial traveller
in the cigarette trade from premises in St Mary Axe.

At the inquest where he was called as a witness, he stated that along
with Mr Harris and Mr Levy he had stayed later than usual at the
club due to the rain. He continued that they prepared to leave the
club at a time of 1.30 a.m. by his watch and the club clock, and would
have been leaving the building at about 1.34 a.m. About fifteen yards
from the club door they saw Eddowes (he identified her later at the
mortuary by the clothes she was wearing). With her was a man
standing at the Church Passage entry into Mitre Square.

He stated that he was walking a little apart from the other two and
as such he did see the man and identified him as follows.

A man of medium build and sailorly appearance, wearing a pepper
and salt coloured loose jacket, a grey cloth cap with a similar-coloured
peak. He put his height at five feet seven or eight inches and said he
was about thirty years old, with a fair complexion and sporting a
moustache.

The Times, however, reported that Lawende had put his height as
five feet nine inches and said he was of shabby appearance. Lawende
also said that he did not think that he would recognise the man if he
saw him again.

The three statements, if read together, would lend a lot of weight
to the school of thought that the Ripper was a Jew and could be
identified, but fellow Jews would not betray one of their faith to the
authorities.

Joseph Lawende was regarded by the police as a very important
witness, and at the inquest the City Solicitor said that 'Unless the

jury wish it, I have special reason for not giving details as to the appearance of this man.' The Coroner agreed with him and therefore only the clothes which the man was wearing were described.

The police gave a lot of credence to Joseph Lawende's description of the man and believed that he had described the Ripper. Did this indicate that the description fitted a known associate of Eddowes or a man that the police already suspected?

Major Henry Smith, the Acting Commissioner of the City of London Police, said in his memoirs that he regarded Lawende as a more reliable witness, because he refused to be led by the questions put to him, was not interested in the relationship to the previous murders, and stated that he doubted his ability to recognise the man if he saw him again.

At approximately 1.40 a.m. Police Constable James Harvey came along Duke Street and down Church Passage in the process of walking his beat. He was called as a witness to the inquest and stated that he did not enter Mitre Square, and saw and heard nothing suspicious. When asked about the time he said that he had estimated from himself having taken the actual time from the Post Office clock in Aldgate.

I would suggest that PC Harvey was actually a number of minutes earlier than his estimate and believe that by 1.40.a.m. the murderer had already killed Eddowes and was in the process of committing the atrocities. I propose that Catherine Eddowes went up Church Passage to her death within a couple of minutes of seeing Lawende and his colleagues.

The reason for this assumption is that otherwise he would not have had sufficient time to carry out the described mutilations to the body.

Police Constable Edward Watkins's beat took him along Duke Street, Creechurch Lane, Leadenhall Street, St James's Place, Mitre Street, and Mitre Square, and took him between twelve and fourteen minutes to patrol.

At a time he put at 1.42 a.m. to 1.44 a.m. he entered Mitre Square and at 1.45 a.m., he discovered the body in the south-west corner of the square. He said that he had passed through the square at 1.30 a.m. and at that time it was empty.

He immediately crossed the square to Kearley and Tonge's warehouse and alerted the watchman George James Morris, a retired policeman who also gave evidence at the inquest.

In his evidence Morris stated that the warehouse door was open and he had not heard any sounds emanating from the square. He confirmed that ordinarily he heard the policeman's footsteps, but had

heard nothing until PC Watkins came into the warehouse at around
1.45 a.m. He stated in evidence that PC Watkins had called out 'For
God's sake, mate! Come to assist me.' Morris said that he picked up
his lamp and followed, asking 'What's the matter?' To which Watkins
had replied 'Oh dear! There's another woman cut to pieces.'

He said that after seeing the body, he ran to Aldgate to fetch a
policeman, where he found Police Constables Harvey and Holland.
In the meantime PC Watkins remained with the body, as was the
procedure for the discovering or first arriving policeman.

Doctor Sequeira, who had a surgery at Number 34 Jewry Street,
said that he was alerted to the situation by PC Holland, and put his
arrival at the scene as 1.45 a.m., though it was almost certainly later.
He pronounced the body dead but did not examine it closely, as the
arrival of the police surgeon Dr Gordon Brown was imminent. At the
inquest to which he was subsequently called, he said that he concurred
with the evidence given by Dr Brown, but on being questioned further by the Coroner, he stated that in his opinion the murderer didn't
show any particular skill, and that he had not been seeking any particular organ when he extracted the kidney and the uterus.

The Station Inspector who was on duty at Bishopsgate Police
Station on the night of the murder was Inspector Edward Collard,
who was called to the inquest. In giving his evidence he stated that he
was called to the murder scene at Mitre Square and that he timed his
arrival at 2.03 am. He then proceeded to organise an immediate
search of the district and the house-to-house enquiries of the following day. Before leaving Bishopsgate Police Station, it was he who
had sent for the police surgeon, Dr Brown.

A table of Eddowes's movements would read as follows.

Witness	Where seen	With whom	Time
PC Hutt	Bishopsgate Police Station	Released from custody	1.00 a.m.
Lawende, Levy and Harris	Entrance to Church Passage	Talking to a man	1.35 a.m.
PC Harvey	Came along Duke's Place and down Church Passage	Saw no one	1.40 a.m. probably earlier
PC Watkins	Mitre Square	Found body	1.45 a.m.
Dr Sequeira	Mitre Square	Examined body	Arrived 1.45 a.m. probably later
Inspector Collard	Police Station	Informed of murder	1.55 a.m.
Inspector Collard	Mitre Square	Arrived at scene	2.03 a.m.
Dr F. Gordon Brown	Mitre Square	As above	2.07 a.m.

Dr Brown arrived at the scene no more than a few minutes after Inspector Collard and gave his initial examination findings, thus:

The body was on its back, the head turned to the left shoulder, the arms by the side of the body as if they had fallen there. Both palms upwards, the fingers slightly bent. The left leg extended in a line with the body. The abdomen was exposed. The right leg was bent at the thigh and knee. The throat cut across.

The intestines were drawn out to a large extent, and placed over the right shoulder. They were smeared over with some feculent matter. A piece of about two feet was detached from the body and placed between the body and the left arm, apparently by design. The lobe and auricle of the right ear was cut obliquely through. There was a quantity of clotted blood on the pavement on the left side of the neck, around the shoulder and upper part of the arm, and fluid blood-coloured serum, which had flowed under the neck to the right shoulder, the pavement sloping in that direction.

The body was quite warm; no death stiffening had taken place. She must have been dead probably within the half hour. We looked for superficial bruises, and saw none. No blood on the skin of the abdomen or secretion of any kind on the thighs. No spurting of blood on the bricks or pavement around. No marks of blood below the middle of the body. Several buttons were found in the clotted blood, after the body was removed. There was no blood on the front of the clothes. There were no signs of recent connection.

When the body arrived at the mortuary in Golden Lane, some of the blood was dispersed through the removal of the body to the mortuary. The clothes were taken off carefully from the body. A piece of the deceased's ear dropped from the clothing.

I made a post mortem examination at half past two on the Sunday afternoon. Rigor mortis was well marked. The body was not quite cold. There was green discolouration over the abdomen.

After washing the left hand carefully, a bruise the size of a sixpence, recent and red, was discovered on the back of the left hand between the thumb and the first finger. A few small bruises were evident on the right shin, of older date. The hands and arms were bronzed. There were no bruises on the scalp, the back of the body or the elbows.

The face was very much mutilated. There was a cut about a quarter of an inch through the lower left eyelid, dividing the structures completely through. There was a scratch through the skin on the left upper eyelid, near to the angle of the nose. The right eyelid was cut through to about half an inch.

There was a deep cut through the bridge of the nose, extending from the left border of the nasal bone down near to the angle of the jaw on the right side of the cheek. This cut went into the bone and divided all the structures of the cheek except the mucous membrane of the mouth.

The tip of the nose was quite detached from the nose by an oblique cut from the bottom of the nasal bone to where the wings of the nose join onto the face. A cut from this, divided the upper lip and extended through the substance of the gum over the *right* upper lateral incisor tooth. About half an inch from the top of the nose was another oblique cut. There was a cut on the *right* angle of the mouth, as if the cut of a point of a knife. The cut extended an inch and a half, parallel with the lower lip.

There was on each side of the cheek, a cut which peeled up the skin, forming a triangular flap about an inch and a half.

On the left cheek there were two abrasions of the epithelium under the left ear.

The throat was cut across to the extent of about six or seven inches. A superficial cut commenced about an inch and a half below the lobe, and about two and a half inches below and behind the left ear, and extended across the throat to about three inches below the lobe of the right ear. The big muscle across the throat was divided through on the left side. The large vessels on the left side of the neck were severed. The larynx was severed below the vocal chord. All the deep structures were severed to the bone, with the knife marking the intervertebral cartilages.

The sheath of the vessels on the right side was just opened. The carotid artery had a fine hole opening. The internal jugular vein was opened an inch and a half, not divided. The blood vessels contained clot. All of these injuries were performed by a sharp instrument like a knife, and pointed.

The cause of death was haemorrhage from the left common carotid artery. The death was immediate, and the mutilations were inflicted after death.

We examined the abdomen. The front walls were laid open from the breast bone to the pubes. The cut commenced opposite the enciform cartilage. The incision went upward, not penetrating the skin that was over the sternum. It then divided the enciform cartilage. The knife must have cut obliquely at the expense of the front surface of that cartilage.

Behind this, the liver was stabbed as if by the point of a sharp instrument. Below this was another incision into the liver of about two and a half inches, and below this the left lobe of the liver was slit through by a vertical cut. Two cuts were shewn by a jagging of the skin on the left side.

The abdominal walls were divided in the middle line to within a quarter of an inch of the navel. The cut then took a horizontal course for two and a half inches towards the right side. It then divided round the navel on the left side, and made a parallel incision to the former horizontal incision, leaving the navel on a tongue of skin. Attached to the navel was two and a half inches of the lower part of the rectus muscle on the left side of the abdomen. The incision then took an oblique direction to the right and was shelving. The incision went down the right side of the vagina and the rectum for half an inch behind the rectum.

There was a stab of about one inch on the left groin. This was done by a pointed instrument. Below this was a cut of about three inches going through all the tissues making a wound of the peritoneum about the same extent.

An inch below the crease of the thigh was a cut extending from the anterior spine of the ilium obliquely down the inner side of the left thigh and separating the left labium, forming a flap of skin, up to the groin. The left rectus muscle was not detached.

There was a flap of skin formed from the right thigh, attaching the right labium and extended up to the spine of the ilium. The muscles on the right side inserted into the frontal ligaments were cut through.

The skin was retracted through the whole of the cut in the abdomen, but the vessels were not clotted. Nor had there been any appreciable bleeding from the vessels. I draw the conclusion that the cut was made after death, and there would not be much blood on the murderer. The cut was made by someone on the right side of the body, kneeling below the middle of the body.

I removed the content of the stomach and placed it in a jar for further examination. There seemed very little in it in the way of food or fluid, but from the cut end partly digested farinaceous food escaped.

The intestines had been detached to a large extent from the mesentery. About two feet of the colon was cut away. The sigmoid flexure was invaginated into the rectum, very tightly.

Right kidney pale, bloodless, with slight congestion of the base of the pyramids.

There was a cut from the upper part of the slit on the under surface of the liver to the left side, and another cut at right angles to this, which were about an inch and a half deep and two and a half inches long. The liver itself was healthy.

The gall bladder contained bile. The pancreas was cut, but not through, on the left side of the spinal column. Three and a half inches of the lower border of the spleen, by half an inch, was attached only to the peritoneum.

The peritoneal lining was cut through on the left side, and the left kidney carefully taken out and removed. The left renal artery was cut through. I should say that someone who knew the position of the kidney must have done it.

The lining membrane of the uterus was cut through. The womb was cut through horizontally, leaving a stump of three quarters of an inch. The rest of the womb had been taken away with some of the ligaments. The vagina and cervix of the womb was uninjured.

The bladder was healthy and uninjured, and contained three or four ounces of water. There was a tongue-like cut through the anterior wall of the abdominal aorta. The other organs were healthy.

There were no indications of connection.

I believe the wound in the throat was first inflicted. I believe she must have been lying on the ground.

The wounds on the face and abdomen prove that they were inflicted by a sharp pointed knife. And that in the abdomen, by one six inches long.

I believe the perpetrator of the act must have had considerable knowledge of the position of the organs in the abdominal cavity, and the way of removing them. The parts removed would be of no use for any professional purpose. It required a great deal of medical knowledge to have removed the kidney and to know where it was placed. Such knowledge might be possessed by someone in the habit of cutting up animals.

I think the perpetrator of this act had sufficient time, or he would not have nicked the lower eyelids. It would take at least five minutes. [I personally find it difficult to accept that the cuts on the eyelids would have taken five minutes to inflict, or is Dr Brown indicating that the whole of the act would have taken at least five minutes?]

I cannot assign any reason for the parts to be taken away. I feel sure that there was no struggle. I believe it was the act of one person.

The throat had been so instantly severed that no noise could have been emitted. I should not expect much blood to have been found on the person who had inflicted these wounds. The wounds could not have been self-inflicted.

My attention was called to the apron. It was the corner of the apron, with a string attached. The blood spots were of recent origin. I have seen the portion of an apron produced by Dr Phillips, and stated to have been found in Goulston Street. It is impossible to say it is human blood. I fitted the piece of apron, which had a new piece of material on it that had evidently been sewn onto the piece I have the seams of the borders of the two actually corresponding. Some blood and apparently faecal matter was found on the portion found in Goulston Street. I believe the wounds on the face to have been done to disfigure the corpse.

One cannot overstress the comprehensiveness of the report and the insight which it gives into the Ripper's modus operandi.

The post mortem undertaken by Dr Brown was attended by Doctors Phillips, Sequeira, and Sedgwick Saunders.

I would like once again to thank the authors of *The Jack the Ripper A to Z* for this punctuated extract of the complete report from which they extracted the relevant information and removed all irrelevant and repetitious comment.

Returning to the night of the murder. At approximately 2.15 a.m., Superintendent Foster and Inspector McWilliam arrived on the scene and were later joined by Major Henry Smith.

City Police Sergeant Jones found the following items beside the corpse of Catherine Eddowes: a mustard tin, containing two pawn tickets, one for John Kelly's boots and another for a shirt given to her by Emily Birrell. He also found three buttons and a thimble.

There is in existence a full inventory of Eddowes's clothing and possessions. This was taken at the mortuary and included twelve pieces of white rag, some of which were slightly bloodstained. This could suggest that at one time there were more than twelve pieces, and that the bloodstains could have come from the hands of the Ripper as he selected pieces to clean the blood from his hands. There is no evidence to support this statement.

At 2.20 a.m. PC 254A Long, who had been drafted in to supplement H Division's investigation of the murders, stated that he was passing through Wentworth Model Dwellings but did not notice the piece of bloodstained apron at this time. This agrees with the testimony of DC Halse, and the times suggest that they must have just missed each other.

At a time of 2.55 a.m. Police Constable Alfred Long, at the Wentworth Model Dwellings, Goulston Street, discovered the previously mentioned bloodstained piece of Catharine Eddowes's apron and noticed some writing on the wall immediately above it. This writing is what is now known as the 'Goulston Street Graffiti'.

Superintendent Arnold, when he arrived at the scene, deduced that the graffiti was not linked to the murder, and made a judgment that if it was left, it would probably be interpreted as a clue and revive the anti-Semitism that prevailed in the area. As implied by their name, the Wentworth Model Dwellings were only recently built, and were predominantly inhabited by Jews.

Sir Charles Warren, the Metropolitan Police Commissioner, authorised the removal of the graffiti, and a constable who had been standing in readiness furnished with a wet sponge removed the writing on the order of Superintendent Arnold.

The graffiti immediately became a point of contention and controversy with regard to the content and wording of the original.

PC Long in noting it down wrote 'The Jews are the men that will not be blamed for nothing' (he did not however spell the word 'Juwes').

Detective Constable Halse noted the wording as 'The Juwes are not the men that will be blamed for nothing'.

DC Halse said at the inquest that he had responded to George Morris's whistle at 1.58 a.m. along with Detectives Outram and Marriot. Halse said that he directed an immediate search of the area, and then returned to Mitre Square via Goulston Street, which he passed at approximately 2.20 a.m., and did not notice the graffiti or the piece of apron. He then went with Detective Hunt to Leman Street Police Station, and was directed back to the graffiti site.

DC Halse, who was a City of London policeman as opposed to a Metropolitan policeman, said at the inquest that he thought that the graffiti, which was written in chalk, had been done recently, and suggested that it be photographed, so that a print existed that could be used for subsequent examination. When this suggestion was refused by the Metropolitan Police, who stressed the anti-Semitic feeling in the area, coupled with the fact that the Petticoat Lane traders would see the graffiti as they arrived for the Sunday morning market, DC Halse suggested that only the top line (containing the word 'Juwes') should be removed, but he was overruled.

For this reason I am personally inclined to believe that the true version of the graffiti was that of DC Halse who, having highlighted the fact that the inference of the wording could be removed by elimination of the top line, must have scrutinised the phrase more expertly and appeared to be more observant than his Metropolitan police counterparts. Whether or not the graffiti has any connection with Jack the Ripper remains a mystery.

It must be noted that the torn piece of apron is the only clue that has been definitely identified as being left by the Ripper, and if the observant DC Halse is to be believed, and the apron was not present in Goulston Street when he previously passed through the site at 2.20 a.m., then the Ripper was still in the area for a minimum of 35 minutes after the discovery of the body.

The inquest was presided over by Samuel Frederick Langham, on 4 and 11 October, at the Golden Lane Mortuary.

Doctor William Saunders was called as a witness at the inquest – he stated that he had attended the post mortem examination, and had analysed the contents of the dead woman's stomach, finding no trace of any poison. He added that he agreed with Doctors Sequeira and Gordon Brown that the murderer had shown no significant anatomical skill in his mutilations, nor had he had any design on a particular organ. This however, as can be seen by the statement of Gordon Brown, completely conflicted with Brown's own view of the situation, and he had stated on a number of occasions that the murderer possessed anatomical knowledge. He specifically chose to mention the difficulty in removing a kidney from the front.

Dr Sequeira, in giving his evidence at the inquest, reported that he agreed with the evidence given by Dr Brown, but concluded that in his opinion, the murderer showed no skill in extracting the kidney and uterus, and agreed with Dr Saunders that the murderer had not been seeking any particular organs.

Doctor Bagster Phillips, who also attended the post mortem, told the *Evening News* of 1 October that the Eddowes murder was not by the same hand that killed Stride.

James Blenkingsop, a nightwatchman in St James's Place, told the *Star* of 1 October, that a respectably dressed man had approached him at about 1.30 a.m. on 30 September, asking if he had spotted a man and woman going through the Place. Blenkingsop replied that he had seen some people pass, but had not taken any notice. He was not called as a witness to the inquest.

John Kelly, who had lived with Eddowes for a number of years, said at the inquest that he had read about the pawn ticket in the name of Birrell being found on the body in Mitre Square, and had gone to the police. It was Kelly who had identified the body. *This would imply that until Kelly had seen the connection in the newspaper article, he had not bothered to search for Catharine or locate her whereabouts. This may be thought of as unusual, but not if Kelly was the one who had murdered her.*

The Times of Wednesday 3 October carried this report . . .

Last night between 9 and 10 o'clock, a labouring man, giving the name of John Kelly, of 55 Flower and Dean Street, . . . a common lodging house, entered the Bishopsgate Street Police Station, and stated that from what he had been reading in the newspapers he believed that the woman who had been murdered in Mitre Square was his 'wife', He was at once taken by Sergeant Miles to the mortuary in Golden Lane, and there identified her as the woman, to whom he subsequently admitted he was not married, but with whom he had cohabited for seven years.

Major Henry Smith, the Assistant Commissioner of the City Police, and Superintendent Foster were telegraphed for, and immediately went to the Bishopsgate Street station. Kelly, who was considerably affected, spoke quite unreservedly, and gave a full statement as to his own movements and those of the ill-fated woman, as to whose identity he was quite positive. In this statement he was borne out by the Deputy of the lodging house, Frederick Wilkinson, who knew the poor woman quite well, and who had just seen the body. Kelly, in answer to questions, stated that the last time he saw her . . . referring to her as Kate . . . was on Saturday afternoon. The last meal she had with him was a breakfast which she had obtained by the pledging of his boots for 2s. 6d. Asked if he could explain how it was that she was out so late on Saturday night, he replied that he could not say. He left her in the afternoon believing that she would return to him at the lodging house in Flower and Dean Street. He had told her to go and see her daughter, and to try and get 'the price of a bed for the night'. 'Who is her daughter?' he was asked, to which he replied 'A married woman. She is married to a gunmaker, and they live somewhere in Bermondsey, King Street, I think it is called, but I never went there.' He was then asked if he knew the murdered woman's name, and if he could explain the meaning of the initials 'TC' on her arm. He at once replied that Thomas Conway was the name of her husband, but he could not state whether Conway was dead or alive, or how long, in the latter case, she had been living away from him. Being asked why he had not made inquiries before, relative to her absence on Saturday night and since, he replied that he thought that she had got into some trouble and had been locked up, and he thought he had better wait. She was given to drinking. He had cautioned her not to stay out late at night on account of the previous murders. The reason which had induced him at length to call at the police station was his having read about pawn tickets being found being found near the murdered woman relating to pledges in the names of Kelly and Birrell. Further questioned on this point, he repeated the references to the pledging of his boots with a pawnbroker named Jones, of Church Street, and stated that the ticket for the other article (a flannel shirt), pledged in the name of Emily Birrell, had been given to them by the latter, who had been with them hopping, and who had slept in the same barn with them. He further stated that he and the murdered woman were both Londoners, and that the latter was born at Bermondsey. They had just returned from hopping at a place which he was understood to call Hunton, adding that it was about two miles from Coxheath in Kent. To the question how he obtained his living, he replied, 'I job about the markets now.' He added that he had worked pretty constantly for a fruit salesman named Lander for over 12 years. He and 'Kate' had, he said, gone through many hardships together, but while she was with him he 'would not let her do anything bad'. He was asked if he knew whether the woman had any relatives besides the daughter mentioned, to which he replied that, 'Kate's' sister was living in Thrawl Street, Spitalfields, with a man who sold farthing books in Liverpool Street.'

At the inquest Frederick Wilkinson, the Deputy at 55 Flower and Dean Street, gave his evidence accordingly . . .

I have known deceased and Kelly for the last 7 or 8 years, they passed as man and wife. They lived on very good terms. They had a few words now and again when she was in drink. Deceased got her living by hawking about the streets and cleaning amongst the Jews. When they were there they were pretty regular in their rent. She did not often drink; she was a very jolly woman. I never saw Kelly drunk. I saw deceased on Friday afternoon when she returned from hopping. I did not see Kelly. She went out on Friday night. I saw her again on Saturday morning along with Kelly between 10 and 11. I did not see deceased again until I saw her in the mortuary. She was generally in bed between 9 and 10 at night when they stopped there. I did not know her to walk the street. I never knew or heard of her being intimate with anyone but Kelly. She used to say she was married to Conway and her name was bought and paid for. She was not at variance with anyone that I know of. She was quite sober on Saturday when I last saw her. When Kelly came in on Saturday night between half past seven or eight I asked him 'Where's Kate?' He said 'I have heard she's been locked up,' and he took a single bed. A single bed is 4d; a double bed is 8d.

In reply to questions asked by Mr Crawford the City Solicitor Wilkinson answered . . .

I should say it was four or five weeks since they slept together at this house, they had been hopping. I am quite positive he never went out on Saturday night. On the Saturday morning she was wearing an apron, she was not dressed in anything particular. No stranger came in between 1 and 2 on Sunday morning to take a bed. I cannot recollect whether any stranger came in at 3 o'clock.

When questioned, John Kelly gave this statement whilst under oath . . .

I have seen the body of the deceased, I knew her as Catherine Conway. I have known her for seven years and have been living with her the whole of that time. She used to sell a few things about the street. She lived with me at 55 Flower and Dean Street, a common lodging house. I was last in her company on Saturday last at 2 o'clock in the afternoon in Houndsditch. We parted on very good terms. She said she was going over to see if she could see her daughter Annie, at Bermondsey, a daughter

she had by Conway. She promised me to be back by 4 o'clock
and no later. She did not return. I heard she had been locked
up at Bishopsgate, *I was told by two women*. I made sure she
would be out on Sunday morning. It was for a little drop of
drink. I never suffered her to go out for immoral purposes. She
was occasionally in the habit of drinking slightly to excess. She
had no money about her when I left. She went over to see her
daughter with a view of getting some money. I was without
money to pay for the lodging at the time. I know of no one
with whom she was at variance or likely to injure her. I do not
know whether she had seen Conway or whether he was living. I
never saw him.

When questioned by the jury as to her usual hours he responded,
'She usually returned about 8 or 9 o'clock.'
In answer to a further question from Mr Crawford he stated . . .

I do not know of anyone with whom she had been drinking. She
left me some months ago in consequence of a few words. She
only remained away for a few hours. She told me her daughter
lived at King Street, Bermondsey. We have lived in the same
house for some years. On Friday night we did not sleep together.
That night she went into the Casual Ward at Mile-End. We did
not sleep the whole of that week at the lodging house. We were
hop-picking until Thursday. We both went to the Casual Ward
on Thursday night at Shoe Lane. I saw deceased on Saturday
morning at 8 o'clock. She had some tea and coffee which she had
bought after I pawned my boots. She was sober when we parted.
She had never brought money to me in the morning that she has
earned at night. My wife pawned the boots. The date is the 28th.

*If John Kelly was Jack the Ripper, he was aware that Eddowes was
locked up in Bishopsgate Police Station, as he admits that he was told of
this by two women. He was also aware that she had been shouting her
mouth off about claiming the reward for naming the Ripper. He would
therefore have needed to silence her.*

*This must also be coupled with the fact that the last murder before
the double event was on the day before Kelly and Eddowes went hop-
picking in Kent. It is a big coincidence that the Ripper was quiet from
8 September until the 30th, while Kelly was away from Whitechapel.
Wilkinson, the Deputy, stated that Kelly had told him that Eddowes had
been locked up.*

George Clapp was called as a witness at the inquest. He was a caretaker at Number 5 Mitre Street, and his bedroom overlooked the square. He said that he heard nothing on the night of the murder.

Metropolitan Police Constable Long in giving evidence stated that he had, after discovering the piece of cloth (apron) made a complete tour of the staircase and landings, looking for an injured person. He did not at that time know that a murder had been committed.

Mrs Eliza Gold was Catharine Eddowes's sister. She said at the inquest that Catharine was of sober habits, and had last lived at Number 55 Flower and Dean Street. She further testified that her sister earned her living as a 'hawker or pedlar'.

Frederick Foster was employed as Surveyor to the City of London Police. He presented plans of Mitre Square together with maps of the area and specified the location of the graffiti. He pointed out the Ripper's route from Mitre Square to Goulston Street, and suggested that the Ripper's destination might have been Flower and Dean Street.

PC George Hutt stated in evidence that he had seen Eddowes turn left on leaving the police station at 12.55 a.m. When asked, he estimated that it was about an eight-minute walk from there to Mitre Square.

Emily Birrell, a friend of Catherine Eddowes, met her and Kelly when they came back from hop-picking in Kent. She gave her a pawnbroker's ticket for a man's shirt. The ticket was found in the mustard tin beside Eddowes's body, and on reading the newspaper reports she had come forward to identify herself to the police.

An article in *The Daily Telegraph* of 12 November 1888 described how two people who were in St James's Place on the night of the murder had seen Eddowes at the end of the covered entry to the square, talking to a man about thirty. He was described as having a fair moustache. The report carried on to say that the City Police had made attempts to trace the described man which had proved unsuccessful.

The entry described in this sighting is not the same one described by Lawende, Harris and Levy, as the point at which they say they had seen Eddowes is not visible from St James's Place.

Two firemen also told Superintendent Foster that they had been manning the night fire station in the Orange Market, and had neither seen nor heard anything unusual from the area.

There is further evidence that Eddowes may have been seen by a City Police Constable, in the company of a man, after her release from Bishopsgate Police Station.

Detective Superintendent Alfred Lawrence Foster was attendant at the murder site in Mitre Square, shortly after the death of Catharine Eddowes. He was also the officer who had taken care of Joseph Lawende, when he had been hidden away prior to giving evidence at the inquest. It is blatantly obvious from this that Lawende's testimony and description were given paramount importance by the senior police officers of the day.

On 16 October 1888, George Lusk, the proprietor of a building and decorating business, received through the post a letter and a human kidney, both supposedly sent by the Ripper.

Lusk was a widower with seven children, who resided at Number 1 Tollit Street, Alderney Road. He was elected Chairman of the Whitechapel Vigilance Committee on 10 September of that year.

The letter is now commonly referred to as the 'Lusk Letter' or the 'From Hell Letter' and the text is as follows:

> From hell
>
> Mr Lusk
> Sor
> I send you half the kidne I took from one women
> prasarved it for you tother piece I fried and ate it
> was very nise I may send you the bloody knif that
> took it out if you only wate a whil longer
>
> signed   Catch me when
>   you can
>   Mishter Lusk

The original letter has been lost, along with a photograph which is also missing. On a number of occasions the letter has been analysed by graphologists. Their findings in general have indicated that the writer may indeed have been the real Jack the Ripper, or most definitely a person who would be capable of the atrocities which were committed.

Further information is also apparent on analysis.

1. Why did the writer put 'Mr' at the start of the letter and yet put 'Mishter' at the end?
2. 'Sor' and 'Mishter' are phonetic spellings of the two words, if the writer was of Irish extraction or wanted the reader to think that he was.
3. I would rule out the trade of butcher in my investigations, as a butcher would know how to spell knife and kidney.

4. The word 'women' is also the phonetic spelling of a singular female as pronounced by the lower classes of the day.
5. 'tother' and 'prasarved are also dialect pronunciations of the two words, 'tother' being an abbreviation of 'the other', and 'prasarved' being a substitute for 'preserved'.
6. 'nise' is once again a natural spelling of how the word is pronounced, and similarly 'wate' could be categorised this way.
7. 'whil' is not how you would spell the word if you did not have the education, that would be 'wile' and I would say that the same applies to the word 'nife'. In spelling it as in the letter they have created a word where the 'I' has been put in to make a sound like 'eye'.

All of this is immaterial if the letter was sent to confuse. I believe that some of the words could have been deliberately spelt wrongly. I believe this because some rather more complicated words have been spelt correctly, when to the uneducated, they are more prone to be mistakenly written. I refer to 'half', 'piece', 'fried', 'bloody', and 'signed'.

However, in argument against this, I would ask you to view the chapter on the Letters (Chapter 15). In doing so you will see that such mistakes are not a rarity. What kind of man wrote the letter?

In his book *The Complete Jack the Ripper*, Donald Rumbelow includes an analysis from a Canadian graphologist named C. M. Macleod, who states within his evaluation: 'I would say he was in fact a latent homosexual (suggested by lower zone strokes returning on the wrong side of the letter) and passed as a man's man: the roistering blade who made himself the life and soul of the pub, and sneered at women as objects to be used and discarded' – a description which may be nearer to one of the major suspects, Montague John Druitt, than we can prove.

From this information it can be inferred that the Ripper was only semi-literate, or conversely that he was masking his true education by deliberate mistakes. Neither of which helps us in our quest to identify him. But if we conclude that the letter was from Jack the Ripper, in his own hand, and written to the standard of which he was capable, then a lot of the suspects can be eliminated from our conclusions.

Let us now move to the kidney which accompanied the letter. The kidney was allegedly half of the left kidney of Catharine Eddowes, and was received by Lusk on 16 October. It had been preserved in 'spirits of wine', and arrived in a three-inch square cardboard box, wrapped in brown paper. The box had a postmark on it, possibly that of 'London E'.

Lusk initially treated it as a hoax, but was persuaded to hand it over for medical examination, and thereafter Doctor Thomas Horrocks Openshaw examined the specimen.

Dr Openshaw was a consulting surgeon, who had taught anatomy at London Hospital and at the time was Curator of London Hospital's Anatomical Museum. He described it as a woman's kidney preserved in 'spirits of wine'.

The Daily Telegraph of Saturday 20 October 1888 reported thus . . .

A statement which apparently gives a clue to the sender of the strange package received by Mister Lusk was made last night by Miss Emily Marsh, whose father carries on business in the leather trade at 218 Jubilee Street, Mile End Road. In Mr Marsh's absence, Miss Marsh was in the front shop, shortly after one o'clock on Monday last, when a stranger, dressed in clerical costume, entered, and, referring to the reward bill in the window, asked for the address of Mr Lusk, described therein as the President of the Vigilance Committee. Miss Marsh at once referred the man to Mr J. Aarons, the treasurer of the committee, who resides at the corner of Jubilee Street and Mile End Road, a distance of about thirty yards. The man, however, said he did not wish to go there, and Miss Marsh thereupon produced a newspaper in which Mr Lusk's address was given as Alderney Road, Globe Road, no number being mentioned. She requested the stranger to read the address, but he declined, saying, 'Read it out', and proceeded to write something in his pocket book, keeping his head down meanwhile. He subsequently left the shop, after thanking the young lady for the information, but not before Miss Marsh, alarmed by the man's appearance, had sent the shop-boy, John Cormack, to see that all was right. This lad, as well as Miss Marsh, gave a full description of the man, while Mr Marsh, who happened to come along at the time, also encountered him on the pavement outside. The stranger is described as a man of some forty-five years of age, fully six feet in height, and slimly built. He wore a soft felt black hat, drawn over his forehead, a stand-up collar, and a very long black single-breasted overcoat, with a Prussian or clerical collar partly turned up. His face was of a sallow type, and he had a dark beard and moustache. The man spoke with what was taken to be an Irish accent. No importance was attached to the incident until Miss Marsh read of the receipt by Mr Lusk of a strange parcel, and then it occurred to her that the stranger might be the person who despatched it. His enquiry was made at one o'clock on Monday afternoon, and Mr Lusk received the package at eight pm the next day. The address on the package curiously enough gives no number in Alderney Road, a piece of information which Miss Marsh could not supply. It appears that on leaving the shop, the man went right by Mr Aaron's house, but did not call. Mr Lusk has been informed of the circumstances, and states that no person answering the description has called on him, nor does he know anyone at all like the man in question.

The Press with their poetic licence are credited with adding the word 'Ginny' to their reporting of the incident and Dr Openshaw wrote a letter to *The Times* to this effect.

According to one Joseph Aarons, Mr F. S. Reed, a medical attendant, said that the members of the Vigilance Committee initially took the kidney to Dr Frederick Wiles, who operated a surgery at Number 56 Mile End Road. Dr Wiles was unavailable and so Mr Reed examined it himself, pronouncing it to be a human kidney which had been preserved in spirits of wine. He in turn took it to Dr Openshaw, and declared on his return that it was the left kidney of a woman accustomed to drinking, who had died at the Mitre Square murder. As previously stated, Openshaw denied having made any such statement.

Dr Henry Sutton was described by Major Henry Smith, the Acting Commissioner of the City of London Police, as 'one of the greatest authorities living, on the kidney and its diseases'.

Sutton reported to Smith that he would pledge his reputation, that the kidney had been immersed in spirits within a few hours of its removal from the body. This in essence eliminated the possibility of its origin having been the dissecting room, as any body held remained intact for a day to await an inquest.

Dr Saunders told the press, relating to the kidney, that 'It was a pity that some people have not the courage to say they don't know. He went on to say, that there was no difference between a male and female kidney, and emphasised that the right kidney (the one remaining in the body) was normal and as such, the left kidney would also be the same. He continued to say that the liver of the dead woman was healthy and gave no indications that the woman drank. He concluded by inferring that in his opinion it was a typical student's prank.

Dr Frederick Gordon Brown, who conducted the post mortem, describes the right kidney as being 'pale, bloodless, with slight congestion at the base of the pyramids'.

Bright's Disease was quite common at the time. It was a name given to various types of kidney disease, and so called after Doctor Bright, of London, who was the person who first described the disease. It is a 'diffuse nephritis', and appears in an acute and chronic form, the acute form being due to the action of cold or toxic agents on the kidneys, and characterised by inflammatory changes in the epithelial, vascular, or intertubular tissues of the kidneys, respectively varying in intensity as such different forms are recognised.

N. P. Warren is the author of the book *A Postal Kidney*. He is also a practising surgeon. In his research he has established beyond any reasonable doubt that Major Smith was correct in describing the right kidney of Catharine Eddowes as showing signs of Bright's Disease.

He believes that the Ripper had surgical skill, and that the Lusk kidney was the left kidney of Catharine Eddowes. He further remarks that he believes, from experience, that the kidney is so difficult to expose from the front of the body, that the murderer must have had some anatomical knowledge. This was also confirmed by the statement made by Dr Brown, who said that the kidney had been carefully extracted.

Professor James Cameron, a pathologist, suggested that the London Hospital drawings and photographs of Eddowes indicate that the murderer was right-handed due to the abdominal incision having a drag to the right. I do not agree with this conclusion. I would concede that it is more likely, but to make a decision based solely upon this one fact regardless of not knowing where the murderer was situated when making the incision is somewhat audacious.

Interest in the kidney was revived when Major Henry Smith wrote his memoirs, in which he stated that he had shown the kidney to Henry Sutton, the expert previously mentioned, and in Sutton's opinion the kidney was not charged with fluid as it would have been in a body given to the hospital for dissection purposes, and further that it showed signs of Bright's Disease. He further suggested that the length of the renal artery still attached would complement the length of artery which was reported as remaining in the body.

Certain similarities with the other murders exist in the murder of Catharine Eddowes which were not present in the killing of Elizabeth Stride.

The throat was cut as deeply as Annie Chapman's and Mary Ann Nichols's.

As with their murders, the throat had been cut from the victim's left to right, and as with the others the throat had been cut across twice.

The abrasions on the neck, below the left ear, are also similar to those found on Chapman and Nichols.

The cuts used by the murderer are not those of a skilled surgeon, but are a mixture of knowledgeable extraction and frenzied attack.

Maybe the killer attended the inquest on Annie Chapman, and on hearing Dr Phillips's testimony as to the excellence in the way some of the mutilations were carried out, decided that in the next killing (i.e. that of Catharine Eddowes) he would adopt a more amateurish attack, and introduce only isolated instances of adeptness. This would fit in with his ego battle with the authorities.

Dr Sequeira's time of arrival appears to be the one that doesn't fit in with the others, and as such, I suggest that he arrived later than he stated.

My own conclusion on the murder would be that, due to the extent of the mutilations and in consequence, the time they would take to perform, then the arrival of PC Watkins prompted the retreat of the Ripper. It was said by the watchman, Morris, that he never heard the tread of the police constable's footsteps. I therefore suggest that the Ripper timed the duration of the copper's beat and murdered Eddowes at a time that gave him a sufficient period to carry out the mutilation of the body. He then left Mitre Square by another exit.

If, as put forward, the Jews were holding back some vital information, perhaps Levy may have known the identity of the Ripper.

Lawende's description was withheld at the inquest, and Harris stated that he would not be able to identify either the man or the woman. This is too good a secret to be kept, especially as there was a reward on offer for information. I believe that if the identity was known, then sooner or later someone would have leaked the name to the police. However, as will be seen later in the book, when we examine the Suspects, this would indeed fit in with certain known facts.

Let us now review the information and assemble our findings:

1. The killer was the same person who murdered Chapman and Nichols, and therefore Catharine Eddowes was most definitely a victim of Jack the Ripper.

2. We know of the one-time existence of some files which belonged to the City Solicitor, Henry Homewood Crawford. He was in partnership with Samuel Chester at Number 90 Cannon Street. The files which he possessed could include the withheld description given by Lawende, together with other information which failed to come out at the inquest.

3. The inference with regard to the kidney is that all the mutilations were carried out in a short space of time, and in poor lighting conditions. This would make specific mutilations, if deliberate, even more difficult than reported.

4. It would appear that, as per modern serial killers, the extent of the body mutilations was progressively increasing with the number of victims.

5. There was no evidence of spurting of blood around the body. This could once again go with the theory that the heart had stopped prior to the mutilations, or that the Ripper staunched or directed the flow with a cloth, or some other item.

6. The throat was cut from behind the left ear, to a place level with the right ear lobe. I question the fact that this could be achieved, if the body was not lying dormant, and use this to reinforce the argument that the victims were strangled prior to the mutilations. This also proves that if the body was lying face up, and the killer worked from between the legs, then it is virtually impossible to perform this cut with the right hand.

7. If the Ripper worked as has been suggested from the side of the body, then it negates the evidence given, that the abdominal cut dragged to the right.

8. If the mutilations were not performed from between the legs, then why (with all of his victims) did he place the legs akimbo (legs spread apart and bent upwards and outwards from the knees?

9. If we look at the police sketches of the bodies, then it is noticed that the right arm is by her side and slightly away from the body. If the Ripper performed the mutilations from the side of the body then he would have been kneeling on the arm of his victim.

10. The absence of blood on the skin of the abdomen, or secretion of any kind, would tend to intimate that the area had been wiped clean, but in the Victorian age no forensic test could accomplish

anything from the residue of anything left on the body. The only reference to this is by Dr Brown, who stated 'there were no signs of recent connection'. One reason that is left is that the killer, having strangled the body and cut the throat, then performed an act of masturbation on the body prior to the mutilations, and cleaned it away before commencing the abdominal atrocities.

11. Some form of package or bag must have been used to remove the missing organs from the scene of the crime. This would account for the police keeping a special eye out for persons carrying such bags and packages, but we do not have any positive evidence that anyone was stopped and searched whilst carrying a bag. Indeed, the only police constable who did detain a man for this very reason was rebuked by his superiors . . .

As a conclusion to this chapter we must ask how we can possibly have any sympathy for the plight of the police when we read of the ineptitude with which Sergeant White dealt with the situation described in his report below. This may have been as close as the police ever got to catching the Ripper, but with the prevailing situation of panic and the public derision which the police as an entity were suffering, surely anyone with an ounce of common sense would have stopped the gentleman in question and given him an impromptu interview; or if, as is implied, the character was acting suspiciously, would have detained him for questioning. If he had, and the account is true, Sergeant White might well have caught Jack the Ripper.

His report stated:

For five nights we had been watching a certain alley just behind the Whitechapel Road. It could only be entered from where we had two men posted in hiding, and persons entering the alley were under observation by the two men. It was a bitter cold night when I arrived at the scene to take the report of the two men in hiding. I was turning away when I saw a man coming out of the alley. He was walking quickly but noiselessly, apparently wearing rubber shoes, which were rather rare in those days. I stood aside to let the man pass, and as he came under the wall lamp I got a good look at him.

He was about five feet ten inches in height, and was dressed rather shabbily, though it was obvious that the material of his clothes was good. Evidently a man who had seen better days, I thought, but men who have seen better days are common enough down East, and that of itself was not sufficient to justify me in stopping him. His face was long and thin, nostrils rather delicate, and his hair was jet black [it's hard to tell in the dark, even with the benefit of a street lamp]. *His complexion was inclined to be sallow*, and altogether the man was foreign in appearance. *The most striking thing about him, however, was the extraordinary brilliance of his eyes. They looked like two very luminous glow worms coming through the darkness.* The man was slightly bent at the shoulders, *though he was obviously quite young – about 33 at the most –* and gave one the idea of having been a student or profess-ional man. His hands were snow white, and the fingers long and tapering.

As he passed me at the lamp I had an uneasy feeling that there was something more than usually sinister about him [during the Ripper crisis, that should have been enough to detain him], and I was strongly moved to find some pretext for detaining him, but the more I thought it over, the more I was forced to the con-clusion that it was not in keeping with British police methods that I should do so. My only excuse for interfering with the passage of this man would have been his association with the man we were looking for [and he still never pulled him in], and I had no grounds for connecting him with the murder. It is true I had a sort of intuition that the man was not quite right [and he still never pulled him in]. Still, if one acted on intuition in the police force, there would be more frequent outcries about inter-ference with the liberty of the subject, and at that time the police were criticised enough to make it undesirable to take risks.

The man stumbled a few feet away from me, and I made that an excuse for engaging him in conversation. He turned sharply at the sound of my voice, and scowled at me in surly fashion [and he still never pulled him in], but he said 'Good night' and agreed with me that it was cold.

His voice was a surprise to me. It was soft and musical, with just a tinge of melancholy in it, and it was the voice of a man of culture – a voice altogether out of keeping with the squalid surroundings of the East End [you have to wonder whether he would have stopped this man even if he had been carrying the knife in his hand].

As he turned away, one of the police officers came out of the house he had been in, and walked a few paces into the darkness of the alley, 'Hello! What is this?' he cried, and then he called in startled tones for me to come along [and he still never thought to detain the man]. The policeman who raised the alarm after the murder of Catharine Eddowes was PC Watkins.

In the East End we are used to shocking sights but the sight I saw made the blood in my veins turn to ice. At the end of the cul-de-sac huddled against the wall, there was the body of a woman, and a pool of blood was streaming along the gutter from her body. It was clearly another of those terrible murders. I remembered the man I had seen, and I started after him as fast as I could run, but he was lost to sight in the dark labyrinth of East End mean streets.

If this was the quality of staff which the police were using to catch the Ripper it is no wonder that he escaped capture. Another criticism of the police was raised by the question: how did the man and his victim gain access to the site without the knowledge of the two watching policemen?

The answer was forthcoming after the interview of the two concerned, and by all accounts the incident did come to the attention of Sir Robert Anderson.

They had not been present when the man entered the alley, and admitted to being absent for a short while. With the importance of the Ripper investigation and the fact that the action of these two policemen had probably prevented his capture, then there should be some evidence of their censure, and an example should have been made of their neglect to their duty. It is these facts which bring me to the conclusion that the particulars included in this report must be viewed with an element of caution, and that the event may not have had anything whatsoever to do with the Ripper case, but also, the comprehensiveness of the report may have been an effort by Sergeant White to make amends for his incompetence in not stopping anyone who had left the area under surveillance.

The description bears an uncanny resemblance to Druitt, as would the culture of the voice. If we look at existing photographs of Druitt, I do not apologise for mistakenly saying that his features could be confused with those of foreign origin, and Druitt did have dark hair.

The description of the site does not match any of the known sites accurately, though I would tend to favour Mitre Square as the described location. White comments to the gentleman on the weather being bitterly cold which would tend to eliminate the earlier murders, and the latest murder took place in November, but that was indoors, and was not discovered until the following morning.

Martin Howells and Keith Skinner in their book *The Ripper Legacy* state that on the morning of 30 September 1888 the weather conditions were unprecedented, the temperature in London having fallen to just above freezing point. This would lend further credence to the Eddowes murder date, as it must be accepted that this is exceptionally cold for the end of September.

CHAPTER SEVEN

Mary Jane Kelly

Details of the early life of Mary Jane Kelly are at best scarce, and what is known is of second-hand origin, relying primarily on information she passed on to her friends and acquaintances during the period in which she lived in London. She was apparently born in Limerick, in 1862 or 1863, and moved to Wales whilst still young. Her father worked in an ironworks company in Caernarvonshire. She grew up as part of a large family, and had numerous brothers but only one sister. Her brother Henry supposedly joined the Scots Guards.

When Mary Jane was the tender age of sixteen, she married a Welsh miner called Davies, who was killed in a pit explosion in the early 1880s. Kelly moved to Cardiff where she took up prostitution, and did not arrive in London until 1884.

According to a Mrs Carthy, a landlady from Breezer's Hill, Ratcliffe Highway, with whom she had lodged for a time, a previous landlady from St George's Street had accompanied Mary to a French lady's residence in Knightsbridge, to collect some expensive dresses which Kelly had left there. This was a high-class brothel in London's West End. And Kelly did claim to have spent some time with a gentleman friend in France. She claimed not to have liked it so had come back to England.

Mrs Carthy also stated that Kelly had left Breezer's Hill, late in 1886, going to live with a man who worked in the building trade. This was probably Joseph Fleming, with whom she was associated at this time, and who occasionally visited her when she was living with Joseph Barnett at the time of her death.

Kelly had a variety of aliases which included Marie Jeanette, Black Mary, Fair Emma, and Ginger. But all of her contemporaries in London knew her as Mary Jane Kelly, with the exception of Joseph Barnett who called her Marie Jeanette.

Barnett, a Billingsgate porter, had met Kelly in Commercial Street during the Easter of 1887, and had lived with her from that time at an assortment of addresses, the last of which was Number 13 Miller's Court.

Barnett lost his job in 1888, and this caused friction in his relationship with Kelly. It was after an argument on 30 October, that Barnett moved out of their Miller's Court room. The argument centred on Barnett's complaining about them having to share the room with other prostitutes, and Barnett went to lodge at Mr Buller's house in Bishopsgate.

Kelly and Barnett separated nine days before her murder but he continued to visit her on a daily basis and still gave her money.

He said that he visited her on 8 November between 7.30 p.m. and 8.00 p.m., only to find her in the company of another female. He stated that he left about 8.00 p.m. and returned to Buller's boarding house, remaining there for the rest of the evening.

Living in Miller's Court was Lizzie Albrook who stated that she was a friend of Kelly's. She said that she was with Kelly when Barnett had called on her, and put the time of his visit between 7.30 p.m. and 7.45 p.m. Albrook also stated that Kelly had said to her 'Whatever you do, don't you do wrong, and turn out as I have.' She further believed that Kelly would not have gone out that evening if she had not needed the money so badly.

Mrs Maria Harvey was called at the inquest as a witness, and said that she had slept with Kelly on the Monday and Tuesday of the week she died, and had been with her on the Thursday when Barnett had called, which had prompted her to leave.

A widow named Julia Venturey lived at Number 1 Miller's Court, with a man by the name of Harry Owen. In testifying she stated that Joe Barnett was kind to Kelly, and gave her money. She continued to say that it was Kelly who had broken the window, when she had been drunk, a few weeks before. Further testimony revealed that Kelly had another lover, also named Joe, who was a costermonger, and who abused Kelly for living with Barnett. Venturey stated that Mary Kelly was frightened of this man. She completed her evidence by saying that on the night of the murder she had slept through the night and had not heard anything untoward.

This Venturey may have been the Julia who impelled Barnett to leave Miller's Court owing to her forever being in their room.

On Wednesday 7 November, after purchasing a halfpenny candle from John McCarthy's grocery shop at Number 27 Dorset Street, she was seen in Miller's Court by Thomas Bowyer, in the company of a young man, who he described to the police as 'twenty-seven or twenty-eight, with a dark moustache and very peculiar eyes'. He stated that the man was very smart and showed very white cuffs, and a rather long white collar.

On Thursday 8 November, little is known of her early movements save what has already been described, but various sightings of her have been reported.

Elizabeth Foster told the newspapers that she had been with Kelly in the Ten Bells, a public house on the corner of Fournier Street and Commercial Street, on the night of her murder.

Further rumour has it that she was in the Britannia public house on the evening of her demise.

Somewhere around 11.45 p.m. to midnight, Mary Ann Cox, a widow, residing at Number 5 Miller's Court, saw Kelly return home, accompanied by a blotchy-faced man with a carroty moustache. She said the man was carrying a quart of ale and Kelly was singing. She also said that she heard footsteps leaving Miller's Court around dawn. Mrs Cox accepted at the inquest that the footsteps could have belonged to a policeman patrolling his beat. She said at the time of the sighting, Kelly was wearing a Linsey frock and a red knitted shawl. She was drunk, and told Cox that she was going to sing. She was heard by several people between midnight and 1.00 a.m. singing 'Only a violet I plucked from my mother's grave'.

At 2.00 a.m. Kelly was again sighted in Commercial Street by George Hutchinson, who she stopped to talk to. Hutchinson said that she asked him for sixpence. She then carried on towards Aldgate.

Hutchinson lived at Victoria House, Peabody Buildings, Commercial Street, and at the time of Kelly's death he was unemployed.

He attended the inquest on Kelly, but he also made the following statement at Commercial Street Police Station.

At 2.00 a.m. on Saturday 9 November, I was coming by Thrawl Street, Commercial Street, and just before I got to Flower and Dean Street, I met the murdered woman Kelly, and she said to me 'Hutchinson, will you lend me sixpence?' I said 'I can't, I have spent all my money going down to Romford.' She said 'Good morning, I must go and find some money.' She went away towards Thrawl Street. A man coming in the opposite direction to Kelly, tapped her on the shoulder and said something to her, they both burst out laughing. I heard her say 'Alright' to him and the man said 'You will be alright, for what I told you.' He then placed his right hand around her shoulders. He also had a kind of parcel in his left hand, with a kind of strap around it. I stood against the lamp of the Queen's Head public house, and watched him [the Queen's Head was situated on the corner of Fashion Street and Commercial Street]. They both then came past me, and the man hung down his head, with his hat over his eyes. I stooped down and looked him in the face. He looked at me stern. They both went into Dorset Street. I followed them. They both stood at the corner of the court for three minutes. He said something to her. She said 'Alright my dear, come along, you will be comfortable.' He then placed his arm on her shoulder and she gave him a kiss. She said she had lost her handkerchief. He then pulled out his handkerchief, a red one, and gave it to her. They both then went up the court together. I then went to the court to see if I could see them, but I could not. I stood there for about three-quarters of an hour, to see if they came out. They did not, so I went away.

George Hutchinson said that the man was of respectable Jewish appearance. He wore a long dark coat, with an astrakhan collar and cuffs, a dark jacket and trousers, a light waistcoat, dark felt hat which was turned down in the middle, spats, a linen collar and a black tie with a horseshoe pin, and a thick gold chain. He said that the man was about 5 feet 6 inches tall, and was aged thirty-four or thirty-five. He had dark hair and eyelashes and a pale complexion, and his moustache was light with curled-up ends.

He added that he stood under the sheltered entrance to Crossingham's lodging house, and neither the man nor Kelly came out of the house during his stay.

Inspector Abberline interviewed a laundress by the name of Sarah Lewis, who lived at Number 29 Great Pearl Street. She said that she had rowed with her husband and had gone to stay the rest of the night with a Mrs Keylers who lived at Number 2 Miller's Court. She stated that the time was 2.30 a.m., because she had checked it by the Spitalfields Church Clock as she went by. Lewis declared that she saw 'a man standing over against the lodging house, on the opposite side of Dorset Street'. This is most likely to have been George Hutchinson, as it fits in with what he claimed in his own statement. She also said that a young man passed along the street with a woman. She described the man as wearing a high round hat and said that she recognised him as the same man who had frightened her and a friend, on the previous Wednesday in Bethnal Green Road.

At the inquest, which she attended and was called as a witness, she said that the man had propositioned her and her friend, and had asked either one of them, he did not mind which, to follow him. A more comprehensive account states that they followed the man down a passage, after he said that he would treat them, but that when he put down his black bag, and started looking for something in his coat, they had run away. She put the sighting on the night of Kelly's murder as being near to the Britannia public house. She at no time stated that the woman he was with was Mary Jane Kelly.

A woman, quoted only as Mrs Kennedy, told the *Star* that she had gone to Dorset Street, Miller's Court, to stay with her parents. She had put the time as between 3.00 a.m. and 3.30 a.m. She stated that she saw a respectably dressed and intoxicated young man, with a dark moustache, talking to a woman, and continued that it was the same man who had frightened her in Bethnal Green Road the previous Wednesday. The young man said 'Are you coming?' and the woman turned away, and that there was a poorly dressed woman without a hat, standing close. Mrs Kennedy was not called as a witness.

Obviously, by the similarity of the two accounts, it has been mooted that Sarah Lewis and Mrs Kennedy were the same person, and this gains credibility when you take into account that *The Times* reported that Inspector Abberline had interviewed her, as he did Sarah Lewis. However, Sarah Lewis did say that the man had frightened her and a friend, so maybe this was the friend. Either way, the *East London Advertiser* was still referring to Mrs Kennedy a full three weeks later, and Sarah Lewis had been reported by the press at the inquest. Another point to consider is that Sarah Lewis reported seeing a man in the lodging house doorway, whereas Mrs Kennedy did not, and why? Because she would not have seen Hutchinson, who would have left before she arrived.

Detective Constable Walter Dew, who knew Kelly well, is reported to have said that Kelly was good-looking, and could be seen around the district, usually with friends, and that she always wore a clean white apron, and never wore a hat. Was she therefore the hatless woman referred to by Mrs Kennedy?

At a time of about 4.00 a.m., Sarah Lewis, Mrs Kennedy and Elizabeth Prater all reported hearing a shout of 'Murder'.

Mrs Prater, a witness at the inquest, who lived in the room above Mary Kelly, was the estranged wife of William Prater, having been deserted by her husband five years before. She knew Kelly well, and said that she had returned home at about 1.00 a.m. on the morning of

9 November. She said that she had stood in the archway into Miller's Court, beside McCarthy's grocery shop, waiting for the man she lived with. He had not turned up, so she had gone indoors. She said she saw and heard nothing suspicious.

She was awakened by her cat running over her neck, and remembered hearing a cry of 'Murder' coming from somewhere. She judged the time to be later than 4.00 a.m., because that was the time at which they normally put out the lodging house light.

Thomas Bowyer, an Indian Army pensioner, worked for John McCarthy the grocer collecting the rents on his properties.

He went to Kelly's abode to collect rent arrears of thirty shillings; this amounted to Kelly being seven weeks in arrears. The time was 10.45 a.m., and when he knocked at the door there was no answer. At the window there hung a coat which acted as a curtain and also served to reduce the wind caused by the broken window. Boyer was able to draw back the edge of the coat and look into the room. (Kelly and Barnett used to open the door by putting their hand through the opening and springing the latch.)

What he saw was the terribly mutilated body of Mary Jane Kelly, which lay on the bed. He then ran immediately to inform McCarthy, who returned with him to the scene of the crime. McCarthy sent Bowyer to the Commercial Street Police Station, and they arrived at Miller's Court.

As with the others let us now recap on the sightings of Mary during the night she would be killed.

Witness	Activity of Mary Kelly	Time
Joe Barnett	Visited Kelly at Miller's Court	7.30 p.m. to 8.00 p.m. Thursday evening
Hearsay	May have been drinking in Ten Bells	Unspecified Thurs. evening
Maurice Lewis	In Horn of Plenty with Joe Barnett	Unspecified Thurs. evening
Mary Ann Cox	Going home with blotchy-faced man	11.45 p.m. Thurs.
Several witnesses	She was in Miller's Court singing	12.00 midnight to 1.00 a.m. Friday
George Hutchinson	Met Kelly in Commercial Street. He watched her pick up a client.	2.00 a.m.
George Hutchinson	Waited for 45 minutes, then went back home	2.45 a.m.
Mrs Kennedy, Sarah Lewis & Liz Prater	From the room above Kelly's room they all heard a shout of 'Murder'	4.00 a.m.
Thomas Bowyer	Went to Miller's Court and discovered the body	10.45.am

During the investigation into the Ripper murders, the use of blood-hounds to track the murderer had been discussed, and to this end Edwin Brough, a breeder from Scarborough in Yorkshire, had arrived in London with two dogs, for the purpose of conducting a trial. We now know that the dogs had not proved to be a resounding success in following a trail in central London, and a decision had already been taken against their use.

Among the officers at the scene were Inspectors Abberline and Reid, who had been alerted to the murder and summoned to the scene by a telegram sent by Inspector Walter Beck, who was the Station Inspector on duty at Commercial Street. Beck had also sent for Dr Phillips, immediately after being informed of the murder. Other officers present at the site, throughout the morning at one time or another, were Sergeant Godley, DC Walter Dew, and Sergeant Bodham.

Dr Phillips said he was summoned at 11.00 a.m. and reached the murder site at 11.15 a.m. He stated that he looked through the window and satisfied himself that the body was dead, and determined that there was no other inhabitant of the room, who may require assistance. Inspector Abberline arrived about 11.30 a.m. and ordered the sealing off of Miller's Court. After discussion with Dr Phillips, a telegram was despatched to Commissioner Charles Warren, requesting that the dogs be used to track the perpetrator. Warren had by this time resigned, but it was not announced until the day of the murder. They waited in vain for some information as to the use of the dogs or guidance of some description until the time of 1.30 p.m., at which time Superintendent Arnold, who was by now present, ordered the door to be opened.

Dr Phillips, on entering the room, felt obliged to remark that on entering the room the door struck the table to the left of the bed. He conducted a cursory examination, at which he determined that the uterus was missing. This was later retracted after he had conducted the post mortem.

Dr Thomas Bond, who was the Police Surgeon to A Division, sub-mitted a report on Mary Jane Kelly which indicates that it was a description of the murder scene prior to the removal of the body. This report was only found in 1987, and reads as follows:

The body was lying naked in the middle of the bed, the shoul-ders flat, but the axis of the body inclined to the left side of the bed. The head was turned on the left cheek. The left arm was close to the body with the forearm flexed at right angles and lying across the abdomen. The right arm was slightly abducted from the body and rested on the mattress, the elbow bent and the forearm supine, with the fingers clenched. The legs were wide apart, the left thigh at right angles to the trunk and the right forming an obtuse angle with the pubes.

The whole of the surface of the abdomen and the thighs was removed, and the abdominal cavity emptied of its viscera. The breasts were cut off and the arms mutilated, by several jagged wounds, and the face hacked beyond recognition of the features. The tissues of the neck were severed all down to the bone.

The viscera were found in various parts, viz: the uterus and kidneys with one breast were under the head, the other breast by the right foot, the liver between the feet, the intestines by the right side, and the spleen by the left side of the body. The flaps removed from the abdomen and the thighs were on a table.

The bed clothing at the right corner was saturated with blood, and on the floor beneath was a pool of blood about two feet square. The wall by the right side of the bed and in line with the neck was marked with blood, which had struck it in a number of separate splashes.

Dr Phillips made a report to the inquest which stated:

The mutilated remains of a female were lying two-thirds over towards the edge of the bedstead nearest the door. She had only her chemise on, or some under linen garment. I am sure that the body had been removed subsequent to the injury which caused her death, from the side of the bedstead which was nearest the wood partition, because of the large quantity of blood under the bedstead, and the saturated condition of the sheet and the palliasse, at the corner nearest to the partition. The blood was produced by the severance of the carotid artery, which was the immediate cause of death. *This injury was inflicted while the deceased was lying at the right of the bedstead.*

[*Please note that this injury was inflicted at the right hand side of the bedstead. Unless the bed was moved away from the partition in order for the Ripper to get into position, the infliction of this injury by a right-handed assailant is nigh on impossible.*]

Dr Bond continued his report with the post mortem examination, at which he attended together with Dr Brown. His post mortem report read thus:

The face was gashed in all directions, the nose, cheeks, eyebrows, and ears being partly removed. The lips were blanched and cut by several incisions running obliquely down the chin. There were also numerous cuts, extending irregularly across all the features.

The neck was cut through the skin and other tissues, right down to the vertebrae, the fifth and sixth being deeply notched.

The skin cuts in the front of the neck showed distinct ecchymosis.

The air passage was cut at the lower part of the larynx through the cricoid cartilage.

Both breasts were removed by more or less circular incisions, the muscles down to the ribs being attached to the breasts. The intercostals between the 4th, 5th and 6th ribs were cut through and the contents of the thorax visible through the openings.

The skin and tissues of the abdomen from the costal arch to the pubes were removed in three large flaps. The right thigh was denuded in front, through to the bone, the flap of skin, including the external organs of generation and part of the right buttock. The left thigh was stripped of skin, fascia and muscles as far as the knee.

The left calf showed a long gash through skin and tissues to the deep muscles, and reaching from the knee to five inches above the ankle.

Both arms and forearms had extensive and jagged wounds.

The right thumb showed a small superficial incision about one inch long, with extravasations of blood in the skin, and there were several abrasions on the back of the hand moreover showing the same condition.

On opening the thorax it was found that the right lung was minimally adherent by old firm adhesions. The lower part of the lung was broken, and torn away.

The left lung was intact: it was adherent at the apex and there were a few adhesions over the side. In the substances of the lung were several nodules of consolidation.

The pericardium was open below, and the heart absent.

In the abdominal cavity, was some partly digested food, of fish and potatoes, and similar food was found in the remains of the stomach, attached to the intestines.

Whilst it has been put forward that the extraction of the heart through the severed diaphragm showed a degree of medical skill, I myself feel that this particular murder showed that the Ripper indeterminately mutilated the body, and that any semblance of possession of skill was purely by luck rather than good judgement.

I feel that in performing the mutilations the Ripper removed things haphazardly and without any premeditation. I further believe that with regards to Catharine Eddowes, he would have recognised the kidney, as a kidney, only after its removal, and I think I can justifiably claim that most people know where the heart is situated.

The description of the injuries was also published in the *Illustrated Police News*:

The throat had been cut across with a knife, nearly severing the head from the body. The abdomen had been partially ripped open, and both the breasts had been cut from the body. The left arm, like the head, hung to the body by the skin only. The nose had been cut off, the forehead skinned, and the thighs, down to the feet, stripped of flesh. The abdomen had been slashed with a knife across downwards, and the liver and entrails wrenched away. The entrails and other portions of the frame were missing, but the liver etc., it is said, were found placed between the feet of the poor victim. The flesh from the thighs and legs, together with the breasts and nose, had been placed by the murderer on the table, and one of the hands of the dead woman had been pushed in her stomach.

The injuries to the face and neck made it impossible to discern whether, as is now thought, the Ripper strangled Kelly prior to cutting her throat, or indeed partially strangled her. However, her fingers were clenched, which is an accepted indication of strangulation.

On the police inspection of the room it was discovered that there had been a fire in the grate, and evidence existed that it had used clothing as part of the fuel. The heat from this fire had melted the solder at the spout and handle of a kettle which was on the grate. Inspector Abberline drew the inference that the fire had been lit to illuminate the room, yet Kelly's clothes were neatly folded on a chair at the foot of the bed.

Maria Harvey provided the solution to the clothes, when she stated that in Kelly's room she had left two men's shirts, a boy's shirt, a black crêpe bonnet, a child's petticoat, a man's overcoat and a pawn ticket, and that the only thing which she had got back was the overcoat. Walter Dew stated that the overcoat was hung up at the window, like a curtain. Among the ashes in the fire were the remains of a woman's bonnet.

Numerous stories circulated reporting the various theories propounded at the time, and in the *Star* of 10 November 1888, Joseph Barnett told that she had a little boy living with her, who was six or seven years old. The question arises, could Maria Harvey have been the prostitute who Barrett complained was living with Kelly and himself, and did she have a son? She definitely specified a boy's shirt among the clothes which appear to have been burnt on the fire.

There is a school of thought which believes that Mary Kelly was not the body in 13 Miller's Court, and this is explored later in the book. Maurice Lewis told the Press of the day, that he had seen Kelly, about 10.00 a.m. on the morning of November the 9th, in the Britannia public house, with the man that she lived with. This is a number of hours after the estimated time that the murder was supposed to have been committed.

Caroline Maxwell, who was called as a witness at the inquest, testified that she had known Kelly for about four months, and said she had seen her standing on the corner of Miller's Court between 8.00 a.m. and 8.30 a.m. on the morning of 9 November. Kelly had told her that she had 'the terrors of drink on her'. Maxwell said that she should try a drink to put herself straight, to which Kelly said, she had already done so and had vomited it back up. Maxwell also said that she saw Kelly again about an hour later, outside the Britannia, talking to a stout man in dark clothes and a plaid coat.

Whilst both of these sightings appear at first glance to be a case of mistaken identity, it must be noted that the sighting by Maurice Lewis fits in with the second sighting by Caroline Maxwell. It must further be appreciated that Lewis stated that he had known Kelly for about five years. He called the man she was with 'Danny'. Joseph Barnett's brother was called Danny. And we must not forget that Maxwell actually claimed to have spoken to Kelly, and she also gave a description of the man she was with.

Unlikely as this is to be true, it does raise the question that if a body was opened up to the extent Kelly's body was, then could a reliable estimate be made as to the time of death, and could the body parts have cooled a lot quicker than expected, thus allowing an error to be made in the assessment of the time of death? One of the ways the doctors of the day used to assess the time of death was by the contents of the stomach. This has been found to be very unreliable.

If this is the case then the same margin of error could apply to all the accepted Ripper victims except for Elizabeth Stride.

A chestnut seller named Mrs Paumier who was working her patch on the corner of Widegate Road and Sandy's Row, said that a man of about 5 feet 6 inches dressed in a black coat, speckled trousers, and a black silk hat, walked past her on the morning of the murder and remarked, 'I suppose you have heard about the murder in Dorset Street.' She said that she had. The man supposedly grinned and replied 'I know more about it than you do', and then carried on down Sandy's Row. Mrs Paumier said that he had a black moustache and carried a black shiny bag, and she believed him to be the same man who had accosted her friend Sarah and another woman. Could it be that she was relating the particulars of the incident involving Sarah Lewis and Mrs Kennedy on Bethnal Green Road?

It has been mooted throughout the years since the Ripper murders, that more than one person was responsible for the acts. This is supposed to originate initially from the Home Secretary of the day, a man named Henry Matthews, who in answer to a Parliamentary Question stated, 'In the case of Kelly, there were certain circumstances which were wanting in the earlier cases, and which make it more probable that there were other persons who, at any rate after the crime, had assisted the murderer.'

The circumstances to which he is referring, can only be the excessive amount of blood which may have been on the clothes of the Ripper after Kelly's murder, and we must assume that the people he lived with must have noticed the bloodstains and must therefore have shielded him.

Mary Ann Cox was a witness at the inquest into Mary Kelly's death. A niece of hers told author and highly respected Ripper theorist Daniel Farson (he discovered the very important document the Macnaghten Memorandum) that: 'on the night of the murder of Mary Kelly, my aunt, who was very young and just married with one child, was standing at her door, waiting for her husband, who was a bit of a boozer. She saw Mary coming through the iron gate with this gentleman, a real toff. Mary was always bringing home men, mostly seamen from a pub called the Frying Pan, singing and holding their arms, with a bottle of gin under her arm. This night, as they got under the lamp in the court, they stopped. Mary's words was, 'All right love. Don't pull me along'. My aunt said they were only a few yards away from her at the door, she said she saw him as plain as looking at her hand. He was a fine-looking man, wore an overcoat with a cape, high hat, not a silk one, and Gladstone bag. As they went into the house, Mary called out Goodnight to my aunt.'

There is no evidence to suggest that any of this was true, and it must therefore be treated with caution.

Dr Roderick Macdonald, who officiated at the inquest of Kelly, conducted the whole proceedings in a single day, 12 November 1888, at Shoreditch Town Hall. He closed the proceedings as soon as he established sufficient evidence had been given to substantiate the 'cause of death', at which time he requested the jury to come to a conclusion, saying 'There is other evidence which I do not propose to call, for if we at once make public every fact brought forward in connection with this terrible murder, the end of justice might be retarded.'

The jury accepted the offer, and concluded the proceedings.

Mary Kelly was buried at Walthamstow Roman Catholic Cemetery, on 19 November 1888. Hundreds of people attended her funeral, but members of her family were conspicuous by their absence.

In analysing this information, a number of things come to mind, which promote questions, and require to be listed for discussion.

1. The young man is described by Mrs Kennedy as intoxicated. It is highly unlikely that someone with the intentions of the Ripper would be drunk. So we can perhaps assume that either this man was pretending to be drunk, or he was very unlikely to be the Ripper.

2. There were two women in Dorset Street at 3.00 a.m. to 3.30 a.m. on the morning of the murder. Was the woman without the hat Mary Kelly, and when the first woman, who must have been wearing a hat, turned away, did the gentleman then approach Mary Kelly, and was he her murderer? (The witness specifically stated that the second woman was not wearing a hat. This was quite uncommon, but it is stated that Kelly never wore a hat.)

3. If Mary Kelly and Barnett frequently opened the door by putting their arm through the broken window and springing the lock, then why did McCarthy have to burst the door open? If it was a mortise lock which prohibited McCarthy from opening the door via the broken window, then the Ripper must have locked the door and therefore the key must have been found, or when it went missing, it had been taken by the Ripper, at a previous assignation with Kelly in preparation for their next and final meeting. Was this Barnett?

4. We must also appreciate that, with the door locked and Kelly in a state of undress, we may conclude that she knew the murderer

and felt safe with him. If she had taken part in sex, and had taken a reasonable quantity of drink, then she may have involuntarily fallen asleep, and thinking that she was secure, she was therefore not aware of the onslaught until it had commenced.

5. There was a lot of blood, provoking the theory that the killer choked Kelly until she lost consciousness and commenced the mutilations before death. It must be remembered that the heart would have stopped pumping blood around the body once it had stopped beating. Contrary to this assumption, it has been previously explained that the hands of the victim being clenched are a known indication of strangulation.

6. Did the killer murder her by strangulation while he was still undressed from being in bed beside her, and did he then light the fire in order to see better in order to mutilate the body? If the candle was lit, this would not have provided sufficient light for the Ripper's need.

7. If the kettle was on the grate, then it is unlikely that the burning of the clothes could have generated sufficient heat to melt the solder on the spout and handle. Solder has a reasonably low melting point but would not have been used as a jointing medium if the manufacturer was not confident that it was good enough for the job. I can however think of no reason why the Ripper would need to place the kettle on the fire.

8. As previously mentioned, if a body was subjected to the extent of mutilation that Kelly's was, to what extent could the cooling of the body be accelerated, and how much of a mistake could the attending doctors have made when assessing the time of death.

9. To conclude the evaluation of the murder of Mary Kelly I would like you to consider the following points.

a) Nobody admitted to knowing the name of any of the men who were seen with Kelly, only Maurice Lewis, who said it was Barnett's brother Danny, and timed his sighting hours after Kelly was supposed to be already dead.

b) I believe we can eliminate any sightings witnessed inside a public house, as it would have been far too public a place for the Ripper to pick up a victim.

c) Why didn't the Ripper burn Kelly's clothes? I believe that the reason is that he had been in bed with Kelly and his own clothes were on the chair on top of Kelly's. He then carried out his dirty deed and then got dressed. It was only at this time that Kelly's clothes were exposed.

d) Is the time of the murder to be accepted as that time when witnesses heard the cry of 'Murder'? It was after all heard by three separate people.

e) Did the killer lock the door behind him? If this was the case then Mary Kelly had not lost the key, but only told Joe Barnett that she had. Another explanation would be that her murderer had the key. This would be most unlikely unless the killer was Joe Barnett. The fact that the door was locked is the only logical reason explaining why it had to be forced open. The broken window would have been visible to everyone at the scene, and so much time was wasted waiting, before the door was opened, surely somebody would have had the presence of mind to investigate the possibility of the door being opened via the window, especially as this is a common way for burglars to gain entry to premises.

As a conclusion, I am certain that Mary Jane Kelly was indeed a victim of Jack the Ripper.

CHAPTER EIGHT
More unlikely victims

Annie Farmer

Annie Farmer was born in 1848, and at the time of her attack, was separated from her husband, who earned his living as a trader.

On 20 November 1888, she propositioned a client, whom she described to the police as 'wearing a suit of shabby nature', but added that he was of genteel nature.

She took the gentleman to her lodgings in Satchell's lodging house, which was situated at Number 19 George Street, in Spital-fields, where he paid for a bed for both of them.

At approximately 9.30 p.m., a scream was heard and a fully-dressed man ran out of the building.

Annie went down to the lodging house kitchen, bleeding from a cut in her throat. A number of men were present in the kitchen, and they went off in pursuit of the assailant.

Her attacker raced along George Street and into Thrawl Street, where he came upon two cokemen. He shouted 'What a fucking cow' as he passed them, and they then lost sight of him as he mingled with other passers by. He was never found.

Annie claimed the man had attacked her for no apparent reason, but the police, on interviewing her, discovered that the cut was only superficial, and had been inflicted with a blunt blade, quite unlike the modus operandi of the Ripper. They further discovered that she had been hiding coins inside her mouth, and concluded that she had got into an argument with her client over money. She had managed to get the money into her mouth, and refused to release it. The attacker had probably cut her to make her open her mouth and release the money. Or Annie had cut her own throat very slightly and then screamed, and accused her assailant of being Jack the Ripper.

Annie was never seriously entertained as a Ripper victim, and in-vestigations into the crime were dropped after only a short time. She was not killed by her assailant, and was not a victim of Jack the Ripper.

Rose Mylett

Born in 1862, Rose Mylett was known by a number of aliases. She was married to an upholsterer called Davis, to whom she bore a son, and was known to some as 'drunken Lizzie Davis'.

They commenced their married life living with Rose's mother at Pelham Street, Baker's Row, Spitalfields. From there they moved to George Street, and thereafter they lived in the Poplar District.

On 19 December she was seen by a nightwatchman named Charles Ptolomay, in conversation with two sailors in Poplar High Street. The time was 7.55 p.m., and Rose was heard to say 'No, No, No' in her reply to a question.

At 2.30 a.m. on the following morning, Thursday 20 December, Rose was stood outside the George, a public house in Commercial Road, and was seen by a woman named Alice Graves, who described her as being drunk.

At 4.15 a.m., in the yard of a builders' merchant named George Clarke, which stood between Number 106 and Number 108 Poplar High Street, her body was discovered by PC Robert Goulding. She had died only recently, as it was a cold December morning and yet PC Goulding said that the body was still warm. There were no visible signs of injury, and she had not apparently been interfered with. In her possession she had one halfpenny.

The post mortem was carried out by Doctor Matthew Brownfield, who was the Metropolitan Police Surgeon for K Division, who described the body thus:

Blood was oozing from the nostrils, and there was a slight abrasion on the right side of the face. On the neck there was a mark, which had evidently been caused by a cord drawn tightly round the neck, from the spine to the left ear. Such a mark would be made by a four-thread cord. There were also impressions of thumbs and middle and index fingers of some person, plainly visible on each side of the neck. There were no injuries to the arms or legs. The brain was gorged with an almost black fluid blood. The stomach was full of meat and potatoes, which had only recently been eaten. Death was due to strangulation. Deceased could not have done it herself. The marks on her neck were probably caused by her trying to pull the cord off. He thought that the murderer must have stood at the left rear of the woman, and, having the ends of the cord around his hands, thrown it around her throat, crossed his hands, and thus strangled her. If it had been done in this way, it would account for the mark not going completely round the neck.

The findings of Dr Brownfield were immediately questioned, when given at the inquest. The inquest procedure was conducted by Wynne Baxter, and held in the Poplar Coroner's Court.

The police contended that the mark on the neck had not been of sufficient severity to cause the execution to be by ligature strangulation. No observation of a struggle or footprints, or marks of any description, to indicate an attack, had been found. This would have been apparent because the ground in the yard was soft underfoot. The body had been laid in a natural position. There was no trace of Rose having taken alcohol, so the perception given by Alice Graves that she was drunk, must have been mistaken.

Dr Robert Anderson, the Metropolitan Police, Assistant Commissioner, asked Dr Bond to attend the body and submit a report. Bond at first agreed with Brownfield's findings, that she had been strangled with a ligature of some description, but he later revisited the body, after he was urged to reconsider his opinion by Dr Anderson.

The results of this visit conflicted totally with his and Dr Brownfield's previous findings.

He stated that Mylett had choked to death while drunk, and determined that the mark on her neck, was caused by the stiff velvet collar which she had worn.

Wynne Edwin Baxter, the presiding coroner, completely dismissed Dr Bond's evidence and the jury brought in a verdict that Rose Mylett was murdered by person or persons unknown.

Regardless of whether the doctors were correct in their original assessment of the cause of death, or whether the subsequent statement of Dr Bond which was disallowed by the coroner was right, it can clearly be seen that this killing did not bear the mark of the Ripper. It was only ever included, in my opinion, so as to make the legend of Jack the Ripper more infamous. Consequently, like most other serious people who view the case, I conclude that the jury were correct in their verdict. One fact which helps with this assumption is the evidence that the brain was gorged with blood. So as not to detract from the previous post mortem examinations carried out by Dr Bond, I will state in mitigation that he made his examination well after the murder had been committed.

Alice McKenzie

Alice McKenzie was born in the town of Peterborough in the year of 1849. At the time of her death, Alice lived with an Irish porter by the name of John McCormack, who worked for a tailoring firm in Hanbury Street.

They lived as man and wife from 1883, and at the time of her death were staying at Tenpenny's lodging house, which was situated at Number 54 Gun Street, Spitalfields.

Tenpenny's was run by the Deputy, a woman called Elizabeth Ryder, who was the wife of Richard Ryder, who earned his living as a cooper.

McKenzie was a known prostitute, who also worked as a washerwoman, and at times did some charring for some of the better off Jewish families of the East End of London.

McKenzie and McCormack spent the night of 15 July together, and on the morning of the 16th, McCormack got up and as usual went to work. Alice spent the day in the lodging house until approximately 4.00 p.m. when McCormack came home from work slightly drunk, and went to bed. He gave Alice one shilling and eight pence, telling her that she could spend the shilling on herself and to pay for their bed for the night with the other eight pence. He stated that this was the last time he seen Alice alive, although there is some conjecture that the two of them had a row later in the evening. This was the testimony of Elizabeth Ryder, who said that McKenzie had left the lodging house at around 8.00 p.m.

McCormack finally awoke properly, and on going down to the lodging house kitchen, discovered that Alice had not paid their lodge for the night, a fact about which he was extremely annoyed.

Also living in the lodging house was a blind boy by the name of George Discon. On the night of her death McKenzie spent part of the evening with him, at the Cambridge Music Hall. After seeing the blind boy back to the lodging house, McKenzie then went out again, to keep a rendezvous with a man she had met at the music hall and had arranged to meet later in the evening.

Alice was on her way along Flower and Dean Street when she met Catherine Hughes, who was with two other women friends, Margaret Franklin and Sarah Marney. They were sitting on the steps of a lodging house. The time of this meeting was put at 11.30 p.m. to midnight.

At 12.50 a.m. on the morning of Wednesday 17 July, Police Constable Walter Andrews was walking his beat along Whitechapel

High Street when he happened to look down Castle Alley. He spied what he first thought was a bundle close to a lamp-post on the western side of the alley about 90 to 100 yards down the street, and went down to investigate. He found Alice McKenzie's body lying across the pavement. She had been stabbed in the throat, and her skirt was pulled up revealing blood over her stomach and thighs.

PC Andrews heard the sound of footsteps and met Isaac Lewis Jacobs, who was on his way to eat his supper. Andrews had spoken to Jacobs about ten minutes earlier. He instructed Jacobs to remain with the body and went off to inform Sergeant Badham, who responded to the sound of his police whistle. Sergeant Badham arrived at the scene and approximately ten minutes later, Inspector Reid arrived at the murder site accompanied by PC Allen. Reid was the head of the Metropolitan Police H Division C.I.D., having succeeded Frederick Abberline in the position in late 1888. He stated at the inquest that coins found underneath the body were similar to those found in the Annie Chapman Case. He further commented on the fact that, on his arrival, the blood was still flowing into the gutter, but stopped doing so shortly after his arrival.

Dr Bagster Phillips arrived at the murder site at approximately 1.15 a.m. and made a brief examination of the body, before arranging for its removal to the mortuary. His initial examination at the scene of the crime revealed:

The woman was lying on her back, face turned sharply to the right – her right arm was enveloped by her shawl which extended to the ends of the fingers. Her forearm was flexed and lay across her chest. Her left arm was also flexed and the hand rested on the shoulder. The left side of the neck incised, the wound jagged and exposed. Clothes were turned up revealing the genitals. A wound to the wall of the abdomen, apparently not opening the cavity.

Later that day he conducted a very comprehensive post mortem, and accompanied it with a very comprehensive report, which included these main points.

The throat had been stabbed twice rather than cut. The two wounds were about two inches deep and inflicted from above when the body was probably laid on the ground; these wounds had been caused by a sharp cutting instrument, by someone who knew the position of the vessels or at any rate, where to cut. He determined that these injuries were the cause of death.

The bruising on the chest lent itself to the fact that the murderer held the woman down while he stabbed her.

There was a jagged wound in the abdomen extending from the chest to the navel, down the right side. This wound, which pierced the skin and subcutaneous tissues, had not penetrated the abdominal cavity, the wound having been made by a series of cuts.

Other cuts were evident around the genital area, and he stated that all these wounds had been inflicted after death.

Dr Phillips expressed his belief that the instrument used was of a smaller nature than that used in the 'Whitechapel murders', and he further noted within his report, that Dr Gordon Brown who had attended the post mortem, had expressed his concurrence in the conclusions presented.

In concluding his report Dr Phillips stated:

After careful and long deliberation I cannot satisfy myself on purely anatomical and professional grounds, that the perpetrator of all the 'Whitechapel Murders' is our man. I am on the contrary impelled to the contrary conclusion in this, noting the mode of procedure and the character of the mutilations, and judging of motive in connection with the latter.

I do not here enter into the comparison of the cases, neither do I take into account what I admit may be almost conclusive evidence in favour of the one man theory, if all the surrounding circumstances and other evidence are considered, holding it as my duty to report on the post mortem appearances, and express an opinion only on professional grounds, and based upon my own observation.

Dr Bond, who was sent to make an examination of the body again, drew different conclusions from those of Dr Phillips, saying:

I see in this murder, evidence of similar design to the former Whitechapel murders, viz: sudden onslaught on the prostrate woman, the throat skilfully and resolutely cut, with subsequent mutilation, each mutilation indicating sexual thoughts and a desire to mutilate the abdomen and sexual organs.

I am of the opinion that the murder was performed by the same person who committed the former series of Whitechapel murders.

We do not know whether or not Dr Bond's conclusions were being made so as to alarm the public concerning the continuing existence of the Ripper. However, if his conclusions were correct, then some of the suspects lose their importance. If a leading doctor, who was a friend of at least one of the leading Metropolitan Police officers, still thought that the Ripper was at large, then I believe he would have been privy to the thinking of the leading police officers in the case, and therefore, in my opinion, they also did not believe that they had identified the Ripper. This is the main conclusion which I would draw from the evidence of Dr Bond.

As to the murder itself, I am personally of the opinion and tend to accept, that this murder did not bear the mark of the earlier murders. The frenzied attack was not present in the mutilations, and the throat was not slashed but stabbed. We cannot totally reject Jack the Ripper as a suspect, as it is commonly accepted that serial killers do change their modus operandi.

An interesting point was that PC Allen who was called to the scene by Sergeant Bodham stated that on his beat he had met PC Andrews, and had gone up Castle Alley and stood under the very lamppost where the body was found, and had eaten a snack, twenty minutes before the body was found.

We can draw certain information from this occurrence. If PC Allen ate his snack under the lamp-post at 12.30 a.m., and then walked the 90 or 100 yards back to Commercial High Street, the time would have been circa 12.35 a.m. when he resumed his beat. If he had then turned in the correct direction, he would have quite probably walked into Alice McKenzie and her murderer coming up the street, but he did not and so they were not in sight. This means that Alice and her killer had to reach the alley, walk the 100 yards down the alley, and then the murder had to be committed, and the murderer had to walk back up the alley and get out of sight, all before PC Andrews appeared on the scene.

Alice McKenzie was killed by 'a person or persons unknown', as determined by the jury at her inquest. In my personal opinion and that of most noted Ripperologists, the person was not Jack the Ripper.

A further observation, to supplement the supposition with regard to Dr Bond is: if the senior police ranks were so convinced that the Ripper was either interred, dead, in a lunatic asylum, or even identified, shortly after the murder of Mary Kelly, then why were so many extra policemen still patrolling the area, looking for him? Confirmation of this is in the 'Home Office files' itemising the expenditure and sanctions of payments for extra officers drafted in from other divisions.

The Pinchin Street murder

Pinchin Street is a short road situated in the parish of St George's in the East, in the East End, and runs east to west from Backchurch Lane to Christian Street. The north side of the road consisted of paling fencing, which shielded Pinchin and Johnson's Oil and Paint Works. The street did not have any houses and was known by the local community as 'Dark Lane'.

On 10 September 1889, part of a woman's body, consisting of the torso and the arms, and covered with a chemise, was found by Police Constable William Pennett. The constable was patrolling his beat when he saw a bundle. His attention was drawn to the bundle by the smell which it was giving off. The bundle was wrapped in sacking and under a railway arch.

Constable Pennett summoned assistance, and arrested two sailors and a bootblack, who were sleeping rough, under the railway arches. The head and legs of the body were never discovered, and the corpse was never positively identified, though it was mooted that it was a prostitute called Lydia Hart, who at the time of the find had been missing for a few days. To support the identification I can confirm that Lydia Hart was never seen again alive. The abdomen was split by a cut, and the legs and head had been severed in a similar fashion to another female body, which had been found in the Thames, close to Battersea Park and the Embankment. They also bore a resemblance to the body discovered in the 'Whitehall Mystery'. This body was found on 3 October 1888, in a remote vault of the New Scotland Yard which was at the time under construction, and was the headless body of a woman. The body was examined by Percy C. Clark on 10 September 1889, and the post mortem was performed by Dr C. A. Hibbert.

On 12 September 1889, Dr Phillips examined the body, and though the press reported that the stomach was mutilated in a manner similar to that of the Ripper murders, and also the estimated time of death was placed as the anniversary of the murder of Annie Chapman, this was not regarded as the responsibility of the Ripper by most of the investigating officers.

Melville Macnaghten took a keen interest in the case because truthfully, along with the murder of Frances Coles, it was the only murder to be even loosely associated with the Ripper on which Macnaghten had an input.

Melville Macnaghten was a close friend of Commissioner Monro, but he did not become a police officer until six months after the murder of Mary Kelly, so that all of his reflections have been formed with the benefit of hindsight and post all the Ripper murders.

The investigating officers in the case contain some familiar names. They include Inspector Reid, Sergeant Godley, Sergeant Thick, Sergeant White, Inspector Moore, Inspector Pattenden, and Inspector Swanson. They interviewed various suspects and followed numerous lines of enquiry, all to no avail, and the Pinchin Street murder was never solved.

It does however have certain outstanding questions which link it to the Whitechapel murders.

1. The head was removed. Jack the Ripper on a number of occasions attempted to sever the head of his victim, when carrying out his mutilations. He may have been trying to accomplish this, but it is more likely that he slashed the neck so severely, and with such manic force, that the head nearly came away from its structures. If he fully intended to remove the head completely, then he had ample opportunity in some of his previous murders to accomplish this.

2. The abdomen was indeed mutilated, but not to the extent of the accepted canonical victims of the Ripper. It would not have taken him more than five seconds longer to eliminate any doubt as to the identity of the killer.

3. Did the killer mutilate the face and legs so badly that he removed them altogether during his extensive mutilation of the body? It is far more likely that as stated, the hands were well formed and showed no signs of manual labour, and that the head was removed primarily to prohibit identification of the body. It is likely that the legs were removed for one of two reasons, the first being that there was a telltale scar which could have been used to identify the body, which would possibly have led to the apprehension of the culprit. The second, and in my opinion far more likely, is that it made it a lot easier for the murderer to dispose of the corpse: i.e. without the head or legs, the package for disposal would be a lot smaller,

An interesting point is that the estimated date of the murder was put as 8 September 1889; this is exactly one year, to the day, after the murder of Annie Chapman.

In conclusion can I say that when the information is weighed for and against the probability of this murder being the responsibility of Jack the Ripper, I think we must come down on the side of the sceptical, and I do not believe that Jack carried out the Pinchin Street Murder.

Frances Coles

The final murder that was to be attributed to Jack the Ripper, was that of Frances Coles, who was the daughter of a cobbler/bootmaker.

Frances was born in 1865, and had finished up living in the Bermondsey Workhouse, at the time of her murder.

Frances worked for a wholesale chemist until the year 1884, when she started to make a living working as a prostitute.

She was found at 2.15 a.m. on the morning of Valentine's Day 1891, in Swallow Gardens, an alley running between Chamber Street and Rosemary Lane. It was a dark and squalid place and was situated in the vicinity of the place where the 'Ray Fair' was held, and had the reputation of being one of the worst areas of Victorian London.

When Coles was found by Police Constable Ernest Thompson, she was bleeding from a cut to the throat, but was still alive. This would prove that the assault had not long been committed. PC Thompson was an inexperienced copper and had only recently commenced walking the beat.

With the attack having just taken place then there was a distinct possibility that the murderer was still in the vicinity, and as the constable bent down over the bloody mass, he stated that he heard the sound of footsteps coming from the direction of Swallow Street. Initially he contemplated giving chase, as would have been the natural thing to do, but the police force had set down procedures, and one of these dictated that the first officer to arrive on the scene or discover a body, was to remain with the victim.

Nine years later, in 1900, PC Thompson was himself murdered by Barnett Abrahams, who stabbed him during a disturbance at a coffee stall.

Returning to the murder of Frances Coles: on the night of her death she had quarrelled with a seaman at her lodgings, at around 11.30 p.m. At 12.30 a.m., the seaman had left the lodging house. This man was James Thomas Sadler, who had been paid off from his ship on 11 February, and who had been in the company of Frances, for the previous two days.

At 12.35 a.m. Coles also left the lodging house and went to Commercial Street, where she met Ellen Gallagher, and went off with a man in a cheesecutter hat, who had given Gallagher a black eye.

At 2.00 a.m. in the morning Sadler was found by the police, having by his appearance been on the receiving end of a good hiding.

Three railway carmen were walking through the railway footpath called Swallow Gardens at a time of 2.10 a.m.; they stated that they heard nothing but did see a man and a woman. One of the carmen, a man named Knapton, said that he shouted 'Good night' to them.

On being interviewed, another of the carmen, by the name of 'Jumbo Friday', stated that the man he had seen looked like a ship's fireman, and that the woman had been wearing a distinctively shaped bonnet, which he identified as similar to the one found near the body of Frances Coles.

The police soon found Sadler, who admitted that he had spent the previous day in the company of Coles, and who had been in the vicinity of the crime. He was charged with her murder.

When he realised that he was going to be charged with all of the Ripper murders, he appealed to the Stoker's Union, who engaged Wilson and Wallace Solicitors to fight his case.

Sadler had been heavily bloodstained when he had turned up at the lodging house at 3.00 a.m. in the morning. When he was refused a bed for the night, he had then gone to the London Hospital in order to gain treatment for his wounds. The time was put at 5.00 a.m.

At the inquest, when the Crown presented its case against Sadler, his counsel immediately produced seven witnesses who were prepared to testify to his whereabouts at the time of the murder, and furthermore, to confirm that the bloodstains were the result of him having been engaged in a number of fights during the course of the evening and night.

The prosecution's case finally fell apart when Thomas Fowles and Kate McCarthy admitted that they had been the couple who were seen by the three carmen. Sadler left the court a free man.

The inquest was held at the Working Lads Institute in Whitechapel, under the jurisdiction of Coroner Wynne Baxter.

The murder of Frances Coles was the last murder to be linked to Jack the Ripper, *and it must again be said that if the police were so convinced that the Ripper was out of commission, either through drowning or as inferred, an inmate in some jail or lunatic asylum, then why did they try, albeit unsuccessfully, to construct a case against Sadler for which the intention was to convict him of the Whitechapel Murders?*

In my opinion the police had no idea as to the identity of Jack the Ripper, and were still searching for the culprit.

It is most possible that Sadler did indeed murder Frances Coles. He had a history of violence, and indeed, sold his knife for one shilling to a seaman called Campbell on the day following the murder. It may also have been the man in the cheesecutter hat, but if so then why isn't any further mention made of this man? If he had been a genuine suspect then surely the police would have questioned him to their satisfaction. He could have been identified by Ellen Gallagher, who would have gladly helped with his identification in retribution for the black eye.

No, I believe that Sadler was a better prospect for the murderer. He had an argument with Coles, and he probably blamed her for the fact that whilst they were out drinking, he had been assaulted and robbed. He may have thought that Coles was responsible for arranging his mugging; this type of thing did go on.

With regard to our investigation, it has no great bearing. Due to the format of the murder, the fact that no mutilation or attempted mutilation took place, and the victim was not strangled prior to having her throat cut, then this murder was not committed by Jack the Ripper, and Frances Coles was definitely not a Ripper victim.

Mortuary photograph
of Elizabeth Stride

Mortuary photograph
of Annie Chapman

Mortuary photograph
of Martha Tabram

Mortuary photograph
of Catharine Eddowes

Eddowes's face: rough diagram

Eddowes's body: sketch of position

Eddowes's body:
mortuary sketch

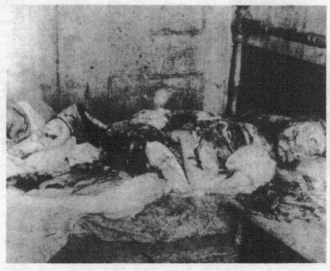

Mary Kelly: Scotland Yard photograph

Back yard of 29 Hanbury Street

George Yard buildings

PART TWO

The Suspects

CHAPTER NINE
Whitechapel in 1888

To obtain an insight into the mind of Jack the Ripper, it is important that we understand and review the conditions which prevailed in East London at the time of the murders.

This involves looking into the Whitechapel and Spitalfields areas, and appreciating the way of life and the squalor in which the populace of these areas existed. We must further address the situation with regard to housing, health, and the sanitation which was all too evident in this part of London.

The term 'East End' was invented around 1880, and was quickly adopted by the Press, to denote a shabby area filled with degradation, and inhabited by prostitutes, thieves, Jews, and any kind of undesirable, whose existence and income dictated that their very survival was their primary ambition.

The area had sprung up on demand after the creation of the railways and docks, which increased the trade of the City of London in both exports and imports.

In this area of London, wages were minimal, and an awful lot of the families existed on the breadline. The men and women tended to lose their revulsion from their living conditions by taking refuge in drink, and public houses abounded on every corner, to cater for this need.

The houses in the East End were of two and sometimes three storeys in height, with some manufactured from stone but a great number still made from wood. The streets had no proper roads, and sanitation if it existed was often just a pit in the cellar. Water was provided by a standpipe from which the residents filled jugs and carried them to their homes.

A large proportion of the penniless families lived in a single room, which was invariably rented either by the week or daily at a fee of fourpence to eightpence per night; it was customary for the families to be evicted for non-payment of rent when the amount owed became unacceptable, or for the family to 'do a runner'.

A lot of the people lived from day to day and purchased a bed for the night at one of the numerous lodging houses that cluttered the area.

Most of the terraced dwellings were joined to one another over an alleyway, which extended for the depth of the premises, and gave access to a backyard, which contained the water tap.

Rubbish littered the streets, as there was no organised collection of the refuse as we have today. Drunken brawls frequently took place; sometimes these fights were between men and women, and this was accepted as a normal occurrence.

The men went in their hundreds, to line up for what work there was, at the London Dock gates. They stood at the gates waiting for them to open and the bell to ring, announcing that work was available and labour was required. The selection was accomplished by the allocation of labour tickets, which were frequently just thrown into the pack of men. Those who came up with a ticket were the ones who had secured a day's toil; the remainder of the men drifted away, only for the performance to be repeated on the following day.

As is evident from this description, the supply of labour vastly exceeded the demand, and this was reflected in the amount of pay they received, which was low. The regular dock workers' maximum potential earnings were about thirty shillings a week, but most of the dockers were lucky to average one third of this.

The 1887 statistical survey showed that within this squalor, and in Whitechapel alone, 67,865 people eked out a living.

Further statistics indicated that the annual rate of births per thousand people was 36.9, and the annual death rate per one thousand head of capita was 25.2. Another disturbing fact was that out of every 1000 births, 173 babies would die before reaching the age of one year.

In the late Victorian age, hospitals were places to be avoided if at all possible. They were not looked upon as places of curing, but as places where people died, and medical treatment was carried out with little regard for any pain inflicted upon the patient. Antiseptics were not in general use, hygiene was of a very poor standard, and sepsis was common throughout the hospitals. The surgeon operated in a black frock coat, which had upon it remnants of the filth and blood collected by years of use, and as can be seen from the following extract from the *East London Observer* of 30 June 1888, the standards were more that of an abattoir than what we would today expect from a hospital:

Mr Joseph Boxall deposed that in July last, his daughter whilst attempting to save a child from being run over, was kicked by a horse. She was taken to the London Hospital, and was sent from there to a convalescent home in Folkestone, from which the witness removed her on the 11th instant. She died however on Wednesday last.

Evidence from Dr Edward Birdoe deposed that on Thursday, the 14th, he was called to the deceased on an order from the Relieving Officer. He saw the deceased, who with her friends, seemed rather embittered at what they considered the bad treatment she had received at the London Hospital. The deceased told him that the doctors had put her under chloroform, for the purpose of, as they said, examining her leg. Instead of doing merely this, however, they amputated her leg just above the knee. This was done without the consent of the deceased or her parents. A short time afterwards it was found that to save her life, it was necessary to amputate the rest of her leg, and this was done with the consent of the deceased

Witness advised her to go to the Infirmary, but she refused, on the grounds that she had a horror of going into any more public institutions. She sank and died on Wednesday last. The cause of death was shock, consequent upon the second operation. A juryman said that the consent of the parents of the girl ought to have been obtained for the first operation. Nobody was present from the hospital, but the jury refused to adjourn the enquiry, one saying that it was the second operation that had caused the death. The jury returned a verdict in accordance with the medical evidence.

It can be seen from this extract, how easily death was accepted. It must be stressed that not all hospitals operated with such a callous disregard for life.

It can so be seen, that in this area of London, the entrepreneurs ruled the economy with a greedy hand. Fuel costs were high, as was the cost of lighting, and therefore in order to compete favourably, the controllable overheads were kept to a minimum, and especially the labour costs. In this way, profits were maximised, as the cheap cost of labour was used to offset the need for investment in somewhat expensive capital equipment, and a sweatshop economy was thus maintained.

Women were even worse off than the men, and were firmly rooted at the bottom of the pile. If they had any work, then it was long hours for even lower wages, and a typical female worker would start at 8.00 a.m. and finish at 7.00 p.m., that is, unless she was required to work overtime, which could place her finishing time as late as 11.00 p.m., and sometimes all through the night. For this work which took various forms, including button making, india rubber stamp machinists, perfumers, spectacle makers, lantern slide makers, and tie makers, to name but a few, she was paid for a wage the princely sum of five shillings, and very often less.

It is therefore little wonder that prostitution was viewed as the easy way out of this quandary, whereby a relatively good-looking young female could make a decent living, and the older wretches could still find men who would pay them the price of a few gins or a night's lodging, for the use of their bodies.

It was into this despicable poverty and degradation that Jack the Ripper was born. He would walk the streets in search of a suitable victim, and when selected, he would take her up one of the many alleys, or up the passages between houses, in fact anywhere quiet and dark would suffice, and there he would carry out his foul executions. There were always willing women available as the abject poverty created the need for money and food, and then many of the women would then go home to their single cramped rooms, with enough money earned to feed the children for another day.

Let us now take this a step further, and look at the Ripper victims in the context of their surroundings. Firstly let us inspect the streets in which the victims lived and died.

Martha Tabram: Star Place, Commercial Road
It was a commercial road both in name and function. Running from Aldgate to Limehouse, and contained a mixture of shops, houses, tenement blocks, coupled with factories and spattered with a number of warehouses. It joined Whitechapel High Street at the same point as did Leman Street, Church Lane, Union Street, Plumbers Row, Settles Street, and New Road, all of which joined it from the north, and Gower's Walk, Berner Street, and Cannon Street joined it from the south. To the east it crossed Burdett Road where it carried on as the East India Dock Road.

Another place associated with Martha Tabram was Flower and Dean Street. In fact this street was the place where three of the potential Ripper victims lived at one time or another, and if I am mistaken, and Elizabeth Stride was indeed a Ripper victim, then that would make four. The others were Martha Tabram, Mary Ann Nichols and Catharine Eddowes.

Flower and Dean Street ran between Commercial Street and Brick Lane, and contained a variety of lodging houses and 'dosses'. These places allowed men and women to sleep together, providing that the bed was paid for, and so they encouraged cohabitation for sexual purposes, and thereby performed the same function as a brothel. Donald Rumbelow tells us that at this time there were 233 of these common lodging houses in Whitechapel alone, and between them they accommodated around 8,500 persons.

It was a no go area for a lone policeman, and was once described as the most dangerous street in the whole of London.

If we take the murder site of Catharine Eddowes (Mitre Square) as a starting point, and make our way through Goulston Street where the graffiti was discovered, this was then regarded by Frederick Foster, the City Surveyor, as the most likely destination of Jack the Ripper, after he had murdered Eddowes.

Martha Tabram was known to frequent and regularly use certain public houses. These are among the most likely places where a would-be murderer could have selected his victim without creating undue attention towards himself.

The Two Brewers, in Brick Lane, was where Martha met the two guardsmen on the night of her death, and was probably used at irregular intervals by all of the Ripper victims. The same claim can be made for the Frying Pan, which stood on the corner of Brick Lane and Thrawl Street. All the Ripper victims at some time lived within three hundred yards of both these pubs.

The White Swan stood on Whitechapel High Street, and was the last premises that Martha Tabram was seen in.

Mary Ann Nichols lived in Number 18 Thrawl Street up until one week before her death, and from then on at Number 56 Flower and Dean Street.

In Thrawl Street, she shared a room with three other women, for a fee of fourpence per night. It was the next street down from Flower and Dean Street, and was situated between Commercial Street and Brick Lane. It included numerous lodging houses, tenement buildings and light workshops, and was frequented by a mixture of drunks, ruffians and thieves.

At Number 56 Flower and Dean Street, which was designated as a dosshouse, Nichols rented a bed, in which she probably slept with a man whom she had picked up off the street and who had paid for the price of the bed, as this was the generally accepted norm.

The pubs that Nichols frequented were the same ones as the other

Ripper victims, and just like some of the films tend to depict, all the Ripper victims probably knew one another by sight.

Nichols's murder site was Buck's Row. This stood to the east of Whitechapel, and ran from Brady Street to Baker's Row. It was some three-quarters of a mile walk from where she was staying at the time of her death.

Annie Chapman, who I regard as the third victim of the murderer, lived for most of the last few months of her life at Crossingham's lodging house, whose address was Number 35 Dorset Street. Number 35 stood opposite Miller's Court, the home and the death site of Mary Jane Kelly, and was within two minutes walk of Thrawl Street and Flower and Dean Street.

Hanbury Street, where she met her death, ran east to west from Commercial Street to Baker's Row, the murder site of Number 29 being towards the west end. It was fronted on the ground floor by 'Mrs Hardiman's cut meat shop'. Access to the yard at the rear was obtained via a passage running the full depth of the building. It was here that Annie Chapman was discovered with her throat cut.

In order to clarify the type of street that it was, I quote a letter to *The Times* dated 14 September 1888, entitled 'The state of Whitechapel'. It outlines the dangers confronting the everyday users of this byway:

Sir

May I add to what as already been said on this subject! Yesterday at 11.00 a.m., a gentleman was seized and robbed of everything, on Hanbury Street. At 5.00 p.m., an old man of seventy years was attacked and served in the same manner in Chicksand Street. At 10.00 a.m. today, a man ran into a baker's shop, at the corner of Hanbury Street and King Edward Street, and ran off with the till and its contents. All of these occurred within a hundred yards of each other, and midway between the scenes of the last two horrible murders.

Yours faithfully,

J. F. S.   Sept. 13th

The East London Advertiser had again warned that 'the murderous lunatic' who issues forth at night like another Hyde, to prey upon the defenceless unfortunate class, would attack again, and that three successful murders will have the effect of whetting his appetite further. *The Advertiser* was quite obviously at this time including Emma Smith as a Ripper victim.

The forecast however proved to be prophetic, as on the same morning at 6.00 a.m., the body of Annie Chapman had been discovered in the yard to the rear of Number 29 Hanbury Street.

This raises in itself the question as to what time *The Advertiser* went to press, and was the forecast too prophetic?

The pubs we know Annie Chapman frequently drank in were the Black Swan, which was situated at Number 23a Hanbury Street, and the Ten Bells, which stood on the corner of Commercial Street and Fournier Street. Again, both of these pubs were within 200 yards of Flower and Dean Street, and were probably frequented by other Ripper victims.

Elizabeth Stride, who I do not believe was a victim of the Whitechapel murderer, nevertheless lived, at the time of her demise, at Number 32 Flower and Dean Street and had previously lived at Number 33 Dorset Street. She was a frequent visitor to the Queen's Head, which was to be found on the corner of Commercial Street and Fashion Street, and the Bricklayer's Arms, situated in Settles Street – once again, both within easy reach of Flower and Dean Street.

Catharine Eddowes, the fourth Ripper victim, lived with *John Kelly* in a lodging house in Flower and Dean Street, and as such will have frequented the same public houses as the other victims.

Her murder site was Mitre Square, which as previously stated was situated toward the eastern side of the City of London, and from our epicentre of Flower and Dean Street, was approximately 800 yards. Though this is not a long way, going this far was probably prompted by the extreme amount of police activity in the Spitalfields market area, *or it may have been for a totally different reason.* The police at this time were randomly stopping men in the street and questioning them on their reasons for being in the area, and what was their destination, so his chances of being caught in the act decreased if he moved outward away from the Flower and Dean Street area.

The East London Advertiser of 24 November ran an article written by 'Rambler', which added a supernatural dimension to the site of Mitre Square. Supposedly discovered by accident whilst he was consulting an old historical manuscript, it read:

It seems that there was an old monastery, in the sixteenth century, on the spot where Mitre Square is now situated. As was not uncommon in those days, the morality of the monks was not of the highest order, and in addition to many other crimes, one of the fraternity put the finishing touches to his wickedness, by murdering a woman who he had smuggled into the monastery, at the foot of the altar. A curse was pronounced on the spot, and it was on the same place where the altar used to stand, that the unfortunate woman Eddowes was murdered. The writer of the story asserted in his letter, that there is a plan of the old monastery in the British Museum, which enables the spot to be accurately identified.

Due again, probably, to the increased police activity, the Ripper appeared to go to ground during the month of October, and for a period of forty days no further murders were committed. However, as we all know, apathy soon shows its head and things once again lapse into indifference, and so it came as no real surprise when on 9 November 1888, Mary Jane Kelly's dismembered corpse was discovered in Number 13 Miller's Court.

Miller's Court was reached by a small alleyway to the side of Number 26 Dorset Street, which itself stood within 200 yards of Flower and Dean Street.

The main pubs which were used by Mary Kelly were the Britannia, which stood at the corner of Commercial Street and Dorset Street, the Queen's Head, where she was seen by George Hutchinson on the night of her murder, and the location of which has already been described under the paragraph on Elizabeth Stride, and possibly the Horn of Plenty, which was sited at the corner of Crispin Street and Dorset Street. At the risk of repeating myself, all of these are within close proximity to our now frequently quoted Flower and Dean Street.

The reader will have probably noted that all the previously mentioned locations are also closely situated to Crossingham's lodging house, which was to be found at Number 35 Dorset Street. This place continually appears as a regular haunt, frequented by a large number of persons associated with the Ripper case.

Now that we have established the locations of the various places where the victims lived and leisured, we will move on to the suspects for the identity of Jack the Ripper, and the police involvement and coverage of the Whitechapel murders.

As a terminus to this chapter, may I assure you that all the locations identified will continue to appear throughout the book as we analyse the police investigation, and identify the primary Ripper suspects. I hope that this chapter, in conjunction with the map, has assisted you in forming your conception of the area, and has helped to establish a picture of the squalor, immorality and general degradation which existed in late nineteenth century east London.

CHAPTER TEN

The doctors under suspicion

Doctor Stanley

There are numerous suspects who at one time or another have been
nominated as Jack the Ripper, and I could not evaluate them all, even
if a separate book were to be devoted to them alone.

In order to rationalise the list, I have extracted the most frequently
named individuals, and having examined the implications made
against these suspects, I have evaluated their guilt or innocence as I
myself see it. I have further catalogued any questions or points
which I feel require attention and further investigation.

One of the most commonly held views over the hundred years
since the Ripper murders were committed, has been that the Whitechapel murderer was a doctor, surgeon, or physician whose brain
became unhinged and who turned the knives that he used to heal,
into the mutilating instruments which committed five murders.

The concept of the Doctor Ripper probably commenced with the
rumour that the murderer carried his knives in a type of black bag,
similar to that which was carried by the medical men of the day, and
indeed by the medical profession of today. The medical doctors who
attended the murder sites, and those who performed the subsequent
post mortems, must shoulder a large proportion of the blame for
this story gaining credibility. In giving their evidence at the various
inquests, they described the mutilations as having been performed
with 'surgical skill', or as 'deftly and skilfully performed'. Doctor
Gordon Brown, when speaking of the killer of Catharine Eddowes,
stated in response to a question, that the Ripper possessed 'a good
deal of knowledge as to the positions of the organs'. In the case of
Annie Chapman's murder, Doctor Bagster Phillips referred to the
Ripper as an expert.

If we closely examine the medical evidence, it is quite obvious that
the wealth of opinion of the medical profession was that the Ripper,
if not an expert, nor a person with a high level of medical knowledge,

such as a student, was a killer who certainly possessed a degree of anatomical knowledge.

In 1929, the first book written in modern times which attempted to solve the mystery of Jack the Ripper, was written by Leonard Matters, an Australian journalist, who asked the question, how could any mystery be solved, when nobody seemed to be careful about the facts before attempting to suggest a solution?

His solution to the problem was to name a Harley Street surgeon called Dr Stanley, who he stated was a brilliant doctor who had attained wealth and renown due to his medical knowledge and surgical skill. He was in great demand as a teaching professor, and commanded large fees for his consultations.

Stanley's practice had the patronage of the rich and famous, and he himself specialised in the study of cancer, which at this time was in its infancy.

He lived with his wife and son in Portman Square, and had great hopes that his son would exceed his own distinguished achievements.

Life took a turn for the worse for Dr Stanley when his wife died, but this only served to increase the lavish affection which he gave to his son. His character at this time took an apparent change, and it is said that he became withdrawn and sullen in his manner. The only time that his spirits are said to have lifted, was when he was in the company of his son.

The young man, in turn, achieved success in his university studies, and was regarded by his peers as a man of outstanding talent, and with a brilliant career in the making. His father assisted him in his advancement, ensuring that he met all the right people and attended all the correct social gatherings. The father furnished his son with ample resources to engage in the social circuit of the day, and this was to prove his ultimate downfall. The reason for this was that the son had an appetite for the good things in life and indulged himself in the pursuits of wine, women and gambling.

It was reported that on the night of the varsity boat race of 1886, the son of Dr Stanley met a lady named Marie Jeanette in the Café Mon-ico, and was instantly infatuated with her. As the night progressed the son partook of an ample quantity of drink and was in undoubtedly high spirits. At the end of the evening he and Marie Jeanette went off together and the young man spent the night with her.

If he had been more sober, he might have realised that Marie Jeanette was a prostitute, and as a result of him having sex with her he was running a terrible risk of contracting a sexual disease.

The son reaped the reward of his folly, discovering the profession of his lady friend when it was too late and he had already contracted syphilis.

He informed his father of the situation, and his parent engaged the top medical men in the field in an attempt to cure his son. As the disease progressed, and it became all too apparent that the son was destined to die of the disease, Dr Stanley extracted the name of the woman from his son, and was given the address of the place where they had met. The name given by son to father was Marie Jeanette Kelly, which as we know was an adopted alias of Mary Jane Kelly, and the one she had purported to use frequently, after her return from a visit to France with a gentleman friend.

Leonard Matters conjectured that Dr Stanley made a vow at his dying son's bedside, to track down the woman responsible, and to kill her. Immediately upon the death of his son Stanley set out to fulfil his promise.

He commenced his search in Wardour Street in Soho, at an address that had been used by Kelly, and found that Mary Jane no longer commanded the favour of the more illustrious areas of London, and having slipped from grace, was now living in the East End of London.

Matters goes on to describe how Dr Stanley commenced to make frequent visits to Whitechapel in order to study the patrols and the methods of the police. He did so dressed in a long dark coat so as not to appear conspicuous, and enable him to blend into the background.

After he had gained the confidence of anonymity, he set about his task. On the night of 6 August 1888 Matters places Dr Stanley as roaming the streets of Whitechapel until the early hours of the morning. At approximately 3.30 a.m. he turned along Osborne Street and spotted a prostitute in the road ahead. He approached her and struck up a conversation which culminated in an arrangement being reached. He and the prostitute adjourned to George Yard, where Stanley asked her if she knew Marie Jeanette Kelly, and was given a negative response. He immediately slit her throat, and as such Martha Tabram became the first Ripper victim.

Leonard Matters goes on to state that in a frenzy he then proceeded to stab the body a total of thirty nine times. Doctor Killeen, however, does define the wounds as including five in the liver, two in the spleen, five in the left lung, two in the right lung, one in the heart, and six in the stomach. He went on to say that at least thirty eight of these wounds were performed by a right-handed person.

The placing of the wounds does tend to have a high proportion inflicted within the critical areas of the body and does lend weight to at least a knowledge of where these vital organs were situated.

Doctor Stanley then consulted the press for a number of days, in order to monitor the reaction to his first encounter, and next ventured out on the night of 30 August. He again roamed the streets until he met Mary Ann Nichols in Buck's Row. He presented her with the same question and on receipt of the same reply, despatched her in a similar fashion, and left the scene unnoticed.

He then let the tumult die down for a week before making his next incursion into the East End. This was on 7 September. He wandered the streets but had difficulty in locating a prostitute who was unaccompanied and it took him until 5.30 a.m. before he came across a suitable woman in Hanbury Street. He put the same question to her and received a similar response to his enquiry. He had resolved at the outset that he would kill all of the prostitutes whom he confronted, and considered that he was doing everyone a favour by ridding the world of these women; and so, with his now customary efficiency, he despatched poor Annie Chapman to her grave.

Once again the Ripper allowed three weeks to elapse in order for the heat to abate, and then he again set about his gruesome business. On the night of 29 September he resumed his patrol of the Whitechapel streets.

Shortly before 1.00 a.m. on the morning of 30 September, Stanley asked his question of a prostitute named Elizabeth Stride, and once again he was greeted with a negative response. He cajoled the woman into following him into Dutfield's Yard in Berner Street and was in the process of cutting her throat when Louis Diemschutz pulled into the entrance to the yard in his horse and cart. Diemschutz discovered that the horse would not willingly enter the yard, and after prodding about with his whip he felt something soft on the ground. It immediately struck him that it could be his wife and so he dismounted and ran into the club in order to fetch help and to obtain a light with which to illuminate the area and identify the obstruction. Doctor Stanley, who was still in the yard, chose this time to make good his escape from the scene of the crime.

A narrow escape, however, did not serve to quell his thirst for blood, and in a frustrated condition he resumed his search for another victim. He had not long to wait, and at 1.35 a.m. he encountered Catharine Eddowes, who had only recently been released from police custody. He engaged Catharine in conversation at the Duke's Place entrance to

Mitre Square. During their discussion three men passed by and after they had disappeared from view he suggested that he and Eddowes go into Mitre Square to have sex.

He asked his question as to the identity and whereabouts of a Marie Jeanette Kelly and was elated when Eddowes confirmed that she knew of a Mary Jean Kelly who was a prostitute and who lived in Dorset Street. The Ripper had the answer which he had been waiting for, and he was excited at the prospect of a future confrontation with Kelly. He knew that the police constable would soon return on his beat and so he quickly killed Eddowes and horribly mutilated her body and face with his knife.

As the policeman was approaching the alley, Stanley left the square by one of the other exits.

The next day, the newspapers were full of the story of the previous night's double event, and Stanley knew that he must wait for a while before killing Kelly. He allowed five weeks to pass, during which time he followed the movements of Kelly, and the tension and hate inside him festered. By this time he was beyond the point of reason and could wait no longer, and he was also well aware that the vigilance and attitude of the police had begun to slacken.

On the night of 8 November he once again went on the rampage. He watched Kelly enter her room in Miller's Court with a client and waited in the shadows for him to leave. Having allowed the client to vacate the premises, and letting a suitable time elapse for him to get out of the vicinity, he entered Mary Kelly's room and bolted the door behind him. The effects of the sex and the drink had ensured that Kelly was asleep and so Stanley placed his hand over her throat and awakened her. He narrated the full story of what Kelly had done to his son, and finished with the statement 'I am Jack the Ripper, and I am going to kill you.' Kelly had the time to shout the one word 'Murder!' and then the Ripper's knife split open her throat. The demented doctor then proceeded to mutilate the body beyond all recognition, and after finishing his task he left Whitechapel forever.

This was how Leonard Matters interpreted the murders, and the way in which Doctor Stanley had carried them out. He concluded his story by claiming that Dr Stanley had fled to Argentina. The author claimed that whilst he was working there, he had discovered the confession in one of the local Spanish newspapers.

Another physician, who reported to have trained under Doctor Stanley in London, received a letter which read:

Dear Sir

At the request of a patient, who says you will remember him as Doctor Stanley, I write to inform you that he is lying in the hospital in a dangerous condition. He is suffering from cancer, and though an operation has been performed successfully, complications have arisen, which make the end inevitable.

Dr Stanley would like to see you. Instructions have been given to the reception room to waive all regulations in your case, and admit you at once to Ward V, where the patient is lying in bed number 28.

Yours truly

José Riche

Senior House Surgeon

On receipt of the letter, the one-time student attended the hospital to visit Dr Stanley, and was told by the doctor that he would like to clear his conscience. Dr Stanley then went on to state that he had committed the Whitechapel murders in order to avenge the death of his son, who had been, in his own words, 'ruined by Mary Kelly'. He continued, 'He died an idiot, and all my hopes died with him. I murdered all those women! I am Jack the Ripper.' Dr Stanley then died.

Colin Wilson is a world-renowned authority on the Ripper. He received a letter from a 'Mister Lee', who lived in Torquay. It stated that:

In 1888, Dad was employed by the City of London Corporation, at the City Mortuary. Among his duties was to collect all the bodies of the persons who died in the City of London, and bring them to the City Mortuary. When an inquest was necessary, he prepared them for post mortem by Mr Spilsbury. His immediate superior was Doctor Cedric Saunders [Mr Lee was referring to Dr William Cedric Saunders, the Medical Officer of Health for the City of London and the coroner for the City.]

Doctor Saunders had a very special friend, a Dr Stanley, who used to visit the mortuary once a week. Whenever he saw Dad, he always gave him a cigar.

One day Dr Stanley arrived, and passing Dad, said to Dr Saunders, 'the cows have got my son. I'll get even with them.'

Very soon afterwards the murders started. Dr Stanley still visited the mortuary during this time, but as soon as the murders stopped, he was never seen again.

Dad asked Dr Saunders whether Dr Stanley would be coming again. The answer was 'No'. When pressed by Dad, Dr Saunders said 'Yes, I believe he was Jack the Ripper.'

As a tailpiece to this, I am told that in the 1920s *The People* newspaper published a paragraph one Sunday which read 'A Dr Stanley, believed to have been Jack the Ripper, has died in South America.'

This theory of Leonard Matters is riddled with errors and unsubstantiated statements and before any credibility whatsoever can be attached to it, there must undoubtedly be a great deal of further investigation into the claims, in order to clarify the following:

Did a real Doctor Stanley ever exist? At the time of writing no concrete proof of his existence has been discovered.

A check must be made to see if any doctor by the name of Stanley (either Christian name or surname) vacated a practice in Harley Street or the West End of London in the year 1888 or 1889.

Did a London hospital in 1888 have two doctors on its staff both having the same surname, and therefore the practice arose of referring to one of them by his Christian name? I know that the chances of this are very slim but we must eliminate every avenue of investigation. Verification of this could be done by researching the names of the London doctors of the day, and seeing if this situation could possibly arise. This would require to be done as it is supposed that the title Doctor Stanley is purportedly used as a substitute for the real name of the doctor, so the search could prove fruitless. However we do have the letter of Mr Lee who it must be admitted had no real reason to lie about what was relayed to him by his father.

The newspapers in Buenos Aires, and *The People* newspaper, need to be reviewed, in order that statements made by Matters can be confirmed or refuted.

If this information was forthcoming and the true identity of the doctor could be established, then further research could be undertaken to establish his guilt or innocence. However, once again I must put the cat among the pigeons and say that this is highly unlikely, as the common belief is that Dr Stanley was probably a figment of Leonard Matters's imagination. Edmund Pearson, an eminent American crime writer, espoused the opinion concerning the Dr Stanley theory, that 'it bore about the same relation to the facts of criminology, as the exploits of Peter Rabbit and Jerry Muskrat do to zoology.

The whole basis of Leonard Matters theory is based on the fact that Dr Stanley's son caught syphilis from Mary Jane Kelly in the April of 1886, and died a pitiful figure, riddled with the disease, at a time that had to have been before August of 1888, in order for the death to have a relationship to the Ripper murders.

Having looked at this scenario, this is extremely unlikely. Syphilis is, as we all know, a venereal disease, which in the 1889s was incurable. It is caused by a spiral-shaped bacterium called spirochaete, is almost exclusively transmitted by sexual contact and manifests itself in the form of three separate phases.

The initial phase, chancres (sores, ulcers) form at the area of infection, normally the genitals. These are usually succeeded by inguinal buboes (painful swellings of the glands of the groin), and they become evident within a few days of contact.

The second stage, or constitutional affectations, is indicated by a generalised rash, ulcers in the mouth and throat and also on the genitals, accompanied by copper-coloured eruption on the skin. These go together with acute pains in the bones and nerves.

The disease will then go into recession, and the third stage may take up to twenty years to become apparent. This third stage causes damage to the heart, eyes, brain and the skin. On the outbreak of this stage death normally occurs within three or four years.

As can be seen from the above time scales, Dr Stanley's son, if indeed there was one, definitely did not die from syphilis, as two years would not have allowed the disease to complete its killing cycle.

Another reason for disbelief in the Dr Stanley theory is that Mary Kelly, although undoubtedly a heavy drinker, and in the early stages of pregnancy, did not have syphilis.

It is impossible for anybody to positively identify Jack the Ripper as over a hundred years have passed and everybody associated with the case is long ago dead. All that researchers can do is to obtain and analyse the existing information and the new information which is infrequently unearthed, and with this information, present a case which would convict in a present-day court of law, or withstand the scrutiny of the critics' analysis. (There may be another way which I will outline later in the book.)

It is, however, possible to prove beyond all reasonable doubt that a certain person was *not* the Ripper, and as such the motive and death of his son, coupled with the absence of any corroborative evidence to support his claims of a deathbed confession, then it is time to drop the Leonard Matters/Dr Stanley theory until such time as somebody unearths a more substantial proof to support the story.

The author's conclusion is that unless some drastic new information is uncovered which will radically alter my opinion of the elusive Dr Stanley, then I can only conclude that this man was definitely not Jack the Ripper.

Doctor Merchant

In 1972 *City*, the City of London police magazine, ran an article entitled 'Jack the Ripper – the mystery solved'. The author of this piece was B. E. Reilly. In the article he expounded the theory that a Dr Merchant (assumed to be a pseudonym) could possibly have been Jack the Ripper. It linked this infamous Dr Merchant with the identity of a doctor who was taken into custody by Metropolitan Police Constable Robert Spicer on the night of the double murder of Elizabeth Stride and Catharine Eddowes.

In March of 1931, Spicer wrote to the *Daily Express*:

> I had worked my beat backwards, and had come to Heneage Street, off Brick Lane. About fifty yards on the right down Heneage Street is Heneage Court, and at the bottom of the court was a brick-built dustbin. Both Jack and a prostitute named Rosy were sitting on the dustbin. She had two shillings in her hand, and she followed me when I took Jack on suspicion. He turned out to be a highly respected doctor, and gave a Brixton address. His shirt and cuffs still had blood on them. Jack had the proverbial bag with him (a brown one). This was not opened and he was allowed to go.
>
> I saw him several times after this at Liverpool Street Station accosting women, and I would remark to him, 'Hello Jack! Still after them?' He would immediately bolt.
>
> He was always dressed the same, high hat, black suit with silk facings, and a gold watch and chain. He was about 5 feet 8 or 9 inches, and about twelve stone, high forehead and rosy cheeks.

The woman Rosy must have been quite beautiful to command a fee of two shillings, when that amount of money was about four times the normal payment.

B. E. Reilly researched into the background of doctors from the Brixton area who had died or disappeared from the registers at or around the year of 1888. He discovered one such doctor whom he chose to call Merchant, because his true surname was too common.

Reilly was able to establish that his doctor was the only Brixton doctor to die shortly after the last murder.

Merchant has been subsequently established to be one Frederick Richard Chapman, who was born in 1851 in Poona, India, and who travelled to London from a provincial practice in 1886, after completing his training and performing a spell at the Fever and Smallpox Hospital in Hull. Chapman was a qualified and practising surgeon.

I can well understand Mr Reilly's initial refusal to announce the true name of his suspect, as the Jack the Ripper story already contains a more than adequate number of persons named Chapman, and one more would only serve to increase the confusion.

He died in 1888, a poor man, of a septic tubercular abscess. It is interesting to note the additional information supplied by PC Spicer to the *Daily Express* reporter who had interviewed him and who stated that there were eight or nine inspectors all employed on the Ripper case already at the police station when he fetched in the suspect, and that he (Spicer) was reprimanded for the arrest of a respectable doctor, and the doctor was allowed to leave the station without the police opening his bag.

In the report to the *Daily Express*, Spicer stated that the doctor had rosy cheeks, and this is a known characteristic of chronic tuberculosis.

Mr Reilly maintains that the risks taken by Jack the Ripper in respect of the later killings, by continuing to murder when the streets of Whitechapel were literally littered with policemen, indicates the actions of a desperate man, and that a doctor, knowing that he was terminally ill, would be of the psychological disposition to endure these risks.

The reliability of the testimony of PC Spicer must be questioned and challenged. It is known that he was discharged from the police force in April 1889, after serving only two years, the reasons for his dismissal being that 'he was found to be drunk whilst on duty and the unnecessary interference with two private persons' rendered him unfit for the police force. In essence, he was too much of a liability.

One interesting fact which was unearthed by Mr Reilly in his research was that Frederick Richard Chapman was found to have a connection with Liverpool, from which one of the Ripper letters, regarded by some as genuine, was posted.

My own opinions tend to dismiss Dr Merchant as a serious Ripper suspect, for the following reasons:-

The only connection to the Whitechapel murders at present is the fact that the doctor just happened to die shortly after the last murder. There isn't any proof that the doctor is the same person who was apprehended by PC Spicer, and the story of Spicer himself is not sufficiently endorsed to be considered anywhere near to being infallible.

Spicer states that he saw the doctor several times after his initial confrontation, at Liverpool Street Station, accosting women. This does not really comport with the facts, because the doctor died shortly after his arrest by PC Spicer.

Dr Frederick Richard Chapman died of a septic tubercular abscess, and at the time of the Ripper murders the disease was in its final stages. If we then take time to analyse the report given by Doctor Thomas Bond to Dr (later Sir) Robert Anderson, the Assistant Commissioner of the Metropolitan Police C.I.D., then doubt must also be cast on Chapman possessing the physical capabilities to carry out the murders.

Dr Bond's report read thus:

The murderer must have been a man of physical strength, and of great coolness and daring. There is no evidence that he had an accomplice. He must, in my opinion, be a man subject to periodic attacks of homicidal and erotic mania, the character of the mutilations indicate that the man may be in a condition, sexually, that may be called satyriasis. It is of course possible that the homicidal impulse may have developed from a revengeful or brooding condition of the mind, or that religious mania may have been the original disease, but I do not think that either hypothesis is likely. The murderer in external appearance is quite likely to be a quiet inoffensive-looking man, probably middle-aged and neatly and respectably dressed. I think he must be in the habit of wearing a cloak or overcoat, or he could hardly have escaped notice in the streets, if the blood on his hands or clothes were visible.

Bearing in mind the type of woman he was attacking (she would be capable of defending herself), and the fact that he had to strangle her before carrying out the relevant mutilations, I doubt whether a man suffering from this condition, and in such an advanced state, would have been capable of the attacks.

Furthermore, on considering the time limitations, in some instances the Ripper had to beat a somewhat hasty retreat, and at times may have been required to scale fencing etc. Can we really accept that a man whose condition would have subjected him to persistent coughing fits, and knowing that the more common areas of the body which the disease attacks are the lungs, bones and joints of the body, especially the hip joints and spine, I find it impossible to accept that a person in this condition could be Jack the Ripper.

Doctor Pedachenko

It has been mooted that no less a person than the Queen's own personal physician was responsible for the Ripper murders. Sir William Gull M.D., F.R.C.P., F.R.S., is however to be discussed later in the book, and so we will dismiss him at this time, and concentrate on our next subject doctor.

Doctor Alexander Pedachenko was born in 1857 in Tver, a province in Russia, with the capital city, also called Tver, situated in a plain on the Volga, approximately one hundred miles north-west of Moscow.

Before moving to live in Glasgow, he had worked for a while at the maternity hospital in Tver. According to Donald McCormick, he served as a member of the Russian secret service, but McCormick cannot furnish proof to support a lot of his statements, as in 1985 a lot of his research papers were given to another researcher who has never returned them.

The involvement of Pedachenko commenced with the assertion by writer and journalist William Le Queux, that after the assassination of Rasputin in 1916, the government of the day 'handed to me in confidence, a great quantity of documents, which had been found in a safe in the cellar of his house, in order that I might write an account of the scoundrel's amazing career'. Le Queux stated that contained within the papers was the greater part of a manuscript, in French, written by Rasputin, and which contained a section on the crimes of Jack the Ripper. He went on to write the book on Rasputin, but did not include the portion on Jack the Ripper; however, prior to returning the documents to the authorities, he copied the Ripper manuscript.

The manuscript implied that the Ripper was a doctor named Alexander Pedachenko, who had gone to London and lived in

Westmorland Road in Walworth, with his sister, and this provided
a base from which to carry out his Whitechapel exploits.

Pedachenko supposedly came to London at the instigation of
Ochrana, the Russian Secret Police, and committed the murders at
their behest, so as to discredit the Metropolitan Police.

He was assisted in the murders by an accomplice named 'Levitski',
who acted as a lookout, and by a woman named 'Winberg', whose
function was to strike up a conversation with the proposed victim
and put her off her guard, so that Pedachenko could kill her. The
story continues that after completing his task, and with the resignation of Sir Charles Warren, he was spirited back to Moscow by the
Ochrana, where, after the attempted murder of a woman called
'Vogak', he was sent to a lunatic asylum, where he died.

Johann Nideroest, who was born in 1885 of German/Swiss parent-
age, frequently sold information to the press. He allegedly told
the Ochrana that Pedachenko was the Ripper, having received the
facts from an anarchist called Nicholas Zverieff. Le Queux in turn
claimed that this report from Nideroest was contained within the
Rasputin manuscript, which he said transposed the sequence of
events. 'The report of Nideroest's discovery amused our Secret
Police greatly, for, as a matter of fact, they knew of the whole
details at the time.' [They would, having supposedly sent him over
here in the first place.]

Donald McCormick quotes an article in *The Glasgow Evening
News* of 27 November 1947, referring to Hector Macdonald Cairns
as being in possession of a document written by Rasputin, which
named Dr Pedachenko as the Ripper, and provided corroborative
evidence to enforce the claim. It has however been established that
a G.D.K.McCormick was the supplier of the information on which
the newspaper printed the article, which I believe is too much of a
coincidence to ignore.

In 1957 a book was published by Rupert Furneaux. Its subject
was a St Petersburg doctor named Panchenko, who was approached
by Patrick O'Brien de Lacy, who in turn had married the daughter of
a wealthy Russian general called Buturlin. In order to secure
the wealth of his in-laws, de Lacy decided to murder them by intro-
ducing cholera and diphtheria germs into the food of his father- and
mother-in-law, and also the brother of his wife. De Lacy offered
Panchenko 620,000 roubles to supply the germs and assist him with
the murders. The plan came to an abrupt halt when de Lacy, in
telling his mistress of the plan, was overheard. Following the death

of his son, General Buturlin was informed, and de Lacy and Panchenko were both arrested, and subsequently tried and convicted. De Lacy was imprisoned for life, and Panchenko was sentenced to fifteen years.

More research needs to be done, but with the known and substantiated involvement in other murders, it is remotely possible that Panchenko and Pedachenko could be the same person. I believe any research into this fanciful connection is only completed in order to confirm the elimination of this unlikely suspect.

Another person involved in the theory is a Prince Serge Belloselkski, who is alleged to have shown McCormick a lithograph copy of the *Ochrana Gazette* of January 1909, which read:

Konovalov, Vassily, alias Pedachenko Alexey, alias Luiskovo Andrey, formerly of Tver, is now officially declared to be dead. Any files or information concerning him, from district sections, should be sent to the Moscow Central District of Ochrana. Such information, photographs of identification details, as may still exist, might refer to Konovalov, Pedachenko, or Luiskovo, either individually or collectively. If documents held by you do not contain these names, they should also be examined for any information concerning a man answering the description of the above, who was wanted for the murder of a woman in Paris in 1886, and for the murder of five women in the east quarter of London in 1888, and again for the murder of a woman in Petrograd in 1891.

Konovalov's description of the wanted man is documented as follows:

Born 1857 at Torshok, Tver. Height medium, eyes dark blue, profession Junior Surgeon. General description: usually wore black moustaches, curled and waxed at ends. Heavy black eyebrows. Broad shouldered, but slight build, known to disguise himself as a woman on occasion, and was arrested when in women's clothes in Petrograd, before his detention in the asylum where he died.

McCormick, in his book entitled *The Identity of Jack the Ripper*, refers to a letter sent by Sir Basil Thomson, who was Assistant Commissioner of the Metropolitan Police from 1913–1919. This letter contains the wording 'In Paris recently, I learned in talks with the French, that they had always thought that the Ripper was a

Russian named Konovalov, who used the alias 'Mikhail Ostrog', under which name Scotland Yard knew him as an ex-convict and medical student.

As we can now see, McCormick includes the above letter from Sir Basil Thomson in the first edition of his book, and the letter implies that the person we know as Konovalov/Pedachenko is in fact one of the prime Ripper suspects known as Mikhail Ostrog. It is interesting to note that in the revised edition of 1970, this phrase is notably omitted from the letter and no mention of Ostrog whatsoever is made or implied.

When we take a closer look at Ostrog in the next chapter, you will no doubt notice that besides anything else, Ostrog did not match the requisite description and was 24 years too old to be confused with Pedachenko.

As to this date, Donald McCormick has not produced any evidence to support his theory to be examined by any independent authority, and with the exception of Le Queux, none of his sources have ever been traced. The information must, in my personal opinion, be viewed with extreme scepticism, as must the actual existence of Dr Pedachenko. I leave you to draw your own conclusions.

William Le Queux may never have received any documents from the Russian Government, and Rasputin is almost certain to have had no input into the documents on the Ripper. Le Queux states that it was transcribed in French, but it is known that Rasputin did not have knowledge of the French language. His daughter has spoken to Colin Wilson (author and noted Ripper expert); she insists that her father had no interest in 'great Russian criminals', which was the alleged subject of the documents.

With regard to the Ochrana transcript of 1909, Donald Rumbelow (a highly respected Ripper authority) argues that in issuing a request for information, if indeed they did so, Ochrana are admitting doubt as to the identity of the man who had died in the asylum. A salient point to make. Also McCormick states in his theory that the information previously mentioned as having been extracted from the *Ochrana Gazette*, was done so from the 9 January edition of 1909. We must draw attention to the fact that within this information, on two occasions it refers to 'Petrograd', and yet in news reports from Russia in 1914 the town is still referred to as St Petersburg.

The only person to whom one can lean when assessing the Pedachenko theory is Donald McCormick himself, and yet none of the corroborative documents and evidence which he uses to support his case have ever been produced. In fact, on two occasions he has declined invitations, for various reasons, to meet accredited Ripper researchers and theorists, in order to discuss his theory.

His connection with Ostrog is just one of many idiosyncrasies in his reasoning, and the lack of consistency in his arguments encourages doubt as to the credibility of his theory.

Until some reliable documentary support is forthcoming, it is my opinion that Dr Pedachenko should be ignored as a suspect, and a good start would be for someone to establish some proof that the gentleman ever existed at all.

Mikhail Ostrog

Michael, or Mikhail, Ostrog was born in 1833, and throughout his life he assumed a number of aliases, among which were Bertrand Ashley, Ashley Nabokoff, Count Sobieski, Doctor Grant, and numerous others.

He assumed these identities in order to carry out his chosen way of life which was a confidence trickster, who extorted money from unsuspecting people by posing as a respectable member of society.

Little is known of his early life, and various police records of his escapades describe him as Russian, a Polish Jew, and just plain Polish.

He stood above average height at 5 feet 11 inches, with brown hair and grey eyes, and it was his normal practice to dress in a semi-clerical outfit.

Throughout a dubious career, he assumed the mantle of respectable professions, and claimed that he had fled Russia after killing another man in a duel.

The first we hear from him is in 1863, when he swindled a group of people in Oxford, and was sentenced to ten months in prison. He performed this scam under the identity of Max Grief. Upon his release he almost immediately resumed his illicit ways, and was convicted of a minor offence in Cambridge, for which he was imprisoned for a further three months.

In July of 1864, this time under the name of Count Sobieski, the exiled son of the King of Poland, he swindled the gentle but gullible folk of Tunbridge Wells, and was apprehended and tried, after which he received a prison sentence of eight months, for fraud.

In 1866, after winning an acquittal on fraud charges in Gloucester, he retreated to Kent, where he stole a gold watch and other effects from a lady named Esther Carpenter, of Maidstone.

Ostrog carried on this busy life of fraud and theft until, when he appeared in Chatham for the theft of two expensive books, Mr Justice Chandler sentenced him to seven years penal servitude, observing in his sentencing that leniency had proved to be ineffectual.

This spell in prison put Ostrog out of commission until he was released in May of 1873 on a 'ticket of leave', which was a form of parole. Prison had not helped to reform him, and his career in crime continued, as we know that within one month of his release he had fled from Woolwich with some valuable silver stolen from a Captain Milner.

He continued this way of life, and in 1874 at Buckinghamshire Quarter Sessions, he was imprisoned for a period of ten years. An indication that he was indeed capable of violence is the fact that, on his arrest by a superintendent at Burton-on-Trent, he attempted to shoot a revolver whilst at the police station, and was only prevented from doing so by having the weapon turned upon him.

The offence in question was the stealing of a tankard from George Biggs at Woolwich Barracks. He was pursued and apprehended by cadets. At Woolwich Court, he was described as 'well educated and gentlemanly'. It must be stated here that, when apprehended, he was wearing cricket dress and had dropped a Gladstone bag in the chase.

He claimed in his defence that he was innocent of any crime, and had been on his way to play cricket, when taken by an attack of sunstroke. He felt the urge to run in a race, and he considered that this was what he was doing when the cadets were chasing him.

Still further into the case, he informed the court that he was going to France, and picking up his overcoat, he attempted to leave, saying that he was a medical doctor, and that this type of scandal could bring about the ruination of his career.

In September 1887, Ostrog was tried at the Old Bailey, and despite a plea of insanity (Dr Hillier, a witness, remarked that 'he was only shamming'), he was found guilty, and sentenced to six months hard labour. During the serving of his sentence he was transferred to the Surrey Pauper Lunatic Asylum, where he was said to be of 'manic disposition'. He was, however, released on the completion of his sentence, on 10 March 1888.

At the height of the Jack the Ripper murders, his whereabouts were again being sought for having 'failed to report', which he had been required to do under the terms of his release. In reporting this failure to report, the police refer to him as a dangerous man, who appears to have disappeared at this time.

It appears to most Ripperologists that any link between Ostrog and the Whitechapel murders is purely conjecture. There is no evidence to place him in the area at the time of the murders, and he was only named by Donald McCormick in his book entitled *The identity of Jack the Ripper*, the implication of which we have discussed in the evaluation of Pedachenko.

On the other hand, when the Macnaghten Memorandum was discovered in 1959, it became quite apparent that Melville Macnaghten, who was a senior police officer, strongly suspected Ostrog, and placed him in a list of three men whom he regarded as the prime Ripper suspects.

It must be recognised that the Macnaghten Memorandum was compiled in 1894, by a man who was privy to the entire inside information and thinking of the investigation team. He was also one of the inner circle, who would have been one of those privileged to any information which may have been withheld from public knowledge.

As I have stated earlier, Macnaghten was Assistant Chief Constable C.I.D., from 1890 to 1893, and had been promoted to Chief Constable at the time when he wrote his memorandum. As such, he will have known the thoughts, suspicions, and evidence of all of the involved officers, and would have been well placed to make an educated assessment. He wrote of Ostrog:

> A mad Russian doctor and a convict, and unquestionably a homicidal maniac. This man was said to have been habitually cruel to women, and for a long time was known to have carried about with him surgical knives and other instruments. His antecedents (criminal records) were of the very worst, and his whereabouts at the time of the Whitechapel murders could never be satisfactorily accounted for. He is still alive.

Three statements bear more discussion: that Ostrog 'was said to have been habitually cruel to women', and that 'he was known to carry about with him surgical knives and other instruments'. Is this an assumption by Macnaghten, or did he have evidence to support these accusations? If the latter, then it has still to be discovered and as such there has been no mention of these inferences in any other Ripper papers.

The other statement: 'he is still alive'. This suggests that in 1894, at the time which Macnaghten was writing, Ostrog's whereabouts was probably known, and yet no record of him has been found to exist after October of 1888. If we then couple this with Macnaghten's inclusion of the statement that 'his whereabouts at the time of the Whitechapel murders could never be satisfactorily accounted for', it would tend to suggest that there is an implication that Ostrog may have been withdrawn from society at some time, and placed in detention under an assumed name.

If this is so, then more research is required to ascertain the whereabouts of Ostrog for the period immediately after the murder of Mary Jane Kelly, and to definitely establish his origin as a Polish or Russian Jew, as these simple statements could account for the end of the Ripper murders, and also for the subsequent disappearance of Ostrog, from this time onwards.

There is evidence that a Jew, who was one of the witnesses who saw Catharine Eddowes with a man just prior to her murder, identified a fellow Jew as the man with Eddowes whilst at a seaside home, and said that the said man was removed to an asylum. Depending upon further evidence being uncovered, it is not beyond belief that Ostrog could have been the identified party.

Following this evidence it may become more apparent that the case against Ostrog is a lot stronger than has previously been assumed.

The argument against Mikhail Ostrog being Jack the Ripper is the acute lack of evidence placing him in the area of Whitechapel at the time of the murders. It is possible that he was there under a previously unknown alias. Ostrog, it must be remembered, was fifty-five years of age at the time of the murders and does not fit any of the descriptions of known sightings of prospective guilty parties, except for the man seen leaving the pub in Berner Street, which we have previously covered, and he does seem to fit the description of the man described in the report which appeared in the *People's Journal*, shortly after the death of Stephen White in 1919.

White had been a C.I.D. Sergeant in H Division, Whitechapel, at the time of the murders. It turned out that White was one of the policemen who were on the streets of Whitechapel in disguise during the murders, and the following purports to be an extract from one of his reports:

> For five nights we had been watching a certain alley, just behind The Whitechapel Road. It could only be entered from where we had two men posted in hiding, and persons entering the alley were under observation by the two men. It was a bitter cold night when I arrived at the scene to take the reports of the two men in hiding. I was turning away when I saw a man coming out

of the alley. He was walking quickly but noiselessly, apparently wearing rubber shoes, which were rather rare in those days. I stood aside to let the man pass, and as he came under the wall lamp I got a good look at him.

He was about five feet ten inches in height, and was dressed rather shabbily though it was obvious that the material of his clothes was good. Evidently a man who had seen better days. This also matches a description given of John Pizer, but one thing differs. Pizer was a short man who was only about 5ft. 4in., this is a full six inches less than the man described, and what follows is far more descriptive of someone like Montague John Druitt.

His face was long and thin, nostrils rather delicate, and his hair was jet black. His complexion was inclined to be sallow, and altogether, the man was foreign in appearance. The most extraordinary thing about him, however, was the extraordinary brilliance of his eyes. The man was slightly bent at the shoulders, though he was obviously quite young, about 33 at the most, and gave one the idea of having been a student or professional man. His hands were snow-white and the fingers were long and tapering.

As the man passed me at the lamp I had the uneasy feeling that there was something sinister about him, and I was strongly moved to find some pretext for detaining him: but the more I thought it over, the more I was forced to the conclusion that it was not in keeping with British police methods that I should do so. [This just doesn't appear to ring true, and sounds fabricated.]The man stumbled a few feet away from me, and I made that an excuse for engaging him in conversation. He turned sharply at the sound of my voice, and scowled at me in surly fashion, but he said 'Good night' and agreed with me that it was cold.

His voice was a surprise to me; it was soft and musical, with just a tinge of melancholy in it, and it was the voice of a man of culture, a voice altogether out of keeping with the squalid surroundings of the East End.

The complete transcript is printed and analysed earlier in the book but the description could have portrayed Ostrog, if indeed he looked a lot younger than his age.

Major Arthur Griffith's book was published in 1898 and entitled *Mysteries of Police and Crime*. The author was a distinguished crime historian and was also an Inspector of Prisons. His comments regarding the identity of Jack the Ripper (one of which could also mirror our man Ostrog) he wrote in the above-named book.

The general public may think that the identity of Jack the Ripper was never revealed. So far as actual knowledge goes, this is undoubtedly true. But the police, after the last murder, had brought their investigation to the point of strongly suspecting several persons, all of them known to be homicidal lunatics, and against three of these they held very plausible and reasonable grounds of suspicion. Concerning two of them the case was weak, although it was based on certain colourable facts. One was a Polish Jew, a known lunatic, who was at large in the district of Whitechapel at the time of the murders, and who, having afterwards developed homicidal tendencies, was confined in an asylum. This man was said to resemble the murderer by the one person who got a glimpse of him – the policeman in Mitre Court. The second possible criminal was a Russian doctor, also insane, who had been a convict both in England and Siberia. This man was in the habit of carrying about knives and surgical instruments in his pockets; his antecedents were of the very worst, and at the time of the Whitechapel murders he was in hiding, or at least, his whereabouts were never exactly known. The third person was of the same type, but the suspicion in his case was stronger, and there was every reason to believe that his own friends entertained grave doubts about him. He was also a doctor in the prime of life, was believed to be insane or on the borderline of insanity, and he disappeared after the last murder, that in Miller's Court, on 9 November 1888. On the last day of the year, seven weeks later, his body was found floating in the Thames, and was said to have been in the water for a month. The theory in his case was that after his last exploit, which was the most fiendish of all, his brain entirely gave way, and he became furiously insane and committed suicide.

The third person is unquestionably another reference to Druitt, and once again they call him a doctor. I am beginning to wonder whether it is Druitt they are talking about as it is criminal in itself that the prime suspect would be wrongly accredited in his profession, unless it was done deliberately.

The second person could once again be our friend Ostrog, as it appears to describe the uncertainty of his movements and his antecedents quite accurately.

My conclusion is that whilst Ostrog was 55 years old, it is contended that he looked younger than his years, but his photograph does not bear out this observation. I still maintan that Ostrog has proven himself to be a credible suspect and should not be readily dismissed at this time.

Doctor Sanders

Doctor John William Smith Sanders was the son of an Indian Army surgeon, who died in 1867. He was born in 1862, and attended the London Hospital as a student in 1879. Hospital records show that in 1881, he 'became ill and was placed in an asylum', and the hospital examination book indicates that he retired due to ill-health. The existence of medical records for February 1887 points to the fact that Sanders's condition had worsened to the point that he was subject to sudden attacks of violence, that he frequently assaulted friends and family, and that he generally was of violent behaviour. He was committed to the Holloway Asylum.

On 19 October 1888, compilation reports sent by Chief Inspector Swanson, a Scotsman who had only just assumed the responsibility as the desk officer in charge of the Ripper investigations, and who had previously been the C.I.D. officer in charge of the case, was sent to the Home Office. In the report on the murder/progress of Annie Chapman, was the following: 'Enquiries were also made to trace three insane medical students who had attended the London Hospital; result: two traced, one gone abroad.'

These reports prompted a Home Office memo, which requested: 'Please see Mr Wortley's memo on Sir Charles Warren's letter. Shall the police be asked at the same time for a report as to what has become of the third insane medical student from the London Hospital, about whom there is a good deal of gossip in circulation?'

On 29 October 1888, in a letter to Sir Charles Warren, the Home Office requested the following: 'Reference is made to three insane medical students, and it is stated that two have been traced, and that one has gone abroad. Mr Matthews would be glad to be informed of the date when the third student went abroad and whether any further enquiry has been made about him.'

Inspector Abberline provided the reply for Warren, in a report which offered: 'I have to state that searching enquiries were made by an officer in Aberdeen Place, St John's Wood, the last known address of the insane medical student named John Sanders, but the only information that could be obtained was that a lady named Sanders did reside with her son at Number 20, but left that address to go abroad some two years ago.'

John Sanders, prior to his internment, lived with his mother in 20 Abercorn Place, and Laura Tucker Sanders, his mother, continued to be listed as the occupant.

This prompts the coincidence that a woman named Sanders also lived in Number 20 Aberdeen Place and had gone abroad, or was it just a mistake in the address by Inspector Abberline?

If the mistake was Inspector Abberline's, and the officer had actually enquired at Number 20 Abercorn Place, then Laura Sanders can no longer have been resident there; otherwise he would have met her or at least any other person who was occupying the premises.

Either way, there is no evidence to confirm that John Sanders had left the asylum, and therefore, being thus incarcerated during the period that the murders took place, he must in all reality be eliminated as a suspect.

Severin Antoniovitch Klosowski
[alias George Chapman]

Severin Antoniovitch Klosowski, alias George Chapman, was born in Nagornak in Poland, in 1865, of a father named Antonio and a mother Emile. He was a student at the Praga Hospital in Warsaw, and after qualifying as a Junior Surgeon in 1887, he came to England, where he worked for Abraham Radin, a barber, in the West India Dock Road.

I feel I must explain that the profession of barber was not limited in those days to the act of cutting hair and shaving customers. It included the performance of minor surgery, such as the removal of warts and the treatment of cuts and abrasions etc.

Chapman, as we will now call him, left the West India Dock Road in 1888, commenced work on a self-employed basis from a premises in Cable Street, and by 1890 was known to be employed in a barber shop, in the basement of the White Hart, a public house which stood on the corner of Whitechapel High Street and George Yard. In 1889, he married Lucy Baderski, and in April of the following year they produced a son.

In 1890, they had emigrated to New Jersey in America, where they split up, Lucy returning to England alone. Chapman did not follow until the middle of 1891.

On his return Klosowski took up with a woman named Annie Chapman. This was not the Ripper victim, as she was already dead, and had been so for three years, nor as far as we know was it any relation to her. It was at this time that Klosowski adopted her surname and from this time onward he was known as George Chapman.

He continued to work as a barber in West Green Road, and carried on in this vein until around 1895, at which time he renounced his profession, and proceeded to earn his living as a publican.

This change in his profession also brought about an alteration in the personality of Chapman, as over the next six years he proceeded to murder three women with whom he lived.

He had split with Annie Chapman by this time and had commenced living with a woman called Isabella Spink. She financed him in taking over a public house in City Road, as the landlord. The year was 1896, and in December of the following year Isabella Spink died.

In 1898, Chapman employed a barmaid called Bessie Taylor, who also took ill and died. The doctors did not find anything untoward in the circumstances of the death, and the year of 1901 sees Chapman employ another barmaid in his pub named Maud March.

When Miss March also died, her mother, suspecting foul play, went to the police, and further investigations were made into the case. It was subsequently found that all three women had passed away as a direct result of antimony poisoning, and Chapman was charged with murder. In April of 1903, Chapman was found guilty of murder and was hanged for his crimes.

In 1903 Inspector Abberline was interviewed by the *Pall Mall Gazette*, with regard to the claim that the recently executed George Chapman was also the notorious murderer Jack the Ripper.

The reporter stated that Abberline was in the process of writing a letter to Sir Melville Macnaghten, which referenced Chapman as a 'highly likely Ripper suspect' and said:

> I have been struck with the remarkable coincidences in the two series of murders that I have not been able to think of anything else for several days past, not in fact since the Attorney-General made his opening statement at the recent trial, and traced the antecedents of Chapman before he came to this country in 1888. Since then, the idea has taken full possession of me, and everything fits in and dovetails so well that I cannot help feeling that this is the man we struggled so hard to capture fifteen years ago.

You will note from this, that in Abberline's opinion Jack the Ripper was still at large, and had not drowned in the Thames or been placed in an institution or died of natural causes or disease. This would serve to eliminate a number of prominent suspects if correct.

Abberline gave the reasons that will already be evident to the reader: that Klosowski had arrived in England shortly before the murders had begun, and that they had stopped about the same time as he moved to America. Chapman fitted in with the 'skill' theory, having trained as a surgeon. Abberline further reported that whilst in America his wife had stated that he had attacked and threatened her with a long knife.

He went on to describe that similar murders had taken place in America whilst Chapman was there, and stated that his only reservations were that Chapman was only 23 years old in 1888, whereas the witnesses had all described the man they had seen as much older than this. In a further interview with the Gazette, Abberline said that:

> You can state almost emphatically, that Scotland Yard is really no wiser on the subject than it was fifteen years ago. It is simple nonsense to talk of the police having proof that the man is dead. I am, and always have been, in the closest touch with Scotland Yard, and it would have been next to impossible for me to have not known about it. Besides, the authorities would have been only too glad to make an end out of such a mystery, if only for their own credit.

> [Abberline continued] I know that it has been stated in certain quarters, that Jack the Ripper was a man who died in a lunatic asylum, a few years ago, but there is nothing at all of a tangible nature to support such a theory.

When prompted about the theory that the Ripper had been a medical student who had drowned in the River Thames, Abberline followed with:

> I know all about that story. But what does it amount to? Simply this. Soon after the last murder in Whitechapel, the body of a young doctor was found in the Thames, but there is absolutely nothing, beyond the fact that he was found at that time, to incriminate him. A report was made to the Home Office about the matter, but that it was 'considered final and conclusive', is going altogether beyond the truth; the fact that several months after December 1888, when the student's body was found, the

detectives were told to hold themselves in readiness for further investigations, seems to point to the conclusion, that Scotland Yard did not in any way consider the evidence to be final.

So now we have a little bit more information which intimates that Scotland Yard still thought that the Ripper was at large, long after the last murder had been committed.

This latter mention of the body in the Thames seems to refer to one of the main culprits, a man named Montague John Druitt, whom we will discuss later in the book, but I believe I should point out at this time that Druitt was not a doctor, but a barrister, and it was not immediately after the final murder that he committed suicide in the River Thames.

Sergeant George Godley was the officer who arrested Chapman for the murders for which he was hanged, and was also a prominent member of the team that investigated the Ripper murders. Abberline is supposed to have said to him after Chapman had been convicted, 'I see you've got Jack the Ripper at last.'

It is hard to imagine that a murderer who committed crimes with such ferocity as the Whitechapel murders could stop his activities with such abruptness, and then recommence, a number of years later, and also change to poison as the inflicting medium. These people murder for the buzz which they get out of the killing, and more often than not the sexual fulfilment which it brings. I know that killers can change their modus operandi. After all, the Yorkshire Ripper did so, and when asked, he responded that he felt like a change, but the make-up of the Ripper, his mental state, would not have allowed him to cease killing for any length of time. I do agree with what Abberline said about Scotland Yard. If the police had apprehended the Ripper, they couldn't have kept it secret. Someone would have blabbed to the Press, and too many people would have been a party to the secret for it to remain a secret for long. Also it was a feather in their cap, so why in heaven would they want to keep quiet the fact that they had caught the most infamous killer of the day?

Wolf Levisohn, an acquaintance of Klosowski/Chapman, is reputed to have told Inspector Abberline that Klosowski was more interested in building up a business, and was not the Ripper, and a far more likely suspect was a barber in Walworth Road, who was seen in Commercial Street on 29–30 September 1888. This is purely conjecture, and no value should be attached to this claim.

It is also considered likely that Inspector Abberline was not as well informed as he considered himself to be. We have seen in the previous paragraphs where Abberline has tripped up on information to do with the case; a simple example would be: What if Sanders had indeed been Jack the Ripper, and when the check of the premises was carried out, he had sent the officer to the wrong address? We are looking at a situation whereby the murderer may have escaped justice because of the incompetence of the investigating officer. I personally believe that Fred Abberline was not the super sleuth who is portrayed on the screen, and nobody has unearthed any evidence of his worthiness of this mantle.

The higher echelons of the police administration did keep a lot of this information to themselves, but if they had identified Jack the Ripper, that secret would have been too important to the public interest for it to remain a secret. All those who knew would have had to engage in conversation concerning the case, with associates and acquaintances, and not divulge the secret to a close friend or member of the family. This is too much to ask. The Prime Minister would have to be told, the Home Secretary would be part of the cover-up, and he would have been required to lie to Parliament, and it is understood that Queen Victoria took a close interest in the progress of the case. No, the only persons who knew the identity of Jack the Ripper are the murderer himself and his victims.

Neil Shelden is a highly respected researcher into the Whitechapel murders. In the Ripperana magazine of the summer of 1993, he reported that the results of his researches into Severin Klosowski had shown that he was not employed by the barber below the White Hart pub until 1890.

In *The Ripper A to Z*, written by Paul Begg, Martin Fido and Keith Skinner, they state that this discovery by Nick Shelden demolishes the theory of Klosowski as the Ripper entirely. Whilst I have not seen Nick Shelden's evidence, unless it states categorically where Klosowski was at the time of the murders, it does not get him totally off the hook. I will eliminate George Chapman as a suspect if the evidence places him in a location where he could not possibly have committed the murders.

However, I must concede that the link between Chapman and the Whitechapel murders is now very thin, and as such it reinforces my opinion of Inspector Abberline. A lot more information needs to be unearthed before Chapman once again attains the standing of a credible suspect.

If I am mistaken about Inspector Abberline then I sincerely apologise. Chapman was the man whom it was said that Inspector Abberline most suspected of the crimes, and in order to make such a claim, there may have been other information which alerted his suspicions and which we are not aware of.

Doctor Thomas Neil Cream

The final doctor who I propose to look at is the notorious poisoner Neil Cream.

It was reported that as the trapdoor of the gallows opened and Neil Cream fell, he is reputed to have shouted 'I am Jack the . . . ' The hangman James Billington is reported to have sworn to the authenticity of Cream's last statement.

Cream was born in Glasgow in the year 1850, and went to Canada in 1854, when his parents emigrated. He graduated from McGill University in March of 1876. It is probable that his first murder was that of his wife, whom he had married in September of 1876, and who died less than a year after the marriage.

In October of that year, Cream came to London for the first time, and studied obstetrics at St Thomas's Hospital. Obstetrics is the study and treatment of women during pregnancy, childbirth, and afterwards.

He returned to America, and the next we hear from him is in May of 1879 when he was investigated after a girl died from an overdose of chloroform, while being attended at his surgery. The official verdict was that the girl had died from chloroform administered by a person or persons unknown.

In 1880 a young Canadian named Mary Anne Faulkner died at the hands of Cream, while he was performing an abortion. He was tried for murder but found not guilty.

The fact that he had been tried for murder did not deter Cream, who next murdered Daniel Scott, who just happened to be the husband of his mistress. We do not know the reason, but two days after the burial of Daniel Scott, Cream sent a telegram to the coroner, indicating his suspicions of foul play. The body was exhumed, and on investigation was found to contain a large dose of strychnine, and after further enquiries, Cream was arrested and put on trial for his murder. He was found guilty this time and sent to prison 'for the term of your natural life, and one day of each year to be kept in solitary confinement'.

There is little need to go any further with this, as it is not until ten years later, on 12 June 1891, that Cream was released from the State Penitentiary at Joliet, Illinois, having been given a pardon by the governor, Joseph Fifer.

A short time after his release, Cream's father died and he inherited the sum of $16,000, which enabled him to return to England.

Within two weeks of his arrival in England, Cream had poisoned his first victim, a woman by the name of Ellen Donworth. He then proceeded to write a letter to the Deputy Coroner saying that he had evidence that would apprehend the guilty party, for a fee of £300,000. It was signed with the name A. O'Brien. He wrote a second letter to one of the partners in the firm of W. H. Smith & Son, accusing him of the murder and offering to defend him. He signed this particular letter H. Bayne.

Throughout his career as a poisoner, Cream continually wrote letters, which in the final analysis assisted in his apprehension and conviction. He went on to kill Matilda Glover, Alice Marsh, and Emma Shrivell, and apparently told his warders, whilst in the condemned cell, that he had murdered numerous other women.

The two things which stand in the way of Thomas Neil Cream being Jack the Ripper are firstly, the modus operandi that was used: Cream murdered remotely, and read about his exploits, whereas the Ripper got his thrills from the mutilation of the bodies immediately after killing them, and was present at the deaths of his victims. Cream's method did not involve any contact with his victims. He did not kill in a frenzy of excitement brought about by the possibility of being seen or caught; Cream gained his satisfaction and kicks from the pleasure in knowing that his victims would die in agony from the effects of the strychnine.

The second reason is undoubtedly the major stumbling block to any theory involving Cream. During the time of the murders in 1888, he was incarcerated in the Illinois State Penitentiary in Joliet, thirty miles from Chicago, from November 1881 until his release in June 1891. This term in prison has been addressed, but no research has yet shown that Cream achieved an earlier release than the date shown.

I therefore suggest that there is really no reason to suppose or suspect that Dr Thomas Neil Cream was Jack the Ripper, and propose that the claim which he half made on the scaffold was prompted by his innate need to be famous.

Doctor Francis Tumblety

A recent suspect to come under scrutiny is Francis Tumblety, who was born in Ireland but moved to America with his parents when he was just a child. The family set up home in Rochester, New York and Tumblety learned about medicines from a Doctor Lispenard who from all accounts did not carry a good reputation himself.

Tumblety left Rochester and set himself up as a 'herb doctor' in which he made lots of money and was very successful. He came to light as a Ripper suspect through a letter written by Chief Inspector John Littlechild, who at the time of the Whitechapel murders was the head of a secret department at Scotland Yard.

In 1913, in answer to a letter from G. R. Sims, who was a well-connected journalist, he penned the following reply.

8 The Chase
Clapham Common S.W.
23rd September 1913

Dear Sir

I was pleased to receive your letter which I shall put away in 'good company' to read again, perhaps some day when old age overtakes me and when to revive memories of the past may be a solace.

Knowing the great interest you take in all matters criminal and abnormal, I am just going to inflict one more letter on you on the 'Ripper' subject. Letters as a rule are only a nuisance when they call for a reply but this does not need one. I will try and be brief.

I never heard of a Dr D in connection with the Whitechapel murders, but amongst the suspects, and to my mind a very likely one, was a Dr T. He was an American quack named Tumblety and was at one time a frequent visitor to London, and on these occasions constantly brought under the notice of police, there being a large dossier concerning him at Scotland Yard. Although a 'psychopathia sexualis' subject, he was not known as a sadist, but his feelings toward women were remarkable and bitter in the extreme, a fact on record. Tumblety was arrested at the time of the murders in connection with unnatural offences and charged at Marlborough Street, remanded on bail, jumped his bail, and got away to Boulogne. He shortly left Boulogne and was never heard of afterwards. It was believed he committed suicide, but certain it is, that from this time the 'Ripper' murders came to an end.

With regard to the term 'Jack the Ripper' it was generally believed at the Yard that Tom Bullen of the Central News was the originator, but it is probable that Moore, who was his chief, was the inventor. It was a smart piece of journalistic work. No journalist of my time got such privileges from Scotland Yard as Bullen. Mr James Monro when Assistant Commissioner, and afterwards Commissioner, relied on his integrity. Poor Bullen occasionally took too much to drink, and I fail to see how he could help it, knocking about so many hours and seeking favours from so many people to procure copy. One night when Bullen had taken a 'few too many' he got early information of the death of Prince Bismark and instead of going to the office to report it sent a laconic telegram 'Bloody Bismark is dead'. On this I believe Mr Charles Moore fired him out.

It is very strange how those given to 'contrary sexual instinct' and 'degenerates' are given to cruelty. In the case of the man Harry Thaw (and this is authentic, as I have the boy's statement) Thaw was staying at the Carlton Hotel, and one day laid out a lot of sovereigns on his dressing table, then rang for a call boy on pretence of sending out a telegram. He made some excuse and went out of the room and left the boy there and watched through the chink of the door. The unfortunate boy was tempted and took a sovereign from the pile and Thaw returning to the room charged him with stealing. The boy confessed. When Thaw asked him whether he should send for the police or whether he should punish him himself, the boy, scared to death, consented to take his punishment from Thaw, who made him undress, strapped him to the foot of the bedstead, and thrashed him with a cane, drawing blood. He then made the boy get into a bath in which he placed a quantity of salt. It seems incredible that such a thing could take place in any hotel, but it is a fact. This was in 1906.

Now pardon me – it is finished. Except that I knew Major Griffiths for many years. He probably got his information from Anderson who only 'thought he knew'.

Faithfully yours,

J. G. Littlechild

After a chequered and somewhat bizarre career, Tumblety made his way to London. He was arrested on 7 November 1888, and was charged nine days later with gross indecency and indecent assault, on four separate counts. The offences involved the use of arms, and he was bailed on 16 November. Whilst on bail awaiting trial, Tumblety fled to France and from there back to America. Whether or not the word had been put out by the British police or not is debatable, but his connection with the Ripper case was published in the American Press before he had arrived back.

Inspector Walter Andrews arrived in New York on business connected with the Ripper case but on which there is no definite proof that it was in connection with Tumblety. The connection however gains credence if we are to believe that Scotland Yard had requested samples of his handwriting. By this time Tumblety had fled New York and was in hiding in the provinces, and his involvement with the Ripper case ceases.

His undoubted homosexuality has for some heightened his credibility as a suspect, but the fact that he appears to have been in police custody for the night that Mary Kelly was murdered seems to rule him out. (If you didn't do one of these murders then you didn't do any of them.)

The police file which included Tumblety is missing and until that resurfaces I will keep my options in relation to Francis Tumblety open. I do not however think of him as a serious Ripper suspect, and believe he would have been more intent on saving his own skin with regard to his impending court case than on retaining any involvement in the Whitechapel murders.

*   *   *

The reason for the extent of research and conjecture into the probability of Jack the Ripper being a doctor revolves around the assessment as to whether the murderer possessed anatomical knowledge, and was the extent of anatomical knowledge required to perform the mutilations of the victims sufficient for it to warrant a doctor or surgeon?

This is variously based on the injuries inflicted, but mainly on the removal of the organs, and the speed at which the mutilations were carried out. These do not necessarily require a doctor's knowledge to carry out, but the use of a commonly used phrase would suffice for description. That phrase is 'He was no stranger to the knife'.

Other persons, in their books, have considered this part of the mystery a lot more comprehensively than I could hope to achieve, without a definite result. I can only suggest that the interest which continues to abound in attempting to identify Jack the Ripper could maybe prompt the British Medical Council to approach the problem and perhaps evaluate the medical evidence at a seminar or meeting. It would certainly help facilitate a more comprehensive understanding if a number of specialist doctors could inspect the documentary material and impart their collective verdict on the medical efficiency of the Ripper. This would allow any future evaluation to have the benefit of an educated decision.

From a personal point of view, the fact that the Ripper was able to identify specific organs puts him one up on most of the ordinary populace of today, and in the Victorian era the internals of the body were known to a very small percentage of the people. I believe that previous persons who have evaluated whether or not the Ripper had anatomical knowledge have given a massive amount of the British population a lot more credit than they deserve, not least myself. Not many people can correctly identify the internal parts of the body with any real accuracy, and to do it in the dark and under the pressure of discovery makes it all the more complicated.

The Ripper must certainly have had some anatomical knowledge or else we must reassess all the medical information and dictate that they were all purely random mutilations. In a personal opinion the very fact that he took Catharine Eddowes's kidney influences my vote enormously.

CHAPTER ELEVEN

The royal connection

In the November 1970 issue of *The Criminologist*, an article was published which was written by Doctor Thomas Edward Alexander Stowell.

In this article, the Ripper suspect under scrutiny was referred to as 'S', and the reference given that he was 'an heir to power and wealth, and his family had for fifty years earned the love and admiration of large numbers of people, by its devotion to public service'.

Stowell and Colin Wilson, whom I have referred to earlier, had lunched together at the Athenaeum in 1960, after Wilson had published a series on Jack the Ripper, in the *Evening Standard*.

Colin Wilson admits that the passage of time has dulled his memory of the details of the meeting, but this remains the first occasion when 'S' was connected with the Whitechapel murders.

The identity of 'S' is Prince Albert Victor Christian Edward, Queen Victoria's grandson, and heir presumptive to the throne of England.

Wilson said that he remembered the gist of the conversation as being that Stowell had seen some papers belonging to Sir William Gull, the royal doctor, which had been shown to him by Gull's daughter, Mrs Caroline Ackland.

The papers apparently revealed that contrary to what was thought, and reported at the time, Prince Albert Victor had not died from influenza in 1892, but had passed away in a mental home near Sandringham, the cause of death being given as 'softening of the brain, due to syphilis'. Stowell inferred that the prince had been Jack the Ripper, and that in order to avoid the scandal, a cover-up had been established. The papers further revealed the details of the Cleveland Street Scandal of 1886, in which members of the upper classes were accused of sodomising the telegraph boys, and detailed that the Duke of Clarence (the title by which Prince Albert Victor was more commonly known) had been among those questioned. This intimated that Albert Victor was a homosexual, and Stowell carried on to say that among the writings there were mysterious hints about the Ripper.

The article in *The Criminologist* left it in no doubt, as to who the suspect referred to as 'S' purported to be. Stowell reported that 'S' had been a keen huntsman, and that he had undergone sexual arousal when watching the post-hunt cutting up of the deer. He had speculated that the prince had contracted syphilis, not from a prostitute, but from a male who had accompanied him on a world cruise in 1880, when he was just sixteen years of age.

When the prince was twenty-two years old, the Cleveland Street scandal broke into the newspapers, and owing to the implication of Albert Victor in the affair, he was again sent on another cruise. On returning from this voyage in 1888, the prince commenced the killing of the Whitechapel prostitutes. Stowell continued with his hypothesis that the prince was caught on the night he murdered Stride and Eddowes, but subsequently escaped, and was apprehended after the killing of Mary Jane Kelly.

The prince was then placed in the care of Sir William Gull, who successfully slowed down the process of syphilitic decay until 1892, when the prince finally succumbed to the disease and died.

Stowell did not stop there but went on to imply that because of the rumour and newspaper coverage, which maintained that the Ripper was surgically skilled, Sir William Gull came under suspicion, and that he had been seen on more than one occasion in the vicinity of Whitechapel, at the times when the murders were committed.

There is also the story concerning the well-known medium Robert James Lees, who is supposed to have identified the Ripper, and this further implicated Gull.

With regard to the Ripper case, Lees is supposed to have been seated on a bus travelling along the Bayswater Road, when he felt that the murderer was close. He realised that the man sitting opposite him was Jack the Ripper, and as such he followed the man back to his home, which was a mansion in the West End. (Gull lived in a large house at Number 74 Brook Street, Grosvenor Square.) Lees then went to the police, and they accompanied him to the house. The police told Lees that he must be mistaken, as the house belonged to a most eminent physician, who had among his patients members of the Royal Family.

Subsequently, the doctor's wife was interviewed, and is said to have expressed concern as to her husband's sanity, and that he had been absent from home on the nights of the Whitechapel murders.

Armed with this information, the police placed the house under surveillance, and detained the doctor when he left the house late one evening, carrying a black bag, which was found to contain a very sharp knife, of the type capable of inflicting the mutilations carried out on the victims. Why this should be odd, I do not know, as Sir William was a renowned doctor and surgeon. The story ends with Gull having been placed in a mental institution, where he died.

Stowell informed Colin Wilson that Sir William Gull's papers had contained references to Prince Albert Victor, one of which was that the Duke had arrived at Gull's house after one of the murders, with blood on his shirt.

It is not impossible that Lees was consulted by the police, or approached the police himself. Lees's diaries are retained in Starstead Hall, and contain the following entries:

2 October – offered services to police, to follow up East End murders – called a fool and a lunatic. Got trace of a man from a spot in Berner Street.

3 October – went to the police again – called a madman and a fool.

4 October – went to Scotland Yard, the same result as previously, but they promised to write to me.

Cynthia Legh wrote an article in a magazine called *Light*, in which she said that she had known Lees from 1912, and confirmed the story saying that Lees had three times been rejected in his bid to help the police, but went on to describe how Queen Victoria had interceded on his behalf, and instructed the police that they should accept his help. The remainder of the story follows the line above, but adds that after the doctor was placed in custody, and put in an asylum, he was so under an assumed name, and a beggar who died in Seven Dials on the same night was buried in his place. The queen supposedly then requested Lees to leave the capital for a period of five years, and for the duration of this period he was granted a pension.

Enquiries made by the Society for Psychical Research in both 1931 and again in 1948, failed to supply any connection with Lees and the police. Eva Lees (daughter) was supposed to possess documentary evidence proving the award of a pension to her father, for his assistance in solving the Whitechapel murders, together with a gold cross said to have been a gift from the prostitutes of Whitechapel and now in the possession of his granddaughter.

A further story which I feel obliged to include, and which also serves to implicate Prince Albert Victor, was written by Stephen

Knight after he interviewed Joseph Sickert. He claims that the prince had secretly married Sickert's grandmother Annie Elizabeth Crook, and that, on the marriage being discovered, a scandal was averted by placing Crook in a lunatic asylum, the marriage never again being mentioned.

The murders were committed by Sir William Gull and associate Freemasons, at the behest of the Government, led by Lord Salisbury. The reason for the murders was that the clandestine marriage had produced a child. Mary Jane Kelly was employed secretly as a nurse-maid to the child, and had related to her fellow prostitutes the details of the marriage, in addition to which she had supposedly attempted to blackmail the government. All of this is pure conjecture, and in my opinion a complete fabrication. No corroborative evidence of any description has ever been found to lend any credence whatsoever to this story.

Joseph Sickert himself confessed in 1978 to the *Sunday Times*, that he had fabricated the whole Masonic tale, and that the whole thing was a hoax.

When considering the involvement of Prince Albert Victor, it is important that we place things in perspective and make you aware of some facts that shoot the theory in the foot.

Due to the modus operandi of the Ripper, it is virtually certain that Mary Ann Nichols, Annie Chapman, and Catharine Eddowes, were murdered by the same person, and that same person most definitely murdered Mary Jane Kelly. If therefore we can establish the where-abouts of a probable suspect for the time of one or two of the murders, then it is quite reasonable to discard this person as a suspect. I there-fore submit the following information which is extracted from Court Circulars and diaries and which pertains to the movements of Prince Albert Victor on the following dates.

29 August to 7 September 1888 – the Prince was staying as a guest of Viscount Downe, at Danby Lodge, Grosmont in Yorkshire.

7 September to 10 September 1888 – the Prince was at the Cavalry Barracks in York, having gone to stay there after his visit to Viscount Downe.

27 September to 30 September 1888 – the prince was in Scotland and no less a person than Queen Victoria includes an entry in her journal for 30 September, that she and Prince Albert Victor lunched together.

2 November to 12 November 1888 – the Prince was staying at Sandringham.

It can be seen from analysing these dates, that only for the murder of Mary Jane Kelly could the prince have realistically been present at the site of the murder at the time of death. All of the above have documentary proof, and it would involve a truly massive exercise in deception to have doctored the evidence to conceal the involvement of the prince, as too many people would have needed to be involved in the ruse, including Queen Victoria herself.

For this reason we can declare the prince innocent of any personal involvement in the crimes committed on the dates for which he has a phenomenally good alibi, and the thing about the Ripper murders was that if you didn't do one of them then you didn't do any of them.

As other people have pointed out numerous times before me, the attraction of the Jack the Ripper solution becomes more attractive, the further the suspect is situated up the social ladder. This is all well and good providing that in making the accusations there is a modicum of proof attached to the hypothesis, which in the case of Prince Albert Victor there definitely is not.

Sir William Gull's involvement tends to dissipate with the absolution of Prince Albert Victor, as it was primarily with this story that he became implicated. However, there is the Lees involvement and the implications of this still to discuss.

I propose that Sir William Gull is innocent of the Ripper murders for the following reasons:

At the time of the murders he was seventy-two years of age, and with physical deterioration more pronounced than it is today, I suggest that at that age he would have been physically incapable of meeting the capabilities required of Jack the Ripper: i.e. the strength and athleticism displayed to subdue and strangle a woman of the streets, who herself was quite capable of self-defence against anyone but a reasonably strong and comparatively fit man.

The Ripper made quick exits from some of the murder scenes, by climbing over fences so as to appear on the streets at a place a reasonable distance from the murder. Gull would not have had the requisite mobility to carry this out.

Sir William was nearing the end of his life; he had already exceeded the expected life span of a male in Victorian times, by a number of years, and would have been well past the age where he would partake in extensive physical exercise. He had experienced problems with his health and would have been semi-retired at the time of the murders.

The year previous to the Whitechapel murders, Sir William had suffered a minor stroke, which would have slowed him down and compelled him to adjust his life-style. This opinion is enforced by documentary evidence that he was slightly paralysed down his right-hand side.

With all due respect to previous theorists and the fact that I myself thoroughly enjoyed the television portrayal by Michael Caine, any serious Ripper searcher must discount Sir William Gull as Jack the Ripper.

CHAPTER TWELVE

Unfashionable suspects

John Pizer [alias Leather Apron]

At the height of the Ripper murders, it was noted that upward of 1200 letters a day were being delivered to the police, and though the vast majority of these letters were hoaxes, all had to be read, analysed and if they proved to have any degree of substance, to be investigated.

A lot of these letters implicated local persons, who, whether by the grudge of the writer or the action of their behaviour, had been reported, and then questioned by the police and included in the Ripper progress reports.

Due to the element of panic within the community, hearsay was rife and it was highly likely that anyone indulging in conversation about the murders, either too frequently or in too much detail and depth, could well be reported to the police, and be subjected to subsequent investigation.

One such suspect was Leather Apron. After the murder of Mary Ann Nichols, the police enquiries and interviews of the local prostitutes came up with a character who had habitually accosted and threatened the prostitutes of the area, extorting money from them with threats that they would be ripped open if they did not comply with the demands.

On 8 September, after the discovery of Annie Chapman's body in the backyard of Number 29 Hanbury street, the speculation increased when it was discovered that close to the body when it had been found was a leather apron. The police intensified their efforts thinking that when the identity of this person was revealed then this would be their man.

Three days before, on 5 September, the *Star* had described him as a short, thickset man, aged 38 to 40 years old. He had black hair, a black moustache, and an exceptionally thick neck. He wore a close-fitting cap and a leather apron. He carried a sharp knife, and frequently threatened, 'I'll rip you up'. He was reported as having glinting eyes and a repulsive smile, and was of a generally sinister and frightening appearance.

The Evening News *described him as having a florid complexion, a small moustache and side whiskers [no beard] and who showed 'more than an ordinary amount of intelligence for a man of his class'.* Emanuel Violenia picked him out straight away in an identity parade but his evidence was somehow discredited. Before the identity parade, he had described the man to the police as '*a man of short stature, with black whiskers and a shaven chin*'.

It should further be emphasised that all the local prostitutes knew of him and therefore he should have proved easy to locate. In the end, it was probably from the prostitutes that the information came, that he could be found in and around the Princess Alice public house which was situated in Commercial Street.

He was additionally identified as a boot finisher, and was said to have a friend called 'Mickeldy Joe', and was a Jew. He could also regularly be seen at Crossingham's lodging house, a fact which was confirmed by Timothy Donovan, the Deputy, who said that he had ejected him for threatening behaviour to a woman, before the murders had started.

A *Star* reporter who went to the lodging house in Brick Lane in search of Leather Apron, found Mickeldy Joe, who refused to identify Pizer as Leather Apron. The other patrons who were present at the house also declined to reveal his identity and refused to confirm whether he was a regular visitor there. Whether this was due to the fact that they were frightened of the man, or that they knew of his innocence and refused to condemn him, the reporter went away without his confirmation.

On 7 September, C.I.D. Inspector Joseph Henry Helson wrote a weekly report to Scotland Yard in which he stated:

> The enquiry has revealed the fact that a man named Jack Pizer, alias Leather Apron, has for some considerable period, been in the habit of ill-using prostitutes in this and other parts of the metropolis, and careful search has been and is continued to be made to find this man, in order that his movements may be accounted for on the night in question, although at present there is no evidence against him.

This report proves that Pizer was implicated as Leather Apron prior to the murder of Annie Chapman in Hanbury Street, as this did not take place until 8 September and this was the murder where a leather apron was discovered near the body, so would only serve to implicate him further. We now know for certain that the apron actually belonged to one of the residents, a previously mentioned John Richardson.

Because of the Jewish link, 8 September produced a reaction against the Jewish community in the area. The discovery of Annie Chapman's body sparked off attacks against the Jews and heightened the search for Leather Apron/John Pizer.

A Miss Lyons reported that on Sunday 9 September, she had met a strange man in Flower and Dean Street, who had arranged to meet her in the Queen's Head, on the corner of Fashion Street, at 6.30 p.m. She remarked that while they were having a drink, the man had said 'You are about the same style as the one that was murdered', and further into the conversation he had added 'You are beginning to smell a rat', at which time he had left.

Miss Lyons said that she had followed him but that he had spotted her and had quickened his pace, which ended in her losing sight of him. She claimed that he was exactly like the papers had described him, down to the *glinting eyes and the repulsive smile*.

This man was never identified, though it must be said that any connection is extremely loose, and he can confidently be ignored unless some other drastic information is produced which further implicates him.

On 10 September, the police investigation into Pizer's whereabouts bore fruit. Police Sergeant Thick and another officer called at a house at Number 22 Mulberry Street, and John Pizer answered the door. He was taken into custody, along with his leather work knives and hats, and removed to Leman Street Police Station. He was then put into an identification parade, but several women who supposedly knew him failed to identify him.

If he was such a significant-looking individual then this was virtually impossible, unless, if he was such a brutal character as his actions and the police records appear to confirm, it could have been a simple case that they were too frightened to identify him, being well aware of the consequences should they do so. It must be noted that it may have been the presence of Mickeldy Joe at the lodging house which exacted a similar reaction from the men there, so the intimidation of the women must have been even more daunting.

He was held in custody, but there being no further evidence found against him, he was released.

Donald Rumbelow goes further when he says that when searching the house at which Pizer was arrested by Sergeant Thick *they found five sharp long-bladed knives and several old hats, an unfortunate reminder that Pizer made hats.* Remember also that Timothy Donovan stated that when he had last seen Pizer, he had been wearing a deerstalker hat similar to that worn by Annie Chapman's killer. It may have nothing at all to do with the case, but Mary Nichols boasted of her new hat. Where would a woman of such limited means have obtained the money for a new hat when she couldn't even afford the fourpence needed for her bed on the night she was murdered?

On 14 October, he was present at the inquest into the death of Annie Chapman conducted by Wynne Baxter. In answer to the first question, he confirmed that he was indeed Leather Apron, and on being questioned further, it became apparent that on the night of the murder of Mary Ann Nichols, *Pizer had been staying at Crossman's lodging house in Holloway, and at 1.30 a.m. he had been in the Seven Sisters Road, in conversation with a Metropolitan policeman concerning the big fire on the London Docks,* which had occurred on that night. Seven Sisters Road was a number of miles from Mary Ann Nichols's murder site. As I have stated, whoever committed one of the murders committed the lot, and the coroner and the police were obviously of the same understanding, for as soon as this fact had been definitely established, Pizer was dismissed and the police released him from any suspicion.

On the night of the Chapman murder, Pizer stated that he was at home, having been there since the preceding Thursday night, a full two days prior to the murder of Annie Chapman. He said that he had remained there until his arrest by Sergeant Thick on 10 September.

When pressed for the reason for this he stated that he had known that false accusations were being made against him, and was scared to leave the house for fear of being attacked. His alibi was confirmed by his brother and the other persons who lodged at Number 22 Mulberry Road.

When he was subsequently interviewed by the Press, Pizer said that he did not know that he was referred to as Leather Apron, and this fact was borne out by family friends and neighbours, who were also questioned.

After the furore involving Leather Apron, it is reported that John Pizer was amply recompensed by the Press, who had fuelled the suspicion that he was Jack the Ripper.

John Pizer died in July of 1897, still living at Number 22 Mulberry Street.

It is inconceivable that the police still regarded John Pizer as a likely Ripper suspect and this after having him in their custody. Prisoners did not have the same rights as they possess in today's society, and as such if they had any suspicions that Pizer was the Ripper they would not have released him back into the community, to allow him to commit the ensuing murders. It must also be noted that the alibis which got him off the hook were supplied by friends and family, and are not as cast-iron as first glance would suggest.

It would be a nice sealer to any remote aspirations that Pizer was the guilty man, if the policeman with whom he had the conversation in the Seven Sisters Road, had left written confirmation of their meeting, but the day and the time were accepted by the Coroner at the inquest so doubtless the officer in question had corroborated the story in some way. But, as can be seen by the poem in the Letters chapter (Chapter 15) later in the book, there is talk about the writer having treated a policeman, and this could have been interpreted as having bribed him.

It is for this reason and the evidence outlined above that I would be tempted to put it to you that John Pizer, alias Leather Apron, was totally innocent of the Whitechapel murders, and was definitely not Jack the Ripper, but that certain communication which has come to light during my investigations prohibits me from saying this. It is a poem, the implications of which are addressed in the Letters chapter, and for this reason I cannot totally eliminate John Pizer as Jack the Ripper, and believe that he must be included as one of the prime suspects for the title of Jack the Ripper.

The Butcher

Whilst only one butcher has been specifically entertained as a Ripper suspect, there remains a suspicion that the trade of butcher could have adequately furnished the necessary training to account for the erudite mutilations. The only butcher ever to come under suspicion was Joseph Issenschmidt.

Issenschmidt was an early Ripper suspect who had, in the initial stages of the investigation, aroused strong suspicions in the police. These suspicions were cultivated due to his having spent time in Colney Hatch Mental Asylum, during 1887, coupled with the fact that on 11 September 1888, two doctors, named Cowan and Crabb, reported to the police that they believed that Issenschmidt was the Whitechapel murderer.

The butcher was lodging at Number 60 Milford Road in the district of Holloway, in a house which was owned by a Mr George Tyler. When questioned, it became apparent that he was frequently absent from the house at unsociable times, and had been missing on the night that Annie Chapman had been murdered.

The police commenced their investigation of the butcher and in doing so discovered that he had left his wife. They watched his lodgings, and after satisfying themselves of his unusual behaviour, they detained him on 13 September, and having ascertained that he was indeed a dangerous lunatic, he was incarcerated in the infirmary at Fairfield Road. The investigations continued, and it was revealed that his business had failed about a year previously.

Mr Tyler, who had kept a log of his movements, said that he frequently left the house in the early hours, and did not return until some hours later.

Detective Sergeant Thick had attempted, but without any appreciable success, to ascertain Issenschmidt's movements on these nightly excursions, and as such reported as much.

The *East London Advertiser* carried a report on 22 September 1888, concerning the arrest of a suspect, and reported as follows:

> The Holloway lunatic who is detained on suspicion in connection with the Whitechapel murders, is a Swiss named ISENSCHMID.
>
> Some time ago he kept a pork-butcher shop in Elthorne Road in Holloway, and he is known in the trade as a 'cutter-up'. Some years ago, it seems, he had sunstroke, and since then he has been subject to yearly fits of madness. These fits have usually come on in the latter part of the summer, and on several occasions his conduct has been so alarming that he has been carried off to Colney Hatch. One of his delusions is that everything belongs to him. He has called himself the King of Elthorne Road. On several occasions he has threatened to 'put people's lights out', as he expressed it, and more than once, the landlord of the shop had been warned not to approach his lunatic tenant. One of the alarming practices of Isenschmid when he is mad, is his continual sharpening of a long knife, and his disappearance from home for a few days has not been unusual. He went mad some weeks ago, and his frightened wife got an order for his detention in a lunatic asylum, but Isenschmid could not be caught. It may be only a

curious coincidence, but the mad pork butcher closely answers the description of the man who was seen on the morning of the [third] murder, near the scene of the crime, with bloodstains on his hands.

Issenschmidt was now in custody, and this fact was to prove beyond any shadow of a doubt that he was not the Whitechapel murderer, as, whilst he was incarcerated, the Whitechapel murders continued.

It is therefore safe to assume that despite his undoubted lunacy, Joseph Issenschmidt was not Jack the Ripper.

The training of a butcher would certainly furnish him with the skill and speed required to perform the Ripper mutilations, as is the possibility of the murderer being a Jewish 'Shochet'.

A letter written by a London slaughterman to the police, in October of 1888, outlined the fact that the dexterity of the trained butcher, together with the speed at which he is capable of executing his craft, would surprise the medical profession. It also explained that 'the throatscutting technique used by the slaughtermen was completely *au fait* with the technique used in the murders'.

I have not personally read this letter, as I was unable to find it, but if by this the writer is confirming that the throat was cut with a double slash, as in the Ripper murders, then this would greatly add to the probability of the Ripper being a butcher or slaughterman. I propose to investigate further the method of slaughter used by the contemporary butcher of the 1880s.

We must appreciate that the importation of cattle into London during this time was an important part of the industrial base of the East End. There was an abundance of abattoirs situated in the area, and the amount of blood generated by these establishments, who generally worked on a twenty-four hours a day basis, would have been enormous. It is further recorded, that animals were frequently slaughtered in the streets.

Queen Victoria herself had concluded that, there being a possibility that the murderer worked on one of the numerous cattle boats that came into the capital, an investigation should be made in that area, and Major Smith, who was the Acting Commissioner of the City of London Police, claimed to have visited every butcher's shop in the city.

Extensive investigations were thus being undertaken in this field, and it was recognised by the constabulary, that persons working in these establishments would be expected to be covered with a certain amount of blood, and would undoubtedly be seen on the streets in such a state.

Chief Inspector Donald Swanson, in reporting progress, on 19 October 1888 stated that 'seventy-six butchers and slaughterers have been visited, and the characters of the men employed enquired into'.

It must be further noted that the slaughterman/butcher would have indeed been described as 'no stranger to the knife'.

All of this tends to add fuel to the fact that a butcher would have been ideally suited to the modus operandi of Jack the Ripper, and I believe more comprehensive research requires to be done into this possibility.

Donald Rumbelow has done a great deal of digging into the possibilities of a butcher being responsible for the Whitechapel murders, but has yet to uncover a named contender. Rumbelow is a conscientious and scholarly researcher, who has unearthed vital information on the Whitechapel murder case and is regarded as somewhat of a mentor on the subject of Jack the Ripper. If the information is there, then he will be the favourite to find it.

My conclusion is that there is ample evidence to indicate that a butcher could have been Jack the Ripper, but no evidence is available at the time of writing, which points to a specific individual. Information appertaining to the Ripper case, is continuously being unearthed, and as such we must be patient with the progress of the researchers, who frequently discover documents which bring about reconsiderations of the parameters of the case.

If the butcher of the day, when slaying a beast, did so with a double cut of the throat, in order to minimise the suffering of the animal, or to sever certain ligatures that could not be accomplished with a single cut, then the case against the butcher would be greatly enhanced. And this in turn could encourage a Ripperologist, to research in this direction, with a probability of a higher degree of success. That research may unearth a butcher suspect who had some credibility, and therefore would be worthwhile. As it now stands, no butcher who has been investigated was Jack the Ripper.

CHAPTER THIRTEEN

The prime suspects

In 1894, on 13 February, the *Sun* newspaper commenced a series of articles on a man named Thomas Cutbush, and his suggested link to the Whitechapel murders. In response to these articles, Sir Melville Macnaghten wrote a memorandum, in which he assessed the merits of Thomas Cutbush as a likely Ripper, and went on to describe three suspects who, in his opinion, were far more likely to be guilty of the Whitechapel murders than Cutbush himself.

It must be appreciated that this document was written by a man who at the time of writing was no less than the Chief Constable of the Metropolitan Police.

The privilege which this position brought would have undoubtedly included that he was in receipt of all of the known information on the Whitechapel killings, including, that which was of restricted circulation and was not discussed with the rank and file or the press. He was therefore in a very advantageous position to assess the evidence, and formulate an educated opinion on the identity or likelihood of a named individual being the Ripper.

Macnaghten named three primary suspects in his documents, and included a paragraph on each, outlining the identity of the suspect and describing, somewhat briefly, why the man was regarded as a likely Jack the Ripper.

Sir Melville, as he was at this time, would have had the benefit of formulating his opinion, not only with the complete documentary evidence, but with the added benefit of consultation with all of the senior officers involved in the case, and would have been in a far more comprehensive position with regard to the facts, than someone making a similar evaluation whilst the murders were being committed.

For this reason his memorandum has been, and must be, greatly respected, and has been the yardstick from which the case has been appraised for a number of years. Having got that out of the way, let us see what he actually wrote.

The three suspects named by Macnaghten were:

Montague John Druitt, a barrister. In the memorandum Mac-naghten mistakenly names him as a doctor. So much for being well informed. However he may have not wanted to reveal the true occupation of the suspect, for reasons which I will explain later.

Aaron Kosminski, a Polish Jew who was resident in Whitechapel.

Michael Ostrog, whose real name was Mikhail, but English pro-nunciations were frequently adopted by foreign immigrants.

Ostrog we have already covered, in the part of the book devoted to doctors, and we will now evaluate the information and evidence which we possess on the other two men, commencing with Mont-ague John Druitt.

The 'Macnaghten Memorandum', as these papers have now come to be called, is described in a later chapter of the book.

Montague John Druitt was born on 15 April 1857, at Wimborne, in Dorset. He was one of seven children, and his father was a practising doctor named William.

1870 was a dramatic year for young Montague. He won a scholar-ship to Winchester, which was the high point of his year, but his mother was taken ill, and her health deteriorated badly.

At Winchester he was recognise as having outstanding sporting ability, with a specific penchant towards the game of cricket, and 1876 saw him representing his school, in a cricket match played at Lords, albeit, on the bad side, it was also the year that his father was forced into retirement by ill-health. Montague, in the same year, was granted a scholarship to study at New College, Oxford, and he commenced his university education reading classics, later that same year.

In 1880 Druitt graduated from Oxford with a B.A. Third Class Honours Degree.

After achieving a degree of success in the college Debating Society, Montague chose to pursue a career in Law, and whilst continuing with his studies, he obtained a position of Assistant Master at Mr George Valentine's School at Number 9 Eliot Place, in Blackheath.

It was in this year 1881 that he commenced his association with Morden Cricket Club. He was later appointed Treasurer of the club, and continued to be a member until his untimely death.

In 1882, Druitt was admitted to the Inner Temple, but found that his earnings from teaching did not match his expenses of living and the costs of maintaining his legal studies, and so he borrowed some money from his father, in order to offset this hardship.

In 1883, Montague John Druitt was nominated and elected a member of the Marylebone Cricket Club (the M.C.C.), the most prestigious cricket club in the world.

Druitt's good years continued to be marred by bad news, and 1885, which in April saw him called to the bar, also saw his father die from a heart attack only a few months later.

Whether or not Druitt had fallen out with his father at some time or other, is not documented, but it is likely, because even though his father left an estate valued in excess of sixteen thousand pounds, Montague was not included in the beneficiaries. The main beneficiaries of his father's will were his mother, three sisters and an elder brother, William Harvey.

On being accepted at the bar, he joined the chambers of a Mr Jeff, of Number 9 King's Bench Walk, but he continued to teach at the school in Eliot Place.

As a barrister, he was attached to the Western Circuit, but he did not assume the responsibilities of a courtroom lawyer, and whether by preference or necessity, he worked on a part-time basis as a 'special pleader'.

A special pleader did not deliver a courtroom brief, as he was not ordinarily a bar-accepted barrister. Instead, he confined his efforts to the tuition and guidance of law students, and the attendance at cases which were settled in chambers, or if not through arbitration.

Druitt continued in this vein for the next couple of years, and found time to indulge in his favourite sport of cricket, in each of the seasons up to his death.

Contrary to popular belief, although his law career was proving to be less than an outstanding success, he was able to earn a comfortable living by integrating his legal and teaching duties.

It has been generally assumed that Druitt was a somewhat abysmal failure as a barrister, but Paul Begg, in his book *Jack the Ripper, the Uncensored Facts*, points out that if all of his finances are analysed, and the relevant expenses are taken into consideration, then Druitt could not possibly have amassed his estate value at death, by the income from his teaching position alone, and though not making a magnificent success of his law career, he must have earned a reasonable amount from legal fees in order for him to maintain his requisite lifestyle and attain the asset value which he possessed at his death.

At the end of the Michelmas term of 1888, Druitt was dismissed from his teaching post for being 'in serious trouble at the school'. The reason for his dismissal has never been uncovered, though the fact that it was nothing to do with his finances, and that it was an 'all boys school', has suggested to some that Druitt was a homosexual, and the reason for his dismissal was that something incriminating had occurred at the school, which had prompted the termination of his appointment.

If however Druitt's law career was not as lucrative as we are led to believe, then the healthy state of his finances tells us that another reason for his dismissal could have been what is today referred to as 'financial irregularities'. Both reasons could explain his subsequent suicide – i.e. the disgrace brought about by the public exhibition of his misdemeanours. It could further explain the fact that none of this was made public after his death. The old adage 'Don't speak ill of the dead' would, or could have been, the maxim.

Suffice to say, that on the last day of the year of 1888, the body of Montague John Druitt was dragged from a section of the River Thames, adjacent to Thorneycroft's Torpedo Works in Chiswick, by one Henry Winslade, a waterman. The body, which was fully clothed, had in its pockets four large stones, when it was examined on the spot by Constable George Moulson.

At the inquest, which was held in the Lamb and Tap in Chiswick, and at which Thomas Diplock officiated, PC Moulson testified that on searching the body he had found two bank cheques drawn on the London and Provincial Bank, one of which was for fifty pounds and the other for the sum of sixteen pounds. He had further found two pounds and ten shillings in gold coin, seven shillings in silver, and two pence in bronze. Further questioning revealed that the body also had in its possession a first-class season ticket for the train from Blackheath to London, and the return portion of a ticket from Hammersmith to Charing Cross. Other items recovered from the body and identified as belonging to Druitt were a gold chain and adornment, a silver watch, a pair of gloves and a white handkerchief.

It was estimated that the body had been in the water for about one month. This would have fitted in with the date on the Charing Cross ticket, which was reputed to be 1 December. If this is true, then it could establish the exact day of his death, as it can be assumed that the return portion was intended to be used when purchased, and it would only require to determine what type of return tickets were available and on sale in 1888, i.e. weekly/daily etc.

William Druitt, the elder brother of the deceased, also gave evidence at the inquest. He was a solicitor who practised in Bournemouth. He stated that he had heard from a friend on 11 December, that his

brother had not been seen for over a week. Armed with this intelligence he had travelled to London on being informed, and had made
enquiries with the purpose of tracing his brother. During the course
of these enquiries, he had discovered that Montague had been dismissed from the school by Mr Valentine, the Principal. When he had
gone to his brother's address, he had found among the possessions a
note which read: 'Since Friday I felt I was going to be like mother, and
the best thing for me was to die!' Is this the entire contents of the
suicide note?

The following account is originally taken from the 5 January 1889
edition of the *Acton Chiswick and Turnham Green Gazette*.

Shortly after midday on Monday, a waterman named Winslade,
of Chiswick, found the body of a man, well dressed, floating in
the Thames off Thorneycroft's. He at once informed a constable
and without delay, the body was conveyed to the mortuary.
On Wednesday afternoon Doctor Diplock, the Coroner, held
the Inquest at the Lamb and Tap, when the following evidence
was adduced. William H. Druitt said he lived at Bournemouth,
and that he was a solicitor. The deceased was his brother, who
was thirty-one last birthday. He was a barrister-at-law, and an
assistant master at a school in Blackheath. He had stayed with
the witness at Bournemouth for a night, towards the end of
October. Witness heard from a friend on 11 December that
deceased had not been heard of at his chambers for more than a
week. Witness then went to London to make enquiries, and at
Blackheath he found that the deceased had got into serious
trouble at the school, and had been dismissed. That was on 30
December [this was obviously a misprint and should have read
30 November]. Witness had deceased's things searched where
he resided, and found a paper addressed to him [produced].

The Coroner read this letter, which was to the effect 'Since
Friday I felt that I was going to be like mother, and the best
thing for me was to die.' Witness continuing, said deceased had
never made any attempt on his life before. His mother became
insane in July last. He had no other relative [this was a lie; Druitt
had numerous other relatives].

Henry Winslade was the next witness; he said that he lived at
Number 4 Shore Street, Paxton Road, and that he was a waterman. About one o'clock on Monday he was on the river in a
boat, when he saw the body floating. The tide was at half-flood

running up. He brought the body ashore and gave information to the police. PC George Moulson, 216T, said he searched the body, which was fully dressed, excepting the hat and collar. He found four large stones in each pocket in the top coat, £2 10s in gold, 7s in silver, 2d in bronze, two cheques on the London & Provincial Bank (one for £50 and the other for £16), a first-class season ticket from Blackheath to London (South Western Railway), a second-half return, Hammersmith to Charing Cross (dated 1 December), a silver watch, a gold chain with silver guinea attached, a pair of kid gloves, and a white handkerchief. There were no papers or letters of any kind. There were no marks of injury on the body, but it was rather decomposed. A verdict of suicide whilst in unsound mind was returned.

So ended the life of Montague John Druitt.

There is only one real argument that furnishes any speculation that Montague John Druitt was the Whitechapel murderer, and that is his inclusion in the Macnaghten document. That speculation is based totally on the fact that the person who highlighted his suspected involvement was a senior police officer, who wrote his famous memorandum in 1894, over five years after the last murder and, as I have stated previously, with hindsight and the benefit of access to all the known evidence and investigative documentation that had been generated both during and after the Ripper's reign of terror.

In 1959, Daniel Farson discovered the Aberconway version of the memorandum, which named Druitt as a probable Ripper culprit, and described him as:

> Mr M. J. Druitt, a doctor of about 41 years of age and of good family, who disappeared at the time of the Miller's Court murder, and whose body was found floating in the Thames on 31 Dec: i.e. 7 weeks after the said murder. The body was said to have been in the water for a month or more – on it was found a season ticket between Blackheath and London. From private information I have little doubt but that his own family suspected this man of being the Whitechapel murderer; it was alleged that he was sexually insane.

As it can be seen from the full transcript of the Macnaghten Memorandum later in the book, Macnaghten goes on to implicate

Druitt by implying that after the final murder his brain gave way totally and he committed suicide. He then conjectures, that after much careful and deliberate consideration, he is inclined to exonerate the last two, but he has always held strong opinions regarding No 1 [Druitt].

This appears at first glance to be poppycock; there is not even the slightest piece of information or evidence to link Montague John Druitt to the Whitechapel murders. There is no evidence or even hearsay which places him in the area of Whitechapel at the time of any of the murders, and if we look at his known movements, we find Annie Chapman was murdered between 5.30 a.m. and 6.00 a.m. on the morning of 8 September. At 11.00 a.m. on that morning, Druitt was playing cricket at Blackheath. Hardly the behaviour of a person who was on the verge of madness or indeed who had brutally murdered a prostitute in Whitechapel a mere five hours earlier.

Druitt was a first-class cricketer, and as such he could only have maintained that standard by having some element of discipline in his life, especially the night before a game. Remember that we are talking about a man who went through a first-class education with the benefit of two scholarships.

On 1 September, the day after the murder of Mary Ann Nichols, Druitt was again playing cricket, this time at Canford in Dorset.

Macnaghten goes on to say that after the Miller's Court murder his brain gave way totally. On 19 November, 10 days after the carnage in Miller's Court, Druitt attended a Board meeting of the cricket club, where he proposed 'that an acre of land be taken behind the grandstand, at a similar proportionate rent to that paid for the present land. The proposal to be referred to a committee to report.'

We are asked to believe that this was a man in the trauma of despair of going insane, who had murdered at least five women by this time, and less than two weeks later would commit suicide. But this is not so. This is the behaviour of a man who as yet has not been found out, who was earning a good living, who was a respected member of society, had a good social life, was a member of the M.C.C., was envied because of his sporting prowess, and may have also had a niggling doubt in the back of his mind concerning the insanity in his family, and who also had a secret.

I suggest that the reason that M. J. Druitt committed suicide was to avoid the humiliation of being exposed as a felon or homosexual. On 1 December he had lost his job, he was probably going to be ostracised from his circle of friends. He would undoubtedly lose his position as treasurer of the cricket club (especially if he had embezzled funds from the school) and if this was the reason for his dismissal then the cricket club would commence an investigation into its affairs, which could have resulted in a deficiency in their own accounts. The humiliation (if true) to a man of his standing and ability, coupled with the embarrassment to his family, must have depressed him to an extent that he saw the only way out to be to kill himself, which he did by filling his pockets with stones and jumping into the River Thames.

The only link between Druitt and the Whitechapel murders is that he happened to die at a similar time as the murders ceased, and as we know, the police were still investigating the crimes long after Druitt was dead, so they weren't as convinced as Melville Macnaghten that the Ripper was already dead.

There is no mention of Druitt in any of the files prior to the end of the Ripper murders. The only reason that I believe he is the prime suspect, is that everybody appears to be avoiding or ignoring the fact that he was not a doctor. I could understand the confusion if he was one of the other suspects who earned their living as a labourer of some sort, but not when the man's profession was a barrister. This tends to make me think that his identity was known to the police and that his suicide prevented his arrest. I personally believe that some time after the death of Mary Kelly, the police were looking for Druitt but could not find him, and before they could, he committed suicide.

The memorandum must only be used as a reference document, and Macnaghten himself does not inspire confidence in anyone who uses the memorandum as a basis for the Ripper identification. In itself, it is riddled with doubt and mistakes:

It refers to Druitt as a doctor . . . wrong.

It says that he was 41 years old . . . wrong.

It attempts to imply that Druitt died about 7 weeks before his body was found, in order to place the time of his death closer to the last of the Ripper murders. A rail ticket for 1 December was found on his body, and he seemed to have been in circulation up until the end of November at least. He was sacked on 30 November.

The memorandum refers to private information – this is tantamount to saying 'It's true, but I can't relay my source.' As I have previously stated, the Ripper case was so high-profile, and captured people's imagination all over the world, that if a solution was on the file it would have been impossible to keep it a secret.

It says that he has little doubt that his own family believed Druitt to be Jack the Ripper. There is no proof or evidence to support this statement, not one shred.

It alleges that Druitt was sexually insane. Once again there is no proof whatsoever to warrant this allegation.

It then proposes the theory that Druitt's brain gave way and that he committed suicide after the Miller's Court murder. If we are to believe that Druitt was so callous as to attend committee meetings after the last murder, and we are to believe that he played cricket after two of the murders, then why should someone so clinical choose to commit suicide. It is far more likely that he would have carried on as normal – as he had after the previous murders. If it had been during the cricket season when the last murder had taken place, I would have put my money on him going for a game of cricket; he'd have probably played a blinder.

It then goes on to say that after much careful and deliberate consideration, I am inclined to exonerate the last two. This phrase could be replaced with 'My guess is'.

My conclusion is that Macnaghten must have had a clue as to who the Ripper was. Sir Melville, due to his position, would have had access to all of the Ripper documentation. But there is no mention in the Ripper files of Montague John Druitt, and so his implication must have arisen after his death or conversely must have been the reason for his death. If this is not so then on the information available it definitely could not be placed at the door of Montague John Druitt.

I do, however, for the reasons outlined above, believe him to be a prime suspect for Jack the Ripper. Everybody refers to him as a doctor, and yet his background was well known. There was contact between his brother and the authorities; surely the mistake would have been corrected by someone in authority, but everyone appears to accept his occupation as doctor. I must question as to whether this misapprehension was deliberate.

It does not matter how much proof you have that an individual committed a certain crime. If that person dies before he is tried, then none of the evidence is worth a jot. The suspect has not been tried and found guilty of the crime so cannot therefore be accused of it after his death.

Druitt has another thing which I believe could link him to the Ripper and that is – modern thinking tends to place the Ripper as a right-handed person, and the majority of people believe that the mutilations were carried out from the right hand side of the body, with the corpse lying lengthways, thus inflicting the wounds with the right hand. If this is so, then why did the Ripper take the trouble to bend and open the legs of his victims? I personally believe, like the earlier Ripper pundits, that the Ripper was a left-handed person. The police sketches of the bodies *in situ* show the right arm of the victim being laid parallel to the body and roughly straight. If the Ripper had worked from the side of the body then he would have had to get the arm out of the way or else he would have had to kneel on it. No matter which way you look at it, the right arm becomes a problem if the mutilations were inflicted from the right hand side of the body. Also it must be appreciated that if the Ripper was right-handed and worked from between the legs then it is extremely difficult for him to perform the throat-cutting sequence as it is contained within the post mortem examinations that the throat was definitely cut from the victims left to right. A similar problem arises with the right leg.

I believe that the Ripper was left-handed and first strangled his victims by pressing down on the throats; this would account for the orientation of the thumb marks and the finger marks as described in the post mortem reports. The marks on the left side of the victim's neck are specified as being higher than those on the right. A left-handed person would place his left hand above his right when pressing down on his victim's throat.

The throat was cut twice, from the victim's left to right, as stated in the post mortems. If the body was laid down, then it is very easy for this operation to be performed by a left-handed person, but in order for a right-handed person to perform this feat his wrist would have to be at a very awkward angle for him to achieve left to right cut. I will not go any further into this at present but try it yourself to appreciate how difficult it would be for a right-handed assailant.

This is where the connection with Druitt comes in. if you look at the most famous photo of Montague John Druitt you will see that he is sat on a chair reading a book. Look carefully; he is holding the book in his right hand, thus allowing him to turn the pages with his favoured left hand. If you're left-handed, try it; you will find that you are more comfortable with the book in your right hand. Now look at the way he is sat. His legs are crossed with the left leg over the right, once again the pose of a person who favours his left side. It is more natural for a left-footed person to cross his left leg over his right. It is possible to do it the other way, but not as natural.

The connection between Druitt and the Ripper is that I believe that Druitt was left-handed.

The second suspect mentioned by Macnaghten was Aaron Kosminski. Aaron was a hairdresser; he was born in 1864 in Poland, and
came to England in 1882. At the time of the murders he was resident
in Sion Square, Whitechapel. Sir Melville Macnaghten describes
him thus:

> Kosminski, a Polish Jew, and a resident in Whitechapel. This
> man became insane owing to many years' indulgence in solit-
> ary vices. He had a great hatred for women, especially of the
> prostitute class, and had strong homicidal tendencies. He was
> removed to a lunatic asylum about March 1889. There were
> many circumstances connected with this man which made him
> a strong suspect.

Once again we must take issue with Macnaghten's memorandum
and question the credibility of its inferences.

He states that Kosminski became insane owing to many years
indulgence in solitary vices. You may have noted that at the time of
the Whitechapel murders Kosminski was only 24 years of age, and if
doubts about the year of his birth hold to be true (it may have been
1865) then he was only 23 years old.

I do not think that with the adult influences present in his life and
the abject poverty encountered throughout his childhood, Kosminski would have had sufficient time to engage in the solitary vices to
such an extent to enable him to be described as having indulged for
many years. Furthermore, it must be considered that at the time of
the murders Kosminski had only been in England for six years. I
instead choose to believe that Aaron Kosminski came to England
by agreement with his brother, who was already resident in Sion
Square, and that self-abuse had nothing whatsoever to do with his
insanity.

As stated by previous Ripper historians, Aaron Kosminski was admitted to Mile End Old Town Workhouse Infirmary for treatment
in July of 1890, and was noted as having been insane for two years.
He was, however, only kept in confinement for a period of three
days, after which he was discharged under the supervision of his
brother, who was named Wolf. I must ask: why is there no solid
evidence of his having been under investigation for the previous
nineteen months? And secondly, if he was placed into an infirmary,
and suspicion that he was Jack the Ripper was conjectured, do you
think by any stretch of the imagination that he would have been
allowed to be released back onto the streets?

Macnaghten carries on to say that Kosminski had a great hatred of the prostitute class, and had strong homicidal tendencies, yet this diagnosis is by no means confirmed by Doctor Houchin, who was the medical doctor who certified Kosminski into the Colney Hatch Asylum in 1891. Houchin stated that Kosminski 'declares that he is guided and his movements altogether controlled by an instinct that informs his mind, he says that he knows the movements of all mankind, he refuses food from others because he is told to do so, and he eats out of the gutter for the same reason.'

He is described at this time by the doctors of Colney Hatch as answering questions fairly, but inclined to be reticent and morose. They also state that he refused to be bathed. Kosminski was examined, and notes kept of his condition, and although they say that his disposition went from being apathetic to that of noisy excitement, they also described his habits as being clean and his health as fair.

It is noted, however, that on one occasion he had attacked an attendant with a chair, but at this time the man was admittedly in a state of mental deterioration, and his sanity continued to deteriorate to such an extent that on 13 April 1894, he was sent to the Leavesden Asylum for Imbeciles. Kosminski did however survive until 1919, and even then the cause of death was gangrene.

By this evidence it can be seen that in the year 1888 Kosminski's mental condition was not as yet in marked deterioration, and it is not until as late as 1893, a full five years after the murders, that he is first recorded as being of violent behaviour. Even on this isolated occasion, we are not told the circumstances of his outburst. The tolerance in asylums was not as liberal as it is today, and control of the inmates took preference over any treatment. Kosminski could have been provoked into the attack, or something untoward may have triggered it. I must ask myself in all truthfulness whether if I had been in a state where my behaviour was monitored whether the records would show me as relapsing into violent behaviour at some time or other, and I must admit that I have lost my temper a lot more than once within the last five years.

There is an absence of any mention in his notes with regard to Macnaghten's statement that he was violently anti-prostitutes, and furthermore, another conflict with Macnaghten's opinion is that throughout the records no reference is made of him being in the slightest bit homicidal.

Once again, in an attempt to link the suspect with the murders, Macnaghten fetches the date of Kosminski's confinement closer to the date of the last Ripper murder. There is no evidence of the confinement of Kosminski in 1889, and when assessing the modus operandi of the Ripper, we must point out that, if Kosminski was not incarcerated until the February of 1891, then he had remained on the streets of Whitechapel for a further period of over two years, during which time he had not committed any further murders; this is extremely unlikely for a killer of the type of the Ripper.

Macnaghten finishes with: 'There were many circs [circumstances] connected with this man, which made him a strong suspect', yet he fails to outline even one or two of these circumstances, in order to add weight to the statement. This is not in keeping with a person who is convinced of his logic, and once again it has the air of guesswork and the manufacturing of conclusions from coincidence.

Chief Inspector Donald Swanson, who was in charge of the Whitechapel murders investigation up until October of 1888, had a personal copy of Sir Robert Anderson's memoirs, called *The Lighter Side of My Life*. In this personal copy, Swanson made certain notes in the margins and at the end of the book. This has over the years came to be known as the 'Swanson Marginalia'. In a reference to Kosminski in the notes, it reads:

> Continuing from page 138. After the suspect had been identified at the 'Seaside Home', where he had been sent by us with difficulty, in order to subject him to identification, and he knew he was identified, on suspect's return to his brother's home in Whitechapel he was watched by police (City C.I.D.) by day and night. In a very short time, the suspect, with his hands tied behind his back, was sent to Stepney Workhouse and then to Colney Hatch, and died shortly afterwards.

We must appreciate, when analysing this statement, that Swanson's recollections were being submitted to paper a full twenty years after the events, and certain facts would have became muddled with the passage of time, but the statement still carries the conviction that the suspect mentioned was Kosminski, even though Swanson mistakenly thought that Kosminski had died shortly after his committal to Colney Hatch.

Swanson's recollection was based on an extract from Anderson's memoirs where he wrote: 'I will merely add that the only person who had ever had a good view of the murderer unhesitatingly identified the suspect the instant he was confronted with him; but he refused to give evidence against him.' With regard to this statement, I must take contention with the reasoning behind it. Whilst we appreciate that the Jews were loath to hand over one of their own to gentile justice, after identifying the suspect, and if indeed this proved beyond all reasonable doubt that he was the Ripper, then intense pressure would have been placed on the witness, to certify his identification in a court of law. Senior police officers would have had consultations with prominent Jews, including the Chief Rabbi, who had been previously consulted on other matters and aspects of the case.

The police in essence had so much to lose and nothing to gain from the refusal of the witness to identify the suspect, that a case would have been brought against him, to fetch the matter to the notice of the newspapers and hence the public, and so implicate the witness, and harry him into testifying. The public were hounding the police for their inefficiency and lack of progress, and the press were badgering for an arrest, and if a chance of the apprehension of Jack the Ripper was the prize, then anything other than full cooperation would not have been tolerated.

I will leave it there, for you to form your own opinion, but a more comprehensive analysis can be undertaken from the transcript of the Macnaghten Memorandum, the Swanson Marginalia and the section including the findings and thoughts of Sir Robert Anderson and Major Henry Smith, which are all to be found in a later chapter of the book.

My own personal opinion, which I have forced upon you throughout this chapter, is that I do not find that there is sufficient evidence to incriminate Kosminski, and the evidence which is available tends to absolve him of the crimes. The dates and times do not knit together, and there isn't any information that successfully implicates Kosminski or even calls into question his whereabouts at the time the crimes were committed, and yet Macnaghten appears to confirm that there were ample reasons and circumstances for believing Kosminski was the Ripper. I hate once again draw your attention to the fact that as previously stated the police were still searching for the Ripper up until four years later, and if they had caught him or they had known that he had died then this wouldn't have been the case. Jack the Ripper was someone who has yet to be mentioned and was never a part of the police investigation nor ever considered as a suspect.

New suspects continuously come to light, as further evidence is discovered. This evidence either implicates a new suspect or allows the revaluation of the existing evidence, which in turn serves to incriminate the new suspect.

One such person who has emerged in the last few years is James Maybrick, who was born in 1838, and was a well-known Liverpool cotton broker. Maybrick died in 1889, of arsenic poisoning, which was supposedly administered to him by his wife Florence. Florence was tried and convicted of his murder, but the conviction failed to recognise that Maybrick had used arsenic, along with other such substances, for a considerable period, in an effort to increase his manly prowess (it was supposedly an aphrodisiac) and to act as a general stimulant. This has raised a doubt whether the conviction of Florence was indeed a travesty of justice.

Maybrick had not been entertained as a Ripper suspect until the discovery of what is now known as the 'Maybrick Journal'. This journal takes the form of 63 pages of a Victorian scrapbook, from which the first 48 pages are missing.

The journal was first made public by a Mr Michael Barrett, a former scrap dealer from Liverpool, who received it from a drinking companion, a Mr Anthony Devereux.

Devereux assured Barrett that the journal was genuine, but refused to tell him from where and from whom he had obtained it, and under what circumstances. Devereux himself died in August of 1991; a good length of time elapsed before the journal was fetched into the public eye.

The contents of the journal are supposed to cover the activities of Jack the Ripper from April 1888 until May of 1889. If its contents are genuinely true, then it boasts a more than adequate amount of evidence to place beyond doubt the fact that it was referring to James Maybrick; and once again, if genuine he is the undoubted author, as it refers to Battlecrease House, the Maybrick family home, and further refers to his wife Florence and her lover Brierly. It further mentions the names of the children Bobo and Gladys, plus numerous other credentials which support the allegations.

It is a comprehensive document explaining how and why James Maybrick committed the murders, admitting his trips to London and cataloguing his increasing dependence on drugs.

It outlines the manner in which he killed the victims, and if it was authentic and the facts correct, it supports the popular appraisal that the Ripper executed five canonical murders, the victims of which are Mary Ann Nichols, Annie Chapman, Elizabeth Stride, Catharine Eddowes, and Mary Jane Kelly. It mentions the Goulston Street Graffiti, and describes the reason why he allowed the police to believe that the Ripper was a Jew. But! If it was written a number of years after the murders then it would include similar accuracy as any genuine document.

The journal further identifies Maybrick as the writer of the 'Dear Boss' letter, and makes various statements concerning the police refusal to release all of the known information concerning each murder. It further identifies what the writer regards as certain little clues which he left for the police. What a load of cobblers. It is widely acknowledged that the 'Dear Boss' Letter was composed by a journalist in order to promote sales of his newspaper.

The first person who Michael Barrett approached with the journal, was Doreen Montgomery, of the Rupert Crew Literary Agency. She in turn contacted the investigative writer Shirley Harrison, and commissioned her to write a book based on the journal; but first the provenance of the journal had to be established.

With this in mind the journal was taken to the British Museum, and inspected by the section which specialises in the authentication of documents. They also sought the opinion of Jarndyce Antiquarian Book Dealers. Both stated that there was not any evidence that the journal had been forged, but did not confirm categorically that the journal was genuine.

South Gryphon Publishers eventually purchased the publishing rights, after the work had been inspected by a number of publishing companies.

In 1992, Mr Robert Smith set out to prove that the document was genuine, and submitted the journal both for testing by scientific analysis, and for examination by handwriting experts.

The results of these tests, verified that the paper and the ink used, were both compatible with materials available in 1888–1889. This in essence proved nothing, as the paper was part of a Victorian scrapbook, which had been cut up to the extent that the first 48 pages of the book were missing, and the presence of gum on parts of the cut out portions which remained in the book, indicated that it had at one time been utilized as a photograph album or something very similar. This could mean that the photograph album could have been legitimately purchased, and the age determined by the photographs contained within. The analysis of the ink did not reveal its age, only that the constituents were similar to those available in 1888. If Mr Devereux was a printer, he would have had ample knowledge of the composition of the ink in the 1880s, and might indeed have had access to some original ink from that period, having obtained it from old stock or friends in the trade. The type of nib used to perform the writing is still readily available to this day, if you look in the right places.

With regard to the graphological analysis: this was undertaken by Anna Koren, who had been commissioned to inspect the writing by Paul Feldman, who was interested in making a film of the events contained within the journal, providing that the contents proved to be genuine.

Whilst I do not dispute the expertise of Anna Koren, I would request to know how the writing was presented to her, whether by individual and non-related words, or small passages taken at random. If the journal was given to her as a complete item, I would maintain that it is difficult to retain impartiality if you are confronted with a passage of writing which describes the murder and mutilation of a Jack the Ripper victim. In such circumstances it must be extremely difficult not to search the writings for evidence of compatibility, rather than adopt an unbiased inspection of the script.

With regard to the letter formations in the journal, being similar to those in the 'Dear Boss' letter, which Maybrick claims to have written, I contend on two counts.

The 'Dear Boss' letter and part of the journal referring to the letter were supposedly written on the same day, and if we are to believe the journal, then both written by the same hand. Why then in both of these documents is the style of handwriting so different? Regardless of whether we believe that certain letter formations indicate similarity, the writing for this part of September should be more or less identical.

The same argument can be promoted for the fact that the journal was examined by Doctor David Forshaw, a forensic psychiatrist, who ascertained that the writing might have originated from a serial killer.

The journal was further inspected and discussed by some eminent Ripper historians, who examined the contents, and found that there was nothing contained within the document, with regard to the historical facts, that immediately judged it to be a forgery. But if we think about it, any forgery worth its salt would surely adhere to the facts of the case, otherwise it would be totally pointless writing the thing in the first place.

The Ripper historians who were consulted were Paul Begg, Melvyn Fairclough, Martin Fido, Martin Howells, Donald Rumbelow, Keith Skinner, and Richard Whittington-Egan. All are respected in the field and all more than adequately qualified to make an educated judgement, and I do not think a single one of them totally committed themselves to the authenticity of the document.

A further consideration is that a lot of the knowledgable Ripperologists now accept that a journalist named Best was the author of the 'Dear Boss' letter, and let's face it, both of them couldn't have written it.

I contend that if the journal is a forgery, then it was undoubtedly assembled from information gleaned from the books on the Whitechapel murders, which these people have written, and as such all the facts should be accurate.

I further stumbled across two pieces of information at the time of the investigation of the journal, and I believe that when the quest for authenticity was under way, these two pieces of information were meant to be discovered, but their existence could not be prompted in any way by either the author of the journal or the seller, so they remained secret.

These two documents would have undoubtedly lent a great deal of weight to the Maybrick case had they been uncovered at the time of the publication. I still possess copies of these two documents, and they are not the 'Liverpool Letters'.

Further research undertaken by Shirley Harrison and her partner Sally Avery, established that on the eighteen dates of the duration of the journal, where Maybrick's movements can be verified, no conflict exists with the information contained within the journal. This is a point in the journal's favour, but may also be explained by the astuteness of the writer of the journal having researched Maybrick's movements prior to penning the document.

The *Sunday Times*, who had made known that they were interested in serialising the story, together with Warner Books, who were bidding for the American rights to the book, appointed independent experts to scrutinise the journal. Both found that the document was a forgery, and the *Sunday Times* published its findings in September 1993.

A further examination of Maybrick's will was compared with the journal. It indicated that both were not written by the same person. Pro-journal believers then questioned the authenticity of Maybrick having written the will. The results of 'ion migration' tests which were done by Doctor Rod McNeill indicated that the document was probably written between 1912 and 1933. These findings have been subject to devaluation by the pro-journalists, but it bears stating that even though they are reasonably diverse in their dating, neither of them, nor the time in between, would allow the document to have been written by James Maybrick. He was dead.

Scotland Yard investigated the journal in 1993, to establish if a fraud had been committed, and after extensive investigations, they concluded that there had been no criminal intent in the publication of the document, and the Crown Prosecution Service intended no action in this direction. However, they did intimate that the document was a forgery, and put its manufacture as being in the last ten years, and its source as Liverpool.

In July of 1992, Mr Albert Johnson purchased a gold watch from Stewart the Jewellers, of Wallasey in Cheshire. He thought nothing about it, but on inspection in 1993, he found on the inner side of the case the signature J. Maybrick, along with the words 'I am Jack', and the initials of the Whitechapel murder victims. There were two other sets of initials but to date no confirmation has been unearthed as to who they belonged to. I have not seen the watch and so cannot verify the initials, but if they exist I am of the opinion that further research will uncover the owners of these initials, as I firmly believe that the discovery of the watch was anticipated when the journal was written, and Mr Johnson was the unwitting discoverer of the coincidence.

I do not regard the journal as genuine, and my primary reason is that I do not believe that Elizabeth Stride was a Ripper victim, and I also believe in the likelihood that Martha Tabram was.

My doubt is accentuated by the points which I have outlined above, together with the following conditions, which I maintain cast major doubts on the authenticity of the journal.

1. Devereux refused to tell Barrett where he had got the diary from. This could intimate that the journal was stolen, but no such loss has been reported in the interim. In my opinion, if you are confident enough in a person to hand over such a document, then you would be confident enough in that same person to pass on its origin.

2. Rather coincidentally, Devereux died before the knowledge of the journal was made public.

3. Why did Devereux give such a document away? After reading it, he would doubtless have some realisation of its value – unless he knew that it was forged.

4. Devereux was a print worker, and would probably know of the recipe for ink of the 1880s, and may have known where some genuine ink could be located.

5. The family of Mr Devereux had no knowledge of the existence of the diary, and in my opinion, they would have had if he did.

6. The evidence with regard to the general information contained within the diary, which serves to provide and confirm the link with James Maybrick, could have been obtained from the local library or the reporting of the Florence Maybrick murder case.

7. As I have stated previously, I do not regard Elizabeth Stride as a Ripper victim.

8. In the 'Dear Boss' letter, the handwriting differs so much from that of the journal, and if genuine it should not.

9. The handwriting on the will of James Maybrick differs so much from that of the journal.

10. There are far too few crossings out and corrections in the diary, also spelling mistakes are minimal. This has supposedly been written by a person on drugs. The power of concentration disperses with the abuse, and mistakes become more frequent as the memory lapses.

11. I have my own doubts as to the grammar at times appearing to be too modern, and I propose to analyse the contents myself, with regard to the accepted spellings of the 1880s.

12. One thing that I would like to know, is the date when Stewart's the Jewellers purchased the watch, and if they have any record as to whom they purchased it from.

13. The diary wrongly identifies the position of the breasts of Kelly, after their removal by the killer. It states:

> I left nothing of the bitch. I placed it all over the room [wrong], time was on my hands, like the other whore, I cut off the bitches nose, all of it this time. I left nothing of her face to remember her by.
>
> I thought it a joke when I cut her breasts off, kissed them for a while. The taste of blood was sweet, the pleasure was over-whelming, will have to do it again. It thrilled me so. Left them on the table with some of the other stuff. Thought they be-longed there. They wanted a Slaughterman so I stripped what I could, laughed while I was doing so. Like the other bitches she ripped like a ripe peach.

You can see by this extract that he makes particular reference to the breasts being on the table. This is wrong. One breast was under the head, and the other was by the right foot.

14. Michael, his brother, is continuously cursed throughout the journal for his ability to write verse and rhyme. We know that

Michael Maybrick was a gifted composer, known by the name of Stephen Adams. Under this alias he wrote hundreds of songs. Michael was part of a song-writing team and his partner was called Frederick Weatherby. But it was Weatherby who wrote all of the lyrics to the songs, Michael was the one who contributed the melodies for the tunes and had minimal input, if any, into the lyrics. Surely as his brother, James Maybrick would have been aware of this.

15. Having not seen the original journal, I do not know whether there have been any pages left untouched at the back of the book.

The diary intimates that Maybrick lost the urge to kill after being treated by a Doctor Fuller in London.

The journal describes how Maybrick went back to his loving ways, and the writer of the book about the diary points out that the change in the style of writing implies and supports this outlook. Why, if this phase of his life was through, and he had repented of his ways, didn't he destroy the journal?

Maybrick, in the journal, comments that after a confidential consultation with his brother's private doctor, he was diagnosed as having very little the matter with him, and this he accounts for his change in attitude to life. He describes how this change prompts him to get rid of the knife. Why didn't the same reasoning bring about the destruction of the journal?

16. Maybrick refers to two murders he says were committed in Manchester. No record of any such murders has yet been found.

I therefore agree with contemporary opinion and condemn the journal as a forgery. I further reject outright the inclusion of James Maybrick as a suspected Jack the Ripper. If additional evidence appears which serves to implicate him, I shall review my opinion, but until that happens NO! James Maybrick was not Jack the Ripper.

Severin Klosowski
[alias George Chapman]

John Pizer (Pizer said
this was nothing like him)

Montague John Druitt

Neil Cream

Prince Albert Victor,
Duke of Clarence

Sir William Gull

Joe Barnett

Prince Albert Victor,
Duke of Clarence

Sir William Gull

Joe Barnett

PART THREE

*The Jack the Ripper
Investigation*

CHAPTER FOURTEEN

The police investigation

Having evaluated the victims and the suspects, it only remains for me to analyse the police input which assisted in the appraisal of the Ripper case, and to consider the thoughts, philosophy, judgment and opinions of the investigating squad; to analyse the beliefs and viewpoints of the senior Scotland Yard officers; to scrutinise the evidence and related information, which is considered of primary importance in the search for the murderer; and then to tell you who done it.

I have chosen when compiling this section of the book, to do so on the basis of the individual and his specific contribution, and whilst I have endeavoured to put a value on the information, I leave a lot of the assessment to the analysis of the reader.

With this in mind, I shall start with a short description of the Metropolitan Police.

The Metropolitan Police was founded in the year 1829, by Sir Robert Peel, and held the jurisdiction for the whole of London with the exception of the City itself. It was directly responsible to the Home Secretary of the day, and as such was particularly susceptible to political influence and interference.

In 1887, on 13 November, there was a demonstration which formed part of a series of planned marches, organised by the Federation of Radical Clubs, and whose sole purpose was to protest against the coercion and oppression in Ireland.

The destination of this particular march was Trafalgar Square, which had been banned for public meetings by the Police Commissioner.

The Metropolitan Police broke up the demonstration in the area of Parliament Street, with the use of such force and brutality, that the press of the day hounded the force for the extent of the violence used.

The 'Met' had further lost the favour of the people when they had turned out in massive numbers to suppress and restrain the weekly demonstrations carried out by the unemployed, and to put it mildly, at the time of the Ripper murders, they did not compare favourably with their sister force, the City of London Police.

The City of London Police, which was responsible to the City of London Corporation, held the jurisdiction for the area of the city, which was approximately one square mile to the north and west of London Bridge.

Catherine Eddowes was the only Ripper victim whose murder fell under the authority of the City police. They took an active part in the investigation of Jack the Ripper, though they did not totally integrate with their colleagues in the Met. However, they did exchange information with regard to the case; it is said that a common goal was envisaged, and that cooperation between the two forces was commendable throughout the investigation.

The way in which the police set about the investigation was heavily criticised in all areas of the press, and since then has been subjected to harsh treatment by Ripper historians and authors alike.

Their method appeared to be to flood the area of the East End with uniformed police patrols, to undertake house-to-house interviews, and afterwards follow through on any incriminating information which they received.

They further had police officers who were working under cover throughout the murders, and these officers would stop and question people on a random basis, in the hope of gleaning some snippet of information that would prove to be important in incriminating an individual, with an outside chance that this could lead to the apprehension of the culprit.

If there is any major criticism which is warranted, then it could be the subsequent analysis of the information received, and the coordination and cross-referencing of reports and documentation.

So much information was relaying itself back to the investigating C.I.D. Force, that the cross-referencing of the information and coordination between facts that maybe complemented one another, suffered. This is evident by the number of small errors which are evidenced in the surviving material, i.e. the misspelling of names, the wrong addresses, etc., However, if the methods had worked, there would have been no criticism, and anyway, this is still the core method employed by modern police, except we have a lot better coordination, and the increased benefit of greater knowledge of forensic science and the now virtually unchallengeable advantage of DNA, which allows the more successful pursuit of individual clues.

In 1888, forensic science was in its infancy, and they did not even have the benefit of a fingerprinting data bank of known criminals; in fact one of the Ripper letters seeks to inform the police of the existence of this method of detection. Microscopic examination of hair and fibres had not been developed, and of course DNA had not even been thought of.

The accepted way of assessing the time of death was by the estimation of the ambient temperature to that of the body and calculating the length of time it would have taken to reach this temperature. This was also assisted by knowing how long after death rigor mortis sets in, and a measured speculation as to the contents of the stomach.

Medical science did however allow for the assertion of the cause of death, and whether the infliction of any injuries had been before death or posthumous. Analysis of wounds could also be determined, how and with what type of weapon a specific injury had been inflicted, and in which direction the cut had been made.

There was also a certain element of expertise, though limited, in the psychological analysis of an individual's character, and a little was known as to the profile of this type of murderer, which was obtained from an assessment of his modus operandi.

It is becoming increasingly accepted that the method which the Ripper employed to dispatch his victims commenced with his hands around their throats. Whether or not he killed them by strangulation prior to the cutting of their throats, is still under debate.

The reason for the increasing acceptance of this method is the evidence which points to his having performed each murder with a minimal amount of sound. This stood less chance of being achieved if the throat was cut immediately and then an attempt was made to silence the victim. There are also the telltale bruises on the necks of the victims, which tend to indicate the position of thumbs and fingers on the necks.

To actually complete the killing by strangulation is not totally proven. It would definitely have been beneficial for the Ripper to kill them in this way, as it would mean that the heart had ceased to pump the blood around the body, and so the slashing of the throat would have created less of a spurting effect. This in turn would have decreased his chances of becoming stained by the copious quantities of blood which the neck arteries would release. It would further eliminate the need to ensure the position of the head when the wounds to the throat were inflicted.

The argument against this revolves around knowing whether the Ripper had a perverted need to mutilate the body while it still lived, and this would necessitate that he only partially strangled the victim, until consciousness was lost, and then he immediately cut the throat, or else waited until the victim showed signs of resuscitation.

The next step to broach is whether the murderer was left- or right-handed. I must admit that I do not know for certain, but what I do believe is that the mutilations, as described in the medical reports, and particularly those to the neck, would have been far more easily performed on an unconscious person by a left-handed person than by a right.

Let us first look at the evidence. It was impossible to determine in which direction the throat of Mary Jane Kelly was cut, due to the extent of the mutilations, but it is stated that the four other generally accepted victims were cut twice from left to right; this also includes Elizabeth Stride, whose throat was cut from her left to her right, but if you inspect the medical report you will notice that it does not comment on a double cut of the throat, only a single slash. Also it must be noted that the opinion of the medical examiner is that the wound was inflicted from behind. The throat being cut from behind indicates to me the attacker was a right-handed person, and the single cut of the throat means that it was highly unlikely that it was a Ripper murder.

If, as is generally accepted, the Ripper strangled his victim, and then lowered her to the ground, or strangled her whilst she was on the ground, then the obvious position from which to commence the post mortem attack would have been from between the victim's legs.

The evidence states that all of the victims' legs were akimbo (bent at the knee and spread apart) in order to carry out the mutilations. If the throat was cut from this position then it is virtually impossible that it be accomplished by a right-handed assailant. The hand can not be turned sufficiently to accomplish a complete cut around the throat from the victim's left to right.

There are however, two ways in which the Ripper could perform the murder, in which it would be easier for a right-handed person, assuming that the body is already unconscious and lying prone.

1. That the victim was approached from the right-hand side, at the level of the head, and the throat cut across the neck and towards the murderer. He would then need to change his position in order to perform the mutilations to the body.

2. That the murderer strangled the victim, and laid the body down whilst supporting it from behind. He could not have strangled the victim from behind because the thumb and finger marks to the neck would be in the wrong place. He then remained behind the head, and cut the throat from left to right from behind the body, using his right hand, and probably with the left hand on the chin. This would have been the most logical way to cut the throat if the strangulation had not been performed first, and would be a similar attack to those which you witness on many war films. But the marks of strangulation did not allow this attack.

Once again the attacker would require changing position in order to carry out the mutilations.

We must also take note of the murder of Mary Kelly, if we intend to challenge a right-handed Ripper.

Those who support a right-handed Ripper also support the number 1 method of cutting the throat, and say that the Ripper then carried out the mutilations of the bodies whilst kneeling at the right-hand side of the lying corpse. This I will accept is quite feasible for all of the murders excepting Mary Kelly's. Kelly was mutilated on a bed which was placed up against a wall. The killer could not get to the left-hand side of the bed and so to the right-hand side of the victim, unless he removed the bed away from the wall.

Also, the right arm of the victim becomes a problem when working from the right-hand side of the victim. The Ripper would need to place the right arm above the head, in order to get it out of the way, before kneeling down at the right side of the body to cut the throat and carry out the mutilations. Having completed the mutilations he would then need to replace the right hand down the side of the body, in order for it to comply with the artist's sketches of the bodies after death. This I believe is not a credible way to expect the murderer to act, just in order to eliminate a left-handed assailant. The way that I have looked at this scenario is to adopt the opposite approach, and assume that the Ripper was left-handed, and then to perform the murder exactly the opposite to the way in which it is described (i.e. the way of a right-handed person). I came to the conclusion that it was far too complicated to undertake in this way, and that a right-handed person would have slit the throat from right to left, and not in the way that the Ripper did, because Jack the Ripper was left-handed.

We must now discredit the commando-style attack from the rear of the victim, which I have said is feasible if the victim was not strangled first. But the victims were strangled before their throats were cut, and the reason is the presence of the thumb and fingermarks on the neck.

Further evidence of strangulation is supported by the inquests, which indicated that both Annie Chapman and Catharine Eddowes had swollen tongues protruding from their mouths, and Chapman, Kelly, and Elizabeth Stride all had their fists clenched. These are classic physical signs of strangulation having taken place.

This in no way means that I have changed my mind on the Ripper being innocent of the murder of Elizabeth Stride. My main reason for proclaiming his innocence of this murder is as follows.

Elizabeth Stride was the first victim of what is now commonly regarded as the double event, when the Ripper was supposedly interrupted before he completed his foul business, and consequently, an hour later he had gone to Mitre Square and murdered Catharine Eddowes to satiate his lust to kill. If you look at the medical examination of Elizabeth Stride you will see, in the opinion of the doctors, not only was her throat cut from behind, but the knife used in the attack was described thus:

> *He was of the opinion that the cut was made from left to right of the deceased, and from that therefore arose the unlikelihood of such a long knife having inflicted the wound described in the neck. The knife was not sharp pointed, but round and an inch across. There was nothing in the cut to show an incision of the point of any weapon.*

If we review the description of the weapon used in the other accepted Ripper murders, we see that the weapon was at least eight inches in length, with a pointed end. So we must accept that a different knife was used on Elizabeth Stride. This would not attract so much of my criticism if she had been murdered on a different night, but one hour after the murder of Stride, the Ripper horribly murdered and mutilated the body of Eddowes in a similar manner to the other victims and with the same knife as used on the other victims. And now comes the crunch. If Jack the Ripper murdered Eddowes with his usual knife then why did he use a different knife to kill Stride only one hour earlier, when he was already known to be carrying his usual knife?

If the Ripper had murdered them both on the same night and less than an hour apart, then he would have used the same knife.

For this reason I totally reject that the murder of Elizabeth Stride was the responsibility of Jack the Ripper.

CHAPTER FIFTEEN

The Jack the Ripper letters

Held in a file in the Public Record Office at Kew, Richmond, and marked MEPO 3/142, are the Jack the Ripper letters.

These letters vary in content from immature ramblings to chilling communications, and whilst they all purport to be genuine, none of them is regarded as such. I do not propose to include all of the letters in this chapter of the book, as most of them I also believe have no bearing whatsoever on the case. I do however include a selection of letters which I believe require further investigation, because of their content, or because they form an example of a specific point or argument which I would like to impart to our reader.

It must also be borne in mind when evaluating the social standing of the person who wrote the letters, and the identity of Jack the Ripper, if indeed he did write some of the communications, that even though education standards had vastly improved, and many Victorian lower class people could read and write, would they have had access to pen and paper? You can see by some of the examples that the letters were sent on small pieces of paper, and forty years later, schools were still issuing slates to children, when teaching them to write.

In the transcription of the letters I have also attempted to interfere with their content as little as possible. I have left most of the spelling mistakes and retained the lack of punctuation and poor grammar, and have only executed an alteration to the format of the letter in places where it is difficult to comprehend in its original form.

The correspondences that I do include are accepted as part of the Ripper culture, and are as follows.

The 'Dear Boss' letter – this is the most famous letter associated with the Ripper case. It was posted on 27 September 1888, and sent to the Central News Agency from the London E.C. postal area. I have left the wording and grammar similar to that of the original letter. Part of the letter is duplicated here.

Dear Boss

*I keep on hearing the police have caught me but they wont fix me just
yet. I have laughed when they look so clever and talk about being on the
right track. That joke about Leather Apron gave me real fits. I am
down on whores and I shant quit ripping them till I do get buckled.
Grand work the last job was. I gave the lady no time to squeal. How
can they catch me now. I love my work and want to start again. You
will soon hear of me with my funny little games. I saved some of the
proper red stuff in a ginger beer bottle over the last job to write with
but it went thick like glue and I cant use it. Red ink is fit enough I hope
ha. Ha. The next job I do I shall clip the ladys ears off and send to the
police officers just for jolly wouldnt you. Keep this letter back till I do a
bit more work, then give it out straight. My knife's so nice and sharp I
want to get to work right away if I get a chance.*
Good Luck.

> *Yours Truly*
>
> *Jack the Ripper*

Don't mind me giving the trade name
Wasnt good enough to post this before I got all the red ink
Off my hands curse it
No luck yet. They say I'm a doctor now ha ha.

Whilst this letter was treated seriously at the time it was sent, and served to name the Whitechapel murderer as 'Jack the Ripper' as it was the first time that the phrase was used, it is now regarded as almost certain to have been written by a *Star* newspaper journalist. The probable culprit was a journalist named Best, who was described in an article in the magazine *Crime and Detection* in 1966. The writer of the article described the details thus:

> Returning homewards with me, Best discussed murders – the Whitechapel murders in particular. With much amplifying detail he talked of his days as a penny-a-liner on the *Star* newspaper. As a freelance he had covered the Whitechapel murders from the discovery of Tabram. He claimed that he, and a provincial colleague, were responsible for all the Ripper letters, to keep the business alive. 'In those days it was far easier to get details and facts from the police, than today.' Best did not mind me having these facts so many years later, and said a close reading of the *Star* of the time might be informative, and that an experienced graphologist with an open mind would be able to find in the original letters 'numerous earmarks' of an experienced journalist at work; the pen used was called a 'Waverley nib' and was deliberately battered to achieve the impression of semi-literacy and 'National School' training!. Best scoffed at the notion that the 'Ripper' has written a single word about his crimes.

Best definitely did not write all of the Ripper letters and did not appreciate the amount of letters received by the police, otherwise he would not have made this statement.

I see no reason to doubt this statement, as the writer of the article had nothing to gain from telling lies, and years later I can appreciate the irony of Best himself revealing that the Dear Boss letter was in essence manufactured in order to boost sales.

The next communication was posted on 1 October 1888, and takes the form of a postcard. It is written in crayon, and because of its undoubted link to the Dear Boss letter, it is generally accepted that this was composed and penned by the same source, and once again its primary intention was to sell newspapers. It reads:

I was not codding dear old Boss when I gave you the tip, youll hear about saucy Jacky's work tomorrow double event this time number one squealed a bit couldn't finish straight off. Had no time to get ears for police thanks for keeping last letter back till I got to work again.

Jack the Ripper

When they were first published both these epistles were assumed to have come from the murderer, but in later years Sir Robert Anderson and Chief Inspector Swanson both stated that the Jack the Ripper letters were probably written by a journalist, who they could identify, and as such the letters may not have been given a lot of importance during the actual investigation, though they have formed an integral part of the police investigation in all of the popular films about the subject. In point of fact, as I have stated above, a journalist for the magazine *Crime and Detection* printed details of a conversation in which Best, a freelance reporter, admitted the authorship of the letters and even qualified his statement by saying that a 'Waverley nib' was used for the purpose.

The third letter which has been debated, and is the most likely to have originated from the real Jack the Ripper, is the letter which was sent to George Lusk, the President of the Whitechapel Vigilance Committee, and which when delivered, was accompanied by part of a woman's kidney. Lusk received the letter on 16 October 1888

and it is now referred to as the Lusk Letter, or the Letter from Hell.
It reads:

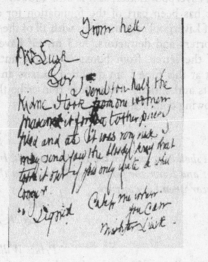

From hell

Mr Lusk
  Sor
I send you half the kidne I took from one women prasarved it for you
tother piece I fried and ate it was very nise I may send you the bloody
knif that took it out if you only wate a whil longer
                    Signed   Catch me when
                                you can
                            Mishter Lusk

The writing was later analysed by a Canadian graphologist named
Macleod, who said of the writer that, he was probably aged 20 to
45 years with a rudimentary education, possibly a heavy drinker,
cockily self-confident. He stated that in his opinion the writing
showed a mind with a vicious drive and great cunning. The writer
would be capable of conceiving and carrying out any atrocity, would
possess sufficient intelligence to hold down a steady job, and be
quite capable of concealing his true personality. I have already
given my own opinions with regard to this letter, in the chapter
devoted to Catharine Eddowes, and as such I have nothing to add to
my earlier opinions.

Another letter which was purportedly sent to the police and the press was the Liverpool Letter, as it is now known.

This letter has been part of the foundation for a case that the Ripper was of Liverpool origin, and as with all of the theories, it also has its supporters and detractors. As I myself have only read the transcript of the letter, from books by fellow authors, I do not consider that at this time I am qualified to pass an opinion on its contents or its authenticity. I therefore transcribe the letter with a minimal following comment.

> Liverpool
> 29th inst.
>
> BEWARE I shall be at work on the 1st and 2nd inst. In 'Minories' at 12 midnight and I give the police a good chance but there is never a policeman near when I am at work.
>
> Yours
> JACK THE RIPPER
>
> Prince William St, L'pool
>
> What fools the police are. I even give them the name of the street where I am living.
>
> Yours
> JACK THE RIPPER

It has been suggested that an event on 1st or 2nd inst cannot be predicted on the 29th inst, but the writer may not have possessed sufficient education to discriminate in this way, and I tend to think that the writer refers to the 1st and 2nd dates of the following month. Either way, I believe the letter to be the work of a hoaxer, and not to be taken seriously.

The next letter which we propose to address was received by Scotland Yard on 25 July 1889, and runs:

> Dear Boss
> You have not caught me yet you see, with all your cunning, with all your 'Lees' with all your blue bottles.
>
> I have made two narrow squeaks this week, but still though disturbed I got clear before I could get to work. I will give the foreigners a turn now I think – for a change – Germans especially if I can – I was conversing with two or three of your men last night – their eyes of course were shut and thus they did not see my bag.

Ask any of your men who were on duty last night in Piccadilly (Circus End) if they saw a gentleman put 2 dragoon guard sergeants into a hansom. I was close by & heard him talk about shedding blood in Egypt I will soon shed more in England.

I hope you read mark and learn all that you can if you do so you may or may not catch

Jack the Ripper

I do not consider this letter to be genuine. It is composed after it was generally accepted that the Ripper was in some way out of commission, and would play havoc with all the known and accepted information on the personality profile of the murderer.

If it is ever proved to be a genuine communication from the murderer then it undoubtedly puts the cat among the pigeons.

Out would go numerous suspects and the vast array of theories would be discredited, but until such times it can safely be ignored.

The next letter is of a disturbing nature and was dated the day after Mary Kelly was found murdered in Miller's Court. It reads:

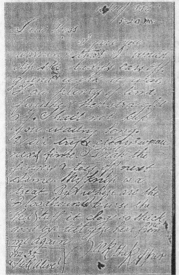

The address on the envelope is as follows:

The Boss
Leman Street Police Station
Whitechapel

10/11/1888
5.20 p.m.

Dear Boss
I gave you warning I would clip the lady's ears off, grand work it was,
Had plenty of time, finished her straight off. Shall not keep you
waiting long, I will try and clear 3 women next time. My knife is a
treat. But where are the Bloodhounds, curse the red stuff it clogs so
thick, goodbye till you hear from me again

Jack
The
Ripper

I'm 35 & still alive

The date of this letter gives it an air of authenticity, until we take
into account that there were no more murders after this letter.
However, the contents of the letter are reasonably accurate in their
substance though without the ring of truth that a genuine letter
would contain, such as a singular fact that only the killer would be
aware of. I am therefore personally inclined to summarily dismiss
it as a hoax letter, but instead I will leave the reader to make up his
own mind.

The next communication which we choose to inspect, was sent on 3
November 88 and is badly written in places, consisting of a jumble of
information, but it can be seen that the word asleep is in an educated
hand. The lettering on the band of paper is probably the police
identification. It was particularly hard to decipher but it reads:

3rd November 88
London

Asleep   Italian
            London docks   Cattleman
                S S Govan
                    Yours Obliging
Will send mi
adress for reward   R H B mate to mum
When you ave
arested hime

                        Whitechapel

This jumble of words seems at first to make no sense. The writing is obviously from someone who struggles to form the words and whose spelling and legibility leave a lot to be desired, I took the offer from the world's greatest armchair detective to help me with the interpretation of the words and the result was as you see above.

If we analyse the contents we find that 'Cattleman' is probably referring to a Cattle Boat which is docked in the 'London Docks', and the 'S S Govan? most likely refers to the name of the ship, i.e. Steamship Govan or something similar . . . . . . The 'R H B' I would hazard is the initials of the sender who is intimating that he will get back in touch after the Italian man has been arrested.

The ship quite obviously had a short name, the 'S.S. G . . .' or at least we are quite certain that the name began with 'G', was of a short length, and probably ended in 'M or N'. I would like to know whether this fits the description of any ship that was docked during the period for each of the murders. I am in the process of investigating this information, and would lend more weight to the note if it conformed to these parameters.

The next sample was addressed to Sir Charles Warren and was stamped as received by the police on 6 October 1888. it reads as follows:

ABS
. . . . ?
Manchester
Dear Sir
I don't think I do enough murders so shall not only do them in White-chapel but in Brixton, Battersea & Clapham. If I cant get enough women to do I shall cut up men, boys & girls, just to keep my hand in practice. Ha! ha! You will never find me in Whitechapel by the description in the papers 5ft 7inches is all wrong. I expect to rip a woman or to on the common at Clapham Junction one day next week. Ha. Ha. ha. I will send you the heart by parcels post.

Ha! Ha!
Bye Bye
Dear Sir
Yours when caught
The Whore Killer

I believe that this letter was a hoax, but that the man who sent it was quite obviously deranged. This letter with its reference to Manchester could I believe have been used to endorse the credibility of James Maybrick's claim to being the Ripper. The handwriting does look reasonably similar to one of the samples of Maybrick's handwriting, but the supporters of Maybrick's claim would have to withdraw their condemnation as to the authenticity of the writing of his will for this to be further discussed.

Our next letter has the postmark London W.C. and was date-stamped by the police 19 Oct. 88. It is addressed to a person named Smith, but the first name or title is questionable as either 'Her, Mr or Mer'. It reads as follows:

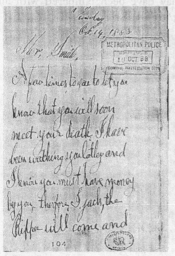

Sunday
Oct 14, 1888
Mer, Smith
A few lines to you to let you know that you will soon meet your death.
I have been watching you latley and I know you must have money by
you, therefore, I Jack the Ripper will come and carve you the same as I
did the other whores in Whitechaple I shall come quite unexpected and
I shant give you time to squeal for my knife is nice and sharp.
Yours truly Jack, the Ripper

As you can see the writer confuses the first word and because he uses the phrase 'the other whores' I would hazard a guess that it was addressed to a specific female. He has made some elementary grammar and spelling mistakes such as 'Whitechaple' and 'latley' but has spelt the words 'unexpected', 'whores', and 'squeal' correctly. If we therefore consider that his spelling could be a little erratic, then I would take a guess that the person to whom the letter was addressed was Mary Smith. If this is so then we do not have a letter from the Ripper, but we do have a threatening letter to Mary Smith. Either way this is not a letter from the real Jack the Ripper.

The next letter appears to have the letters 'FP' or 'TP' in the top left hand corner of the first page and tells a story which is hard to believe. It also appears as if the date may have been tampered with and changed from the 23/11/88 to 23/10/88. It reads:

23/10/88

Dear Sirs
I Jack the Ripper thanks you for your trouble in trying to catch me, but it wont do.
   I suppose you would like to know why I am killing so many women, the answer is simply this. When I was at San Francisco in July 1888, I lent three women from London about £100 sterling to pay some debts they had got into, promising to pay me back in a months time, and seeing that they had a ladylike look I lent the money. Well when the month passed by I asked for my money but I found that they had sneaked off to London. scent of those women that swindled me so basely,

living like well to do ladies on the money they had sneaked from me, never mind that I'll have em yet afore I'm done, damn em, To tell you the truth you ought be obliged to me for killing such a deuced lot of vermin, why they are ten times worse than men.

I remain etc.

Jack the Ripper

Alias

H. S. C. Battersea

This is purely a case of sour grapes. The writer, it appears has, in July of 1888, been fleeced whilst in San Francisco, by three women who, by the gist of it, had used the money which he loaned them to pay for their passage back to London.

The writer if telling the truth, is justifiably angry, and incredibly naïve, and is venting his anger by writing a letter. I believe that is as far as it would go, and do not lay any credibility to this letter being the work of Jack the Ripper

The next letter in our series was once again from Manchester. It was posted on 22 November 88, and the text reads thus:

Manchester

Nov 22 '88

Dear Boss

I am staying in Manchester at present but dressed as a poor man, a navvie. Saw the paper, and you have had a letter from someone signed J. Ripper from Portsmouth soon after I did the last job (Kelly) & have been in Manchester since. Had nothing to do since Kelly but seen Jewess girls everyday will visit London about Sunday ready to begin once again on Monday when i will do another I will tell you all when i get copped. Goodbye old fellow till i return

> *Yours Truly*
> *Jack the Ripper*

This appears to be the letter of a braggart, but once again it is from Manchester. The scribe appears to have been reasonably educated for the Victorian times, and the writing itself is quite legible. There is a constant mistake of using the lower case 'i' and the use of the phrase 'Jewess girls' is grammatically incorrect, but a logical error. The letter intimates that another murder will take place on the Monday following 22 November and as no such murder took place then we are inclined to dismiss the letter as a hoax.

The next letter was addressed to The Inspector at the Police Station at Gypsy Hill. It was dated 6 October 1888, and was found between Princess Road and Selhurst Railway Station. It reads:

6th October 1888
You thought yourself very clever I reckon when you informed the police But you made a mistake if you thought I didn't see you. Now I know you know me and I see your little game, and I mean to finish you and send your ears to your wife if you show this to the police or help them, if you do I will finish you. It's no use you're trying to get out of my way Because I have you when you don't expect it and I keep my word as you soon see and rip you up

Yours truly
Jack the Ripper

[down the side of the letter is written]
you see, I know your address

Once again this appears to be a threatening letter at first glance, but the intimations within the text are frightening. The letter was discovered the week after the double event, and we must question the secret which the writer wants to keep, and is threatening the addressee to make sure that he keeps it. I believe that the recipient of this correspondence had already received the letter and had abandoned it in the place where it was found, intending the police to find it. I do not think from a personal point of view that the writer was Jack the Ripper, and I do not think that there is any reference to the Whitechapel murders hidden within its contents.

We now move on to a letter that was received by the police on 10 October 1888. I have had to enhance large parts of the letter in order to permit its inclusion. And the original hand is only unaltered from the part 'You police are a smart lot'. It reads as follows:

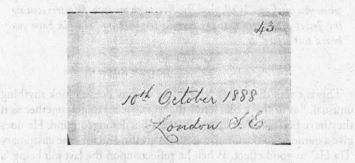

Dear Boss
You will be surprised to find that this comes from yours as of old Jack
the Ripper. Ha Ha. if my old friend Mr Warren is dead you can read
it. You might remember me if you try and think a little Ha Ha. the
last job was a bad one and no mistake nearly buckled and meant it to be
best of the lot curse it, Ha Ha . I'm alive yet and you'll soon find it out.
I mean to go on again when I get the chance, wont it be nice dear old
Boss to have the good old times once again you never caught me and you
never will Ha Ha

You police are a smart lot, the lot of you couldn't catch me one man.
Where have I been Dear Boss you'd like to know. Abroad, if you would
like to know, and just come back ready to go on with my work and stop
when you catch me. Well, good Bye Boss wish me luck. Winters coming
the Jewes are people that are blamed for nothing "Ha Ha have you
heard this before.

yours truly
Jack the Ripper

This is a very disturbing letter. The writing doesn't look anything
unusual, but in the actual letter the words seem to gel together as if
they have been written by someone with a deranged mind. He does
give a quote from the Goulston Street graffiti and uses the customary
'Ha Ha' to good effect. When he reflects upon the last job being 'a
bad one and no mistake' he is referring to the murder of Catharine
Eddowes, which up until this time was by far the worst. *He also says*

'meant it to be the best of the lot'. Could this be that he had a special reason for killing Eddowes?

The letter also indicates a sort of confidence and self-belief, and sardonic mocking of the people who are trying to catch him. He does not use the proper spelling of the word 'Jews' but instead spells it 'Jewes'. When we look into the Goulston Street graffiti, we find that not everyone thought that the Ripper wrote 'Juwes', some thought it was 'Jewes', others 'Jeuws', and we must appreciate that the present-ation of the graffiti in the book, is actually a version copied out by a policeman prior to the writing being removed, and not a photograph of the original. The main point which I would like to make with regard to this letter is the extraordinary way in which the writer writes the word 'and'. Note the extended gap between the 'a' and the 'n'. I have searched through all the papers in my possession but without success because I have seen the word 'and' presented in a similar stretched/flat fashion as it is in this letter, among my copious copies of the Ripper material. Until then, I cannot formulate an opinion as to whether the letter is the work of Jack the Ripper or not.

The following letter was sent to the Central News Agency, in Bridge Street, London on 5 October 1888. It was then passed on to a Mr Williamson, who was the Chief Constable C.I.D of the Metro-politan Police. It reads:

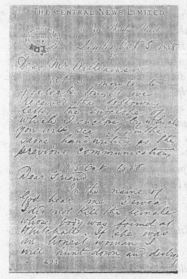
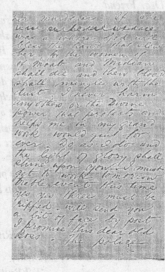

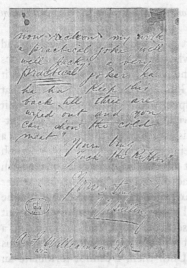

Dear Mr Williamson

At 5 minutes to 9 o'clock tonight we received the following letter; the envelope of which I enclose by which you will see it is in the same handwriting as the previous communications.

5 Oct 1888

Dear Friend

In the name of God hear me, I swear I did not kill the female whose body was found at Whitehall. If she was an honest woman I will hunt down and destroy her murderer. If she was a whore God will bless the hand that slew her, for the women of Moab and Midian shall die and their blood shall mingle with the dust. I never harm any others, or the divine power that protects and helps me in my grand work would quit forever. Do as I do and the light of glory shall shine upon you. I must get to work tomorrow treble event this time, yes yes three must be ripped. Will send you a bit of face by post

I promise this dear old Boss.

The police now reckon my work a practical joke well well Jacky's a very practical joker ha ha ha Keep this back till three are wiped out and you can show the cold meat."

> Yours truly
>   Jack the Ripper"

> Yours truly
>   T J Bulling

This is undoubtedly the work of a religious nut or someone trying to sound like a religious nut, and seeing that we did not get the three murders then I think we can safely assume that it is not the work of Jack the Ripper. By the introduction, it appears that the Central News Agency believed that it is in the same hand as the Dear Boss letter, but as the letter is transcribed, and the original writing is confined to the envelope (which we haven't got), then we are unable to comment on the similarity in the writing. However, even if the writing did match, it would only be another letter sent by a journalist in order to increase circulation.

As an additional piece of information, T. J. Bulling was a journalist who worked for the Central News Agency. He has been previously mentioned in the Littlechild letter but his name was wrongly spelled as Bullen.

The next letter is dated 18 November 1888 and was sent to Inspector Abberline. It reads as follows:

Insp Abberline

18 November 1888

Dear Boss
The police officers 'ave not caught me yet, how can they when I am used to police work. I shall keep on ripping whores till I do get buckled. I want to get to work right away if I get a chance and will do another one

indoors. The last job was a grand one It took me a long time to do. My
knifes so nice and sharp I shall take the next ladys scalp. You will hear
of my funny little games again on Friday night Good Luck
Yours truly
Jack the Ripper

This letter was sent to Insp. Abberline after the last murder was committed. It does refer to the last murder taking a long time, which we are aware is correct. Mary Kelly was by far the most mutilated of all the Ripper's victims. He also threatens to do another murder indoors, and the letter is clearly out to shock. There weren't any more killings after this date, so we must therefore assume that the letter is the work of a crank, and can safely be discounted.

Our next letter was received in October of 1888 and originated from Philadelphia. It is identified with Docket No. 1157 and reads:

286

October 1888
Philadelphia

Docket Nᵒ 1157

Honourablyful
I take great pleasure in giving you my present whereabouts for the
benefit of the Scotland Yard Boys. I am very sorry that I did not have
time to finish my work with the London Whores and regret to state
that I must leave them alone for a short while. I am now safe in New
York and will travel over to Philadelphia, and when I have the lay of
the locality I might take a notion to do a little ripping there. Goodbye
dear friend, I will let you here from me before long with a little more
culling and ripping. I said 20 and I fancy I will make it 40 on account
of the slight delay in operations.

Yours Lovingly
Jack
the ripper

The letter itself is undated, and the only date ascribed to it is that
of October 1888 given by the police. This is a pity, as if it had been
dated after 16 November it could quite credibly have been used
to support the case against Francis Tumblety, if we remember the
police had requested a copy of Tumblety's handwriting, presumably
for comparison.

The hand itself is adequate and the contents somewhat scornful of
the police, both of which traits are credited to Tumblety. It boasts
that he is now safe in New York and that he will travel to Philadelphia; both places are destinations Tumblety is known to have
frequented.

The next letter which we review was allocated the docket number 244 and is acknowledged by the police as received on 24 September 1888. The letter is however dated Saturday 8 December 1888, so it is obvious that the letter must have been written post the last murder. It reads:

Chatham
Saturday
December 8th
1888

Dear Boss
I am still at liberty the last job was not bad in (Whitechapel) but I guess the next will be a (damn) sight worse. The police about here are fine looking fellows I had the pleasure of drinking with one this morning and asked him what he thought about my glorious work I guess I will make a double shuffle of it this time. Me and my pal (you bet) I have got one or two set and soon shall have more (Ha Ha Ha) I can see better specimens in garrison towns, look out in a day or two
    Yours (not yet) Jack the
             Ripper
             (Ha Ha)

This letter was sent long enough after the murders had ended to safely reject it as being by the hand of Jack the Ripper. It appears to be the letter of a person who has a lot bigger opinion of himself than other people would have had. Probably written by a coward who strove for attention, and the pal who he talks of probably didn't exist. This letter was definitely not the work of the Whitechapel murderer.

The next letter is undated and appears to be the work of an exhibitionist. It was received by the police on 9 October 1888 and reads:

I am as you see by this now amongst the slogging town of Brum and mean to play my part well & vigorously amongst its inhabitants I have already spotted from its number, 3 girls, and before one week is passed after receiving this, 3 families will be thrown into a state of delightful mourning Ha. Ha. My bloody whim must have its way, do not be surprised 15 murders must be completed, then I will kill myself to cheat the scaffold. For I know you cannot catch me & may I be even present in your dreams

Jack the Ripper

The contents of this letter are very threatening and obviously the work of some egotist. The letter however refers I believe to Birmingham, and as no murder spree took place during the threatened time, and the murder of Kelly was yet to take place in Whitechapel, I believe that this is unquestionably a hoax letter put together by some sick person but not by Jack the Ripper.

The next missive which we are to review was sourced by the police as 'Neath' and was catalogued as received by them on 4 November 1888, only four days before the night of Kelly's murder. It reads thus:

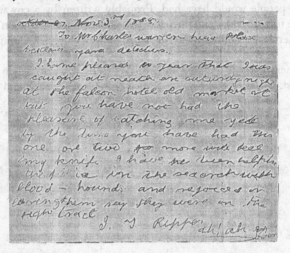

Nov 3rd 1888
To Mr Charles Warren head Police Scotland Yard detectives
I hame [am] pleased to year [hear] that I was caught at neath on
Saturday night at the falcon hotel old market street but you have not
had the pleasure of catching me yet by the time you have had this one or
two more will feel my knife I have been helping the police in the search
with blood - hounds and rejoiced in hearing them say they were on the
right track

J. T. Ripper
ah! ah

The writer has no use whatsoever for punctuation, capital letters and grammar. He wrongly spells the words 'am' and 'hear' yet rightly signifies the words 'pleasure' and 'rejoiced'. This makes me question other assumptions: i.e. that the Ripper deliberately misspelled certain words in order to misrepresent his intelligence and education. He seems to be well informed on the progress of the investigation and even claims to have taken part in the bloodhound trials. Could this have been the actions of a man who thinks himself so superior to the police that he monitored the bloodhound tests for success, to see if they were going to be a threat to him, or is it just the idle boast of a nobody who craves notice?

I will not at this time condemn this letter as a hoax, because whilst it boasts of the police failure to catch him, it does not make the police job any easier by giving any insight into forthcoming murders. This is something that many of the letters which come from the cranks do. I believe that this letter could have been the work of Jack the Ripper.

The next letter which we examine is undated, which is a pity, because the importance of the content depends on when it was written.

It was catalogued as having been received by the police on 10 September 1889, and is postmarked London W.C. The letter itself bears a Metropolitan Police stamp of 13 September 1889. All this seems quite above board until we look at the actual letter which has on it an incomplete date of 'Wednesday 10th 1888 or 1889? This can not apply to the September of 1889 as the 10th in this month fell on a Tuesday. I know the writer may not be as well educated as we may have wished but I do believe that he would have known what the day was when he wrote the letter. It reads:

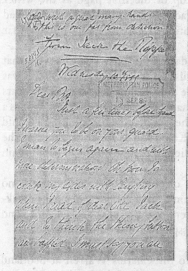
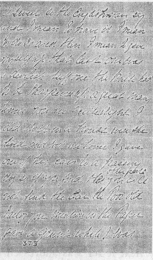

Wednesday 10th 1888

Dear Boss

Just a few lines before hand I warn you to be on your guard I mean to begin again and with more determination Oh how I crack my sides with laughing when I read of dear old Jack and I think the shiny Button are baffled I must say you are a jewel as the Englishman might say, and I mean to have it. I mean to do so and then I mean to give myself up. The last one was a devilish tuff one. The knife had to be sharpened up a great many times you are quite right I did do it in a house were she lived and took me home I gave one of her ears to a passing dog so if you find her other parts you will not find the Ear the poor old sailor who you mentioned gave a grunt while I was [I can write a great many hands this is one] far from detection

From Jack the Ripper

I have placed a portion of the letter in brackets, as I do not believe that this is a relevant part of the message but is just an impromptu boast. The letter ends at the top of the first page as the writer obviously ran out of space. The actual end of the letter should read 'the poor old sailor, who you mentioned, gave a grunt, while I was far from detection'.

As we cannot be certain of the date of the letter I take the view that we cannot therefore summarily dismiss its contents. If the letter was delivered anywhere near the date after Kelly's murder then it bears significance. I am however reasonably confident in discounting it as a Ripper letter, firstly because of the fact that the only murder it could be describing was that of Mary Kelly, and as we know that was the last of the series, and so the prediction that he meant to begin again did not come to fruition.

Once again we find examples of poor spelling, and virtually no punctuation is present, which again demonstrates the danger of making assumptions based on a precept of the Ripper's intelligence and education, and his deliberate misspelling of certain words.

My next letter was addressed to Sir Charles Warren at Scotland Yard. It is undated but bears the postmark of 10 October 1888. and reads:

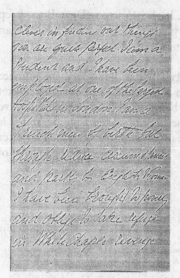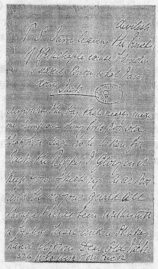

Devilish clever in finding out things you are quite perfect. I am a
Student and I have been employed At one of the largest Hospitals in
London I am a French man by birth but through induce circum-
stances And partly by English Women I have been brought to Poverty
and oblige to take refuge in Whitechapel Revenge disporting the boy
that nearly made me jump Out of my boots poor old chap how sad to be
taken for Jack the Ripper I glory in it, keep your spirits up Dear Bos
and be on your guard all though this has been written with a beating
heart and a shaking hand its from Dear Old Jack. Who wish you luck
P S I am leaving the vicinity of Whitechapel excuse blunder I scarcely
know what I am doing

Jack

I note that the reader mentions the fact that he is a student; this
was a very popular conception which took root after the inquest
reported that the murder and mutilations had shown a degree of
anatomical knowledge. There is no idle boast stating when he
intends to commit the next atrocity, and he even informs us that
he is leaving Whitechapel. He mentions that he is writing the
letter with shaking hands and beating heart but I do not believe he
is Jack the Ripper. The letter is fabricated and does not ring true,
it omits any facts concerning the murders and does not predict
whether or not they are to continue. There is also a degree of

reverence and concern for Sir Charles Warren (Dear Boss, keep your spirits up and be on your guard). This is more advice than threat and is not like our killer at all.

The following out of the ordinary letter was allocated the number 292. It was logged as received on 4 December and assigned docket number 1035. It was sourced as being from Taunton but I believe this to be in error. The envelope is postmarked London and it is addressed to: The Inspector, Leman Street Police Station. The letter itself is dated 10 November 1888. This is the day after the murder of Mary Kelly. It reads:

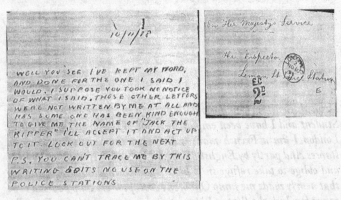

10/11/88

WELL YOU SEE I'VE KEPT MY WORD, AND DONE FOR THE ONE I SAID I WOULD. I SUPPOSE YOU TOOK NO NOTICE OF WHAT I SAID. THOSE OTHER LETTERS WERE NOT WRITTEN BY ME AT ALL, AND HAS SOME ONE HAS BEEN KIND ENOUGH TO GIVE ME THE NAME OF 'JACK THE RIPPER' I'LL ACCEPT IT AND ACT UP TO IT. LOOK OUT FOR THE NEXT.

P. S. YOU CAN'T TRACE ME BY THIS WRITING SO IT'S NO USE ON THE POLICE STATIONS

This letter is very interesting as it one of the few letters that was sent to the police that didn't include the signature Jack the Ripper. It makes a factual reference to the fact that he has kept his word. This could only be with reference to the murder of Mary Kelly, which had only taken place only the day before the letter was sent.

He also states 'I suppose you took no notice of what I said', which would indicate a previous correspondence foretelling the murder and the possibility that it also named the victim. If he had done this there would have been no question that the letter was genuine, but we must also remember that if he had forewarned the police of the name of the victim, they would have at the very least put her under surveillance, and would have captured the culprit either before or after the murder. He does appear to genuinely question the authenticity of the previous letters and derides the police for ignoring his warning, but he also warns of a next victim and we know in retrospect that there wasn't one. So for that reason I do not believe that Jack the Ripper wrote this letter.

The penultimate letter which I include was received by the police on 19 July 1889. it was sent to Mister Monro, who by now was the Metropolitan Police Commissioner. It reads as follows:

Say now boss no 'narrow escape' your officers are lying free I had heaps of time guess I am coming west now for I am a moral man and am determined to put down wholesale whoredom I am going for "lady prostitutes" now, and there are millions

then too some well known card sharper, and other sports will be attended to I have located one a scorcher not far from Portman square who will be found properly carved and his tool ears tongue and ears I shall cut off and send you leaving his guts on the side walk this wont be mean anyway I am a new god to reform abuses and advantage players must be stopped going around – no more crimping at poker and the sucker shall have a look in no more ringing in a cold deck no more reflectors for that boss I guess he may chuck his bugs and lds out for I am to his vile right away, he euchred a mate of mine and so I am going to stick him and others pig sticking I call it shall be around Scotland yard soon I am a 'Foreign butcher' am I you cannot locate me I guess but you see I am an instrument of god for good and when I divide neatly some lilled bosses wife a lady lord guess you will be mad and feel a bit mean and there is no one to squeal for I do it all myself

. . . .

a word of warning beware and protect your low immoral pot bellied prince god has marked him for destruction and "Mutilation", keep your men about pimlico and belgravia – soon there will be two more stiff on the side walks and ladies now

<table>
<tr><td></td><td>*his tool*</td></tr>
<tr><td>*"Jack the ripper"*</td><td>*n.b. other letters not gen*</td></tr>
<tr><td></td><td>*j.t.r.*</td></tr>
</table>

This letter can be safely ignored in our quest for Jack the Ripper. There are some interesting points in it, i.e. the use of the word 'sidewalks' has connotations of America. This would fit in nicely with the hatred he appears to harbour for anyone to do with cards, and games where wagers change hands. He then goes into a religious tirade, attempting to obtain approval and absolution for his crimes (which I very much doubt that he did). This was a man who had probably been cheated and had not received retribution, and so was hitting out at society for his own satisfaction. He was not Jack the Ripper.

The last inclusion I propose to make in this chapter of correspondence is done because I believe it is the type of draft an intelligent Jack the Ripper would send to the police. Another ironic coincidence, which I would credit the real Ripper with the intellect to foresee, is that the letter was received by the Metropolitan Police on 9 November 1889, the first anniversary of the death of Mary Jane Kelly and the end of the killings.

It is very difficult to read and as such I do not believe that anyone has taken the trouble to fathom out this communication previously. I therefore consider that this is the first time that the contents have ever been analysed.

Probably, like myself, previous researchers have seen that it was dated 1889, and immediately dismissed it as a hoax. Only the greatest armchair detective pointed out its relevance, otherwise I also would have ignored it. The individual statements make fascinating reading especially if we substitute a known suspect for the writer.

The letter itself was not dated and is extensive in content. It can not have been created on a whim as it has been made to rhyme, and must consequently have been composed over a period of time, with the objective of the anniversary in mind. To have been penned by an East End resident, as it appears to indicate, would definitely make that resident a well educated man of above average intelligence.

I have taken the liberty of numbering the lines so as to facilitate easier analysis afterwards. It reads as follows . . .

Dear Boss

My first shot to justify myself I now fire	1
You will see by this that I am not a liar	2
Frank Stupid fool, believes me to be insane	3
his next shotlog will be that I' am vain	4
in the papers you sometimes see	5
Letters written by him but not by me	6
He declares an accomplice is concerned	7
That he has to prove and learn	8
He describes my complexion dark with good looks	9
Tells the public he has my boots	10
Togs & suits many of hats I wear	11
And people at me often stare	12
Those spots are bullydogs and not fair	13
The . . . spots I packed 2 pair in High street	14
To pay rent buy food (no gin) but meats	15
The togs have I, 2 suits both dark and blue over coat	16
Hard felt hats and blue ruff on my throat	17
Long hair no beard and none on chin	18
Do neither smoke swill or touch gin	19
I told the man you should try and catch him	20
Say another word old chap I'll you run in	21
Think old donkey, say he can me catch	22

He would soon find in me his match   23

The detectives of London are all blind   24

They know they cannot me search and find   25

I think you should a spark make   26

He would soon be tired and try to escape   27

Operations will begin this month again   28

Despatch the police and good strong men   29

Whitechapel alone is the place   30

The knife is keen quick and leaves no trace   31

My blood boils and with indignation rages   32

To perpetuate more bloody outrages   33

Destitution against which I desperately fight   34

Destroy the filthy . . . . whores of the night   35

Frequenters of Theatres Music Halls and drinkers of hellish Gin   36

Dejected lost cast down ragged mean and thin   37

My knives are sharp and very keen   38

Determined I swear which I mean   39

At Finsbury St Paul's ward near   40

I never dossed the rents are too dear   41

Whitechapel High Street ward near my home [near army home]   42

I always do my work alone   43

Some months hard gone near Finsbury Square   44

An eccentric man lived with an unmarried pair   45

Mad on vivisection (the cutting up of animals) he gave me a treat   46

He would get hold of a dog or cat for a joke   47

With one cut of the knife sever its throat   48

He was very dark, teeth (if new) pocked and marked disease
*   on nose, I did him meet*   49

The tale is false there never was a lad   50

Who wrote essays on women bad   51

I'm not a flash away Belgravian Swell   52

Although self taught I can write and spell   53

The Miller's Court murder a disgusting affair   54

Done by a Polish Knacker rather fair   55

The morn (of the morrow) I went to the place   56

Had a shine but left by haste   57

I spoke to a policeman who saw the sight   58

And informed me it was done by a Knacker in the night   59

The swellish flash away I echo I very often see   60

Treating Whores and asking them to tea   61

One night hard gone I did a policeman meet   62

Treated and walked with him down High Street   63
The letter addressed to 22 Hammersmith Road   64
Was written by some vulgar lying toad   65
Old Frank thinks me a flash away swell   66
A first rate man and in a fine house I dwell   67
A fourpenny doss I have at a common east End dosshouse   68
And do not dine on aristocratic grouse   69
When I by luck some browns and bobs do make   70
Sometimes early, but at others very late   71
He thinks a very large fortune I have got   72
And love to ridicule and me mock   73
He well knowing the reason that I kill   74
The whorish women then I him   75
Money (of which) Sir I have none   76
But I detest ridiculous sarcastic puns and fun   77

J. Ripper
I will write more in a few days

As I have stated, this is a weird story which was held back by the writer until the anniversary of the end of the murders. It is filled with innuendos and clues to the writer. He has an associate called Frank who believes him to be insane. Frank writes letters to the papers accusing him of the crimes. Frank describes the writer in these letters.

He carries on and describes the many hats he wears, and that people stare at him. He says he has long hair and does not sport a beard. Pizer was described by one witness as having 'an unpleasant face that framed an excessively repellent grin'. It is implied that Pizer made hats, and several different hats were witnessed by people at the various murders. If we look at the part of the book devoted to John Pizer you will see that many more of the facts pertain to and describe him. I will therefore analyse the verses as if John Pizer was the writer.

1. I have waited until exactly one year after the date of the last murder before getting in touch with you, and only now am I willing to tell you something about myself. This alone should have alerted some of the more erudite of the more senior Police Officers, who must have suspected that the murders had ceased with the death of Mary Kelly and that later murders were not the work of Jack the Ripper.

2. He states that what we are about to read is the truth. He is telling the reader before he reads the poem that there are

certain inclusions within the verse which serve to prove that the writer is indeed Jack the Ripper. The line itself has the ring of truth about it.

3. Frank thinks I am insane, but he doesn't realise that I know what he is doing. The only man named Frank who has surfaced as a Ripper suspect is Frank Edwards, but due to the affluence ascribed to this man, any correlation is very doubtful.

4. I do not understand the implications of this line.

5. Someone was writing to the papers. This may have been referring to Frank, but also it may be referring to someone who is claiming to be the Ripper.

6. These letters were not written by the writer, but if Frank is the scribe then our writer is well aware that he is writing to the papers.

7. This could be referring to a specific letter which indicates that the Ripper has an accomplice, which is unlikely, or it could refer to Frank implying that he knows our writer is the Ripper or at the very least is involved in some way, but he needs more proof, which is more likely the interpretation of the writer.

8. He needs proof of my involvement.

9. I am swarthy or sun-tanned or even dark-haired. There is an insinuation of immense vanity in the writer describing himself as such. It may be appertaining to a description given by a witness. There were a number of witnesses who gave this description. It may also serve to mislead, by being an opposite or at the very least a description which bears little resmblance to the writer's actual physical appearance. In this respect it could describe Pizer, especially if the writer was being disparaging in his portrayal of his appearance.

10. During the inquest on Mary Connolly a witness named Sarah Colwell stated that she had heard a woman screaming and running.

It appeared to her as if the woman was being attacked as she ran, but she did not hear the sound of any chasing footsteps. This gave rise to the story that the Ripper had rubber-soled boots or rubber strips fixed to his boots so as not to make any noise. This is the only reason that I can think of, to make the boots important to the writer. Did any of the Ripper letters contain a reference to boots? If so this may have been the letter that our writer is referring to.

If we look to John Kelly being the Ripper, then we remember that Catharine Eddowes pawned a pair of Kelly's
boots. Could it be that Frank redeemed these boots from the
pawnbroker? This inference is somewhat vague but could be
important.

11. I have some clothes and suits to wear, and a selection of hats.
When Pizer's lodgings were searched, a selection of hats was
removed, and we must remember that witnesses described the
Ripper as being 'shabbily gentile'.

12. It was said that Pizer's features would attract attention with his
staring eyes, big thick neck and the fixed unsettling grin. He
had the looks that would mark him in a crowd, and remember,
by his own admission he did not laugh or smile as ordinary
people would, but have you looked at the photos of Montague
Druitt who also seems to have shining eyes.

13. Do not understand.

14. . . . .

15. Probably refers to payment received for the packing job in
line 14.

16. He is telling us he owns 2 dark suits and a blue overcoat.

17. He wears felt hats and a blue starched, frilled, or pleated
collar. The blue ruff could also refer to a scarf tied at the
throat.

18. He has long hair, and is clean-shaven. Together with the dark
looks this fits the description given by a number of witnesses
including Mrs Elizabeth Darrell and Police Constable William Smith.

19. He doesn't smoke, nor does he drink beer or gin.

20. The next two lines appear to refer to some conversation he
has had with a policeman concerning the failure to capture
the Ripper.

21. See above.

22. He resents the attitude of the policeman. Calls him a donkey
and boasts that there is no chance of his being caught by such
fools.

23. All throughout this section of the poem he declares his disdain
for the police.

24. He carries on deriding the police and their efforts to apprehend him. The way he refers to London could mean that he is
an outsider who frequents London.

25. See above.

26. See below.

27. He says that if they had a spark of intelligence between them they might be in with a chance of catching him, but even then he would prove to be too much for them.

28. This line and the next few lines read like the aspirations of someone who doubts what he is writing, and doesn't realistically believe that he will carry it out. He threatens to recommence and we know from history that he did not, at least I do not know of any murders in November of 1889. But it could also read as a reminiscence of last year. It may indeed be the swansong of a man who is no longer physically capable of carrying out the murders. It is clear from the content of the verse that the writer is the object of some teasing, and that he resents the fact that he is unable to boast about his being Jack the Ripper, so he may be in poor health at this time. It must also be noticed that he refers to 'Operations will begin'. Could this be that he believes that when he killed he was carrying out an operation, or is it just a turn of phrase used to describe the murders?

29. He tells them to prepare for the restart of the murders.

30. He says that Whitechapel is the place to kill, and that he still has the knife he used in the previous murders.

31. See above.

32. In the next two lines he describes the rage and the need to kill again.

33. See above.

34. He is describing his motivation as being his loathing of the common man and people who booze and revel.

35. He rants about killing prostitutes and whores.

36. He hates people who live for worldly pleasures.

37. This could be further derision of the poor or conversely an expression of how he empathises with them.

38. In this line he talks of the knives being sharp and ready.

39. He is reiterating his threat to start again; maybe as I have said previously, this is just the bravado and swansong of somebody who is now incapable of recommencing the murders and is in poor health. Both Pizer and John Kelly were referred to as being in poor health at the time of the murders. Over the next 12 months they will not have got any better. The preceding 10 lines somehow seem to imply that he would love to continue with the murders. The rage still burning inside him, and the

psychological need to begin again, would have been difficult to control, but even if he was by now incapable of physically murdering anyone then the verse describes the fury that still rages within him. We must also bear in mind that he is aware that Frank is monitoring his movements and must therefore consider that if he were to recommence killing, there is now a greater chance of him being unmasked.

40. He mentions Finsbury and St Paul's and I do not understand the implication of the next two words, but they could just imply that he could not afford to stay in this area.

41. He says he never dossed because it was too dear. He is not saying that all dosshouses are too dear but only that accommodation in Finsbury/St Paul's was too expensive.

42. His home was near Whitechapel High Street Ward. It may also refer to it being located near an Army Home.

43. He says he always works alone; this may not be his killing work but his normal work.

44. He again mentions Finsbury Square.

45. He gives us a clue that a lodger lived there, who was his mentor or who awoke the need to kill in him. Or was he himself the lodger and the male member of the unmarried couple was the vivisectionist?

46. This man used to cut up animals.

47. He says he regarded it as a treat when the man cut a cat's or dog's throat just for fun.

48. See above, but is he referring to himself as the vivisectionist?

49. If this is him, then he has given us a description, and with this description he would certainly have attracted the stares of the public. Pockmarked face, diseased nose, dark complexion. Dark could also suggest his character. At the very least he has furnished us with a description of himself or his mentor.

50. He now says he is lying, but is this the admission that he did not watch the vivisectionist mutilate the animals, that it was himself who started off in this way?

51. He refers to writing essays on bad women (possibly letters to the press). He says he has lied and there is no lad, only him.

52. He tells us he is not a flash Harry from Belgravia, but that he can read and write and has taught himself to do these things.

53. See above, and if correct he is a clever fellow. Pizer was said to be above average intelligence, and John Kelly was referred to

as intelligent. Both would have needed to be well educated to attain the vocabulary required to tell this story in rhyme.

54. He mentions the final murder in the series and reflects on how disgusting it was. How did he know that Mary Kelly was the last victim? The police at this time still treated the next three victims as Ripper murders (the police and Home Office files tell us that). Only the murderer would know when he had stopped.

55. I do not know the inference of 'knacker' but in the dictionaries of the day it could be used to describe a 'saddler', 'a maker of toys', and of course 'a horse slaughterer' or in this instance 'a whore slaughterer'.

56. He says the day after the murder of Mary Kelly he visited the site.

57. Maybe something happened or he was recognised because he left in haste.

58. He says that whilst there he spoke to a policeman. Surely one of the policemen would have remembered this, if indeed the letter had been deciphered and the question asked by superiors. Perhaps I am being over-optimistic, as a year had now passed since the described murder.

59. He again informs us who was responsible for the murder. Again this could be a general description of the mutilation to the body.

60. Is he referring to someone that he thinks is responsible, and telling us he is aware of the identity of this person, or is he talking about himself?

61. He talks about the behaviour of the Toff referred to in line 60.

62. He refers to meeting a policeman not long ago. Was this the policeman Pizer talked to in the Seven Sisters Road on the night of the murder of Mary Nichols?

63. He says he treated the policeman. Does this mean gave him some money, and walked with him down the High Street. This does not have to be Whitechapel High Street.

64. This line refers to a letter addressed to 22 Hammersmith Road. What was at number 22 Hammersmith Road? Did one of the Ripper letters get sent to this address? This could be a most important piece of information. Was it ever investigated? I don't believe so. What existed at this address and what does the census tell us about who lived there and what did he look like?

65. Says it was a liar who wrote the letter to Hammersmith Road. If there is a letter in the files with this address, I have not seen it, but if it can be found then it is most important that the contents be analysed. They may hold the key to the mystery. Is this another dig at Frank?

66. Old Frank makes another appearance. Obviously not liked or trusted by the writer, but Frank thinks the writer some kind of Toff, so we can assume that our scribe dressed better then the average East Ender.

67. The writer is self-opinionated and thinks he is better than others. He is resentful that people whom he regards as less intelligent than himself are better off than him. He is aggrieved at his low position in society, and could have started killing to prove his superior intelligence.

68. He is telling us he lives in one of the East End dosshouses. If the police had checked which ward the Whitechapel High Street was in, and then checked them all looking for a regular named Frank, who was probably an oldish man, then they would have been well on their way to catching this man. (I do not believe that John Pizer stayed regularly in a dosshouse, though I may be wrong, as it is common knowledge that he was not staying at his usual address for the censuses of 1871 and 1881, and there is evidence that the police tried to interview 'Mickeldy Joe' at a lodging house in Brick Lane which was supposed to be a frequent haunt of 'Leather Apron'.) Could this have been the place where Old Frank lived?

69. This refers to his eating habits. He has already stated that he did not drink.

70. He is about to tell us what he does when he has a bit of money.

71. He is telling us that he occasionally works during the day but more often at night.

72. He is saying that at these times, or generally, this is the reason that Frank thinks he is well off.

73. He does not like this man called Frank, and it appears that Frank takes the mickey out of him at certain times. This could mean that our writer is a bit of a loner and keeps himself to himself. Not an outgoing personality who would argue with Old Frank, but a person who would allow the resentment to build up inside him.

74. He says that Frank knows he is the killer and also knows why he is doing it. I wonder whether Frank was being paid

to keep silent. This confirms the reason why the murders did
not restart.

75. He states that he kills prostitutes and would like to kill Frank
    as well. It would be nice to know if a murder of someone called
    Frank took place after the date of this letter, and if so what was
    his address.

76. He now tells us that he has no money at the time he is writing
    the letter. Is this another implication that he may be being
    blackmailed?

77. He tells us a little about his character. He doesn't mix with
    other people very well and does not seem to be capable of
    joining in jokes and general banter. He won't have had many
    mates, if any.

I think you will agree that this is a very strange communication. The
time taken to compose it would have been counted in hours if not
days. The content is uncanny and has the ring of truth about it. It
suggests someone who has a mission and who harbours numerous
hates and inner turmoil.

A lot of the content is ambiguous and confusing, and I do not
profess to be any better than my reader at determining which parts
are important and which are insignificant.

I personally believe that the importance of this document can not
be overstressed, and I further consider that it is a profile of the
person who could and may have committed the murders.

If genuine, as I believe it could very well be, this amounts to a
stunning confession by Jack the Ripper. It also gives an insight into
how he could have been located if the searchers had been clever
enough, and with all of this information at hand, how he still might
be identified.

I believe that from 1889 up until the present day, nobody has taken
the trouble to evaluate the subject matter contained within the verse,
and as such this communication has been ignored for over 100 years.
It must now be up to all of the excellent researchers to scrutinise the
contents and see if we can identify the writer.

That writer could be John Pizer, and if it is he could be the
Whitechapel Murderer.

There is also a non-corroborated story related by R. Thurston
Hopkins in *Life and Death at the Old Bailey*. It relates to a man who is
described as 'Mr Moring' (not his real name), who was suspected by
Hopkins, and who fitted the description given by George Hutchinson. Moring was known to be a drug-addicted poet who was a

friend of Mary Kelly, and the son of an affluent East End trader. Could this be our man?

You can see by the contents that he wants to be caught. If he isn't caught, then he only ever remains an anonymous murderer. He is taunting the police. Part of the text could refer to the fact that they have let him off the hook; lines 22 to 27 could have connotations of this. If it is Pizer then he had been in custody and positively identified, yet he was released after the man Violenia was discredited for some reason. This would have given him a high degree of confidence in his ability to outwit the police.

And finally: I have stated at the beginning that the reason I found this letter so interesting and important was that the writer wrote in the first line '*My first shot to justify myself I now fire*', and he timed the correspondence to arrive on the first anniversary of the death of Mary Jane Kelly, and in doing so coincided with the date we now accept as the end of the Jack the Ripper murders. He is telling the police that he has committed the murders with this first line. Certainly up until 1890 and beyond, the police may have had their suspicions that the murders were over but they continued to hunt for the Ripper. Between the day of Kelly's murder and the date this letter was sent, a further four murders were committed. They were:

Annie Farmer, on 21 November 1888.

Rose Mylett, on 20 December 1888.

Alice McKenzie, on 17 July 1889.

Alice Hart? on or about 10 September 1889.

This poetic correspondence was sent on 9 November 1889.

For all of this time the police were treating these murders as the work of the Ripper, but our writer didn't. He knew when the Ripper murders had stopped, and he waited exactly one year to tell the police. Why? If our writer wasn't Jack the Ripper, then how did he know exactly what date to send the letter on? Only the killer would have known that fact for certain, and it wasn't for some decades later that the number of Ripper attributed murders was generally reduced to five, with Mary Kelly being accepted as the last, on 9 November 1888.

Dr Robert Anderson thought that there were six victims and he was head of the Police C.I.D. Even when he closed the files in 1892, he still believed that there were six.

All of the above murders are included in the Metropolitan Police 'Whitechapel Murders' file, so at the time of the murders must have been presumed to be the work of the Ripper.

I have not included this deliberation in the 'Whodunit' chapter of the book, preferring to allow the reader to evaluate this evidence separately, but I think you will agree that this letter has been wrongly ignored for over 100 years, and the writer I personally believe was Jack the Ripper.

Contained within the Home Office files and dated 10 November is a pardon which has been offered to accomplices and persons who may be implicated in the murders but are not actually Jack the Ripper. The pardon reads as follows:

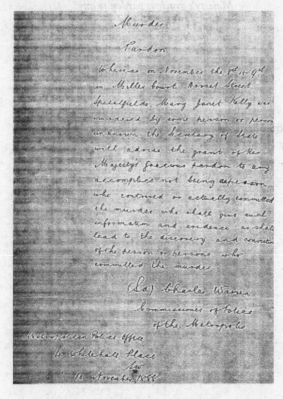

Murder

Pardon

*Whereas on November the 8th or 9th
in Miller Court Dorset Street
Spitalfields, Mary Janet Kelly was
murdered by some person or persons
unknown, the Secretary of State
will advise the grant of Her
Majesty's gracious pardon to any
accomplice, not being a person
who contrived or actually committed
the murder*

> *(Sd) Charles Warren
> Commissioner of Police
> Of the Metropolis*

*Metropolitan Police Office
4 Whitehall Place
SW
10 November 1888*

CHAPTER SIXTEEN

The paperwork

I am absolutely astonished at the lack of Metropolitan Police documentation, and the negligence with which the records have been maintained. This situation has now been rectified, but in the interim important information has been lost and stolen, and is still missing. On initially learning of the extent of the files available on the Ripper case, I was dumbfounded at their scarceness.

The Whitechapel murder investigation lasted for a period of four years, during which time, at its peak, there were over 400 uniformed officers on patrol alone. These were backed by the extensive C.I.D. coverage, senior officer briefings, reports written by investigating officers, thousands of witnesses who were interviewed, and the list goes on. You will be amazed to know that the amount of information retained in the Metropolitan Police files, is negligible. In addition to that which we have already stated, where are the following?

1. Notebooks of the uniformed police, or details of their reports

2. Details and records of interviews. At the very least you would have expected a list of names and addresses of all of the persons who had been interviewed.

3. Logbooks, which were filled in from one shift to the next, or the details of what was passed on, which progress reports, to superiors and the Home Office.

4. Results of house-to-house investigations: which houses had been attended, and which had been missed.

5. Statements of officers of all ranks, as to how their part of the enquiry is progressing.

6. Directions of enquiries.

I would personally have thought that an unsolved case of this magnitude would have generated at the very least, over a period of four years, enough paperwork to fill an average-sized living room, and that after closure of the case, at least 10% of this information should have been retained. Instead, we find that the documentation is numbered by its pages, and when the whole is added together, it is only a minute fraction of the 10% that we envisaged.

For this reason I believe that there must still be in circulation, perhaps in the attics of the descendants of police officers, or hidden in the archives of Scotland Yard, in store-rooms of the doctors involved in the case, in coroners' offices, in newspaper archives etc, a wealth of information which has yet to be discovered.

The City of London police files were lost in the blitz, so they at least have an excuse.

The Home Office files are generally what is expected, but if this mirrors the extent of their enquiries, then the people at the top must have been apathetic beyond belief, and sadly lacking in their curiosity and concern for the people of the East End of London.

Nevertheless, what we have is what we must use. The following is a catalogue of the files which are available and which can be found in the Public Records Office, unless otherwise stated.

Throughout the book I have duplicated some of the reports and memoranda contained within the files and in the chapters to which their content refers.

THE HOME OFFICE FILES

The Suspects File HO/144.220.A49301.A

1. 12 October 1888. Correspondence via the Foreign Office from one E. W. Bonham, the consul in Boulogne. This concerns John Langan, who Bonham suspected of being the Ripper. It was later discovered to be unfounded, and Langan was dismissed from police enquiries.
2. 10 October 1888. A letter from Robert Anderson with regards to a suspect called Donkin. It states that the real name of the cabman's suspect was John Davidson, and that he had satisfied the police with regards to his movements on the nights of the murders. It further includes a copy of details of the enquiries made by Abberline and Superintendent Arnold.
3. 16 October 1888. Verification of the release of the suspect Langan, and justification of his innocence.
4. 23 July 1889. Contains a letter to *The Times* from the Reverend Samuel Barnett with regard to the prevailing vice in Whitechapel.
5. 5 August 1889. Contains a report from James Monro with regard to the letter of Reverend Barnett. There are further references to

the Barnett letter dated 10 September 1889 and 27 September 1889.

6. 1 October 1889. Contains an anonymous letter regarding a doctor who had taken furnished rooms at Number 51 Abingdon Road in Kensington. He had a 'portmanteau containing surgical instruments', and is described as strong, well built, aged 45 to 50 years, 5 feet 9 inches in height with a dark complexion, beard and moustache. Has the identity of this doctor ever been established?

7. 14 October 1889. Contains two letters from one J. H. Hazelwood, alleging that the murders were committed by Police Sergeant Thick. In the margin a note states 'I think it is plainly rubbish, perhaps prompted by spite'.

8. 9 October 1889. Contains a letter from Donald Swanson referring to the letter in number 6, and stressing that the accusations are without foundation, that enquiries into the contents of the letter seem unjustified, and the whole thing appears to be a 'product of an excited imagination'.

9. 11 October 1892. Home Office memo regarding a request by the distinguished 'criminal psychologist' Doctor Arthur MacDonald of Washington, to see all the Home Office and Police medical reports on the Ripper victims. It is noted that the Home Office declined to send him the information.

HO/144/220/A49301.B
[this is a comprehensive file concerning the benefits of providing a reward for information leading to the capture of the Ripper]

1. 31 August 1888. A letter from L. P. Walter and Son, 11 to 13 Church Lane, Spitalfields, recommending that a reward should be offered. Includes a copy of the reply from E. Leigh Pemberton emphasising that the practice of offering rewards had been discontinued.

2. 10 September 1888. Contains a letter from Sir Charles Warren, accompanied by a letter from Samuel Montagu, who was the MP for Whitechapel, and was offering a reward of £100. Warren writes for guidance and instruction from the Secretary of State. Included is a response from E. Leigh Pemberton.

3. 16 September 1888. Contains a letter from the secretary of the Whitechapel Vigilance Committee, Mr Harris, asking that the Home Secretary raise the reward or give his reasons for declining. Also included is the response from Leigh Pemberton.

4. 1 October 1888. Contains notice of a cheque for £300 from the *Financial News*. This is to be given as a reward on behalf of the Government. Also included is a letter from Leigh Pemberton to Henry Matthews, the Home Secretary, in which he states that he has not yet refused the cheque, in case the Home Secretary wishes to reconsider the position. In the letter Pemberton also states that Charles Warren assures him that all is being done to capture the killer, but the outlook is not optimistic. It further reports that the Queen has phoned with a request for information.

5. 1 October 1888. Contains a telegram from a Mr Bulling, informing the Chief Constable, A. F. Williamson, of the £500 reward offer of the Lord Mayor.

6. 2 October 1888. Contains a letter from George Lusk requesting an offer of a reward. Also includes a press cutting from *The Times*, in which is outlined the reply to Lusk from the Home Office. It also contains an article out of *The Daily Telegraph* concerning a man who had sought out George Lusk and threatened him.

7. Contains a letter from Lusk asking that a pardon be offered to anyone who may be involved in the murders but is not the actual assassin. An addition by Godfrey Lushington (a senior civil servant) is included, which states 'There is no reason to suspect an accomplice, quite the reverse. I therefore see no good in offering a pardon.' An observation by Matthews adds, 'Before answering further, send a copy to Commissioner, and request him to inform the Secretary of State whether any useful result could be achieved in his opinion, by the offer of a pardon to accomplices.' The final inclusion is a draft of the reply to George Lusk.

8. 9 October 1888. Contains Commissioner Warren's response to the above request: 'During the last three or four days, I have been coming to the conclusion that useful results would be produced by the offer of a pardon to accomplices. The murderer's relatives or neighbours may have gradually or unwittingly slid into the position of accomplices, and may be hopeless of escape without a free pardon. A letter to Matthews from Lushington outlines the implications of offering a pardon and advises against it. Also contained is a draft of a letter from Matthews, declining the offer of a pardon.

9. 13 October 1888. Contains a communication from Warren to the Home Office, outlining the results of a discussion with the senior officers of the police. It weighs the arguments for and

against the merits of a reward, and states that 'Hope of gain by giving information and help to the police, is a powerful motive with ordinary people.'

10. 16 October 1888. Contains a letter from one William Bencraft, late of Melbourne Fire Brigade, quoting a specific case whereby the provision of a reward was responsible for inciting a crime, and the near-conviction of an innocent man.

11. 17 October 1888. Contains Commissioner Warren's reply to questions raised by Matthews, with regard to the police investigation. (1) Police had not yet exhausted every avenue of enquiry. (2) Anonymous letters still coming in, and one of the logical solutions to the murders is that there may be several persons who are more or less assisting the murderer. (3) 'I look upon this series of murders as unique in the history of our country.'

12. 25 October 1888. Contains the results produced by Warren showing past evidence which favours the offer of a reward, also includes the statements from the Divisional Superintendents.

13. 1 November 1888. Specifies a case of 1860, where a reward induced the actual murderer to frame an innocent person. This led to his own detection. A Home Office addition states that if the murderer had been more skilful in concocting his false accusations, then an innocent man would have gone to the gallows.

14. 10 November 1888. Contains a memorandum stating that the cabinet had decided to offer a pardon to anyone not the actual murderer of Mary Jane Kelly. Also contains a copy of the pardon.

15. November 1888. Contains a report from *The Times* relating to the Home Secretary's answers to questions in Parliament regarding the offer of rewards.

16. 29 November 1888. Contains a Home Office review on rewards from 1878–1884. The file consists of three handwritten documents.

17. Contains a printed version of the above review, entitled 'Memorandum on the question of the rewards by Government in criminal cases'.

18. Contains example copies of reward offers and pardons.

19. 19th July 1889. Contains a question put to Matthews from the *Daily Chronicle* with regard to the offer of a reward or pardon in the Alice McKenzie murder. Also contains Matthews's reply, together with a copy of 17. Matthews's answer states 'The circumstances of the present murder are, so far as known, almost identical with those of last year . . . a total augmentation of 1 inspector,

5 sergeants, and 50 constables was yesterday sanctioned.' The file also includes a memo from Munro which includes a summary of the plain-clothes men patrolling the area at various times during the investigation. It further includes documentation indicating the reduction in the number of officers involved in the case after the murders had stopped, i.e. shortly after the death of Mary Kelly. It makes no mention of the murderer having been caught or dying or being placed in an institution but indicates that the cuts in manpower were prompted by lack of funding.

The nomenclature used is dissimilar to that used in the files but the Home Office system would indicate that two files are missing. One of these files would be dated somewhere between 9 and 13 October 1888, the other after 29 November 1888.

HO/144/220/A49301.C
[this file includes the details and reports from Scotland Yard with regard to the progress and direction of the investigation into the murders]

1. 24 September 1888. This contains a letter from the Secretary of the Whitechapel Vigilance Committee, one B. Harris, who advises the Home Secretary that his refusal to sanction a reward will be given to the public at a General Meeting, and invites the minister to attend. Matthews replies with regret that he cannot attend.

2. 29 September 1888. Contains a letter from a Mr R. J. Neave, accusing the Government of callousness, neglect of duty and apathetic indifference to the murders. There is a note to assist the responder. It states: 'They are trying to make party capital out of the Whitechapel murders. Merely acknowledge.' Neave was the Honorary Secretary of the General Liberal Association in Hampshire.

3. 30 September 1888. Should have included another letter from the Whitechapel Vigilance Committee but the letter is missing. There only remains a minute stating, 'No reason to alter previous decision'.

4. 1 October 1888. Contains a letter from a Colonel Sewell of the Tower Hamlets Militia Division. The letter informs the Home Office that Sir Alfred Kirby, the Commanding Officer of the Militia offers a £100 reward together with 50 men to assist in the investigation of the murders. The offer was respectfully declined.

5. 2 October 1888. Contains information from the Clerk to the Whitechapel Board of Works, requesting that the police presence in the vicinity be increased. Leigh Pemberton replies that the Home Secretary is satisfied that the police are doing everything in their power to apprehend the murderer.

6. 4 October 1888. Contains a communication from Thomas Metcalf, the Clerk of the Whitechapel Vestry, in which he urges the Government to do everything possible to catch the murderer. Matthews has written a minute in which he explains his personal feelings regarding the murders, then adds 'Or simply acknowledge'.

7. 1 October 1888. Containing a letter offering a theory that the murderer escaped through the sewers. The letter was shown to both Warren and Monro, and remarks 'Neither of them think it improbable'.

8. 5 October 1888. A description of George Donkin, sent by the Governor of Newcastle Prison.

9. 4 October 1888. Contains a letter from the former Lord Mayor of London, Sir J. W. Ellis, in which he suggests that a cordon be thrown around all suspicious areas, and the houses forcibly searched. The response comes from Charles Warren: 'I am quite prepared to take the responsibility of adopting the most drastic and arbitrary measures that the Secretary of State can name, which would further the securing of the murderer, however illegal they may be, provided HM Government will support me'.

The reply to this is dated 5 October and comes from Matthews; in it he suggests that searches be conducted of suspicious houses with the owners' permission, and that search warrants be applied for where permission is refused; surveillance to be maintained if the warrant application is rejected. He further requests a report of all the measures taken to date for the detection of the murderer, and asks 'Have any of the doctors examined the eyes of the murdered women? (This is prompted by the misconception that the eye held an image of the last thing it sees before death.)

10. 19 September 1888. Contains a letter from Charles Warren in which he complains of the hindrance to the police investigation and in which he describes the avenues of investigation currently being pursued at the present time. These consisted of: (a) waiting to identify the lunatic Isenschmid [sic] as the man seen by Mrs Fiddymont; (b) a man called Puckridge who was released from

the asylum on 4 August and who was educated as a surgeon. He 'has threatened to rip people up with a long knife. He is being looked for but can not be found yet.' (c) 'a brothel-keeper who will not give her address or name writes to say that a man living in her house was seen with blood on him on morning of murder. She described his appearance and said where he might be seen, when detectives came near him he bolted, got away and there is no clue to the writer of the letter.'

19 September 1888. There is a letter from a man named Sandars (initials J. S.) reporting to Matthews on the above letter. The file also contains two memos of no value to the case.

11. 24 October 1888. Contains Charles Warren's response to a letter of 13 October requesting a report on the details of the invest-igation progress. 'Very numerous and searching enquiries have been made in all directions and with regard to all kinds of suggestions which have been made: they have had no tangible result.' There was also a note from Robert Anderson which stated: 'That a crime of this kind should have been committed without any clue being supplied by the criminal is very unusual, but that five successive murders should have been committed without our having the slightest clue is extraordinary, if not unique in the annals of crime.' He carried on to say that all avenues of investigation had been pursued except for the blat-antly absurd, and that the general public, especially those in the East End, had shown a marked desire to assist in every way, even at some sacrifice to themselves.

In addition, enclosed within the file is a set of reports from Chief Inspector Swanson which are catalogued as follows:

September of 1888. A report on Martha Tabram.

19 October 1888. A report on Mary Ann Nichols.

19 October 1888. A report on Annie Chapman.

19 October 1888. A report on Elizabeth Stride. This last report has within it a reference to the insane student, and asks when he is purported to have gone abroad. The reference to the insane student was first mentioned in page 6 of the report on Annie Chapman.

12. 29th October 1888. Contains a letter from Sir James Fraser, the Commissioner of the City of London Police, which encloses the report on the murder of Catharine Eddowes. (This murder was not within the jurisdiction of the Metropolitan police and was handled primarily by the City Police force.)

13. 6 November 1888. Contains a report from Donald Swanson on the murder of Eddowes. It consists of 11 pages. There is another report from PC Long, referring to the apron and graffiti found in Goulston Street, which is accompanied by a report from Superintendent Arnold explaining his decision to erase the writing. The last report included is from Commissioner Warren, which includes his input into the Goulston Street fiasco and also has within it a copy of the wording of the graffiti.

14. 6 November 1888. Contains a letter outlining answers to questions from the Home Office with regard to the murders and with reference to the reports itemised above.

15. Undated. Contains newspaper reports from *The Times* concerning the inquests of the murder victims.

16. Undated. Contains a report in *The Daily Telegraph* containing Commissioner Warren's letter to the Whitechapel Board of Works. Also included is a copy of the 'Jack the Ripper' letter.

17. 29 November 1888. Contains an analysis of the evidence, a list of the victims (which includes Martha Tabram) showing the time place and date of each murder, plus a list of the injuries. Nothing unusual is included in the contents except a dispute over the time of Chapman's murder, which states: 'Doubtful evidence points to somewhere between 5.30 and 6 a.m., but medical evidence says about 4 o'clock.'

18. 15 October 1888. Contains a letter from Samuel Montagu which appends a petition from the Whitechapel residents asking for the police levels to be increased.

19. 15 October 1888. Contains a letter to Henry Matthews which was wrongly addressed, and was therefore opened by the Post Office. It names a General Brown as a suspect for the murders. On 17 October Commissioner Warren replies saying that General Brown has been questioned and cleared.

20. 10 November 1888. Contains press cuttings regarding the competency of Warren, and also includes his resignation.

21. 11 November 1888. Contains a letter from a Thomas Blair suggesting that police of short stature and as far as possible of effeminate appearance should act as decoys by dressing as women.

22. 10 November 1888. Contains a letter from a Mr Smith from Essex, suggesting that when the murderer is caught he should receive a daily lashing with a cat-o-nine-tails for a period of 12 months prior to his execution.

23. 11 November 1888. Contains a letter from James Young of Merton in which he derides the police. He states that his father was a superintendent, 'and was reckoned about as crafty as any man who ever misapplied his talents in a bad service'. He offers a plan for catching the killer.

24. 13 November 1888. Contains a note from Commissioner Warren stating 'Mr Hales says that Packer believes the murderer to be his own cousin.' Was this ever investigated?

25. 13 November 1888. Contains a letter from Anderson, and a full medical report, plus extracts from a communication from Anderson to Dr Bond, in which he requests the doctor's assistance in establishing whether the Ripper had surgical skill and anatomical knowledge.

26. 16 November 1888. Contains a letter from a James Frederick Brooks with a suggestion that the Government offer a pardon to the murderer, and then renege on the offer after they have him in custody.

27. Missing.

28. 12 March 1889. Contains a letter from an A. H. Skirving, of the Ontario Police, stating that he suspects a prisoner in Chatham Prison, Ontario, by the name of Jack Irwin, to be the murderer. This man was not in the country at the time of the crimes.

29. Missing.

30. 6 May 1892. Contains a letter from Mr Charles Barber who has dreamt that Deeming is the Ripper.

31. Missing.

32. 8 November 1894. Contains a letter from a Dr Gustave Olive from Nantes, in which he requests a copy of Dr Bond's report and refers to the possibility of a similar case in France.

33. 22 November 1894. Contains notification with regard to the above request, that a copy of the report has been despatched.

34. 3 December 1894. Contains a reference to a letter from the Right Honourable E. H. Pickersgill MP, which was published in *The Times* of 23 November, in which he criticises the police over a technical matter concerning a killing in Whitechapel the previous Saturday. The reply intimated that the MP had confused the police with the Public Prosecutor's office and totally misunderstood the regulation under question. (This has no bearing whatsoever on the Ripper case.)

There are a number of references in this section which I have not included within this list, as they are totally alien to the Jack the Ripper case, or they are from idiots and cranks, or they contain intelligence that has no bearing on the actual case. (An example of this would be the letters and reports referring to the provision of cycles to assist the police in catching the Ripper.)

HO/144/220/A49301.D

This section contains a number of documents concerning the case which have found their way into the files via the route through the Foreign Office.

The first five documents concern the personage of Sir Augustus Paget, who was the British Ambassador in Vienna, Austria. They have been forwarded to the Home Office by the Permanent Under-secretary of State to the Foreign Office, Sir Julian Pauncefote. The documents concern a person named Jonas who, it is claimed, managed the affairs of a secret political society, and who believed the Ripper to be an ex-member of this society who had been expelled for denouncing society members to the authorities in New York. It further claimed that the man was now in Britain and was under observation by present members of the society.

The man Jonas would come to London to identify the person, for a fee of £165. The Home Office and the Viennese Authorities both thought the man to be a crank, and the authorities recalled a tale in 1883, when the same individual had warned them of an assassination plot which had failed to materialise.

Sir Augustus Paget believed the story and out of his own money advanced Jonas £165. There were further requests for money which the police in the personage of Deputy Commissioner Monro strongly advised against, and there the story subsides into insignificance. The man Jonas did warn against a proposed London bombing campaign but no action was taken and the bombing campaign never took place. No further mention is made of the man Jonas being able to identify the Ripper.

Commissioner Warren however did write on 12 October 1888: 'As Mr Matthews is aware, I have for some time past been inclined to the idea that the murders having been done by a secret society is the only logical solution to the question, but I could not understand them being done, because the last murders were done by someone desiring to bring discredit on the Jews and the Socialists, or the Jewish Socialists.'

The Civil Servant Godfrey Lushington replied to this communication the following day with: 'I cannot agree with the Commissioner that the only logical solution of the question is that the murders may probably have been done by a secret society.' He also says that he 'cannot understand this having been done by a socialist, because the last murders were evidently done by someone desiring to bring discredit on the Jews and socialists or Jewish socialists. It seems to me on the contrary, that the last murder was done by a Jew who boasted of it.' By the date of this letter, the murder referred to must be that of Catharine Eddowes, and the evidence which Lushington is referring to is probably the Goulston Street Graffiti.

On 6 December a letter was received from a Mr Tomas Romero, in which he writes about and gives a description of a man who he believes to be the Ripper. There is no addition to this letter saying whether the lead was followed up.

A letter was received on 14 December, from a man named George Strachey from Dresden. It concerned information given to him by an American student called J. Lowenheim relating to a Polish Jew named Wirtkofsky who the student had met near Finsbury Park and who had threatened to kill a certain woman and others of her type.

The remainder of the documents included within this file are of little importance to the Ripper Case so I have chosen to eliminate them from the book.

HO/144/221/A49301.E.
This file is dedicated to the use of bloodhounds to help in tracking the killer and other felons. The items include the practicality of using the dogs in the confines of a crowded neighbourhood and the costs of maintaining the dogs. The contents of the file are of little use in assisting any investigation into the Ripper crimes so I believe that it would be of little importance to list them.

HO/144/221/A49301.F.
Consists of a report from Commissioner Warren to Godfrey Lushington, informing him of the murder of Mary Jane Kelly, and advising him that the case is being handled by Anderson, the Assistant Commissioner. It is dated 9 November 1888, so must have been written on the day of the murder.

HO/144/221/A49301.G.

This file has no direct bearing on the attempt to solve the case. It is devoted to expenditure information and I therefore do not intend to bore the reader with its contents.

HO/144/221/A49301.H.

This file provides details of the murder of Rose Mylett, which took place on 20 December 1888. As this is not acknowledged as a Ripper murder then I propose to go no further with the contents of this file.

HO/144/221/A49301.I.

There is only one document of any importance contained within the file. This is a report on the murder of Alice McKenzie, dated 17 July 1889. In the report he states 'I need not say that every effort will be made by the police to discover the murderer, who, I am inclined to believe, is identical with the notorious Jack the Ripper of last year'. Also enclosed within the report is a section by Superintendent Arnold.

The way that the report is worded can be interpreted in two ways: where Monro states 'I am inclined to believe, is identical with the notorious Jack the Ripper of last year', could be taken to imply that this is a copycat of the Ripper murders, in which case it could lend credence to the belief that the police thought that Jack the Ripper was out of commission. It could also be a statement that Monro thought it quite probable that the Ripper had murdered McKenzie. Whether or not this is true does not matter. What does matter, is that if this is Monro's opinion, then he for one did not think that the Ripper had been captured or had died at this time.

HO/144/221/A49301.J.

[this file is missing]

HO/144/221/A49301.K.

This is the last file in the series and is composed of only one, quite interesting, document. The document enclosed is a report from Monro to a Mr J. S. Sanders, the Assistant Private Secretary to the Minister Matthews, and is dated 11 September 1889. It concerns the Pinchin Street murder, where a headless and legless corpse was discovered under an arch. Monro states that the murder could have been the work of Jack the Ripper but he was inclined to the murderer being another person.

The reason for the interest is that despite Macnaghten and other senior police officers, who later in life implied that the identity of the Ripper was known, Monro in September of the following year is allowing an opinion that this murder could quite possibly be the work of the Ripper. Monro was a very senior police officer and would have been privileged to all the top-level information on the Jack the Ripper Murders, and yet he is still persisting that the Ripper is on the loose at this time. The fact that it is extremely unlikely that the Ripper committed the murder is nothing to do with it. It is the inference that he *could* have been responsible that makes the file so interesting and casts doubt upon the credibility of the Macnaghten Memorandum.

THE SCOTLAND YARD FILES

Since these files have become available to the public, they have been consulted on a number of occasions

MEPO3/140 Separate Murders

The documents indicate that they should have started with those of Emma Elizabeth Smith, but these are no longer available, having been stolen in 1983.

Martha Tabram

1. 7 August 1888. 33. Contains a photograph of Martha Tabram.
2. 10 August 1888. 34. Contains a report by Inspector Ellisdon on the discovery of the body.
3. 16 August 1888. 44–48. Contains a report on the identification of the body together with the details concerning the identification parade using Mary Ann Nichols (Pearly Poll) to try and identify the two soldiers who may have been implicated in the murder. The report is compiled by Inspector Reid.
4. 24 August 1888. 49–51. Another report by Inspector Reid. This document gives some details together with the conclusions of the inquest on Martha Tabram.
5. Dated September 1888. 37–43. Contains a report compiled at the request of Commissioner Warren, and conducted by Chief Inspector Donald Swanson. It contains details of the ongoing investigation into the murder of Martha Tabram.

It must be noted that this is very early in the investigation into the Whitechapel Murders, and many would state that the Ripper murders had not yet begun. However, that someone as senior as the Commissioner should personally request a report on an individual murder, giv some idea that even at this early stage the police were under the opinion that there was something out of the ordinary happening in Whitechapel, and there may already have been the suspicion that a killer was on the loose.

6 25 September 1888. 52–59. Contains a report by Inspector Reid with regard to the visit to the Wellington Barracks, in an attempt to identify the soldier seen by Police Constable Barrett.

7. is undated, but probably 7 August. 33. Contains details of the murder of Martha Tabram. The reason I believe it could be 7 August is that due to the nomenclature I think that at one time it may have accompanied the photograph identified earlier in the files.

8. 19 October 1888. 60. Contains the index to the above report by Chief Inspector Swanson.

Mary Ann Nichols

9. 31 August 1888. 239–241. Contains a report from Inspector Spratling, with regard to the discovery of the body.

10. 7 September 1888. 235–238. Contains a report on the murder and identification of Mary Nichols compiled by Inspector Joseph Helson of J Division, Bethnal Green. In the report he states that there is 'no doubt that the murder was committed where the body was found'; he further states that 'in all probability, there was only one murderer.' (By this he is comparing the deaths of Nichols and Chapman only.) He makes mention of a leading suspect at the time and says: 'A man named Jack Pizer, alias Leather Apron, has been ill-using prostitutes in this and other parts of the metropolis, and careful search has been made and is continued to be made to find this man ... though at present there is no evidence against him.'

Annie Chapman

11. 8 September 1888. 9–11. Contains a report on the discovery of the body by Inspector Chandler. The file also contains a briefing from Acting Superintendent West which informs the reader that Inspector Chandler is making investigations into the murder

assisted by Sergeant Thick and Sergeant Leach. A further entry informs us that Inspector Reid is on leave, and that Inspector Abberline has been told to combine the investigations of Annie Chapman and Mary Nichols.

12. 11 September 1888. 12–13. Contains a report by Inspector Styles concerning the visit of two doctors, Crabb and Cowan, and that they suggest that Issenschmidt is the Ripper.

13. 13 September 1888. Missing.

14. 14 September 1888. 16. Contains a report by Inspector Chandler regarding his enquiries at the 1st Battalion of the Sussex Regiment, concerning the portion of an envelope found near to the body of Annie Chapman.

15. 14 September 1888. 17. Contains information regarding the suspect Edward Stanley, and police enquiries made at the London Hospital without success. It also refers to a memo from the Commissioner, and the arrest of Edward McKenna, a short-term Ripper suspect.

16. 15 September 1888. 18–20. Contains a report detailing the progress and results of further enquiries made at the Sussex Regiment by Inspector Chandler.

17. 17 September 1888. 21–23. Contains a report by Sergeant Thick with regard to ongoing enquiries into Issenschmidt.

18. 18 September 1888. 24–25. Contains a report given by Inspector Abberline, in which he tenders the opinion that Issenschmidt is the man seen by Mrs Fiddymont. It also expresses the difficulty of getting access to Issenschmidt for the purposes of confirming identification. A minute from Chief Constable Williamson that he had interviewed the Doctor at the Fairfield Road Asylum. (It was later proved that Issenschmidt had been incarcerated during the time of the murders, and could not have been Jack the Ripper.)

19. 19 September 1888. 26–28. Contains a report by Sergeant Thick regarding his interview with the wife of Issenschmidt.

20. 19 September 1888. 29–31. Contains a report by Inspector Helson, in which he summarises the results of the investigation into Issenschmidt.

21. 19 September 1888. 242–247. Contains Inspector Abberline's report on the current stage in the investigation into Annie Chapman and Mary Nichols.

Elizabeth Stride

22. 4 October 1888. 211. Contains a report referencing the interview of Matthew Packer and his statement in which he told the reporters that he had not been interviewed by the police (a copy of the statement, which was published in the *Evening News*, is not contained within the file).

The report is compiled by Inspector Moore, who states that he had sent Sergeant White to escort Packer to the mortuary to identify the body as that which he had seen.

23. 4 October 1888. 212–214. Contains the report of Sergeant White referenced in the report above.

24. Undated. 215–216. Contains a note from Commissioner Warren confirming the statement which he himself had taken from Packer.

25. 6 October 1888. 203. Contains an extract from the *Daily News*.

26. 29 October 1888. 208–210. Contains part of a letter from the Home Office regarding the evidence of Schwartz and the cry of 'Lipski'.

27. 1 November 1888. 204–206 (nomenclature is out of position). Contains the responses of Inspector Abberline to questions asked by the Home Office, in the letter above. He describes the content of the interview with Israel Schwartz and volunteers the explanation that the term 'Lipski' was a term of anti-Semitic abuse.

28. 5 November 1888. 207. Contains a draft of Anderson's response to the above letter from the Home Office.

Catharine Eddowes

It must be appreciated that the murder of Eddowes was not committed within the jurisdiction of the Metropolitan Police, so therefore the file on her murder is very limited, the details having been held in the City of London police records.

29. Undated. 3–6. Contains photographs of Eddowes only.

Mary Jane Kelly

30. 10 November 1888. 220–223. Contains a report on the murder by Dr Thomas Bond.

31. 12 November 1888. 227–229. Contains the statement by George Hutchinson.

32. 12 November 1888. 230–232. Contains a report on the inquest into the death of Kelly, by Inspector Abberline, and includes his opinion that Hutchinson's statement is true. An ex-tract from *The Daily Telegraph* is included with a preponderance of it based upon

the inquest of Kelly. There is also included in this article further information on Catharine Eddowes, concerning a man who was seen with her approximately ten minutes before the body was found. This man was seen conversing with Eddowes in the covered entry to Mitre Square, by two persons who were in the Orange Market, and who closely observed the man. He is described as aged about thirty with a fair complexion, and a fair moustache. It states that the City Police have been making enquiries in an attempt to find this man for a number of weeks without success.

33. 3 December 1888. 7. Contains an extract from an article in the *Philadelphia Times* which contains a theory, and has no bearing on the facts of the case.

Rose Mylett

There is a file containing some papers of Wynne Baxter, in which he comments on the examinations of the bodies by the doctors. There are also two files, numbered 34 and 35, which contain extracts from articles in the *Daily Chronicle*. Both are dated 28 December 1888.

Alice McKenzie

36. Undated. 259. Contains a photograph of McKenzie.

37. 17 July 1889. 272–273. Contains a report outlining the discovery of the body, and the events immediately following, by Sergeant Badham.

38. 17 July 1889. 274. Contains a similar report as above submitted by Police Constable Andrews.

39. 17 July 1889. 294–297. Contains a report by Inspector Moore.

40. 18 July 1889. 259–262. Contains a medical report by Dr Bond. Among other things the report states: 'I see in this murder evidence of similar design to the former Whitechapel murders. Viz – sudden onslaught on the prostrate woman, the throat skilfully and resolutely cut, with subsequent mutilation. I am of the opinion that the murder was performed by the same person who committed the former series of Whitechapel murders.' This as we know contradicts the earlier analysis of Dr Bond, and is in direct conflict with the opinion of Dr Phillips. (It is becoming apparent that the doctors did not like each other and Bond consistently went out of his way to contradict the opinions of Doctor Phillips. When viewing the medical documentation I believe that Dr Phillips was a first-class doctor, and I personally think that Bond had a bit of a chip on his shoulder.)

41. 19 July 1889. 284–287. Contains a confession to the murder by a man named William Wallace Brodie. The confession is devalued by a note from Inspector Arnold who states that Brodie is of unsound mind.

42. 19 July 1889. 280–281. Contains a request for instructions with regard to Brodie, from Inspector Moore.

43. 19 July 1889. 279. Contains a report from the Convict Supervision Office, confirming that Brodie had previous convictions.

44. 19 July 1889. 282. Contains information concerning Brodie's brothers.

45. 19 July 1889. 283. Contains a report on the investigations undertaken at Brodie's lodgings.

46. 20 July 1889. 288. Contains a summary of the committal proceedings against Brodie at the Thames Magistrates Court. The report is compiled by Inspector Moore.

47. 22 July 1889. 264–271. *Contains a medical report from Doctor Phillips on the murder of McKenzie, in which he states that he does not believe that all of the Whitechapel murders have been committed by the same individual.*

48. 22 July 1889. 275. Contains a witness statement from Margaret Franklin.

49. 22 July 1889. 276. Contains a witness statement from the deputy of the lodging house where McKenzie stayed. Her name is Elizabeth Ryder.

50. 23 July 1889. 277. Contains confirmation from Sergeant Bradshaw that Brodie was in South Africa between the dates of 6 September 1888 and 15 July 1889.

51. 24 July 1889. 278. Contains a written interview, in report by Sergeant McCarthy, of George Dixon, who was with McKenzie on the night she was murdered.

52. 27 July 1889. 277. Contains a communication whereby Sergeant McCarthy confirms that he was unable to verify the alibi of George Dixon.

53. 27 July 1889. 290–291. Contains a report from Inspector Moore in which he states that Brodie had been released, and rearrested for the crime of fraud.

54. Undated. 292–293. Contains part of an article from the newspaper the *Kimberley Advertiser* of 29 June 1889, in which it is reported that whilst under the influence of drink, Brodie had confessed to the Ripper murders.

Pinchin Street murder

55. Contains a map/plan of the district.

56. 10 September 1889. 136–140. Contains Donald Swanson's report on the discovery of the body in which he states, 'There is a marked absence of attack on the genitals, as in series of Whitechapel murders, beginning in Buck's Row and ending in Miller's Court.'

57. 10 September 1889. 170–173. Contains a detailed examination of the body.

58. 11 September 1889. 125–134. Contains a report by James Monro, to J. S. Sandars [the Assistant Private Secretary to the Minister Matthews] in which he reports about the Pinchin Street murder, and iterates that it could have been the work of Jack the Ripper, but he did not think that it was. (By this, we can see that we are now into September of the following year, and a senior police officer is still reporting as if the Ripper is on the loose, and has never been apprehended or is thought to have died.)

59. 11 September 1889. 146–147. Contains a report from Inspector Reid referring to attached reports from Sergeant White and Sergeant Thick, which are not in the file, and which are said to describe certain investigations undertaken by Sergeant Godley regarding bloodstained clothing discovered in Batty Street.

60. 11 September 1889. 141–145. Contains the post mortem report on the body, performed by a Dr Hibbert.

61. 11th of September 1889. 146–147. Contains comments by Dr Hibbert.

62. 11 September 1889. 135. *Contains part of an article taken from the* New York Herald, *in which it is stated that a John Cleary informed the Night Editor of the* Herald *of a murder committed in Backchurch Lane, on 7 September 1889; it asks if Cleary anticipated the finding of the body in Pinchin Street on 10 September. [Pinchin Street ran off Back Church Lane.]*

63. 11 September 1889. 151. Contains a report from Inspector Pattenden, in which he outlines an incident culminating in the removal to the London Hospital of a woman, by the police. He offers this incident as an explanation for the content of Cleary's statement described earlier in the files.

64. 12 September 1889. Contents are missing.

65. 12 September 1889. 153–157. Contains a comprehensive report by Chief Inspector Swanson on the investigation into a man called Leary. (Could this have been confusion with Cleary?)

66. 12 September 1889. 158–159. Contains a report based upon the suspicions of a Mr Miller concerning the man Cleary.

67. 12 September 1889. 160–165. Contains a statement from a news-vendor from Charing Cross, named John Arnold, in which he states that he was John Cleary, and he had been informed by a soldier that another murder had taken place in Backchurch Lane. He gave a description of the soldier as aged 35 to 36 years, 5 feet 6 inches in height, with a fair complexion and a moustache. He further states that the soldier was carrying a parcel (where have we heard that description before?).

68. 12 September 1889. 166–169. Contains case notes on the body by Doctor Phillips.

69. 24 September 1889. 174–175. Contains a progress report by In-spector Moore, with an additional request from Superintendent West that permission be given to bury the body.

70. 30 September 1889. 176–177. Contains a report from Inspector Moore initiated by the one above.

71. 5 October 1889. 178–179. Contains another report from Inspec-tor Moore in which he informs that the body has been preserved in spirits inside a sealed container which was buried on the prev-ious day.

Frances Coles

72. 13 February 1891. 113–116. Contains a report on the discovery of the body, and an opinion from Dr Phillips, that the murder is unconnected with any of the previous crimes.

73. 14 February 1891. 97–108. Contains a comprehensive report by Donald Swanson, in which a statement is contained of James Sadler, who was the leading suspect for the murder, and who had met Coles in a public house named the Princess Alice.

74. 15 February 1891. 119–121. Contains a report on the positive identification of the body by Frances Coles's father James, and her sister Mary Ann.

75. 16 February 1891. 117–118. Contains a report outlining the arrest of James Sadler for the murder of Frances Coles.

76. 18 February 1891. 63–64. Contains photographs of the mur-dered woman.

77. 21 February 1891. 65–74. Contains a report by Chief Inspector Swanson on the interview of a Mrs Sadler.

78. 25 February 1891. 81–82. Contains a witness statement from Kate McCarthy.

79. 25 February 1891. 83–85. Contains a witness statement from a Mr Thomas Fowles.

80. The folio is dated 27 February 1891, but the contents, originally two pages, are missing.

81. 2 March 1891. 75–78. Contains a report from Inspector Moore regarding the movements of James Sadler.

82. 3 March 1891. 79–80. Contains a report, supplementing the one above, and detailing the whereabouts of Sadler from 16 to 20 July 1889. (By the looks of this, the police must have harboured suspicions and possible connections with the murder of Alice McKenzie which took place on 17 July 1889.)

83. [originally consisted of two pages, numbered 86 and 87, both of which are missing. The folio is dated 3 March 1891.]

84. 11 December 1891. 90–91. Contains a report by Donald Swanson with regard to a complaint filed against James Sadler by his wife.

85. 16 December 1891. 92–93. Contains a report of no account to the case.

86. 1 January 1892. 94–95. Contains a character report by Sergeant Boswell on James Sadler, in which he states that Sadler is now the proprietor of a shop, which appears to be doing quite well, and in his opinion Sadler is a man of changed character.

87. 4 March 1892. 96. Contains another report by Sergeant Boswell stating that the Sadler family are once again fighting among themselves.

88. 10 March 1892. 109. Contains a report on the continuing developments within the Sadler household.

89. 9 May 1892. 110. Contains a further report by Boswell regarding the fact that Mrs Sadler has taken out a summons against her husband.

90. 16 May 1892. 111. Contains the result of the court case against James Sadler, in which he was bound over to keep the peace for a period of six months

91. 2 January 1893. 112. Contains a police report on the proposed change of address by James Sadler.

MEPO/3/141

1. 10 September 1888. 175–176. Contains a letter from a Member of Parliament, Samuel Montagu, in which he offers a reward of £100 for information leading to the apprehension of the murderer.

2. 13 September 1888. 173–174. Contains a letter from the Home Office to Commissioner Warren outlining the offer of £100 reward from Samuel Montagu.

3. 19 September 1888. 170–172. Contains a letter from Commiss-
    ioner Warren to Government Minister Henry Matthews.

4. 30 September 1888. 184. Contains a police handout requesting
    information from the public with regard to Annie Chapman and
    Polly Nichols.

5. 13 October 1888. 185. Contains an article from the *Daily Chron-
    icle* which includes within its text the arrest of a Mr John Foster in
    Belfast; the admittance of a somewhat suspicious character to the
    London Hospital; the use of bloodhounds to track down the
    killer; and the allegation that the police believed that the word
    'Juwes' was the Yiddish equivalent of the word 'Jews'.

6. 17 October 1888. 136–137. Contains a petition from the White-
    chapel traders, requesting that the police increase the number of
    officers on the ground.

7. 22 October 1888. 164–166. Contains a breakdown of the number
    of officers already on beats in the area of Whitechapel. It details
    absence of officers on leave and sickness, and culminates in a
    recommendation that the force be augmented by a further 25
    constables. The report is submitted by Superintendent Arnold.

8. 22 October 1888. 167–169. Contains a letter to Commissioner
    Charles Warren from Permanent Undersecretary Godfrey Lush-
    ington, in which he requests information on the extent of prostit-
    ution, the number of brothels and lodging houses within the area.

9. 25 October 1888. 158–163. Contains the reply to the above
    letter from Commissioner Warren, detailing the number of
    brothels as 62, lodging houses as 233, and an estimation of 1200
    prostitutes.

10. 26 October 1888. 138. Contains a request from Commissioner
    Warren that the force be augmented by a further 306 men.
    (Considering the size of Whitechapel, this would make a massive
    police presence within the area, and makes it all the more difficult
    to see why the Ripper was not caught.)

11. 10 November 1888. 150–157. Contains a medical report and
    evaluation from Dr Bond.

12. 29 October 1888. 149. Contains a letter from Godfrey Lushing-
    ton requesting information on the number of inhabited houses in
    the H Division and an estimate of the population of the area. He
    also requests a map.

13–31. Contain various applications for payment of allowances to
    the police who have been drafted into Whitechapel to supple-
    ment the force.

32–135. Are supposed to contain a file on the Suspects in the case, together with reports from the various divisions of the police force prompted by a Scotland Yard request made on 17 January 1889, at which time they made a request for a comprehensive list of all the persons who had been detained/interviewed in connection with the murders from 31 October 1888.

Various researchers who had access to the files, have included information on their content. When the BBC ran a dramatic investigative documentary on the murders, they used the TV policemen, Barlow and Watt from the series *Softly, Softly* to front the programme. The series was co-scripted by Elwyn Jones and John Lloyd. They also co-wrote a book on the subject entitled *The Ripper File*. During their research they consulted the 'Suspect File' and commented on the fact that it contained no information on the three main suspects i.e. Druitt, Kosminski and Ostrog.

This is arguably the most important file in the Scotland Yard records of the case, and we can only hope that at some time in the future the contents will reappear, or the culprit will forward them anonymously to someone like myself, so that the information which they contain can be re-entered into the equation.

The contents of the file appear to have included police reports on at least one hundred men who were questioned by the police in relation to the murders, and who had been highlighted for investigation by members of the public.

The earlier persons who, thank heavens, got a preliminary look at the file, included such valued researchers as Stephen Knight, Colin Wilson, Donald Rumbelow, Melvin Harris, and Robin Odell, and we must rely on their memories and notes to educate us on the contents.

I believe that the most informative book on the facts of the Jack the Ripper case is *The Jack the Ripper A - Z*, which was co-written by Paul Begg, Martin Fido and Keith Skinner, and their book has been a constant source of support in assisting my own labours. I therefore quote in places verbatim from this book, as to the quality and type of information which we know that this file contained.

27 September 1888. Contained information regarding the response of the Bremen Police to an enquiry from Scotland Yard saying 'Evidently the hairdresser Mary is the person referred to'. On 7 August 1888, 'Mary' a male, had completed a seven-year

sentence, and had been rearrested and sent to Oslebshausen, from where he would be released on 7 August 1889.

5 October 1888. Contained a report from the Chief Constable of Rotherham in which he says that a discharged soldier named James Oliver believes a man named 'Dick Austin' to be the Ripper. He calls him 'a perfect woman-hater' who had said that if he had his will, he would 'kill every whore and rip her insides out'.

16 October 1888. Inspector Abberline reports on the unsuccessful appeal to various divisions for any information concerning the man Austin.

19 October 1888. Contained another reference to our friend 'Mary'. Detective Baring from Bremen writes that 'Mary' had been arrested several times, for assaulting women and girls in the breasts and private parts with a sharp instrument. He also tried to rape a young girl in his barber's shop.

19 October 1888. The Chief Constable of Rotherham states that as a result of a second interview with James Oliver nothing interesting was added. He also requests a copy of the Ripper letters.

22 October 1888. Contained a report from Inspector Abberline, that 'Mary' was undergoing a prison sentence of 12 months and 'could not be connected with the recent murders in Whitechapel'. It further notes that 'with regard to the man Wetzel, it has been clearly proved that he was in no way concerned in the matter. He was also under remand at the time that the Berner Street and Mitre Square murders were committed. (We note from this that Abberline included the murder of Elizabeth Stride, which is another indication that Abberline at least thought it to be one of the Ripper murders.)

The man 'Wetzel' was an alias used by Charles Ludwig, who was a Ripper suspect until it was found that he could not possibly have committed the double-event murders, having been in custody at the time.

24 October 1888. Contains another report from the Chief Constable of Rotherham stating that James Oliver believes the Ripper handwriting to be very like that of Austin, 'especially that of the letter (written in steel pen); that of the postcard (written with quill) he does not think so like.'

18 December 1888. Contained a report from the Kingston Police Station that John Hemmings and William Shuber had reported the strange behaviour of one Arthur Henry Mason, of

Kingston, to Police Constable Robert Large No. 548T. Mason was questioned and released.

14 June 1889. Contains a report from Chief Constable S. Richards, in which he outlines certain information given to him by Richard Wingate Baker, of 10 Church Street, Edgware Road, who has stated that he suspects a man named Pierce John Robinson, who had entered into partnership with him five weeks previously. He stated that his suspicions were aroused by the fact that Robinson fell silent during any conversation about the murders, plus the fact that he had sent his mistress, a lady called Miss Peters, a letter expressing 'fear that he would be caught today'.

(Further investigations by Superintendent Waghorn and Superintendent Arnold assisted by Sergeant Thick had revealed that Robinson was a religious maniac and a quack doctor, that he had previously lived at Mile End, where he had committed bigamy. However, his bigamous wife knew that he had been with Miss Peters in Portslade on the night of the murder of Mary Kelly.)

Certain files are missing from the above section, which appear to have contained suspects who the police regarded as serious contenders for the Ripper. The next section seems to contain general enquiries undertaken during the Ripper investigation, but enquiries made after the 17 January deadline, when Scotland Yard had requested the updated information on the number of detainees etc.

13 November 1888. Contains a folio from A Division, of King Street, in which an artist's model named Antoni Pricha was highlighted to Police Constable Maybank No. 61A, by a man named Edward Knight Larkins, who pointed out that he fitted the description of the Ripper. Subsequently after investigation by the police, it was found that Pricha had an alibi for the night of the murder of Mary Kelly, and he was released.

8th of December 1888. Two detectives, Bradshaw and Godley, detained a man, name of Edwin Burrows, who resided at a common lodging house at Victoria Chambers. He was wearing a peaked sailor cap. A Division police knew him and confirmed that he was an occasional vagrant who was struggling to exist on an allowance of £1 a week which he received from his brother; he was therefore released.

A Division, Rochester Row

21 December 1888. Mr Douglas Cow of the company Cow & Co., Merchants, who dealt in india rubber, was turned in by Mrs Fanny Drake of Clerkenwell Street, who stated that he fitted the murderer's description and had grinned frighteningly at her. Cow proved his identity and was released.

A Division, Hyde Park

22 November 1888. A complaint was lodged against an Irishman named James Cornell, by a lady named Martha Spencer, with whom she had taken a walk in the park. She stated that he had frightened her with conversation about the Ripper. Cornell proved his respectability and was released.

B Division, Walton Street

17 November 1888. Richard Watson turned in Oliver Matthews, because Matthews was in the habit of carrying a black bag.

G Division, King's Cross.

12 November 1888. John Avery of Willesden confessed to the murders and said that he would have committed more, had he not lost his bag. He was found guilty of being drunk and disorderly, and sentenced to 14 days hard labour.

13 November 1888. A Massachusetts seaman, name of John Murphy, was brought in from Holburn Casual Ward because a knife had been found on his person, and he was wearing a cloth cap with peak. The circumstances were investigated by Inspector Abberline, and Murphy was released when his account was been found to be correct.

25 November 1888. A man was brought in accused of accosting women at King's Cross Station. He was a Dutchman named Van Burst and was resident at Bacon's Hotel in Fitzroy Square. Enquiries were made which proved to be satisfactory, and he was allowed to go.

25 November 1888. Another resident of Bacon's Hotel was given into custody. He was named Alfred Parent, and was from Paris. He had been turned in by a prostitute called Annie Cook because he had apparently offered her a sovereign if she would go with him, or the sum of five sovereigns if she would spend the night. She had thought the sum suspiciously large. After investigation Parent was released.

28 December 1888. Joseph Denny, dressed in a long astrakhan-trimmed coat, was brought in after he was seen accosting women. He was later released after certain enquiries had been made.

Other files within this section are:

32. 27 July 1889. 148. Contains a letter from Lushington to Monro discussing the letter of Samuel Barnett which was published in *The Times*.

33. 3 August 1889. 145–147. Contains a subsequent report describing the interview with Samuel Barnett, conducted by Superintendent Arnold.

34. 5 August 1889. Contains a reply to the Lushington letter concerning Barnett, from Monro, with the benefit of the information gleaned from the interview given by Superintendent Arnold.

35. February 1894. Contains the most important document, the Mac-naghten Memorandum.

MEPO 3/142

This is a file full of letters purporting to have come from the Ripper, none of which is believed to be genuine. Some of the letters are of chilling content and are the work of persons with warped imaginations. Some were sent to the police, some to the newspapers, and some to various businesses within London. One letter was even washed ashore in a bottle. The file also includes a note from Inspector Moore, who was a leading figure in the Ripper investigation. The gist of the note is that even in 1896 Moore believed that the Goulston Street Graffiti was an example of the Ripper's handwriting and that the correct spelling of the word included in the phrase was 'Jewes', and not 'Juwes' as is the common understanding. He also thought that some of the letters were of genuine origin, but neglected to tell us which.

There is a variety of other information which I have neglected to include as I believe it has no bearing on the search for Jack the Ripper. Doubtless at some time in the future a book will be written which will be devoted purely to the written material available on the case.

CHAPTER SEVENTEEN
The medical evidence

Though I have already identified some of the medical evidence in the specific chapters on each individual murder, I have decided to include this chapter so that the reader may be able to scrutinise all of the medical evidence in a single review, thus making it easier to compare the various injuries and the methods used by the Ripper.

I have further listed a number of my observations on each of the murders, under the appropriate heading of the individual victim, in order that the reader may evaluate my statements, and form their own opinions as to their viability; or they can promote their own point of view with regard to my inferences. I am an amateur, and do not in any way believe that my own conclusions are sacrosanct.

I have given my questions a nomenclature which will allow the reader to consider my presumptions and to forward their opinions and arguments to me at the address provided at the back of the book, on anything to which they may take exception.

The inclusion of this information will allow the reader to formulate his own opinion on matters which are still the subject of controversy, e.g. Did Jack the Ripper possess a degree of anatomical knowledge, and if so, how much?

I hope this gives you the added dimension of actually investigating the crimes for yourself, analysing the information and formulating your own opinion as to the identity of the culprit.

It is generally acknowledged that Jack the Ripper had only five victims. Whilst I possibly agree with the number of his victims, I do not personally believe that the murder of Elizabeth Stride was the responsibility of Jack the Ripper. I have therefore taken the liberty of including Martha Tabram as a potential victim, but in listing the victims I have marked the generally accepted 'canonical victims' with an asterisk so that they can be more easily identified.

The victims under discussion are as follows:

Name	Date of murder	Place of murder
Martha Tabram	7 August 1888	37 George Yard
Mary Ann Nichols*	31 August 1888	Buck's Row
Annie Chapman*	8 September 1888	29 Hanbury Street
Elizabeth Stride*	30 September 1888	Berner Street
Catharine Eddowes*	30 September 1888	Mitre Square
Mary Jane Kelly*	9 November 1888	Miller's Court

I have listed them in the order in which they were killed, and I will evaluate them in a similar order.

Martha Tabram
Doctor Timothy Robert Killeen was called to examine the body at a time he put as 5.30.am.

He estimated that death had occurred about two hours previously, which would place the time of death at around 3.30 am. There were 39 stab wounds, including 5 in the liver, 5 in the left lung, 1 in the heart, 2 in the right lung, 2 in the spleen and 6 in the stomach, the breasts, belly and sexual organs being the main targets. He further stated that 38 at least had been inflicted by a right-handed person, and that only one wound could not have been caused by an ordinary penknife. The exception was a wound to the sternum which was ascertained as having been made by a dagger or sword bayonet.

It was thought that the murder was committed by a guardsman, and certain questions were asked about the extent of anatomical knowledge expressed in the murder.

It must be pointed out that in my own opinion the doctor did not say that the weapon used was definitely a penknife but only that a penknife was capable of inflicting 38 of the wounds. I do not think that the assailant had two knives with him, and swapped them over to commit a single injury, but prefer to lean to the opinion that the same weapon which inflicted the wound on the sternum was itself also capable of inflicting the other 38 injuries.

As to the murder being committed by a guardsman, then, we must review the time period between the soldier being confirmed as having gone with Martha into the yard at 11.45 p.m., and the time confirmed by the policeman Barrett, when he talked to the guardsman in Wentworth Street, which was 2.00 a.m.

Albert Crow, I believe, saw the body at 3.30 a.m., but what happened in the preceding one and a half hours holds the solution, and whether it was a guardsman who murdered Martha Tabram, or Jack the Ripper.

Mary Ann Nichols*

Doctor Llewellyn testified at the inquest that he was called from his surgery at 0400 hours, by PC Neil and pronounced her dead. He noticed that there was only a wine glass and a half of blood in the gutter, but was in no doubt that the body had been killed on the spot.

He found the body lying flat on her back and found her hands and wrists to be quite cold, and determined the body to have been dead no more than half an hour.

PC Thain in lifting the body into the cart that served as an ambulance noticed that the back of the dress was covered in blood.

The body had been washed at the mortuary, when Dr Llewellyn arrived to perform the post mortem, and he was somewhat indignant about this. At the inquest his testimony was reported as follows:

Five of the teeth were missing, and there was a slight laceration of the tongue. There was a bruise running along the lower part of the jaw on the right side of the face that might have been caused by a blow from a fist or pressure from a thumb. There was a circular bruise on the left side of the face, which also might have been inflicted by the pressure of the fingers. On the left side of the neck, about one inch below the jaw, there was an incision about four inches in length, and ran from a point immediately below the ear. On the same side, but an inch below, and commencing about one inch in front of it, was a circular incision which terminated at a point about three inches below the right jaw. That incision completely severed all the tissues down to the vertebrae. The large vessels of the neck on both sides had been severed. The incision was about eight inches in length. The cuts must have been caused by a long-bladed knife, moderately sharp and used with great violence. No blood was found on the breast, either of the body or the clothes. (This would tend to confirm to me that the murderer tore away the clothes before attacking the body with his knife, and did not cut through the clothes when mutilating the body) There were no injuries about the body until just about the lower part of the abdomen. Two or three inches from the left side, was a wound running in a jagged manner. The wound was a very deep one, and the tissues were cut through. There were several incisions running across the abdomen. There were also three or four similar cuts running downwards on the right side, all of which had been caused by a knife which had been used violently and downwards.

The injuries were from left to right, and might have been done by a left-handed person. All the injuries had been caused by the same instrument.

Dr Thomas Bond, the police surgeon to A Division of the Metropolitan Police, was asked later by Dr Robert Anderson, the Assistant Commissioner, to produce a report on the Ripper murders. One of the things that he stated in this report was that Nichols had been attacked from her right hand side.

Mary Ann Nichols was born in 1845 and died on 31 August 1888. She was last seen alive at 2.30 a.m. by Ellen Holland on the corner of Osborne Street and Whitechapel High Street, and her body was discovered at approximately 3.40 a.m. of that morning. From 24 August until 30 August she had been staying at the White House, Number 56 Flower and Dean Street.

Nichols's two front teeth were definitely missing prior to her murder, and it has never been suggested that the Ripper removed her other missing teeth.

Annie Chapman*

Doctor Phillips said in evidence, that he was summoned to examine the body at 6.20 a.m., and arrived at the murder scene approximately ten minutes later. His first observations were that at the feet of the body there was a piece of muslin cloth and a comb in a paper case, which he presumed were the contents of a torn pocket in Chapman's dress.

On attending the inquest on 14 September, in the Whitechapel Working Lads Institute, he gave his evidence as follows:

The left arm was placed across the left breast. *The legs were drawn up, the feet resting on the ground and the knees pushed outwards* (this is referred to as akimbo and indicates to me that the Ripper performed the mutilations from a kneeling position between the legs), the face was swollen and turned to the right, so exposing Annie's left profile. The tongue protruded between the front teeth, but not beyond the lips, and was much swollen. The teeth were perfect as far as the first molar, top and bottom, and very fine teeth they were. The body was violently and terribly mutilated.

The stiffness of the limbs was not marked, but was evidently commencing. I noticed that the throat was deeply dissevered; that the incisions through the skin were jagged and reached right round the neck.

On the wooden paling between the yard in question and the next, smears of blood (corresponding to where the head of the deceased lay) were to be found. These were about fourteen inches from the ground, and immediately above the part where the blood lay that had flowed from the neck.

I should say that the instrument used at the throat and the abdomen was the same. It must have been a very sharp knife with a thin narrow blade, and must have been at least six inches to eight inches in length, probably longer. I should say that the injuries could not have been inflicted by a bayonet or sword bayonet. They could have been done by such an instrument as a medical man used for post mortem purposes, but the ordinary surgical cases might not contain such an instrument.

Those used by slaughtermen, well ground down, might have caused them. He thought that the knives used in the leather trade would not be long enough in the blade. There were indications of anatomical knowledge which were only less indicated in consequence of haste. The whole of the body was not present, the absent portions being from the abdomen. The mode in which these portions were extracted showed some anatomical knowledge. I should say that the deceased had been dead for at least two hours, and probably more, when he first saw her, but it was right to mention that it was a fairly cool morning, and that the body would be more apt to cool rapidly, from its having lost a great quantity of blood. There was no evidence of a struggle having taken place.

He was positive that the deceased had entered the yard alive. A handkerchief was round the throat of the deceased when he saw it early in the morning. He should say that it was not tied on after the throat was cut.

On Saturday p.m. Dr Phillips performed a post mortem examination of Annie Chapman's body at the Whitechapel Workhouse Infirmary Mortuary, which was inferred to be in poor condition by Dr Phillips. The autopsy findings were reported as follows:

He noticed the same protrusion of the tongue. There was a bruise over the right temple. On the upper eyelid there was a bruise, and there were two distinct bruises, each the size of a man's thumb on the forepart of the top of the chest. The stiffness of the limbs was now well marked. There was a bruise over the middle part of the bone of the right hand. There was an old scar on the left of the frontal bone. The stiffness was more notable on the left side, especially in the fingers, which were partly closed.

There was an abrasion over the ring finger, with the distinct marking of a ring or rings. The throat had been severed as before described. *The incisions into the skin indicated that they had been made from the left side of the neck.* There were two distinct clean cuts on the left side of the spine. They were parallel to each other and separated by about half an inch. The muscular structures appeared as though an attempt had been made to separate the bones of the neck. There were various other mutilations of the body, but he was of the opinion that they occurred subsequent to the death of the woman, and to the large escape of blood from the division of the neck. At this point in the procedures Dr Phillips said that, as from these injuries he was satisfied as to the cause of death, he thought that he had better not go into further details of the mutilations, which could only be painful to the feelings of the jury and the public. The coroner agreed, and Dr Phillips continued saying, the cause of death was apparent from the injuries he had described, from these appearances he was of the opinion that the breathing was interfered with previous to death, and that death arose from syncope or failure of the heart's action in consequence of loss of blood caused by severance of the throat.

In answer to subsequent questions put to him by the coroner, Dr Phillips continued. The deceased was far advanced in disease of the lungs and membranes of the brain, but they had nothing to do with the cause of death. The stomach contained a little food, but there was not any sign of fluid.

There was no appearance of the deceased having taken alcohol, but there were signs of great deprivation, and he should say she had been badly fed. He was convinced that she had not taken any strong alcohol for some hours before her death. The injuries were certainly not self-inflicted. The bruises on the face were evidently recent, especially about the chin and sides of the jaw, but the bruises in front of the chest and temple were of longer standing – probably of days. *He was of the opinion that the person who cut the deceased's throat took hold of her by the chin, and then commenced the incision from left to right.* He thought that it was highly probable that a person could call out, but with regard to an idea that she might have been gagged he could only point to the swollen face and protruding tongue, both of which were signs of suffocation.

The body was laid out and washed by Mary Elizabeth Simonds, a nurse, and assisted by Frances Wright. It was done on the orders of the Clerk to the Parish Guardians, and to the extreme annoyance of Dr Phillips, who was of the opinion that it may have hindered the post mortem findings.

Dr Phillips was requested to re-attend the inquest on 19 September by the coroner, Wynne Baxter, who asserted that after consideration, he required that the doctor give a more comprehensive explanation as to the after-death mutilations. Baxter declared that certain medical opinion was in disagreement as to whether the mutilations were indeed posthumous. The following transcript is taken from *The Lancet*.

The abdomen was completely laid open, and the intestines, severed from their mesenteric attachments, had been lifted out of the body and placed on the shoulder of the corpse; whilst from the pelvis, the uterus and its appendages with the upper portion of the vagina and the posterior two-thirds of the bladder had been entirely removed. *No trace of these parts could be found and the incisions were cleanly cut, avoiding the rectum, and dividing the vagina low enough to avoid injury to the cervix uteri* [this sentence alone would serve to convince me that the Ripper possessed a degree of anatomical knowledge], obviously the work of an expert, or of one at least, who had such knowledge of anatomical or pathological examinations as to be enabled to secure the pelvic organs with one sweep of the knife, which therefore must have been at least five or six inches in length, probably more. The appearance of the cuts confirmed him in the opinion that the instrument, like the one which divided the neck, had been of a very sharp character. The mode in which the knife had been used seemed to indicate great anatomical knowledge.

In answer to questions from the coroner: he thought that he himself could not have performed all of the injuries he described, even without a struggle, under a quarter of an hour. If he had done it in a deliberate way such as would fall to the duties of a surgeon, it would probably have taken him the best part of an hour.

The long-term bruising described earlier in the evidence can be ignored, and was most probably the result of a fight which Annie had with Eliza Cooper, when she had taken a beating.

Elizabeth Stride *

Dr William Blackwell arrived at the murder scene at 1.16 a.m. precisely, and determined that Stride had been dead no longer than twenty minutes.

The Police Surgeon, Dr Bagster Phillips, said in evidence that he was summoned at twenty past one, and went to the scene of the murder via the police station in Leman Street, arriving at approximately 2.00 a.m.

In his report he stated:

The body was lying on the near side, with the face turned towards the wall, the head up the yard and the feet towards the street. The left arm was extended, and there was a packet of cachous in the left hand. The right arm was over the belly, the back of the hand and the wrist had on it clotted blood. The legs were drawn up with the feet close to the wall. The body and face were warm to the touch, and the hand cold. The legs were quite warm. The deceased had a silk handkerchief round her neck, and it appeared to be slightly torn. I have since ascertained it was cut, this corresponded with the right angle of the jaw. The throat was deeply gashed, and there was an abrasion of the skin about 1½ inches in diameter, apparently stained with blood, under the right brow.

At 3.00 p.m. on Monday at St George's Mortuary, Dr Blackwell and I made a post mortem examination.

Rigor mortis was thoroughly marked. There was mud on the left side of the face and it was matted in the head. The body was fairly nourished. Over both shoulders, especially the right, and under the collar bone and in front of the chest, there was a bluish discolouration, which I have watched and have seen on occasions since. There was a clean-cut incision on the neck. It was six inches in length and commenced 2½ inches in a straight line below the angle of the jaw, ½ inch over an undivided muscle, and then becoming deeper, dividing the sheath.

The cut was very clean and deviated a little downwards. The artery and the other vessels contained within the sheath were all cut through. *The cut through the tissues on the right side was more superficial and tailed off to about two inches below the right angle of the jaw. The deep vessels on that side were uninjured.*

From this it was evident that the haemorrhage was caused through the partial severance of the left carotid artery. Decomposition had commenced in the skin. Dark brown spots were on the anterior surface of the left chin. There was a deformity in the bones of the right leg, which was not straight but bowed forwards.

There was no recent external injury save to the neck. The body being washed more thoroughly, I could see some healing sores. The lobe of the left ear was torn as if from the removal or wearing through of an earring, but it was thoroughly healed. On removing the scalp, there was no sign of bruising or extra-vasation of blood.

The heart was small, the left ventricle firmly contracted, and the right slightly so, there was no clot in the pulmonary artery, but the right ventricle was full of dark clot. The left was firmly contracted so as to be completely empty. The stomach was large and the mucous membrane only congested. It contained partly digested food, apparently consisting of cheese, potato, and farin-aceous powder. All the teeth on the left lower jaw were absent. Examining her jacket I found that while there was a small amount on the right side, the left side was well plastered with mud.

The coroner then proceeded to ask Dr Phillips some questions, to which the doctor gave the following information.

The cause of death is undoubtedly from the loss of blood from the left carotid artery and the division of the windpipe. The blood had run down the waterway to within a few inches of the side entrance of the club. Roughly estimating it, I should say there was an unusual flow of blood considering the stature and nourishment of the body.

On resumption of the inquest Dr Phillips described further observ-ations:

He had made a re-examination with regard to the missing palate, and from very careful examination of the roof of the mouth he found that there was no injury to either the hard or the soft palate. He had also carefully examined the handkerchiefs, and had come to the conclusion that the stains on the larger hand-kerchief were those of fruit. He was convinced that the deceased had not swallowed the skin or inside of a grape within many hours of her death. The apparent abrasion which was found on washing the flesh was not an abrasion at all, as the skin was entire underneath. He found that the deceased was seized by the shoulders, pressed on the ground, and the perpetrator of the deed was on the left side when he inflicted the wound. He was of the opinion that the cut was made from left to right of the deceased, and from that therefore arose the unlikelihood of such a long knife having inflicted the wound described on the neck. The knife was not sharp-pointed, but round, and an inch across. There was nothing in the cut to show an incision of the point of any weapon.

He could not form any account of how the deceased's right hand became covered in blood. It was a mystery. He was taking it as a fact that the hand always remained in the position he found it in resting across the body. Deceased must have been alive within an hour of his seeing her. The injuries would only take a few seconds to inflict. It may have been done in two seconds. He could not say with certainty whether the sweets being found in her hand indicated that the deed had been done suddenly. *There was a great dissimilarity between this case and Chapman's. In the latter, the neck was severed all round down to the vertebral column, the vertebral bone being enlarged with two sharp cuts, and there being an evident attempt to separate the bones.*

The murderer would not necessarily be bloodstained, for the commencement of the wound and the injury to the vessels would be away from him, and the stream of blood, for stream it would be, would be directed away from him, and towards the waterway already mentioned. He had reason to believe that the deceased was lying on the ground when the wound was inflicted.

I would ask that you note the statements highlighted in italics, and my own opinion, as you know, is that Elizabeth Stride was not killed by Jack the Ripper. The throat was cut by a single slash, unlike the other victims, and the severity of the cut decreased as the knife came across the neck, from the victim,s left to right. I would ask you to bear in mind that Dr Phillips also, did not think that the Ripper killed Stride.

Bagster Phillips also attended the inquest and post mortem of Catharine Eddowes and affirmed that the murder was not by the same hand that killed Stride.

Catharine Eddowes*

Doctor Sequeira arrived at the scene of the crime at 1.45 a.m.. He pronounced the body dead, but did not undertake a close examination, as the arrival of the police surgeon for the area, Dr Gordon Brown, was imminent.

After the evidence of Dr Brown, at the inquest, Dr Sequeira said that he concurred with the findings of Dr Brown, but on being further questioned by the coroner, he stated that 'the murderer did not show any particular skill', and that in his opinion he had not been seeking any particular organ when he had extracted the kidney and the uterus.

Dr Frederick Gordon Brown described his initial examination findings as follows:

The body was on its back, the head turned to the left shoulder. The arms by the side of the body as if they had fallen there. Both palms upward, the fingers slightly bent. The left leg extended in line with the body. The abdomen was exposed. The right leg was bent at the thigh and knee. [This would make it difficult for someone to commit the mutilations from the right side and below the waist, as is one section of contemporary thinking; also the arm being down by the side would prevent the perpetrator getting near to the body.] The throat cut across.

The intestines were drawn out to a large extent, and placed over the right shoulder. They were smeared over with some feculent matter. A piece of about two feet was quite detached from the body and placed between the body and the left arm, apparently by design.

The lobe and auricle of the right ear were cut obliquely through.

There was a quantity of clotted blood on the pavement on the left side of the neck, round the shoulder and upper part of the arm, and fluid blood-coloured serum which had flowed under the neck to the right shoulder, the pavement sloping in that direction.

The body was quite warm. No death stiffening had taken place. She must have been dead possibly within the half hour. We looked for superficial bruises and saw none. No blood on the skin of the abdomen or secretion of any kind on the thighs. No spurting of blood on the bricks or pavement around. No marks of blood below the middle of the body. Several buttons were found in the clotted blood, after the body was removed. There was no blood on the front of the clothes. There was no signs of recent connection.

Dr Brown further examined the body at the Golden Lane Mortuary, and his report reads:

I made a post mortem examination at half past two on the Sunday afternoon.

Rigor mortis was well marked; the body was not quite cold.

There was green discolouration over the abdomen.

After washing the left hand carefully, a bruise the size of a sixpence, recent and red, was discovered on the back of the left hand between the thumb and the first finger. A few small bruises were evident on the right shin of older date. The hands and arms were bronzed. There were no bruises on the scalp, the back of the body, or the elbows.

The face was very much mutilated. There was a cut about a quarter of an inch through the lower left eyelid, dividing the structures completely through, there was also a scratch through the skin on the left upper eyelid, near the angle of the nose. The right eyelid was cut through to about half an inch.

There was a deep cut over the bridge of the nose, extending from the left border of the nasal bone down near to the angle of the jaw on the right side of the cheek. This cut went into the bone and divided all the structures of the cheek except the mucous membrane of the mouth.

The tip of the nose was quite detached from the nose by an oblique cut from the bottom of the nasal bone to where the wings of the nose join onto the face. A cut from this divided the upper lip and extended through the substance of the gum over the right upper lateral incisor tooth. About half an inch from the top of the nose, was another oblique cut. There was a cut on the right angle of the mouth as if the cut of the point of a knife. The cut extended an inch and a half, parallel with the lower lip.

There was on each side of the cheek, a cut which peeled up the skin, forming a triangular flap about an inch and a half.

On the left cheek there were two abrasions of the epithelium under the left ear.

The throat was cut across to the extent of about six or seven inches. A superficial cut commenced about an inch and a half below the lobe and about two and a half inches below and behind the left ear, and extended across the throat to about three inches below the lobe of the right ear. The big muscle across the throat was divided through on the left side. The large vessels on the left-hand side of the neck were severed. The larynx was severed below the vocal chord; all the deep structures were severed to the bone, with the knife marking the intervertebral cartilages.

The sheath of the vessel on the right side was just opened. The carotid artery had a fine hole opening. The internal jugular vein was opened an inch and a half, not divided. The blood vessels contained clot. All of these injuries were performed by a sharp instrument like a knife, and pointed. [It must be noted that the knife used in this murder was pointed as in the other murders, with the exception of Stride. This means that if the same person committed the murders of Stride and Eddowes then he used a different knife for each of the murders, and yet the murder of Eddowes was only 40 minutes after the murder of Stride.]

The cause of death was haemorrhage from the left common carotid artery. The death was immediate, and the mutilations inflicted after death.

We examined the abdomen. The front walls were laid open from the breast bone to the pubes. The cut commenced opposite the enciform cartilage. *The incision went upward* [once again I must draw the reader's attention to the fact that this specific cut is difficult to achieve if undertaken with the right hand and from being positioned on the right hand side of the body, with the right leg raised and bent at the knee], not penetrating the skin that was over the sternum. It then divided the enciform cartilage; the knife must have cut obliquely at the expense of the front surface of that cartilage.

Behind this, the liver was stabbed as if by the point of a sharp instrument. Below this was another incision into the liver of about two and a half inches, and below this the left lobe of the liver was slit through by a vertical cut. Two cuts were shewn by a jagging of the skin on the left side.

The abdominal walls were divided in the middle line to within a quarter of an inch of the navel. The cut then took a horizontal course for two and a half inches towards the right side. It then divided round the navel on the left side, and made a parallel incision to the former horizontal incision, leaving the navel on a tongue of skin. Attached to the navel was two and a half inches of the lower part of the rectus muscle on the left side of the abdomen. The incision then took an oblique direction to the right and was shelving. The incision went down the right side of the vagina and the rectum for half an inch behind the rectum.

There was a stab of about one inch on the left groin. This was done by a pointed instrument. Below this was a cut of about three inches going through all the tissues making a wound of the peritoneum about the same extent.

An inch below the crease of the thigh was a cut extending from the anterior spine of the ilium obliquely down the inner side of the left thigh and separating the left labium, forming a flap of skin, up to the groin. The left rectus muscle was not detached.

There was a flap of skin formed from the right thigh, attaching the right labium and extended up to the spine of the ilium. The muscles on the right side inserted into the frontal ligaments were cut through.

The skin was retracted through the whole of the cut in the abdomen, but the vessels were not clotted, nor had there been any appreciable bleeding from the vessels. I draw the conclusion that the cut was made after death, and there would not be much blood on the murderer. The cut was made by someone on the right side of the body, kneeling below the middle of the body. [As the reader will appreciate, I do not hold with this position for reasons previously explained, also if the assailant was left-handed the same mutilations could have been duplicated from a position between the legs. Furthermore I do not dismiss the fact that at some time during his attack on the body, the Ripper may have moved around the body to position himself over the head kneeling either side of it.]

I removed the contents of the stomach and placed it in a jar for further examination. There seemed very little in it in the way of food or fluid, but from the cut end, partly digested farinaceous food escaped.

The intestines had been detached to a large extent from the mesentary. About two feet of the colon was cut away. The sigmoid flexure was invaginated into the rectum very tightly.

Right kidney pale, bloodless, with slight congestion of the base of the pyramids.

There was a cut from the upper part of the slit on the under surface of the liver to the left side, and another cut at right angles to this, which were about an inch and a half deep and two and a half inches long. The liver itself was healthy.

The gall bladder contained bile. The pancreas was cut, but not through, on the left side of the spinal column. Three and a half inches of the lower border of the spleen by half an inch, was attached only to the peritoneum.

The peritoneal lining was cut through on the left side and the left kidney carefully taken out and removed. The left renal artery was cut through. I should say that someone who knew the position of the kidney must have done it.

The lining membrane over the uterus was cut through. The womb was cut through horizontally, leaving a stump of three quarters of an inch.

The rest of the womb had been taken away with some of the ligaments. The vagina and cervix of the womb was uninjured.

The bladder was healthy and uninjured, and contained three or four ounces of water. There was a tongue-like cut through the anterior wall of the abdominal aorta. The other organs were healthy.

There were no recent signs of connection.

I believe that the wound in the throat was first inflicted. I believe she must have been lying on the ground.

The wounds on the face and the abdomen prove that they were inflicted by a sharp pointed knife and that in the abdomen one six inches long.

I believe the perpetrator of the act must have had considerable knowledge of the positions of the organs in the abdominal cavity and the way of removing them. The parts removed would be of no use for any professional purposes. It required a great deal of medical knowledge to have removed the kidney and to have known where it was placed. Such knowledge might be possessed by someone in the habit of cutting up animals.

I think that the perpetrator of this act had sufficient time, or he would not have nicked the lower eyelids. It would take at least five minutes.

I cannot assign any reason for the parts being taken away. I feel sure there was no struggle. I believe it was the act of one person.

The throat had been so instantly severed that no noise could have been emitted. I should not have expected much blood to have been found on the person who had inflicted these wounds.

The wounds could not have been self-inflicted.

My attention was called to the apron. It was the corner of the apron, with a string attached. The blood spots were of recent origin. I have seen the portion of an apron produced by Dr Phillips and stated to have been found in Goulston Street. It is impossible to say it is human blood. I fitted the piece of apron, which had a new piece of material on it which had evidently been sewn on to the piece I have. The seams of the borders of the two actually corresponded. Some blood and apparently faecal matter was found on the portion found in Goulston Street. I believe the wounds on the face to have been done to disfigure the corpse.

Mary Jane Kelly *

Dr Phillips on entering the room of Kelly felt obliged to remark that the door, on opening, struck the table to the left of the bed. He conducted a cursory examination stating:

> The mutilated remains of a female were lying two-thirds of the way over towards the edge of the bedstead nearest the door. She had only her chemise on, or some underlinen garment.
>
> I am sure the body had been removed subsequent to the injury which caused her death, from the side of the bedstead which was nearest the wood partition, because of the large quantity of blood under the bedstead, and the saturated condition of the sheet and the palliasse at the corner nearest to the partition. The blood was produced by the severance of the carotid artery, which was the immediate cause of death. This injury was inflicted while the deceased was lying at the right of the bedstead.

Dr Thomas Bond submitted his report on Kelly, and stated:

Position of Body
The body was lying naked in the middle of the bed, the shoulder flat, but the axis of the body inclined to the left side of the bed. The head was turned on the left cheek. The left arm was close to the body with the forearm flexed at a right angle and lying across the abdomen. The right arm was slightly abducted from the body and rested on the mattress, the elbow bent and the forearm supine with the fingers clenched. The legs were wide apart, the left thigh at right angles to the trunk and the right forming an obtuse angle with the pubes.

The whole of the surface of the abdomen and thighs was removed, and the abdominal cavity emptied of its viscera. The breasts were cut off, the arms mutilated by several jagged wounds and the face hacked beyond recognition of the features.

The tissues of the neck were severed all round to the bone.

The viscera were found in various parts viz: the uterus and kidneys with one breast, under the head, the other breast by the right foot, the liver between the feet, the intestines by the right side, and the spleen by the left side of the body. The flaps removed from the abdomen and thighs were on the table.

The bed clothing at the right corner was saturated with blood, and the floor beneath was a pool of blood covering about two feet square. The wall by the right side of the bed and in a line with the neck was marked by blood which had struck it in a number of separate splashes.

Post mortem examination

The face was gashed in all directions, the nose, cheeks, eyebrows and ears being partly removed. The lips were blanched and cut by several incisions running obliquely down to the chin. There were also numerous cuts extending irregularly across all the features.

The neck was cut through the skin and other tissues right down to the vertebrae. The 5th and 6th being deeply notched.

The skin cuts in front of the neck showed distinct ecchymosis.

The air passage was cut at the lower part of the larynx through the cricoid cartilage.

Both breasts were removed by more or less circular incisions, the muscles down to the ribs being attached to the breasts. The intercostals between the 4th, 5th, and 6th ribs were cut through and the contents of the thorax visible through the openings.

The skin and tissues of the abdomen from the costal arch to the pubes were removed in three large flaps. The right thigh was denuded in front of the bone, the flap of skin, including the external organs of generation and part of the right buttock. The left thigh was stripped of skin, fascia and muscles as far as the knee.

The left calf showed a long gash through skin and tissues to the deep muscles and reaching from the knee to five inches above the ankle.

Both arms and forearms had extensive and jagged wounds.

The right thumb showed a small superficial incision about 1 inch long, with extravasation of blood in the skin, and there were several abrasions on the back of the hand moreover, showing the same condition.

On opening the thorax it was found that the right lung was minimally adherent by old firm adhesions. The lower part of the lung was broken and torn away.

The left lung was intact: it was adherent at the apex and there were a few adhesions over the side. In the substances of the lung were several nodules of consolidation.

The pericardium was open below and the heart absent.

In the abdominal cavity was some partly digested food of fish and potatoes, and similar food was found in the remains of the stomach attached to the intestines.

This is the main medical input into the injuries and opinions provided by the doctors of the day.

I personally believe that there was a degree of animosity directed towards Bagster Phillips from Dr Bond, and certain of Bond's criticisms were in my opinion partially made to discredit Bagster Phillips.

However, Dr Robert Anderson requested a general report on the murders from Dr Bond. I have taken the liberty of punctuating the text of the report to enable the reader to more easily decipher its content.

The report reads thus:

I beg to report that I have read the notes of the four Whitechapel murders, viz:
1. Buck's Row.
2. Hanbury Street.
3. Berner Street.
4. Mitre Square.

I have also made a post mortem examination of the mutilated remains of a woman found yesterday in a small room in Dorset Street.

1. All five murders were no doubt committed by the same hand. In the first four, the throats appear to have been cut from left to right. in the last case, owing to the extensive mutilation, it is impossible to say in what direction the fatal cut was made, but arterial blood was found on the wall in splashes close to where the woman's head must have been lying.

2. All the circumstances surrounding the murders lead me to form the opinion that the women must have been lying down when murdered, and in every case the throat was first cut.

3. In the four murders of which I have seen the notes only, I cannot form a very definite opinion as to the time that had elapsed between the murder and the discovering of the body. In one case, that of Berner Street, the discovery appears to have been made immediately after the deed – in Buck's Row, Hanbury Street, and Mitre Square, three or four hours only could have elapsed. In the Dorset Street case, the body was lying on the bed at the time of my visit, two o'clock, quite naked and mutilated as in the annexed report.

Rigor mortis had set in, but increased during the progress of the examination. From this, it is difficult to say with any degree of certainty the exact time that had elapsed since death, as the period varies from 6 to 12 hours before rigidity sets in. The body was comparatively cold at 2 o'clock, and the remains of a recently taken meal were found in the stomach, and scattered about over the intestines. It is, therefore, pretty certain that the woman must have been dead about twelve hours. And the partly digested food would indicate that death took place about three or four hours after the food was taken, so 1 or 2 o'clock in the morning would be the probable time of the murder.

4. In all the cases there appears to be no evidence of struggling, and the attacks were probably so sudden, and made in such a position, that the women could neither resist nor cry out. In the Dorset Street case, the corner of the sheet to the right of the woman's head, was much cut and saturated with blood, indicating that the face may have been covered with the sheet at the time of the attack. [Did the Ripper profess a degree of shyness, and get Kelly to hide her eyes while he removed his clothes? He then attacked her while the sheet was pulled over her eyes.]

5. In the four first cases, the murderer must have attacked from the right side of the victim. In the Dorset Street case, he must have attacked in front or from the left, as there would be no room for him between the wall and the part of the bed on which the woman was lying. Again, the blood had flowed down on the right side of the woman and spurted on to the wall.

6. The murderer would not necessarily be splashed or deluged with blood, but his hands and arms must have been covered, and parts of his clothing must certainly have been smeared with blood.

7. The mutilations in each case, excepting the Berner Street one, were all of the same character, and showed clearly that in all the murders, the object was mutilation.

8. In each case the mutilation was inflicted by a person who had no scientific nor anatomical knowledge. In my opinion, he does not even possess the technical knowledge of a butcher or horse slaughterer, or any person accustomed to cut up dead animals.

9. The instrument must have been a strong knife at least six inches long, very sharp, pointed at the top, and about an inch in width. It may have been a clasp knife, a butcher's knife or a surgeon's knife. I think it was no doubt a straight knife.

10. The murderer must have been a man of physical strength, and of great coolness and daring. There is no evidence that he had an accomplice. He must in my opinion be a man subject to periodical attacks of homicidal and erotic mania. The character of the mutilations indicates that the man, may be in a condition sexually, that may be called satyriasis. It is of course possible that the homicidal impulse may have developed from a revengeful or brooding condition of the mind, or that Religious Mania may have been the original disease, but I do not think either hypothesis is likely. *The murderer, in external appearance is quite likely to be a quiet inoffensive looking man*, probably middle-aged, and neatly and respectably dressed. I think he must be in the habit of wearing a cloak or overcoat, or he could hardly escape notice in the streets, if the blood on his hands or clothes were visible. [He wouldn't need the cloak or overcoat, if he wiped his hands and arms before leaving the scene of the crime, or washed them nearby in one of the many standpipes in the area.]

11. Assuming the murderer to be such a person as I have just described, he would probably be solitary and eccentric in his habits; also, he is most likely to be a man without regular occupation, but with some small income or pension. He is possibly living among respectable persons who have some knowledge of his character and habits, and who may have grounds for suspicion that he is not quite right in his mind at times. Such persons would probably be unwilling to communicate suspicions to the police, for fear of trouble or notoriety, whereas, if there were a prospect of reward, it might overcome their scruples.

As I have previously stated the inclusion of this chapter is designed to stimulate the reader in analysing the information and formulating his own opinions based on the information included within the chapter.

I offer you some of the questions which require consideration and hope that you can scrutinise the evidence and evaluate its contents.

1. Did the killer have anatomical knowledge, and if so, to what degree?

2. Which hand did he favour?

3. Were the victims strangled prior to their throats being cut?

4. From which position was the throat cut, i.e. where was the Ripper situated when he commenced the cutting of the throat and the mutilations?

5. Have the fingers got sufficient strength to strangle from behind and prevent the emission of any sound? Ordinarily strangulation from behind would involve the use of the arms, but this would not leave the telltale bruising on the throat.

6. The bruises on the neck and jaw/cheeks of the victims, some of which are identified as thumb prints: would these indicate that the victim was strangled whilst lying on the ground? And if so, would the location of the bruises favour a right- or left-handed assailant?

7. What is the likelihood of error in the estimation of the time of death, when taking into account that the stomach has been opened, and there has been a great loss of blood?

8. It takes a lot of anger and rage to stab a body 39 times. Could Martha Tabram's murder have been a logical start for the Ripper?

9. Do you think that Elizabeth Stride was a Ripper victim?

10. Would the person who killed Martha Tabram be likely to kill again?

11. Is there any inference to be drawn from the fact that it was the right leg of Eddowes that was bent at the thigh and knee?

12. Could some of the cuts on the inside of the body be the result of the initial attack on the outside?

13. *My big question for this chapter is: why did the Ripper cut/tear a section of Eddowes's apron? Could the Ripper have cut himself, in the frenzy of the attack, and did he wrap the piece of apron about his hand? There has to be a reason why he took the piece of apron. If so, could the blood on the piece of apron found in Goulston Street belong to Jack the Ripper? It appears to have been done in haste, and he abandoned the piece of apron in Goulston Street, approximately fifteen minutes walk from the scene of the murder, but at least one hour and a half after the murder was discovered. As I have stated there must have been a reason for him to hang on to the piece of apron for so long a time.*

14. *Nichols – throat was cut twice.*
    Chapman – throat was cut twice.
    Eddowes – throat was cut twice.
    Stride – throat was cut once.
    Kelly – too badly mutilated to tell.
Do you still believe that Stride was a Ripper victim?

I have other questions which would draw their importance from the feedback I receive to the ones above.

All the information listed within this chapter has been transcribed as written, with minimal changes to the vocabulary and grammar. I must therefore absolve myself of the responsibility for spelling and punctuation mistakes.

CHAPTER EIGHTEEN

The main players and supporting cast

In 1886 Sir Charles Warren was chosen to succeed Sir Edmund Henderson as the Commissioner of the Metropolitan Police. Initially, he was a popular appointment, and was well received by the London Press, as the man needed to revitalise and reorganise the London Police Force. This relationship soon soured, as the police mishandled situations and solved the city's problems rather more brutally than was considered acceptable.

Well before the onset of the Whitechapel murders, the *East London Observer* was criticising the efficiency of the 'Old Bill' when it suggested: 'One of the East End representatives might do service by looking into the police arrangements in the East End of London, for there is room for grave doubt whether our end of town has its fair return for money in the matter of police protection.' It went on to give evidence of assaults carried out by night, where 'the guardian of the night' was notably absent. 'Where was the police?' it demanded.

The dissatisfaction continued to gather momentum, and after the murder of Annie Chapman, which was the third killing in a month, the *East London Advertiser* of 15 September 1888 mounted a massive attack on Sir Charles, describing him as 'a martinet of apparently a somewhat inefficient type' who was guilty of 'the double folly of weakening his detective force, and strengthening his ordinary police force, from the ranks of reserve men – and others of a military or semi-military type that destroys two safeguards of a community. It deprives it of a specially trained force, consisting of men of superior intellect and specially adapted powers for detective purposes. It substitutes for the old parish constable, the man with the few years' military service, but with no other qualifications for serving the public. Nothing indeed has been more characteristic of the hunt after the Whitechapel murderer than the want of local knowledge displayed by the police. They seem to know little of the bad haunts of the neighbourhood, and still less of the bad characters that infest them.'

As the murders continued, so the criticism of the police gained momentum, and the pressure increased on Sir Charles Warren to resign.

After the double murders of 30 September, this pressure again amplified, and Warren was accused of going blindly forward without a true sense of direction, contributing to increased inefficiency and demoralising the C.I.D. force.

With the first murder being regarded as that of Martha Tabram, this meant that from 7 August to 30 September, five murders had been committed, and the *East End News* of 5 October, continued the attack:

> The marvellous inefficiency of the police, in the detection, was forcibly shown in the fact that, in the very same block as that containing Mitre Square, in the leading thoroughfare, and at a moment when the whole area was full of police, just after the murder, the Aldgate Post Office was entered and ransacked, and property to the value of hundreds of pounds taken clean away under the very noses of the 'Guardians of peace and order'!

The criticism was not confined to any particular class of society, and Queen Victoria personally intervened, when on 10 November, after the killing of Mary Jane Kelly, she wired the Marquis of Salisbury from Balmoral, saying, 'All these courts must be lit, and our detectives improved. They are not what they should be.' She followed with a letter in which she repeated that 'the detective department is not as efficient as it might be' and went on to offer ideas on how the methods of investigation might be improved. This involvement by her majesty assisted in applying the *coup de grâce* to Warren's police career, and the editor of *Justice* announced that on Tuesday 13 November the Police Commissioner had been ignominiously kicked out of office by the same Tory Home Secretary, amid the jeers and execrations of the whole community. In point of fact, Sir Charles Warren resigned on the day of Mary Kelly's murder, and had been contemplating such an action for a number of weeks beforehand.

Warren was succeeded as Commissioner by James Monro, who had himself resigned as Assistant Commissioner in charge of the C.I.D. over his disagreement with Warren as to who should have total control of the C.I.D., and had undertaken an appointment as unofficial head of the Detective Service, which he held for a period of two months up to his appointment as Commissioner. He held the position of Metropolitan Police Commissioner for a period of two years, at which time he again tendered his resignation, over a dispute on the Police Bill, and his being overruled in the appointment of Chief Constable.

During his time in the senior ranks of the Met. Munro emerged as a person who was respected by virtually every officer who served under him. Everybody agreed on his undoubted ability as a detective, and anybody who committed himself to paper, inevitably spoke of him with high regard.

During his two-year spell as Commissioner, the standing of the police markedly increased, and there was a significant fall in the crime figures, which was attributed directly to his influence.

It is hardly surprising, with all of the internal bickering within the echelons of the police force, and the undoubted ill feeling between Scotland Yard and the Home Office, that the Ripper was not apprehended, and it seems warranted that at the time of the Whitechapel murders, the press were indeed justified in their accusations of inefficiency.

Concerning the Ripper murders, Monro did indeed have a theory, and in 1890 when he was interviewed by *Cassells Magazine*, he stated that 'he had formed a theory on the case', but he did not expound the theory by naming a suspect or relaying implicating evidence.

After retirement, he made a statement to one of his grandsons which included 'The Ripper was never caught, but he should have been.'

Monro gave some papers concerning the Whitechapel murders to his eldest son Charles, and though he did not reveal what the papers contained, Charles informed his brother Douglas that 'the theory contained within the pages was a "very hot potato".' To the present time these documents have not surfaced, and so Monro's theory and suspect have never been investigated.

Dr Robert Anderson assumed the role of Assistant Commissioner in August of 1888, after the resignation of James Monro, and on 6 October he assumed overall control of the Whitechapel Murders, and retained this charge until the closure of the case in 1892.

During his career, Anderson stated on a number of occasions that the identity of the Ripper was known. He himself was described by Major Arthur Griffiths as 'an ideal detective officer, with a natural bias for the work. Of the quickest apprehension, and with the power of close rapid reasoning, of the facts, suggestions, or even impressions. He seizes on the essential point almost by intuition. He is discreet, the most silent and reserved of public functionaries. Someone said he was a mystery to himself. He has perhaps achieved greater success than any other detective of his time.'

However, not everyone held Anderson in such high esteem, and on his retirement, *The Police Review* described him thus:

> Turning to the repute in which Dr Anderson was held in his immediate official circle. His tenure of office was considered to be characterised by the comfortable placidity for which the majority of our public functionaries are remarkable. Moreover, his temperament, so admirably adapted to his social and religious proclivities, was not such as best fits one for the work of the C.I.D.
>
> A biblical scholar of repute, and a literary recluse, such as he is, would hardly be the man to take an active part in fighting the criminal classes of London. Discreet, silent, and reserved though he was according to Major Arthur Griffiths' estimate, he lacked one inestimable quality to success, as Director of the detective staff of the most important police force in the world, and that was just the requisite kind of knowledge of the world and of men. An acknowledged authority on our penal system, it was perhaps, hardly a looked for choice on the part of Home Secretary Matthews.

Anderson assumed his position in Scotland Yard on the day that Mary Ann Nichols was murdered. He regarded it as the second of the Ripper murders and must therefore have counted Martha Tabram as the first victim. Anderson had been advised to take sick leave at the time of his appointment, and assigned the supervision of the Whitechapel murders to Detective Chief Inspector Donald Swanson. He then left for Switzerland on the day that Annie Chapman was killed.

In his memoirs, Anderson wrote that after examination of the evidence, 'We reached certain conclusions which eventually proved correct in every respect.' What exactly these conclusions were, we do not know, but they had nothing whatsoever to do with the identity of the Ripper, because, in a letter to the Home Office on 23 October, he wrote 'That five successive murders should have been committed without our having the slightest clue of any kind is extraordinary.'

In 1910, Anderson published his memoirs, which he called *The Lighter Side of my Official Life*. He did this in serial form in *Blackwood's Magazine*, and on the Whitechapel murders he volunteered:

One did not need to be Sherlock Holmes to discover that the criminal was a sexual maniac of a virulent type; that he was living in the immediate vicinity of the scenes of the crimes; and that, if he was not living absolutely alone, his people knew of his guilt, and refused to give him up to justice. During my absence abroad, the police had made a house to house search for him, investigating the case of every man in the district whose circumstances were such that he could go and come, and get rid of his blood stains in secret. And the conclusion we came to was that he and his people were low-class Jews, for it is a remarkable fact that people of that class in the East End will not give up one of their number to gentile justice.

And the result proved that our diagnosis was right on every point. For I may say at once that 'undiscovered murders' are rare in London, and the Jack the Ripper murders are not in that category, and if the police here had the same powers such as the French police possess, the murderer would have been brought to justice. I will only add here that the Jack the Ripper letter which is preserved in the police museum in Scotland Yard is the creation of an enterprising London journalist.

Having regard to the interest attached to the case, I should almost be tempted to disclose the identity of the murderer, and of the press man who wrote the letter above referred to, provided that the publishers would accept all responsibility in view of a possible libel action, but no public benefit would result from such a course, and the traditions of my old department would suffer. I will only add that when the individual whom we suspected was caged in an asylum, the only person who had ever had a good view of the murderer at once identified him.

Let us now review the contents of this extract from Anderson's memoirs.

1. Anderson says that 'undiscovered murders' are rare in London. If he means that unsolved murders are rare, this is totally against the statistical evidence. As has been implied previously, the efficiency of the police was subject to extensive ridicule. Just let us look at the twelve murders which we have reviewed. We must remove 'Fairy Fay', as there is no conclusive evidence that a murder was ever com-mitted. Then let us ignore the possible six murders which were attributed to Jack the Ripper. That leaves five other killings. Let us now give the police the benefit of the doubt and

eliminate Rose Mylett, on the detail that the police questioned the fact that her death was a murder. This leaves four murders still outstanding – none of which was ever solved. Another piece of information which supports my claim on the inefficiency of the police is that in the year of 1887, in the Whitechapel area alone, Tom Cullen the esteemed Ripper journalist and author wrote the following paragraph:

> In scanning the press for this period one is astounded by the number of reports of women who had been beaten or kicked to death, jumped on until they were crushed, chopped, stabbed, scarred with vitriol, eviscerated, or deliberately set afire. In the preceding year thirty-five murders were recorded in the Home Counties alone, seventy-six murders if we include infanticides, and of this number only eight convictions were secured. The majority of these crimes remaining unsolved forever. Using this as an example, Anderson's statement that 'undiscovered murders in London were rare' is an out-and-out lie.

2. He states that he is almost tempted to disclose the identity of the Ripper, but nowhere in the police files is there any indication that Anderson knew the identity of the Ripper, and if he had given this information to the publishers and the press, they *would* have accepted liability if only for the increased sales which it would have generated. Plus, if he was so sure of the identity, then we must ask if the person named, if still alive, would risk taking the matter further knowing what could come out in any ensuing court case?

3. He states that release of the Ripper's identity would have served no public benefit. What a load of rot. He adds that the traditions of his old department would suffer. Police inefficiency was notorious at the time, and this would have undoubtedly raised the esteem of the police in the eyes of the public and the newspapers, unless the culprit was one of their own.

4. There is also a discrepancy between his volunteering that the suspect was identified in an asylum, whereas Swanson, in his *Marginalia* (later in the book) states that he was identified at the Seaside Home. Yet both appear to be identifying the same suspect.

Anderson does not at any time state the name of his suspect, and releases only that he was a low-class Polish Jew (this is in the book version of his memoirs), from the immediate vicinity of the murders. This could possibly refer to Aaron Kosminski, a prominent suspect, or Aaron Davis Cohen, a little-known one, but it could also apply to another 50,000 people in Whitechapel.

Aaron Davis Cohen was arrested in December of 1888, and was brought before the Thames Magistrates Court by Metropolitan Police Constable John Patrick, being defined as a lunatic at large. He was escorted by PC Patrick to the Whitechapel Workhouse Infirmary at approximately 5.00 p.m on 7 December, and was registered as David Cohen, aged 23 years, of 86 Leman Street.

During his stay at the infirmary he is reported as having attempted suicide, to have been of a violent nature, and to have continuously threatened other patients. He was described as being required to be restrained, otherwise he would cause damage to equipment.

He was transferred to Colney Hatch Asylum, where he was identified as a foreign Jew, and his occupation was listed as 'tailor'.

During this time he was required to be fed by a tube, and was prone to tear the clothes off himself if not prevented.

He was declared dangerous and as such was isolated from the other patients. He continued to be of a reckless nature until it was noted that his personality underwent a marked change on 15 October 1889, when he was taken ill and confined to bed. He died on 20 December 1889.

Martin Fido, an eminent Ripper historian and researcher, names him as Anderson's suspect, but it can be seen that he does not fit the criteria demanded of either Anderson or Swanson, and I tend to agree at the present time that the person Anderson was alluding to was Aaron Kosminski.

On the other hand, another possibility was explored in *The Times* of Wednesday 12 September, in which the following article appeared:

A half-Spaniard and half-Bulgarian, who gave the name of Emanuel Delbast Violenia, waited on the police with respect to this enquiry.

He stated that he, his wife, and two children tramped from Manchester to London with a view of being able to emigrate to Australia, and took abode in one of the lodging houses in Hanbury Street. Early last Saturday morning, walking alone along Hanbury Street, he noticed a man and a woman quarrelling in a very excited manner. Violenia distinctly heard the man threaten to kill the woman by sticking a knife into her. They passed on, and Violenia went into his lodging. After the murder he communicated what he had seen to the poolice. At 1 o'clock yesterday afternoon Sergeant Thicke, assisted by Inspector Cansby, placed about a dozen men, the greater portion of who were Jews, in the yard of Leman Street Police station. Pizer was then brought out and allowed to place himself where he thought proper among the assembled men. He is a man of short stature, with black whiskers and a shaven chin. Violenia, who had been accommodated in one of the lower rooms of the station house, was then brought up into the yard. Having keenly scrutinised all the faces before him, he at once, without any hesitation or doubt whatever, went up to Pizer and identified him as the man whom he heard threaten a woman on the night of the murder. It was then decided, with the approval of Detective Inspector Abberline, that Violenia should be taken to the Whitechapel mortuary to see whether he could identify the deceased woman as the one he had seen in Pizer's company early on Saturday morning. The result is not announced, but it is believed that he was unable to identify her. Subsequently, cross-examination so discredited Violenia's evidence that it was wholly distrusted by the police and Pizer was set at liberty.

Could John Pizer have been Anderson's suspect? If so he was way off the mark because we know that at 1.30 a.m. on the morning of the murder of Mary Nichols, Pizer had held a conversation with a policeman in Seven Sisters Road, which was confirmed and accepted at the inquest. (Seven Sisters Road was a couple of miles from the murder scene, and the policeman had recalled Pizer because it was the night of the fire at London Docks.) But had he really seen Pizer at that time, or was it earlier? Nichols was seen drunk and staggering by Ellen Holland on the corner of Osborn Road and Whitechapel High Street, which means that she wasn't dead, and her body wasn't discovered until 3.40 a.m. Pizer would have had ample time to get back and murder her.

One of the persons in whom Anderson had a great deal of confidence was Dr Thomas Bond, who was the police surgeon for A (Westminster). Due to a certain element of conflict between the reports of the investigating doctors, and with specific regard to the modus operandi and the question of whether the killer possessed anatomical skill, and the extent of that skill, Anderson requested that Dr Bond compile a report as to what his opinions were regarding the Ripper murders. I have covered the contents of this report in the chapter on Mary Kelly and the one containing the medical evidence. My personal opinion of this report is that it was either composed in

conjunction with Anderson or it greatly influenced him in his search
for the Ripper. If Aaron Kosminski was already known and suspected
by the police, then I favour the opinion that the report of Dr Bond
was composed with Kosminski in mind, and if not then the report
assisted in formalising Kosminski as a major suspect.

The only one of the Whitechapel killings which fell within the jurisdiction of the City Police was the murder of Catharine Eddowes,
which took place in Mitre Square on 30 September. Sir James Fraser,
the Commissioner, was on leave at this time and so Major Henry
Smith, who in his absence was the Acting Commissioner, immediately assumed command of the investigation.

Major Smith was a popular man and was much better treated by
the London press, due to his giving the impression that he was much
more open in his relationship with them. He instructed his men to
infiltrate the community by frequenting the pubs and engaging in
social conversation, in the hope of picking up snippets of gossip and
helpful leads that would assist with their enquiries.

In his memoirs entitled *From Constable to Commissioner* he stated:
'There is no man living who knows as much about these murders as I
do', and then proceeded to make numerous errors in his evaluation
of the killings.

He was sceptical of Sir Robert Anderson's claim that he knew the
identity of the Ripper, and he said so. He accused the Metropolitan
Police of conducting a fruitless investigation, and stated that they
had no idea as to the identity of the killer.

Without naming him, Sir Melville Macnaghten wrote:

> Only two or three years ago, I saw a book of police reminisces
> (not by a Metropolitan officer) in which the author stated that he
> knew more of the Ripper murders than any man living, and went
> on to say that during the whole of August of 1888, he was on the
> tiptoe of expectation. That writer had indeed a prophetic soul,
> looking to the fact that the first murder of the Whitechapel
> miscreant was on 31 August of that year of grace.

I must point out at this time, that this date of the commencement
of the Ripper murders is only true if we regard Mary Ann Nichols as
the first victim in the series. If we include the death of Martha
Tabram, then Smith's statement is quite valid.

In the preface of the book entitled *The Trial of George Chapman*,
Major Smith is named as having confidentially told the author, Mr

H. L. Adams, that the identity of the Ripper was indeed known. It
does not elaborate on the establishment of the culprit, but Smith in
his book maintains 'I must admit that the Ripper completely beat me
and every other officer in London; and I have no more idea now than
I had twenty years ago.'

Major Smith was subsequently promoted to the position of Commissioner, City of London Police, and held the post from 1890 until
his retirement in 1901.

Sir Melville Macnaghten, who disputed the claim made by Major
Smith, was born in 1853 and was the son of the Chairman of the
British East India Company. He was educated at Eton and joined
Scotland Yard in June of 1889, as Assistant Chief Constable in
charge of C.I.D.

Macnaghten is very important in the annals of Ripper history, as
he is the author of the Macnaghten Memorandum, which names
three suspects who were high on the list of Scotland Yard.

Major Henry Arthur Griffiths, an eminent crime historian of the
day, wrote of him that he was 'essentially a man of action', and he
continued further: 'It is Mr Macnaghten's duty, no less than his
earnest desire, to be first on the scene of any such sinister cata-
strophe. He is therefore more intimately acquainted, perhaps, with
the details of the most recent celebrated crimes than anyone else at
Scotland Yard'.

The Macnaghten Memorandum comes in two versions; the first
was transcribed by his daughter, and is called the 'Aberconway
version'. This was rediscovered by the author Daniel Farson in 1959,
and takes the form of nine sheets, seven of which are typed and two
in the hand of Lady Aberconway herself. Whilst there are differences
in this version and that held as the 'Scotland Yard version', I tend to
accept that the Scotland Yard version, which is written in the hand of
Macnaghten himself, is the primary copy, and that the Aberconway
version was probably an earlier draft.

The memorandum's original intention was to detract from the
allegations in *The Sun* newspaper about the eligibility of one Thomas
Cutbush as a Jack the Ripper suspect. The full transcript of the
Scotland Yard version is:

Confidential – The case referred to in the sensational story told
in *The Sun* in its issue of the 13th inst., and following dates, is
that of Thomas Cutbush, who was arraigned at the London

County Sessions in April 1891, on a charge of maliciously wounding Florence Grace Johnson, and attempting to wound Isabelle Frazer Anderson, in Kensington. He was found to be insane, and sentenced to be detained during Her Majesty's pleasure.

This Cutbush, who lived with his mother and aunt at 14 Albert Street Kensington, escaped from the Lambeth Infirmary (after he had been detained there only a few hours, as a lunatic) at noon on 5 March 1891. He was rearrested on the 9th idem. A few weeks before this, several cases of stabbing, or 'jabbing' girls behind had occurred in the vicinity, and a man named Colicott was arrested, but subsequently discharged owing to faulty identification. The cuts in the girls' dresses made by Colicott were quite different to the cut made by Cutbush (when he wounded Miss Johnson), who was no doubt influenced by a wild desire of morbid imitation. Cutbush's antecedents were enquired into by Chief Inspector (now Supt) Chis [illegible] by Inspector Race, and by PS McCarthy C.I.D. – [The last-named officer had been specially employed in Whitechapel at the time of the murders there.] Cutbush it was ascertained was born and lived in Kensington all his life. His father died when he was quite young, and he was always a 'spoilt' child. He had been employed as a clerk and traveller in the tea trade, at the Minories, and subsequently canvassed for a Directory in the East End, during which time he bore a good character. He apparently contracted syphilis about 1888, and – since that time – led an idle and useless life. His brain seems to have become affected, and he believed that people were trying to poison him. He wrote to Lord Grimthorpe, and others, & also to the treasury, complaining of Dr Brooks, of Westminster Bridge Road, whom he threatened to shoot for having supplied him with bad medicines. He is said to have studied medical books by day, & to have rambled about at night, returning frequently with his clothes covered in mud; but little reliance could be placed on the statements made by his mother or his aunt, who both appear to have been of a very excitable disposition. It was found impossible to ascertain his movements on the nights of the Whitechapel murders. The knife found on him was bought in Houndsditch about a week before he was detained in the infirmary. Cutbush was a nephew of the late Supt. Executive.

Now the Whitechapel murderer had five victims and 5 victims only; his murders were:

1. 31st August '88, Mary Ann Nichols, at Buck's Row, who was found with her throat cut, & with (slight) stomach mutilation.

2. 8th September, Annie Chapman, Hanbury Street: throat cut, stomach and private parts badly mutilated & some entrails placed around the neck.

3. 30th September '88, Elizabeth Stride, Berner Street. Throat cut, but nothing in the shape of mutilation attempted, and on same day

4. Catharine Eddowes, Mitre Square, throat cut, & very bad mutilation, both of face and stomach.

5. 9th November, Mary Jane Kelly, Miller's Court, throat cut, and the whole of the body mutilated in the most ghastly manner.

The last murder is the only one that took place in a room, and the murderer must have been at least 2 hours engaged. A photo was taken of the woman as she was found lying on the bed, without seeing which it is impossible to imagine the awful mutilation.

With regard to the double murder which took place on 30 Sept., there is no doubt but that the man was disturbed by some Jews who drove up to the club [close to which the body of Elizabeth Stride was found] and that he then, '*nondum satiatus*', went in search of a further victim whom he found in Mitre Square.

It will be noticed that the fury of the mutilations increased in each case, and, seemingly, the appetite only became sharpened by indulgence. It seems, then, highly improbable that the murderer would have stopped in November '88, and been content to recommence operations by merely prodding a girl behind some 2 years & 4 months afterwards. A much more rational theory is that the murderer's brain gave way altogether after his awful glut in Miller's Court, and that he immediately committed suicide, or, as a possible alternative, was found to be so hopelessly mad by his relations, that he was by them confined in some asylum.

No one ever saw the Whitechapel murderer; many homicidal maniacs were suspected, but no shadow of proof could be thrown on any one. I may mention the cases of three men, any one of whom would have been more likely than Cutbush to have committed this series of murders:

1. A Mr M. J. Druitt, said to be a doctor & of good family, who disappeared at the time of the Miller's Court murder, whose

body (which was said to have been upwards of a month in the water) was found in the Thames on 31st December, or about 7 weeks after the murder. He was sexually insane and from private info I have little doubt but that his own family believed him to have been the murderer.

2. Kosminski, a Polish Jew, & resident in Whitechapel. This man became insane owing to many years indulgence in solitary vices. He had a great hatred of women, specially of the prostitute class, & had strong homicidal tendencies; he was removed to a lunatic asylum about March 1889. There were many circumstances connected with this man which made him a strong suspect.

3. Michael Ostrog, a Russian doctor, and a convict, who was subsequently detained in a lunatic asylum as a homicidal maniac. This man's antecedents were of the worst possible type, and his whereabouts at the time of the murders could never be ascertained.

And now with regard to a few inaccuracies and the misleading statements made by *The Sun*. In its issue of 14th Feb, it is stated that the writer has in his possession a facsimile of the knife with which the murders were committed. This knife (which for some unexplained reason has, for the last three years, been kept by Insp. Race, instead of being sent to the prisoner's property store) was traced, & it was found to have been purchased in Houndsditch in Feb '91, or 2 years 3 months after the Whitechapel murders had ceased.

The statement, too, that Cutbush 'spent a portion of the day in making rough drawings of the bodies of women, & of their mutilations' is based solely on the fact that 2 scribble drawings of women in indecent postures were found torn up in Cutbush's room. The head & body of one of these had been cut from some fashion plate, & legs were added to show a woman's naked thighs and pink stockings.

In the issue of the 15th inst. it is said that a light overcoat was among the things found in Cutbush's house, and that a man in a light overcoat was seen talking to a woman in Backchurch Lane, whose body with arms attached was found in Pinchin St. This is hopelessly incorrect! On 10th Sept. '89 the naked body, with arms, of a woman was found wrapped in some sacking under a railway arch in Pinchin St; the head and legs were never found nor was the woman ever identified. She had been killed at least 24 hours before the remains (which had seemingly been brought from some distance) were discovered. The stomach was split up by a cut, and the head and legs had been severed in a manner identical with that of the woman whose remains were discovered in the Thames, in Battersea Park, & on the Chelsea Embankment on 4th June of the same year; and these murders had no connection whatever with the Whitechapel horrors. The Rainham mystery in 1887, & the Whitehall mystery [when portions of a woman's body were found under what is now New Scotland Yard] in 1888 were of a similar type to the Thames and Pinchin St crimes.

It is perfectly untrue to say that Cutbush stabbed 6 girls behind; this is confounding his case with that of Colicott.

The theory that the Whitechapel murderer was left-handed, or, at any rate 'ambi-dexter', had its origin in the remark made by a doctor who examined the corpse of one of the earliest victims; other doctors did not agree with him.

With regard to the 4 additional murders ascribed by the writer in *The Sun* to the Whitechapel fiend:

1. The body of Martha Tabram, a prostitute, was found on a common staircase in George Yard Buildings on 7th August 1888; the body had been repeatedly stabbed probably with a bayonet. This woman had, with a fellow prostitute, been in the company of 2 soldiers in the early part of the evening. These men were arrested, but the second prostitute failed, or refused, to identify them, and the soldiers were accordingly discharged.

2. Alice McKenzie was found with her throat cut (or rather stabbed) in Castle Alley on 17th July 1889; no evidence was forthcoming, and no arrests were made in connection with this case. The stab in the throat was of the same nature as in the case of the murder of

3. Frances Coles, in Swallow Gardens, on 13th February 1891, for which Thomas Sadler, a fireman, was arrested and, after several remands, discharged. It was ascertained at the time that Sadler had sailed for the Baltic on 19th July '89, & was in Whitechapel on the night of the 17th idem. He was a man of ungovernable temper & entirely addicted to drink, & the company of the lowest prostitutes.

4. The case of the unidentified woman, whose trunk was found in Pinchin Street, on the 10th Sept. 1889, which has already been dealt with.

M. L. Macnaghten
23rd Feb. 1894

This memorandum of Macnaghten, once again, only serves to criticise the police for their poor rate of solving crimes. Unless the murderer was a spouse or someone of close connection with the deceased, then there was a good chance that a murderer would not be convicted, or even arrested.

Macnaghten wrote this document in 1894, and it has been the cornerstone of the Ripper investigation since it was first discovered by Donald Rumbelow in 1975. However, as I have previously explained, there are an awful lot of irregularities contained within it.

Major Arthur Griffiths, who spoke so well of Sir Melville Macnaghten, was as stated an eminent crime historian of the day. He wrote, among other things, a trilogy entitled *Mysteries of Police and Crime*, which contained the following passage:

The general public may think that the identity of Jack the Ripper was never revealed. So far as actual knowledge goes, this is undoubtedly true. But the police, after the last murder, had brought their investigations to the point of strongly suspecting several persons, all of them known to be homicidal lunatics, and against three of these, they held very plausible and reasonable grounds of suspicion.

Concerning two of them the case was weak, although it was based on certain colourable facts. One was a Polish Jew, a known lunatic, who was at large in the district of Whitechapel at the time of the murders, and who, having afterwards developing homicidal tendencies, was confined in an asylum. This man was said to resemble the murderer by the one person who got a glimpse of him, the police constable in Mitre Court. The second possible criminal was a Russian doctor, also insane, who had been a convict both in England and Siberia. This man was in the habit of carrying about knives and surgical instruments in his pockets, his antecedents were of the very worst, and at the time of the Whitechapel murders he was in hiding, or, at least, his whereabouts were never exactly known. The third person was of the same type, but the suspicion in his case was stronger, and there was every reason to believe that his own friends entertained grave doubts about him. He was also a doctor in the prime of his life, was believed to be insane or on the borderland of insanity, and he disappeared after the last murder, that in Miller's Court, on 9th November 1888. On the last day of the year, seven weeks later, his body was found floating in the Thames, and was said to have been in the water for a month. The theory in this case was that after his last exploit, which was the most fiendish of all, his brain entirely gave way, and he became furiously insane and committed suicide.

This statement by Griffiths more or less duplicates the results reached by Macnaghten, but it also states that there were several suspects which were narrowed down to the itemised three. I draw the conclusion that the three final suspects were simply the ones who more adequately fitted the bill.

Chief Inspector Donald Swanson was a contemporary and trusted friend of Sir Robert Anderson. He was also the officer directly in charge of the Whitechapel murder investigation, from the day after the murder of Mary Ann Nichols until 6 October 1888, at which time he assumed the position of Desk Officer in charge of the case, but under the jurisdiction and guidance of Dr Robert Anderson who had taken overall charge of the case from then until the closure of the Ripper file in 1892.

Swanson was highly respected by his fellow officers and was described by Melville Macnaghten as 'a very capable officer with a synthetical turn of mind'.

He received a personal copy of Robert Anderson's memoirs, and whilst reading them, he wrote some notes in the margins of the book, and at the end of the book, on the spare leaf at the back. These notes are now referred to as the 'Swanson Marginalia'.

In order to obtain an insight into the esteem in which Swanson was held by Anderson, we must review the importance attached to his role, and the memorandum with which Anderson recommended his appointment to his colleagues. He stated:

I am convinced that the Whitechapel murder case is one which can be successfully grappled with, if it is systematically taken in hand. I go so far as to say that I could myself in a few days unravel the mystery, provided I could spare the time and give undivided attention to it. I feel therefore the utmost importance to be attached to putting the whole Central Office work in this case in the hands of one man who will have nothing else to concern himself with. Neither you nor I nor Mr Williamson can do this. I therefore put it in the hands of Chief Inspector Swanson, who must be acquainted with every detail. I look upon him for the time being as the eyes and ears of the Commissioner in this particular case.

He must have a room to himself, and every paper, every document, every report, every telegram must pass through his hands. He must be consulted on every subject. I would not send any directions anywhere on the subject of the murder, without consulting him. I give him the whole responsibility. On the other hand he should consult Mr Williamson, you, or myself, on every important particular before any action, unless there is some extreme urgency.

I find that a most important letter was sent to Division yesterday without his seeing it. This is quite an error, and should not occur again. All the papers in Central Office on the subject of the murder must be kept in his room and plans of the positions etc.

The first thing which is noted is the confidence which Anderson obviously places in Swanson.

The second and most important, is that Swanson, by virtue of his position and responsibilities, should know more about the Ripper case than anyone else. All of the information concerning the case was passed through him, and it was he who then decided which information was to be passed upstairs. He was the central hub in all channels of communication concerning the Whitechapel murders.

Let us now look at the Swanson Marginalia, in which he comments on the theory of Dr Anderson. In it he says:

Anderson's suspect is neither named nor clearly defined in his printed text, beyond the observations that he is a poor Polish Jew from Whitechapel, whose people would not hand him over to justice, and that 'the only person who ever saw the murderer unhesitatingly identified the suspect the instant he was confronted with him, but he refused to give evidence against him, because the suspect was also a Jew and also because his evidence would convict the suspect, and witness would be the means of murderer being hanged, which he did not wish to be left on his mind. And after this identification which suspect knew, no other murder of this kind took place in London.

He further wrote at the back of the book:

After the suspect had been identified at the Seaside Home, where he had been sent by us with difficulty, in order to subject him to identification, and he knew he was identified, on suspect's return to his brother's home in Whitechapel he was watched by police by day and night. In a short time the suspect, with his hands tied behind his back, was sent to Stepney Workhouse and then to Colney Hatch, and died shortly afterwards.

Kosminski was the suspect.

We must appreciate that Swanson was making these observations a full 20 years after the Whitechapel murders, and as expected there is inevitably wrong information contained within.

I would tend to accede to the fact that the suspect named was indeed Kosminski, relying purely on the statement that the suspect resided with his brother in Whitechapel, and that he was transferred from the workhouse infirmary to the Colney Hatch Asylum, as nobody else passed through the infirmary who could meet the demands of the Marginalia.

The man in charge of the detectives directly investigating the Whitechapel murders was Metropolitan Police Inspector Frederick George Abberline. He was not, as he is frequently described, the officer in charge of the case.

Abberline joined the police force in 1863, and in 1865 he was promoted to Sergeant. He was involved in the investigation into the Fenian movement in 1867, and in 1868 he married Martha, the daughter of a labourer named Tobias Mackness. The marriage was fated, and Martha died in 1868 as a result of consumption.

By February 1888 Abberline was a 'First Class' Inspector of the Met. Police, and had been 12 years married to his second wife Emma, the daughter of a merchant named Henry Beamont.

He was regarded as an efficient officer (we do however know that his attention to detail was somewhat suspect at times), and he was renowned for his knowledge of the murder district and its inhabitants. This made him a most important member of the murder case team.

We have already discussed Abberline's views on Klosowski, i.e. George Chapman, under the section of the book devoted to him, and Klosowski had lived in George Yard, the place where Martha Tabram was murdered, and we must state that even though, in Abberline's opinion, the weight of evidence convicted Klosowski, Abberline did have certain reservations as to the witnesses' descriptions, and the extent to which they differed from the description of Klosowski.

The bulk of the descriptions which were close enough to the time of death to have been taken as those of the Ripper, predominantly described him as being in his thirties, whereas we know that at the time of the murders Klosowski was only 23 years old.

The *Pall Mall Gazette* interviewed Abberline, asking his opinion on the conjecture that the Ripper was a young medical student who was found drowned in the Thames. He responded as follows:

You can state most emphatically, that Scotland Yard is really no wiser on the subject than it was fifteen years ago [he was certainly truthful]. It is simple nonsense to talk of the police having proof that the man is dead. I am, and always have been, in the closest touch with Scotland Yard, and it would have been next to imposs- ible for me not to have known about it. Besides, the authorities would have been only too glad to make an end out of such a mystery, if only for their own credit. I know [he continued] that it has been stated in certain quarters that 'Jack the Ripper' was a man who died in a lunatic asylum a few years ago, but there is nothing at all of a tangible nature to support such a theory! As for the medical student drowned in the Thames, I know all about that story. But what does it amount to? Simply this. Soon after the last murder in Whitechapel, the body of a young doctor was found in the Thames, but there is absolutely nothing beyond the fact that he was found at the time, to incriminate him. A report was made by the Home Office about the matter, but that it was considered final and conclusive, is going altogether beyond the truth. The fact that several months after December 1888, when the student's body was found, the detectives were told to hold themselves in readiness for further investigations, seems to point to the conclusion that Scotland Yard did not in any way consider the evidence as final.

My own opinion on this is, that there is so much perplexity and uncertainty, and so many people within the case give mention to a young doctor or a young medical student, that I think that extensive research should be undertaken into investigating someone other than Montague John Druitt as being this person. How can so many people who were closely associated with the investigations all make the same mistake? Surely someone remembered that the person dragged from the Thames was a barrister and not a doctor. Surely someone interviewed his brother when he came to London to ident- ify the body or even later when it was suspected that he may have been the Ripper. Not everybody's memory can have developed this blank denial and carried on with the deception from then until twenty years later. Some reporter would have heard the story and been despatched to check the facts, and the doctor clanger would have been rectified. Could we be looking for someone else who isn't included in the police files?

Three diaries, purportedly written by Inspector Abberline between 1895 and 1915, provide the basis for the argument of the Royal connection, but these are now generally acknowledged to be forgeries and their contents therefore ignored.

Walter Dew, who at the time of the Ripper murders was a Detective Constable, and who went on to achieve fame as the man who caught Crippen, assists in his memoirs in providing an element of background information concerning the investigation. He implies in his writings that the streets of Whitechapel were extremely heavily patrolled by both uniformed and plain clothes policemen, and verifies that some officers were indeed disguised as women. He further goes on to describe how the police were instructed to stop well-dressed persons who were not known to the constabulary and question them, whilst similar persons who were resident in the area were allowed to go about their business unhindered.

He questions the attitude of his senior colleagues in their approach to the press, which he says caused unnecessary antagonism, and states that 'The police at this time were terribly buffeted. In some cases they did not receive the support they had a right to expect.'

He remembers that after the murder of Annie Chapman, he was sent to review likely escape routes from 29 Hanbury Street, with the destination of Spitalfields market, and relays that the route which he was asked to research was, 'East along Hanbury Street to Brick Lane, then south as far as Princelet Street then west to Spitalfields market'. The author notes as indeed previous authors have also done, that this is a roundabout direction in which to reach the market, which could more easily be attained by going west, straight along Hanbury Street, and would have achieved the destination in less than half of the distance. The author further appreciates that in escaping the scene of a crime the Ripper would want as many corners between himself and the murder site in the shortest possible time, and could not take the chance of walking straight along Hanbury Street with the possibility of being recognised by someone whilst still in the vicinity of the murder.

The Whitechapel investigation was primarily run by H Division of the Metropolitan Police, which had the responsibility for Whitechapel. The officer in charge of H Division was Superintendent Thomas Arnold. He did not take an active part in the murder investigation until the night of the double event. He had previously been on leave.

It was Arnold who was in overall charge of the area, though he had limited input into the actual Ripper case, and his only significant contribution was one of a negative nature, as he was the person responsible for the removal of the graffiti in Goulston Street, prior to it having been photographed, and would not even accept the erasure of the word 'Juwes', and in so doing allow the remainder of the phrase to remain, until the photographer had completed his work.

In February of 1893, in an interview with the *Eastern Post*, Arnold advised: 'I still hold to the opinion that not more than four of these murders were committed by the same hand. They were the murders of Annie Chapman in Hanbury Street, Mrs Nichols in Buck's Row, Elizabeth Stride in Berner Street, and Mary Kelly in Mitre Square.'

The last of these throws his statement into confusion as we know that Kelly was murdered in Miller's Court; but in any event, Arnold had no theory as to the identity of the Ripper, which is just as well considering.

Included in the police officers who were significant in the Ripper investigation, must be Detective Sergeant George Godley. Despite his undoubted commitment to the case, he is not remembered for any theory which he expounded in later life, but only for the arrest of one of the major suspects of the day, and a prominent suspect of many Ripper theorists.

DC Godley arrested George Chapman (Severin Klosowski) for the poisoning of three women, for which he was hanged in 1901.

After the discovery of the body of Annie Chapman, the first senior policeman on the scene was Inspector Joseph Chandler, who as Desk Officer in the Commercial Street Police Station declared that at 6.02 a.m. on the morning of the 8th September 1888, he saw men running up Hanbury Street, they told him of the murder, and he went to the scene of the crime, having first sent for an ambulance from the station, and despatched a runner to inform Dr Bagster Phillips, the police surgeon.

A man who cannot be ignored and whose opinions must command respect, is Inspector Edmund John Reid, who succeeded Abberline as the head of H Division C.I.D.

Reid was a pioneer, and a man of many talents. He was a renowned balloonist, and early parachutist. He was also an accomplished actor and magician, and was the model on which the fictional detective Dier was based by the author Charles Gibbon.

I believe, however, that in the matter of the Ripper case, the man can indeed be ignored, as his beliefs and opinions do not tend to reflect the true ingredients of the murder enquiry, and conflict with the views and opinions of the other leading players.

His conjectures were not accompanied by any proof, and his controversial statements to the press were speculative and mainly supposition. They included:

1. That there were nine Ripper victims, the murder of Frances Cole being the last.

2. That at no time was any part of a body missing.

3. He believed that the Ripper showed no surgical expertise whatsoever (in this he could be correct), and declared that the mutilations were a series of slashes, which were made on the body without any thought or reasoning, and that the Ripper continued to carry on with the attacks long after the body was dead. (I do not think we need his opinion to confirm that Mary Kelly was not alive for the duration of her mutilations.)

4. He did not know of the existence of a list which contained the names of the three primary suspects.

There were numerous other police officers involved with the Ripper enquiry, but none of them had any important contribution to make to either the investigation or the theorising which has taken place since the closure of the files.

I intend therefore to complete this part of the book with my last two named officers. The first is Sergeant Benjamin Charles Leeson.

Leeson did not join the police until 1891, and had only been in the force for one month when the murder of Frances Coles took place. He has been found to be unreliable in a lot of his remarks and grossly inaccurate in others, but he may have reflected the views of the ordinary bobby when he stated:

> I am afraid I cannot throw any light on the problem of the
> Ripper's identity, but one thing I do know, and that is, that

amongst the police who were most concerned with the case, there was a general feeling that a certain doctor, known to me, could have thrown quite a lot of light on the subject. This particular doctor was never very far away when the crimes were committed, and it is certain that the injuries inflicted on the victims, could only have been done by one skilled in the use of the knife.

The last person I shall name is Detective Constable Robert Sagar, who was described by Major Henry Smith with the words: 'A better or more intelligent officer than Robert Sagar, I never had under my command.'

He retired in 1905 with the rank of Inspector, and he played a leading part in the Ripper investigation. In *Reynolds News* of 15 September 1946 Justin Atholl reported:

Inspector Robert Sagar, who died in 1924, played a leading part in the Ripper investigations. In his memoirs he said 'We had good reason to suspect a man who worked in Butcher's Row, Aldgate. We watched him carefully. There was no doubt that this man was insane, and after a time, his friends thought it advisable to have him removed to a private asylum. After he was removed, there were no more Ripper atrocities.

At the time of writing, no confirmation as to the existence of the memoirs of Inspector Sagar have been discovered, but the *Brighton and Hove Herald* of 6 December 1926 stated that his obituary had included a similar opinion. If this is true then I see no reason to doubt the authenticity of the statement.

Sir Charles Warren

Sir Melville Macnaghten

Sir Robert Anderson

Sir Henry Smith

Dr Bagster Phillips

Dr Thomas Bond

George Lusk

CHAPTER NINETEEN

'Whodunit'

No book on the Whitechapel murders would be complete without the inclusion of a theory from the author, and in this philosophy I am no different from anyone else.

I am of the opinion that I have put up a credible case for the guilt of John Pizer. This conviction only came about whilst I was writing the book; before that I had no misgivings about accepting the innocence which most people now pronounce on Pizer. I intend to leave my judgment on Pizer to the reader and will now proceed with my original suspects.

You will also note that throughout the book there are certain phrases and sentences which are highlighted with italics. These are specific sections of the content which I regard as very important in supporting either a theory or one of the following suspects. After reviewing this chapter of the book you will probably need to reflect on these highlighted parts of the text, in order to decide whether you agree that they are important to the case against each individual, which I now put forward.

I intend, however, to adopt the stance of Sir Melville Macnaghten, and see if the argument which I have achieved through my own evaluation of the facts and evidence can convince the reader that I have proven my case for any one of the suspects beyond a reasonable doubt.

This also leaves me open to criticism of my peers, but it may also stimulate further discussion and open up the case, so that is a cheap price to pay.

I must therefore apologise that I am not in a position to be able to isolate one particular suspect, and supply sufficient evidence to establish without doubt the identity of the killer. I will however give my own opinion as to the persons who I believe are the most likely to be the guilty party.

Let us first explode one of the myths of the Jack the Ripper legend. It is a misconception that the Ripper must have held down a steady

job of some description because the Ripper murders were committed
at weekends. Let us therefore take a look at when the Ripper murders were actually committed. The following table will help. I have
taken the liberty of using only the maximum six victims that Jack the
Ripper could realistically have killed. They are as follows:

Name	Date	Day	Time	Place	Comments
Martha Tabram	7 Aug	Tues	3.30 a.m.	George Yard	Out late if he had to work on Tuesday.
Mary Nichols	31 Aug	Fri	2.30 a.m. to 3.40 a.m.	Bucks Row	Early, if he was a a working man.
Annie Chapman	8 Sept	Sat	5.30 a.m. to 6.00 a.m.	Hanbury Street	Could have been on his way to work.
Liz Stride	30 Sept	Sun	1.00 a.m.	Berner Street	Could be a worker or a non-worker.
Catharine Eddowes	30 Sept	Sun	1.45 a.m.	Mitre Square	Could be a worker or a non-worker.
Mary Kelly	9 Nov	Fri	c. 4.00 a.m.	Miller's Court	Out late if he had to work on Friday.

From this it is apparent that if you do not consider Saturday as a
working day, which it was for a lot of manual workers, it still only
works out in favour of an employed person for three of the murders,
and an unemployed person would have been just as likely to commit
these three murders as a man who was employed.

Initially, I do not propose to expound any theory that purports to
name Jack the Ripper, but only submit my opinion and reasoning on
the solution of one of the murders, that of Mary Jane Kelly. It would
then be reasonably safe to surmise that if it can be proven that a
particular suspect committed one of the murders, then we can also
presume his guilt for the rest of the crimes and deduce him to be Jack
the Ripper.

The person who I propose to be responsible for this murder is
Joseph Barnett, and my case against Barnett is outlined thus.

Joseph Barnett, born in 1858, was the fourth child of a fish porter
who died when he was six years old, and whose mother abandoned the
family shortly afterwards. He was raised by his two older brothers,
Denis and Daniel, and his sister Catherine. He attended school until
the age of thirteen, which meant that he effectively received quite a
good education. We know that he could read, because in interview he
stated that he used to read to Mary Kelly.

The family were not well off, but were not considered destitute,
and Joseph, along with his brothers, was employed as a fish porter.

He was described as being fair-haired and blue-eyed and stood about 5ft 7 inches tall. (If we scrutinise the descriptions of the Ripper we will see that he matches the most popular ones to a large degree.)

He met Mary Kelly during the Easter period of 1887, and from then on they lived together in various addresses, until they finally ended up in Miller's Court.

At the inquest and in common knowledge, it was stated that Barnett had left Kelly at the beginning of November 1888; the reason given was that Kelly had allowed other prostitutes to use the room in which she and Barnett were living as man and wife. Barnett did not like this arrangement, and it was the cause of frequent arguments between himself and Kelly, prior to him leaving Miller's Court.

He had lost his job at Billingsgate Market in the July, and subsequently all of the rent on the property had not been paid since that time, and the balance at the time of Kelly's death stood at seven weeks in arrears. Barnett no longer supplied the rent and I believe that this will have caused a lot of the arguments and that in the end, Mary Kelly kicked him out.

With Mary allowing other prostitutes to use the room, he and Mary never enjoyed the luxury of being alone, and the constant presence of other women, and also a child, put untold stress on their relationship.

I suggest that during this time, and in the preceding weeks, the tension which had built up in him, and his resentment of his treatment, triggered him into leaving the room after each argument, and taking it out on the female residents in the area by murdering and mutilating local prostitutes.

Having satisfied himself that the relationship was at an end, and that he could not prevent Kelly from allowing other prostitutes to use the Miller's Court room, he went round to the room to plead with Kelly for one last time

He arrived at Miller's Court at approximately 7.30 p.m. and stated in evidence that he stayed for about half an hour, before going back to Buller's lodging house in Bishopsgate. With his alibi established he returned to Miller's Court, and waited until Kelly had finished her rendezvous and subsequent sexual liaison with the blotchy-faced man and quite possibly with another client.

Kelly let Barnett into the room and he saw that she was drunk. He closed the door, and they both got undressed and went to bed, but not before Barnett had locked the door, using the supposedly lost key.

When Kelly had passed out into a drink-induced sleep, Barnett, who had not taken a drink, remained awake. He got out of bed and lit the candle which Kelly had purchased from McCarthy's. The candle may already have been alight, as it was probably used as a sign for the other ladies that the room was in use, and to stay away. It was November and the room was cold, and so he set alight to the clothes left there by Mrs Harvey, which also gave him more light to perform his murder than that given out by the candle, and whilst still undressed he cut Kelly's throat, having probably strangled her first.

It is also a possibility that he may have waited outside for a suitable length of time and then let himself into the room, to find Kelly already in her drunken slumber.

He then attacked the body, and vented his rage with the mutilations; having completed the horrible assault, he cleaned himself on the bedclothes, and got dressed.

He unlocked the door and left the room, locking the door behind him, and then returned to Buller's to re-establish his alibi.

As I have previously said, I propose that in the prior weeks, being incensed by the presence of other prostitutes living in the room, he had left the room in a fit of temper on four previous occasions, and had at these times committed the other Ripper murders. The start of the murders coincided with him losing his job as a fish porter.

My reasons for the incrimination of Joe Barnett are as follows:

On the door to the room at Miller's Court there was a lock, which opened with a key, and there also appeared to have been a bolt. It was stated at the inquest that the key had been lost for a number of weeks, and that Kelly and Barnett were in the habit of putting their hands through the broken window and releasing the bolt to gain entry. It was also stated that the window was broken on the night that Barnett left Kelly, and was the result of an argument. Barnett and Kelly hadn't been separated for a number of weeks, only a matter of nine or ten days. Why did Barnett need to know that the bolt could be released in this way? He didn't live there any more, so how did he find out, unless he was shown by Kelly? The only other explanation is that the window had been broken in an earlier argument, or else we must ask the question, how did they access the room after the key was lost and before the window was broken? Somebody was lying, unless during that period of time the room was left constantly open.

McCarthy (who was the owner of the building), Bowyer (who was the rent collector), the neighbours, who had gathered outside on the day of the murder, and the policemen present, would all have known that the door could be opened via the broken window by the time it was decided to enter the room. It was hours after the body had been discovered that it was decided to go into the room. Conversely, as soon as the police suggested forcing the door, someone local would have volunteered this information. That is, unless, and a lot more likely, the door was actually locked with the key, in which case the door would have needed to be forced open.

This meant that the last person to leave the room had used the key to lock the door and had taken it with them. Are we expected to believe that a number of weeks earlier, the Ripper had found the key and just happened to know which door it fitted? This is highly unlikely, unless he had witnessed who dropped it. A much more likely premise is that the key was never really missing, but had been retained by Barnett at some time before their break-up. When Barnett left Kelly, or was kicked out, he knew that the key afforded him access to the premises any time he required it.

The inference that Kelly had undressed for her attacker and had neatly folded her clothes and placed them on a chair, would suggest to me that she knew the last man to be in the room, and was comfortable in his company.

Kelly was presumably awake when the clothes were burnt on the fire, as if not, surely her own clothes would also have been destroyed.

Kelly had purchased a candle at McCarthy's. This would obviously have been used as illumination, or as a warning beacon to other women, informing them that the room was already occupied. It does not say whether the candle was found in the room.

The mutilation of the body in a cold room would tend to accelerate the heat loss from a dismembered corpse. It is well noted that a body cools from the inside outwards as well as from the outside in. This would tend to influence the doctor into mistakenly estimating the time of death.

Barnett had ceased contributing towards the rent, when he had failed to influence Kelly in refusing the use of the room to other women.

It has been stated that other women had slept at the house on previous nights; in fact this is quoted as the reason for the break-up of Kelly and Barnett. Why then did none of these women attempt to gain entry to the room on the night of the murder? The only reason is that Kelly had told them that they would not be allowed in. Or had they lied, and come to the door, only to find it locked? These women would have been very wary of admitting to the police that the house was being used for the purpose of prostitution, and McCarthy would not want the police to know that the house was allowed to be used in this way.

The door being locked would have served two purposes in assisting the Ripper. Firstly, it would have protected the murderer from being surprised by a third party whilst carrying out the murder and mutilations; and secondly, it would have stopped the premature discovery of the body by any persons coming to the room after the Ripper had made good his escape.

Barnett was 30 years old at the time of the murders, and as such would have fitted a lot of the descriptions given by witnesses at all of the murders, and especially suspects who were spotted close to the scene of the crime, talking to the victim, and at a time near enough to the time of death to draw the conclusion that he was probably the killer.

I therefore submit as my first suspect Joe Barnett, the jealous ex-lover of Mary Kelly. I believe that in the weeks preceding the murder of Kelly, Barnett frequently stormed out of the room he shared, after arguments brought about by the fact that Kelly had resumed prostitution, also by the presence of other prostitutes in the room and the fact that he had been relegated to second place in her affections. On these occasions he then, in a fit of temper, sought out a prostitute and murdered and mutilated her body to vent his rage.

I believe the most damning evidence is the confirmation that the door was locked (only the last person leaving could have locked it), enhanced by the fact that the key was confirmed as missing at the inquest. In my opinion, the only person who could realistically have held that key is Joseph Barnett.

I must be fair and point out a further explanation for the fact that the key was supposedly missing.

What if the key was never actually missing, but Kelly had only told Joe Barnett that it was? This would leave the way open for Kelly to pick up a client and take him back to the room, lock the door behind them so as they could not be disturbed, undress and place her clothes in a neat pile before getting into bed. Remember that if the witnesses are to be believed, she was in a singing mood that evening. The rest of the scenario remains the same, leaving a totally different Jack the Ripper to lock the door behind him when he left.

I leave you to form your own conclusions as to Joe Barnett being Jack the Ripper. I would only state that, if you accept that Mary Jane Kelly was murdered by Joe Barnett, and, after assessing all of the evidence, you consider Kelly to have been a Ripper victim, then you have but one conclusion to arrive at, and that is whoever killed one of them, killed them all, and that leaves but one conclusion.

Joe Barnett was Jack the Ripper.

My second suspect is also included in Sir Melville Macnaghten's Memorandum, and is arguably the most popular suspect for the role of Jack the Ripper. I am not going to laboriously duplicate the material in the Suspects chapter (Chapter 13) and other parts of the book, and can confidently say that if a *doctor* had been drowned in the Thames at the end of 1888, then none of us would be questioning the identity of this folklore figure. The named doctor would have been accepted as Jack the Ripper.

I will start with a little insight into the character of the murderer given in late September of 1888 by Doctor Henry Sutherland, a lecturer on insanity at the Westminster Hospital, who wrote:

> These murders were committed by some person or persons who were perfectly sane. He was most probably a stranger to his victim, and not bound to her by ties of blood. In all probability he was a poor man. It is well known to experts in insanity that although the anticipation of the deed may long be cherished, yet the act itself is sudden, unexpected, uncomplicated by any subsequent mutilation, or attempt to conceal the act, and very frequently followed by some suicidal attempt. As far as we have yet heard, there have been no suicides in Whitechapel lately, and any reader of the daily papers must be aware how common is this tendency when an insane person has committed a murder.

In the case of Montague Druitt, I do not believe when they speak of insanity they are saying that he was a raving lunatic, but that he had severe mood swings, suffered from acute depression, and above all I consider that he was most probably a homosexual. I believe that was the reason why he had lost his position at Valentine's School. That in itself constituted sexual lunacy in Victorian times.

With regard to his mental state. Donald McCormick in his book *The Identity of Jack the Ripper* is supposed to have contacted a London doctor, whose father was at Oxford with Druitt. This doctor supplied the following, which incidentally only Donald McCormick has seen.

My father always told me that the story about Druitt being the Ripper arose through the barrister being blackmailed by someone who threatened to denounce him as Jack the Ripper to the school at which he worked. Whether this was a heartless hoax, or a cruel method of extorting money from a man who was just recovering from a nervous breakdown, was not clear. There was nothing seriously wrong with Druitt, but he suffered from insomnia and blackouts. This allowed the threats to prey on his mind and paved the way to a further breakdown. He may, under severe stress, have given a muddled account of the threats to his mother.

My father, who was an experienced doctor, was quite convinced he could not have been the Ripper, and that the gold found on his body was originally intended to pay off the blackmailer. He certainly confided in his mother about the whole affair, and she presumably told the police when he was reported missing some time during December 1888. Anyhow, my father was emphatic that Druitt was living in Bournemouth when the first two Ripper crimes were committed.

Why would Druitt have an extortionate amount of money on his person to pay a blackmailer? Let us be reasonable about this. The position of schoolteacher was to supplement his earnings as a barrister. The job in itself won't have been that well paid, and certainly not well paid enough to allow him to pay a blackmailer out of the salary. He would rather have just packed the job in. Furthermore, lengthy discussions have taken place as to how Druitt managed to amass so much capital, if he was such a miserable failure as a barrister. This accretion of wealth becomes even more unlikely if he was also paying monies to a blackmailer as well.

I do believe that the senior police and the Home Office were in receipt of private information, and that at the time of the suicide of Druitt, he was being hunted by the police and would have been arrested if he had lived.

The Scotland Yard files indicate that the manpower used in the case was being reduced from December onwards, and the number of policemen patrolling the beats of Whitechapel had been reduced to half that of the peak cover, despite the fact that the Ripper had previously allowed a period of over five weeks to elapse between the murder of Eddowes and Mary Kelly. This should have sanctioned the level of personnel coverage to be maintained at maximum intensity, until at least the end of the year. That is, unless they were confident that the Ripper murders had ceased. To this end, it is believed that Montague John Druitt committed suicide on or around the first of December.

I believe that his brother told the police something which made them pretty confident that Druitt was the Ripper. Maybe the letter held the clue. The only part which has been published is the section which reads 'Since Friday I felt that I was going to be like mother, and it would be best for all concerned if I were to die.' This letter seems to be very short, and the quoted section appears to be only a small part of the whole.

The letter in total was never published and could have held the key to the confidence with which some senior policemen seemed to be assured that the Ripper was dead. The reason why it may never have been made public was probably that the contents of the letter were unfit to publish and only a small portion was therefore released. This assumption is purely conjecture, and is my opinion only.

In Macnaghten's published memoirs entitled *Days of My Years* he states: 'The Whitechapel murderer, in all probability, put an end to himself soon after the Dorset Street affair in November 1888. *Certain facts pointing to this conclusion, were not in possession of the police till some years after I became a detective officer.*' Later in the book he carries on, 'I incline to the belief that the individual who held up London in terror resided with his own people, that he absented himself from home at certain times and that he committed suicide on or about 10 November 1888.' The identity of the man he is describing is unquestionable even if the date is three weeks early.

This is born out by a statement made by Albert Bachert, a leading member of the Whitechapel Vigilance Committee who stated:

I was given this information in confidence about March 1889. I had complained to the police that there seemed to be too much complacency in the force simply because there had been no further murders for some months.

I was then asked if I would agree to be sworn to secrecy on the understanding that I was given certain information. Foolishly, I agreed. It was then suggested to me that the Vigilance Committee and its patrols might be disbanded, as the police were quite certain that the Ripper was dead.

I protested that, as I had been sworn to secrecy, I really ought to be given more information than this. 'It isn't necessary for you to know any more,' I was told. 'The man in question is dead.

He was fished out of the Thames two months ago and it would only cause pain to relatives if we said any more than that'.

Again I protested that I had been sworn to secrecy all for nothing, that I was really no wiser than before. 'If there are no more murders I shall respect this confidence, but if there are any more I shall consider I am absolved from my pledge of secrecy'

The police then got very tough. They told me a pledge was a solemn matter, that anyone who put out stories that the Ripper was still alive might be proceeded against for causing a public mischief. However, they agreed that if there were any other murders which the police were satisfied could be Ripper murders, then that was another matter.

I never believed the yarn, though I kept my pledge until after the McKenzie murder in 1889. Maybe some police officers kidded themselves that this was the truth, though I have my doubts about that.

Detective Inspector Abberline told me years later that he was quite certain that the story was untrue and that the Ripper remained alive and uncaught.

This should carry a great deal of weight, when we recognise that it comes from the senor detective who was in charge of the investigation, and should be deliberated upon when assessing the content of the Sergeant White report, and the rhyming letter, which are both included earlier in the book.

The reference in the Bachert statement to the date of the McKenzie murder is wrong, but if the statement is correct, then it very much ties in with the fact that the police by then were also scaling down the number of policemen that they had patrolling the streets. They would not have done this unless they knew that there was little chance of another murder being committed.

Because they had not actually caught him, they could not put him on trial, and if he hadn't been found guilty of anything then they did not have the right to denounce him and to release his name to the press and the public. This may have been the reason that everybody has continually made mistakes as to his profession and his age (they always refer to him as a doctor of 41 years, when in fact he was a barrister of 31 years, and some also refer to him as a student and do not give any age).

Bachert puts the date of this interview as March 1889, and states that the body was fished out of the Thames a couple of months

before. If this interview took place towards the end of March, then
it is quite feasible that they are referring to another body which
was fished out of the Thames some time in late January or early
February.

There is no mention of Druitt in any of the police files which were
generated during the Ripper Investigation. Somebody must have
known something. They never just pulled Druitt's name out of a hat.
There must have had some reason to include him as a suspect.

It is further said that in analysing the Ripper murders one would
have expected a murder to have taken place in October, but none
took place during that month. I am led to believe that during the
month of October, Druitt was not in London but was staying with
his brother in Dorset. Hence the gap in the cycle of murders.

George Robert Sims was a journalist who wrote under the name of
'Dagonet' and who was said to have good police contacts, and was
most probably a confidante of Macnaghten. He wrote a column in
The Referee which in 1902 reflected on the Ripper murders saying
that the police in the course of their enquiries had reduced the
suspects from seven to three, by exhaustive enquiries. He continued,
'and were about to fit these three people's movements in with the
dates of the various murders, when the only genuine Jack saved
further trouble by being found drowned in the Thames, into which
he had flung himself, a raving lunatic, after the last and most appall-
ing mutilation of the whole series.

'But, prior to this discovery, the name of the man found drowned
was bracketed with two others as a possible Jack, and the police were
in search of him alive when they found him dead.'

Did this indicate that because he had died and had not been tried
for the murders, that they removed all of the incriminating evidence
contained within the murder files and left only the Macnaghten
Memorandum to dubiously identify him?

Once again we must go to Mr Sims for what appears to be an insight into the impending arrest of the Ripper.

According to Martin Howells and Keith Skinner in their book *The
Ripper Legacy*, they identified that Sims had written the following
piece of information early in December of 1888, and therefore three
to four weeks before Druitt's body was given up by the Thames:

It would be strange if the accession of Mr Monro [he had been
made Metropolitan Police Commissioner after Warren had re-
signed] to power were to be signalised by such a universally

popular achievement as the arrest of Jack the Ripper. From information which has reached me, I venture to prophesy that such will be the case.

My last piece of evidence against Montague Druitt is that, as I have previously stated, I believe the Ripper to have been left-handed. There are two well-known photographs of Druitt which are regularly used in books about the Ripper. If we take the first photograph of Druitt sat reading a book, you will notice that his left leg is crossed over his right. This is a posture which is more comfortable and natural for a left-sided person. A right-sided person would be more at ease with his right leg crossed over his left. For a man, a further reason to be taken into consideration when defining which leg is the more comfortable to cross is on which side the man dresses. It is more usual for a right-handed person to dress to the left. This would make it less comfortable for him to cross his left leg over his right. This is only an observation but one that proves correct to a high degree.

Within the same photo you will further notice that Druitt is reading a book. The book is held in the right hand, allowing the pages to be turned over with his left hand. Once again, this is a position more in keeping with a left-handed person. A right-handed person would be more comfortable holding the book in his left hand, so allowing his dominant hand to perform the act of turning the pages. This condition however is not as prevalent as the first statement, as I know a number of persons who confirm the fact that they are quite comfortable holding a book in their right hand even though they are right-handed.

If we now look at the second photograph you will see that Montague is wearing a tie. On closer inspection it can be seen that the highest part of the knot of the tie is on the right side of his neck, (the left as you look at the picture). This indicates that the knot in the tie has been completed by putting the left portion of the tie over the right. This is also the action of a left-handed person. A right-handed person would ordinarily place the right section of the tie over the left (the shortest side of the tie would be on his left). This would ensure that the highest part of the knot on completion would be on the left side of the neck, opposite to that which the Druitt photo shows. Since the advent of the Windsor knot this condition does not arise as both sides of the tie are more or less equal but in 1888 the Duke of Windsor, who popularised this knot, was not yet born.

I have only seen one example of Druitt's writing, and that consisted mainly of a signature which, because it is practised as a child, can be misleading. His writing however is very much akin to my own (I am left-handed), and the lateral crossing on the letter 't' in his name slopes slightly downward which I believe could indicate a left-handed writer. I do not offer this up as any confirmation or indication of his hand, firstly because I am not a graphologist, and secondly because I am led to believe that in Victorian days there was a stigma attached to left-handedness, and so it was common practice to teach a left-handed person to write with his other hand.

When all of this is added together and rationalised, I believe that Montague John Druitt was a most credible suspect to have been our Whitechapel Murderer 'Jack the Ripper'.

My final suspect is I believe a new one, and I only made the decision to include him when, in the course of writing the book, certain coincidental facts started to appear. He is John Kelly, who was the lover and common law husband of Catharine Eddowes.

He appears to have been a likeable sort of chap and earned his living as a market porter.

It was estimated in 1888 that there were approximately 1200 prostitutes in Whitechapel. Of these, Jack the Ripper killed a maximum of five, and the places where the victims lived could all have been enclosed within a circle of 250 yards diameter. So in my search for the culprit I commenced looking within that circle. After investigating and dismissing numerous suspects who had been previously named, by chance I was reading the transcript of the Eddowes murder and a thought popped into my head.

For the seven years before her death Eddowes and Kelly had been an item. According to Kelly, they had met one another in the lodging house where they both lived, and had hit it off together, so had paired up.

On Sunday 9 September they had set off for the hop fields in Kent. They tried their luck at a place called Hunton near Maidstone. This was a regular jaunt for some of the poorer folk of London. This year they had not been very lucky in finding work and so they started to make their way back to London in the company of a woman named Emily Birrell and her male companion. The couples parted company on the road, because Birrell and her man were going to Cheltenham, but before they separated Birrell gave Catharine a pawn ticket for twopence for a flannel shirt. Eddowes and Kelly arrived back in

London on Thursday 27 September and stayed the night at the Casual Ward at Shoe Lane.

On Friday 28 September Kelly managed to earn 6d (sixpence), of which Catharine took 2d, leaving Kelly the other 4d for a bed at Cooney's lodging house in Flower and Dean Street, which was his regular dosshouse, and Eddowes went on to the Casual Ward at Mile End.

Kelly, for some reason, did not stay at Cooney's that night, but at another dosshouse at Number 52 Flower and Dean street (Cooney's was Number 55). Why was this? Was it to search out another victim? However, at 8.00 a.m. the following morning he was in the kitchen at Cooney's where Catharine found him, she herself having been turned out of the Casual Ward for some unspecified trouble.

In order to obtain some money they agreed to pawn a pair of Kelly's boots, which they did at Smith's pawnbrokers in Church Street. They received the sum of two shillings and sixpence, and purchased some tea and food which they took to Cooney's, and between 10.00 a.m. and 11.00 a.m. they were seen by Frederick William Wilkinson, who was the Deputy of the lodging house, having breakfast in the kitchen.

Two shillings and sixpence, more commonly known as half a crown, had a purchasing power in excess of ten pounds in present-day terms, so it may be assumed that they also bought some drink, as by 2.00 in the afternoon they were once again broke. Eddowes left Kelly in Houndsditch saying she was off to Bermondsey to borrow some money from her daughter Annie, and would be back at 4.00 p.m.

At 8.30 p.m. she was drunk and causing a disturbance outside 29 Aldgate High Street and was taken into custody by PCs Robinson and Simmons. She was taken to Bishopsgate Police Station where she was locked up in a cell to sleep off the effects of the drink. This was the custom in Whitechapel, and the person would be released as soon as they were considered capable of looking after themselves.

According to Donald Rumbelow in his book *The Complete Jack the Ripper*, Kelly had heard that Catharine had been arrested and locked up for being the worse the wear for drink, but at the inquest he stated that he didn't bother to go and look for her, as he knew she would turn up on the Sunday morning, but he did admit to having been told of her whereabouts by two women, and the deputy in his testimony said that Kelly had informed him as to Eddowes being in Bishopsgate police cells. As we know, she was released from custody by Police Constable George Hutt, under the instruction of Sergeant

Byfield, at 1.00 a.m. in the morning, and within an hour of her release her body would be discovered, murdered and mutilated, in Mitre Square.

For what happened after Catharine left the police station I will introduce the report by Donald Swanson, which is most comprehensive and complete.

I beg to report that the facts concerning the murder in Mitre Square which came to the knowledge of the Metropolitan Police are as follows:

1.45 a.m. 30th Sept. Police Constable Watkins of the City Police discovered in Mitre Square the body of a woman, with her face mutilated almost beyond identity, portion of the nose being cut off, the lobe of the right ear nearly severed, the face cut, the throat cut, and disembowelled. The PC called to his assistance a Mr Morris, a night watchman and pensioner from the Metropolitan Police, from premises looking on the Square, and surgical aid was subsequently called in, short details of which will be given further on in the report.

The City Police having been made acquainted with the facts by PC Watkins the following are the results of their enquiries as far as known to Met. Police:

1.30 a.m. The PC passed the spot where the body was found at 1.45 a.m. and there was nothing to be seen there at that time.

1.35 a.m. Three Jews, one of whom is named Mr Lewin (actually Lawende) saw a man talking to a woman in Church Passage which leads directly to Mitre Square. The other two took but little notice and state that they could not identify the man or woman, and even Mr Lawende states that he could not identify the man; but as the woman stood with her back to him, with her hand on the man's breast, he could not identify the body mutilated as it was, as that of the woman whose back he had seen, but to the best of his belief the clothing of the deceased, which was black, was similar to that worn by the woman he had seen, and that was the full extent of his identity.

2.20 a.m. PC 245A Long (this PC was drafted from A Division temporarily to assist H Division) stated that at the hour mentioned he visited Goldstone (Goulston) Street Buildings, and there was nothing there at that time, but at

2.55 a.m. he found in the bottom of a common stairs leading to No. 108 to 119 Goldstone Street Buildings, a piece of a bloodstained apron, and above it written in chalk, the words 'The Juwes are the men who will not be blamed for nothing', which he reported, at the earliest moment, when it was found that beyond doubt the piece of apron found corresponded exactly with the part missing from the body of the murdered woman.

The surgeon, Dr Brown, called by the City Police, and Dr Phillips who had been called by the Metropolitan Police in the cases of Hanbury Street and Berner Street, having made a post-mortem examination of the body reported that there were missing the left kidney and the uterus, and that the mutilation so far gave no evidence of anatomical knowledge in the sense that it evidenced the hand of a qualified surgeon, so that the police could narrow their enquiries into certain classes of persons. On the other hand as in the Metropolitan Police cases, the medical evidence showed that the murder could have been committed by a person who had been a hunter, a butcher, a slaughterman, as well as a student in surgery or a properly qualified surgeon.

The result of the City Police enquiries were as follows:

Beside the body were found some pawn tickets in a tin box, but upon tracing them, they were found to relate to pledges made by the deceased, who was separated from her husband, and was living in adultery with a man named John Kelly, respecting whom enquiry was at once made by Metropolitan and City Police, the result of which was to show clearly that he was not the murderer. Further it showed that the deceased's name was Catherine Eddowes, or Conway, who had been locked up for drunkenness at Bishopsgate Street Police Station at 8.45 p.m. 29th and being sober was discharged at 1 a.m. 30th. Enquiry was also made by the City and Metropolitan Police conjointly into her antecedents, and it was found that there did not exist amongst her relations or friends the slightest pretext for a motive to commit the murder.

At Goldston Street Buildings where the portion of the bloodstained apron was found, the City Police made enquiry, but unsuccessfully, and their subsequent enquiries into matters affecting persons suspected by correspondence or by statements of individuals at Police Stations, as yet without success, have been carried on with the knowledge of the Metropolitan Police, who on the other hand have daily acquainted the City Police with the subjects and natures if their enquiries.

Upon the discovery of the blurred chalk writing on the wall, written – although mis-spelled in the second word – in an ordinary hand in the midst of a locality principally inhabited by Jews of all nationalities as well as English, and upon the wall of a common stairs leading to a number of tenements occupied almost exclusively by Jews, and the purport of the writing being to throw blame upon the Jews, the Commissioner deemed it advisable to have them rubbed out. Apart from this there was the fact that during police enquiries into the Bucks Row and Hanbury Street murders a certain section of the press cast a great amount of suspicion upon a Jew named John Pizer, alias 'Leather Apron', as having been the murderer, and whose movements at the dates and hours of those murders had been supposedly enquired into by Met. Police, subsequently clearing him of any connection with the killings. There was also the fact that on the same morning another murder had been committed in the immediate vicinity of a socialist club in Berner Street frequented by Jews – considerations which, weighed in the balance with the evidence of chalk writing on the wall to bring home guilt to any person, were deemed the weightier of the two. To those officers who saw the chalk writing, the handwriting of the now notorious letters to a newspaper agency bears no resemblance at all.

Rewards were offered by the City Police and Mr Montagu [the MP for Whitechapel] and a Vigilance Committee formed, presided over by Mr Lusk of Alderney Road, Mile End, and it is to be regretted that the combined result has been that no information leading to the murderer has been forthcoming. On the 18th Oct. Mr Lusk brought a parcel which had been addressed to him to Leman Street Police Station. The parcel contained what appeared to be a portion of a kidney. He received it on the 15th Oct. and submitted it for examination eventually to Dr Openshaw, curator of London Hospital Museum, who pronounced it to be a human kidney. The kidney was at once handed over to the City Police, and the result of the combined medical opinion they have taken upon it, is that it is the kidney of a human adult, not charged with fluid, as it would have been in the case of a body handed over for the purposes of dissection to an hospital, but rather as it would be in a case where it was taken from the body not so destined. In other words, similar kidneys might and could be obtained from any dead person upon whom a post-mortem had been made from any cause, by students or dissecting room porter. The kidney, or rather portion of the kidney, was accompanied by a letter couched as follows:

[There then follows a transcription of the 'From Hell' letter, which is printed earlier in the book.]

The postmarks upon the parcel are so indistinct that it cannot be said whether the parcel was posted in the E. or E.C. districts, and there is no envelope to the letter, and the City Police are therefore unable to prosecute any enquiries upon it.

The remaining enquiries of the City Police are merged into those of the Metropolitan Police, each force cordially communicating to the other daily, the nature and subject of their enquiries.

The foregoing are the facts so far as known to Metropolitan Police, relating to the murder in Mitre Square.

Now let us return to the question of the guilt of John Kelly.

According to the Superintendent of the Casual Ward at Shoe Lane, to whom Catharine Eddowes was well known, but who stated that she had not stayed there for a long while, she told him 'I have come back to earn the reward offered for the apprehension of the Whitechapel murderer. I think I know him.' The Superintendent of Shoe Lane warned her to take care she was not murdered, to which she replied 'Oh, no fear of that.'

I believe that Eddowes had come back to name the identity of Jack the Ripper, and the person she intended to name could have been John Kelly.

Look closely at the transcript of the conversation above. It has always been assumed that she intended to name John Pizer, but the inference of 'I think I know him', and 'Oh, no fear of that', seems to propose that Eddowes knew his name, and was certain she felt safe from becoming one of his victims. This could be because she was his woman.

It is a remarkable twist of fate that the day after she boasts about her knowing his identity she meets her own horrific death.

Remember that Eddowes and Kelly went to Kent immediately after the murder of Annie Chapman, and during the time that they were away, no murders took place in the East End.

As I have stated previously, Kelly's main abode was Cooney's lodging house at Number 55 Flower and Dean Street, and the day before the murder he had stayed at Number 52 Flower and Dean Street. Mary Ann Nichols had stayed at the White House for the week before she was murdered. The White House was situated at Number 56 Flower and Dean Street. Elizabeth Stride lodged at Number 32 Flower and Dean Street at the time of her death. This was a central position from which Kelly could select his victims and become on talking terms with them, so that when he met them on the night of the murders they were not alarmed.

Frederick Wilkinson, the Deputy of Cooney's, says 'Catharine was not often in drink and was a very jolly woman, often singing, she was generally in the lodging house for the night between 9 and 10 p.m.' This would have left Kelly plenty of time to commit the murders. We must also allow for the fact that on returning from Kent, Kelly and Eddowes did not stay at the same place, except for the first night when they stayed at Shoe Lane, and that was a Thursday.

If this was the usual, and Eddowes and Kelly were separated some weekends, then this would have afforded Kelly a free rein on these weekends to cultivate his quest for victims.

Catharine Eddowes was murdered in Mitre Square. Was this because she intended to name John Kelly as Jack the Ripper, and so he had to go out of his usual area in order to prevent this happening? Other than this one instance the Ripper never left the confines of Whitechapel and Spitalfields. Are we expected to believe that the Ripper just happened by chance to be passing an area where he had never frequented before and randomly selected a prospective victim, who just happened to be spouting off that she could identify Jack the Ripper? No, Eddowes wasn't just a randomly selected victim, she was marked for death. She had to be killed, just in case she carried out her boast to name the Ripper.

It has been asked why, with the streets being prowled by such a predator, did the police release Eddowes on to those streets at 1.00 a.m. in the morning? Answer: there had not been a murder in the City of London, his exploits had been confined to Whitechapel, and so, what was wrong in releasing a prisoner in this part of the city?

The Ripper, if not well educated, was clever, resourceful and careful. After the murder, he did not panic and immediately leave the area. PC Alfred Long discovered the Graffiti and the portion of Eddowes's apron at 2.55 a.m. in the open doorway of the staircase to numbers 108–119 of the Wentworth Model Dwellings, in Goulston Street. He swore that the apron had not been there twenty minutes earlier. PC Watkins had found the body at 1.45 a.m. So the Ripper was still in the area with the piece of apron on his person a minimum of 45 minutes later. Why?

I think it was because, whilst performing the mutilations, he had cut himself. He had cut off a piece of the apron and wrapped it round his cut hand in order to stem the flow of blood, before fleeing the scene of the crime. He did not want to appear in full view of the public whilst still bleeding. This would trigger an alarm in anyone who saw him, so he waited until after the cut had ceased bleeding, and it was therefore not until later than 2.20 a.m., that he abandoned the bloodstained piece of apron in Goulston Street.

It has been mooted that the piece of apron was cut off by Eddowes to use as a handkerchief. I totally disagree. The police retained a list of Catharine's belongings; among them were listed 1 large white handkerchief, 1 white cotton handkerchief and 12 pieces of white rag. Why then would she use a piece of her apron as a handkerchief? No! it was the nearest piece of cloth the Ripper could see after he had cut his hand. The piece of apron was covered in blood. Doctor Phillips stated at the inquest that 'it was impossible to say that it was human blood on the apron', but he did say that it fitted perfectly to the remainder which was left on the body. He did concede that it was some kind of blood on the apron, and I think that it is safe to assume that it was human blood. What else could it have been? There were no lions or tigers in Whitechapel.

John Kelly was described at the inquest as being 'quiet and inoffensive, with fine features and sharp and intelligent eyes'. It is further known that by October 1888, he was very ill with a kidney complaint, and had a bad cough. The kidney complaint would have given him a sallow complexion. He appears to have been in poor health, and legend has it that they walked from Hunton, Coxheath to London in a single day. This is a distance of 37 miles and is no mean feat for even a fit man.

We know that he was educated because he read in the newspaper that a woman had been discovered with two pawn tickets in her possession.

We are acquainted with the fact that two women had informed him that Eddowes had been locked up in Bishopsgate Police Station. This information was admitted by Kelly himself and was endorsed by Frederick Wilkinson the deputy of the lodging house.

The only person who ever saw the Ripper was Sergeant Stephen White, who said that 'he was slightly bent, and his complexion was inclined to be sallow'; he also said that 'the most extraordinary thing about him was the extraordinary brilliance of his eyes.' Was this John Kelly, and did he die from his illness shortly afterwards?

Remember that Catharine told the police as she was released, 'I'll get a damn fine beating when I get home'. So Kelly was capable of violence when it suited him, and wasn't as quiet and inoffensive as he would have us believe. Eddowes was sufficiently frightened of him to turn away from the direction of Flower and Dean Street when she was released and set off in the opposite direction.

In *The Ripper Legacy* by Martin Howells and Keith Skinner, they include a description by Edward John Goodman of what he believed was a profile of the Ripper. In 1892, Goodman wrote:

> If the truth were known, the so called Jack the Ripper would probably be no vulgar ruffian, repulsive in appearance and destitute of education, but a most respectable person, mild and suave, or cheerful and plausible, in manner, of superior culture and intelligence, possibly a very popular man in his own circle, what is commonly known as a good fellow. In short, the very last person whom ordinary folks would have suspected of such deeds as his.

If I am being fair, this description could apply as well to John Kelly as to Montague John Druitt, and perhaps better.

Remember the only letter which is generally accepted as having originated from the hand of the Ripper. That is the letter 'From Hell', also referred to as the 'Lusk Letter'. It included such Irish terms as 'Sor' and 'Mishter'. Kelly was of Irish Catholic descent.

Lastly, remember once again. The victims would have more than probably known their murderer, as they all appeared to have been at ease with him and quite happily went with him into dark alleys, even at the height of the panic created by the killer.

John Kelly was described as inoffensive and quiet, with fine features. Kelly lived almost exclusively at Cooney's Lodging House at 55 Flower and Dean Street. All of the victims, with the exception of Mary Jane Kelly, lived or dossed in Flower and Dean Street. I do not believe that Jack the Ripper murdered Elizabeth Stride, but if he did, he only became aware of her after she moved into Number 32 Flower and Dean Street (she'd only been there for a week). The one victim who did not live there was Mary Kelly, who lived in Miller's Court, but even this was less than 200 yards from Cooney's lodging house. They probably all drank in the same pubs like the Britannia, the Horn of Plenty, the Ten Bells, the Princess Alice and the Queen's Head.

All the information I have imparted concerning John Kelly may be convincing, but it is all circumstantial, and like all the other suspects there is no concrete evidence against him, but would it influence you if I was to tell you that whilst Kelly and Eddowes were in Kent, a horrible murder took place there (and remember, none took place in Whitechapel)? And would it also complete the case if I confirmed that Kelly died shortly after the murders ended? At present I am unable to do this as I am still researching the life of John Kelly, but I will include the result of my investigations in the second issue of this book, if there is one.

I will once again echo what Sir Melville Macnaghten said.

I have strong opinions with regard to these three suspects but am inclined to favour the last two more than the first.

The final piece of information which I would ask you to consider is the gravity and importance of the following.

If you remember, on pages 82–83 of this book there was a transcript of a statement which was given by a Police Sergeant White, and which is held in the Scotland Yard Files on the case. Earlier in the book I was somewhat critical of Sergeant White for allowing the man who was leaving the alley to go on his way without any effort to stop and interview him.

I do however think that this altercation is of prime importance to the Jack the Ripper case and holds the key to eliminating a number of suspects.

Sergeant White was well thought of by his superiors and had attained the rank of sergeant, so must have possessed a degree of intelligence and initiative. Look at the entries in the Scotland Yard Files to appreciate his close involvement in the case.

If indeed he was telling the truth in his report of the referenced incident, and there is no reason to assume that he was not, as he did not come out of the incident dowsed in glory, then he is very important to the case.

He stated that he got a good look at the man as he passed, and included a description of him in his report of the incident. He therefore did not recognise the man as one of the local villains, and in the course of the Jack the Ripper investigation did not meet him again, otherwise the man would have been arrested or at the very least questioned. I would also assume that anyone brought in for questioning about the murders, who was considered a serious suspect by the police, would have been subjected to the scrutiny of Sergeant White. This I strongly suggest serves to eliminate a lot of the suspects, as they would have been recognised by White either at the time of the incident in the alley or subsequently on the streets of Whitechapel. I would therefore lean towards Jack the Ripper being a person who was not regularly seen on the streets of Whitechapel, but frequented the area only at night and maybe only on the nights on which the murders were committed; this is all presuming that Sergeant White was an honourable and truthful man, and most probably the incident was corroborated by the two policemen referenced in the statement.

If we accept this information then Issenschmidt, Pizer, Kosminski, etc., could all definitely be eliminated, as doubtless White was aware that all were suspects and known villains, and therefore none of them could have been the man whom he saw leaving the alley. But it does not eliminate Montague John Druitt.

Furthermore, surely his superiors arranged for him to attend the inquests of the victims to see if the person whom he caught sight of was present at the proceedings. They would also have arranged for him to encounter all of the implicated persons in the case in order to check that they were not the man he had encountered.

Because of the amount of research which I hope this book triggers, it is impossible to complete the work alone, and I can only hope that I have interested someone, somewhere, enough for them to take up the baton and prove me right or wrong. I will continue to do my bit, but I can now only await the search for further information which may confirm one of the two suspects as Jack the Ripper, or establish who wrote the poem represented in Chapter 15, as I am convinced that this was the murderer.

If I succeed then I promise that I will tell you all, in due course.

THE END

INDEX

If, after reading this book, you wish to enter into correspondence with the author, please write to:

Terry Lynch
4 Trinity Court
Whitehaven
Cumbria CA28 7NB
UK